Jung in the 21st Century
Volume One

This first volume provides an original overview of Jung's work, demonstrating that it is fully compatible with contemporary views in science. It draws on a wide range of scientific disciplines including evolution, neurobiology, primatology, archaeology and anthropology.

Divided into three parts, areas of discussion include:

- evolution, archetype and behavior
- individuation, complexes and theory of therapy
- Jung's psyche and its neural substrate
- the transcendent function
- history of consciousness.

Jung in the 21st Century Volume One: Evolution and Archetype will be an invaluable resource for all those in the field of analytical psychology, including students of Jung, psychoanalysts and psychotherapists with an interest in the meeting of Jung and science.

John Ryan Haule is a Jungian Analyst in private practice in Boston and a training analyst at the C. G. Jung Institute, Boston.

Jung in the 21st Century Volume One

Evolution and archetype

John Ryan Haule

Routledge
Taylor & Francis Group

LONDON AND NEW YORK

First published 2011
by Routledge
27 Church Road, Hove, East Sussex BN3 2FA

Simultaneously published in the USA and Canada
by Routledge
270 Madison Avenue, New York, NY 10016

Routledge is an imprint of the Taylor & Francis Group, an Informa business

© 2011 John Ryan Haule

Typeset in Times by RefineCatch Limited, Bungay, Suffolk
Printed and bound in Great Britain by TJ International Ltd, Padstow,
Cornwall
Paperback cover design by Andrew Ward

This publication has been produced with paper manufactured to strict
environmental standards and with pulp derived from sustainable forests.

British Library Cataloguing in Publication Data
A catalogue record for this book is available
from the British Library

Library of Congress Cataloging in Publication Data
Haule, John Ryan, 1942–
    Jung in the 21st century / John Ryan Haule.
        p. cm.
    Includes bibliographical references. 1. Jungian psychology. 2. Jung,
    C. G. (Carl Gustav), 1875–1961. 3. Archetype (Psychology)
    4. Evolutionary psychology. 5. Coincidence. I. Title. II.
Title: Jung in the twentyfirst century.
        BF173.J85H38 2010
        150.19′54–dc22

                                                                2010014735

ISBN: 978–0–415–57797–7 (hbk)
ISBN: 978–0–415–57798–4 (pbk)

For Ann

Contents

Preface

C. G. Jung has become the most beloved of the original giants of psychoanalysis in the minds of the general public, but his fate in academic circles has been much less impressive. Scientists have generally ignored his contributions, accepting the official Freudian judgment that his theories are mystical and anti-Semitic. For many decades Freud seemed to be the "scientific" psychoanalyst, and views about Jung were based less on fact than on his reputation as the Crown Prince of Psychoanalysis who strayed too far into the realm of superstition to be taken seriously.

Two developments since 1970, however, have uncovered a different and truer Jung. The first of these was Henri Ellenberger's publication in 1970 of *The Discovery of the Unconscious*, where Freud, Jung, Adler, and Janet were placed in historical context, and it came out that Jung had always belonged more to the French-English-Swiss-American tradition in psychology that paid attention to natural and "artificial" (i.e. hypnotic) dissociations in the human psyche. They were the so-called "French School" of psychology that Jung had always claimed to belong to, investigators who were fascinated by the discovery, first, that all of us have simultaneous conflicting subpersonalities; second, that each subpersonality lives in a different world, remembers a different past and strives for a different future; and third, that some of these subpersonalities seem capable of knowing things that appear to be impossible (telepathy, clairvoyance, etc.).

Ellenberger was a tremendous inspiration for me, and I began to study the works of Pierre Janet, Theodore Flournoy, Morton Prince and the other dissociationists (all cited by Jung) who were experimenting with hypnosis a century and more ago. New aspects of Jung's lifework opened up to me, and my concept of the psyche expanded marvelously.

Still, however, I was not sure how "scientific" any of this work was, and I remained skeptical about whether Jung's insights would ever be appreciated by the mainstream of Western thought. At that point, in the late 1990s, I became aware of the new field of Evolutionary Psychology, founded by the married couple, Leda Cosmides and John Tooby. Here were researchers who accepted Jung's view that the human psyche is the product of evolution and that something very much like the archetypes (now called "mental modules") had become the center of discussion.

Here, I thought, were people carrying on the work of Jung—even though they never mentioned his name. As I studied their work, however, I found their ideas more rigid than Jung's and a bit too dogmatic. I began reading the sources that they were citing, and a whole new world opened up for me. What I discovered and how it affects my understanding of C. G. Jung's lifework is the subject matter of *Jung in the 21st Century*.

Volume 1, *Evolution and Archetype*, presents a coherent and unified perspective on Jung's lifework as an outgrowth of the dissociation school of a century ago, with special attention to how the essence of his theories has been rediscovered by contemporary evolutionary science. The nature of the archetypes, the complexes, the role of dreams, relationship between ego and self, the transcendent function—all of these deeply "Jungian" concepts are actually supported by what brain science, the science of animal behavior, paleontology and similar fields have discovered. Working out the details in all of this really does give us a Jung for the twenty-first century, one whose views are dependable, not only because Jungian analysts say they are effective in the consulting room, but also because laboratory work links them solidly with the biology of the human organism.

Volume 2, *Synchronicity and Science*, takes up Jung's *critique* of science for failing to investigate certain matters that it finds to be impossible or embarrassing: the practical value of altered states of consciousness, the reality of parapsychological experiences and the like. In 1896 Jung urged the members of his college debating society to take up the challenge of these things that lie in the "border zones of exact science" and discover what the truth really is. A half-century or so later, in dialogue with Wolfgang Pauli, one of the founders of quantum mechanics, he offered a new vision of the cosmos—of reality in general—one in which life, intentionality (striving for the future) and parapsychology are not embarrassing exceptions to reality as we know it but just as deeply real as everything that we naively take to be self-evident. There is substantiation, too, from physics and biology that Jung's speculations in this realm enjoy a good deal of support.

The Jung described in these two volumes may be a more radical critic of Western culture but a more cautious and astute theorist than many have guessed.

Acknowledgements

I should like to thank my analysands and students at the C. G. Jung Institute, Boston for giving me a chance to work out many of the ideas in this book, and particularly the Psychology, Culture and Religion Group of the American Academy of Religion, which held sessions on Evolutionary Psychology and the Study of Religion at two annual meetings in 2001 and 2002.

Personal thanks for suggestions, responses to early drafts, and the like, go in alphabetical order to Christopher Bamford, Nathaniel Barrett, Louis S. Berger, Michael T. Bradley, Jr., Ann Yoost Brecke, Kelly Bulkeley, Benjamin Campbell, Pamela Donleavy, James M. Haule, David A. Hogue, Gregory Love, Dan Merkur, Holmes Rolston, III, Mary T. Ruffin, Jeffrey Schloss, Sonu Shamdasani, Maxine Sheets-Johnstone, Jeffrey Timm, Cecile T. Tougas, and William S. Waldron.

For their help in publishing, Katherine Boyle, Jane Harris, and Kate Hawes.

Abbreviations

The following works of Carl Gustav Jung are abbreviated for simplicity of reference.

CW   *The Collected Works of C. G. Jung*. Translated by R. F. C. Hull. Princeton, NJ: Princeton University Press. Volumes are identified as *CW1*, *CW2*, etc., followed by the paragraph number in which the citation occurs. Volumes *CWA*, *CWB*, *CWC* are addenda to the *Collected Works*.

FJL   *The Freud-Jung Letters: The Correspondence Between Sigmund Freud and C. G. Jung*. Edited by William McGuire. Translated by Ralph Manheim and R. F. C. Hull. Princeton, NJ: Princeton University Press, 1974.

Letters   *Letters*. Edited by Gerhard Adler with Aniela Jaffé. Translated by R. F. C. Hull. In two volumes: 1973 and 1975. Princeton, NJ: Princeton University Press.

MDR   *Memories, Dreams, Reflections*. Recorded and edited by Aniela Jaffé. Translated by Richard and Clara Winston. New York: Pantheon, 1961.

PJL   *Atom and Archetype: The Pauli/Jung Letters, 1932–1958*. Edited by C. A. Meier, with C. P. Enz and M. Fierz. Translated by David Roscoe 2001.

Sem25   *Analytical Psychology: Notes of the Seminar Given in 1925*. Edited by William McGuire. Princeton, NJ: Princeton University Press, 1989.

Sem28   *Dream Analysis: Notes of the Seminar Given in 1928–1930*. Edited by William McGuire. Princeton, NJ: Princeton University Press, 1984.

Sem32   *The Psychology of Kundalini Yoga*. Edited by Sonu Shamdasani. Princeton, NJ: Princeton University Press, 1996.

Speaking   *C. G. Jung Speaking: Interviews and Encounters*. Edited by William McGuire and R. F. C. Hull. Princeton, NJ: Princeton University Press, 1977.

Chapter 1

The past and future of Jung

This book emerges from equal measures of pessimism and optimism over the future of Analytical Psychology, the "Zurich School" of psychoanalysis that C. G. Jung started a century ago and that I have practiced more than three decades. On the one hand, pessimism: psychoanalysis was a major cultural force in the twentieth century but has waned significantly in recent decades. Its standing as a "science"—once loudly proclaimed but always somewhat questionable—has become precarious with recent advances in brain research.[1] Worse, within the world of psychoanalysis, Jung has generally been marginalized as a "mystic" who dispensed with science in favor of dubious superstitions. Despite such good reasons for pessimism, however, I am also optimistic. Recent developments in evolutionary biology show that the basic tenets of Analytical Psychology are amazingly "consilient" with the most recent scientific theories and the evidence that supports them. The word *consilience* has been given prominence by Harvard sociobiologist E. O. Wilson, to mean that when facts and theories from different disciplines all point in the same direction, they implicitly support one another and jointly contribute to their mutual likelihood of being proven correct. They "create a common groundwork of explanation" (E. O. Wilson 1998: 8).[2]

Consilience convinces us by its cable-like argument. We follow a bundle of evidence strands, all supporting one another so that gaps here and there in some of the strands do no damage to the argument (Lewis-Williams 2002: 102). Much of archaeology, paleontology, evolutionary biology and neurobiology have no choice but to draw their conclusions on the basis of cabling or consilience, and this is precisely the sort of reasoning Jung employed in developing his theory of the archetypes. Jung dreamed of unifying the biological and human sciences at a time when a cabling of those disciplines had little empirical justification. And he did so with amazing prescience. Therefore, the time has come to tell the story of the remarkable consilience between Jung's archetypal psychology and a biology founded on Darwinian principles and augmented by the science of genetics—what biologists today call the "modern synthesis."[3]

But this is only half of the story. Jung was also relentless in challenging the limitations of science, especially its refusal to admit phenomena that are undeniably real, such as life, intentionality and consciousness. From his university years onward, Jung argued that science had to explore its "border zones," especially the phenomena of parapsychology. Later in life he collaborated with one of the founders of quantum mechanics, Wolfgang Pauli, to formulate synchronicity as a cosmic principle. Although the doctrine of synchronicity is not accepted by contemporary scientists, Jung's *argument* for it is consilient with the scientific thinking that solved earlier problems involving "action at a distance," namely magnetism and gravity.

Specialists and dilettantes

Among the three or four hundred books and articles outside the field of Analytical Psychology that I have read in preparation for this study, only E. O. Wilson's *Consilience* and the articles of a diverse group of scholars that call themselves bio-genetic structuralists mention Jung's doctrine of the archetypes as a possible contribution to the synthesis of knowledge.[4] Wilson adds that archetypal theory has never been sufficiently developed (E. O. Wilson 1998: 85). Among Jungian analysts, only the British psychiatrist Anthony Stevens has publicly recognized the problem: "Concepts introduced by Jung more than a half-century ago anticipate with uncanny accuracy those now gaining currency in the behavioral sciences generally" (Stevens 1983: 27). Stevens notes that no theory of psychology can today "command more than esoteric interest if it fails to take account of biology, physics, and neurophysiology." Jungians, however, have been reluctant to investigate such things, remaining satisfied to be "mesmerized by archetypal symbols" (Stevens 1983: 32, 29).

In the end Stevens has been too much a specialist in psychiatry, not only to explore the broad consilience between Jung and the modern biological synthesis, but also to use this knowledge to begin rethinking the doctrine of the archetypes.[5] The job requires a shameless dilettante, hard-working and curious, someone who has a yen for facts and theories and the patience to sift through mountains of them. Jung viewed himself as a dilettante of this type, "constantly borrow[ing] knowledge from others."[6]

As the author of this study, I put myself forward as such a dilettante. No one can master all of the fields of study involved, but the right sort of dilettante might hope to sketch out the confluence of those fields, leaving it to specialists to follow some of the leads into new territory. My own qualifications for surveying diverse fields of science are limited. In 1963, I earned an undergraduate degree in chemistry and biology and later taught high school chemistry. In 1973, I earned a doctorate in religious studies and taught philosophy and religion at university level. More recently I have taught Jung's *Collected Works* nearly every semester for more than twenty years and published several articles on the history, development and import of his thought.

Jung's dream of a fundamental science[7]

Jung's scientific ambitions manifested as soon as he finished his medical degree and accepted an appointment to the Zurich mental asylum, Burghölzli, where he apprenticed himself to Alexander von Muralt and began studying cross-sections of the brains of schizophrenics under a microscope. However, when von Muralt confessed that for him brain dissection was "just a sport" (Shamdasani 2003: 45f), Jung turned to the Word Association Experiment, where he first made a name for himself by establishing the empirical foundations of neurotic dissociation. He found that emotionally charged words organize themselves into "complexes" or subpersonalities.

In this effort, Jung was working in the middle ground between the French dissociation school of Pierre Janet and Freud's brand new school of psychoanalysis (cf. Haule 1984). It led to a six-year-long association between Jung and Freud, in which Jung strove to accept the sexual doctrine of psychoanalysis. The end of that period was heralded for Jung by a dream of a house in which each floor, moving from attic to sub-basement, came from an earlier period of history than the last. He found a pair of skulls in a pit under the basement floor. He discusses this dream a half-century later, shortly before his death in 1961:

> The dream is in fact a short summary of my life—the life of my mind. I grew up in a house two hundred years old, our furniture consisted mostly of pieces about a hundred years old, and mentally my greatest adventure had been the study of Kant and Schopenhauer. The great news of the day was the work of Charles Darwin. Shortly before this I had been living in a still medieval world with my parents, where the world and man were still presided over by divine omnipotence and providence. . . .
>
> I was fascinated by the bones of fossil man, particularly by the much discussed *Neanderthalensis* and the still more controversial skull of Dubois' *Pithecanthropus*. As a matter of fact, these were my real associations to the dream. But I did not dare mention the subject of skulls, skeletons, or corpses to Freud, because I had learned that this theme was not popular with him.[8]
>
> (*CW18*: ¶485f)[9]

For Jung the dream was a clear description of the layered psyche of his later theories. From the year of the dream, 1909, onwards, Jung looked to phylogeny, the evolution of the species, as a basis for understanding the development of the human individual. In the fall of 1913, he wrote a letter to Smith Ely Jelliffe and William Alanson White, the founders of the brand new American journal, *Psychoanalytic Review*: "We need not only the work of medical psychologists, but also that of philologists, historians, archaeologists, mythologists, folklore students, ethnologists, philosophers, theologians, pedagogues, and biologists" (*Letters*, i: 29f). In 1932, the publisher of Rhein Verlag invited Jung to edit a new journal, to be called *Weltanschauung*, in which Jung and his editors were to "fish out from the ocean of specialist science all the facts and knowledge that are of general interest and make them available to the educated public" (*Letters*, i: 106f).

Although *Weltanschauung* never got off the ground, a more limited but related project did, the annual Eranos Conference to which specialists from a variety of disciplines (unfortunately, few from the sciences) met for a week and discussed one another's papers. Meetings began in 1933 and survived for decades after Jung's death at the villa of its benefactress, Olga Fröbe-Kapteyn, near Ascona in Switzerland (Bair 2003: 412ff). Almost simultaneously, Jung established a lectureship at the Swiss Federal Polytechnic Institute, in Zurich, where "psychology should be taught in its biological, ethnological, medical, philosophical, culture-historical, and religious aspects" (Shamdasani 2003: 15).

In the 1930s, while all these "universalizing" activities were going on, Jung stopped calling his school "Analytical Psychology" and began to call it "Complex Psychology": "Complex psychology means the psychology of 'complexities' i.e. of complex psychical systems in contradistinction from relatively elementary factors" (Shamdasani 2003: 14). In this statement, as was often the case, Jung was working in the spirit of William James, whose model of self and reality has been described as "fields within fields within fields" (Barnard 1998: 199).

A look back at twentieth-century social science

By 1900 little had been established that might have formed a scientific foundation for psychology. Neurology had not yet discovered the nature and function of the neuron. Evolution as a theory was not in doubt, but *how it worked* still awaited the rediscovery of Gregor Mendel's work with pea plants.[10] The scientific study of animal behavior (ethology) had to wait for Konrad Lorenz and Niko Tinbergen in the 1930s. Meanwhile, a century of French experiments in hypnosis had shown that the psyche has both conscious and unconscious portions, and that splits between them are variable and possibly related to traumatic events. Upon this poorly defined foundation, Freud intuited a way forward, inventing a theory of psychotherapy that was compelling, controversial, and vaguely scientific-looking, although rather isolated from the scientific mainstream. Harvard psychologist, J. Allan Hobson, summarizes the situation this way:

> It was owing to the initially slow growth of neurobiology that psychoanalysis diverged from the experimental tradition. And it is owing to the currently explosive growth of the brain sciences that a reunification of psychoanalysis and experimental psychology may now be contemplated in a new, integrated field called cognitive neuroscience.
>
> (J. A. Hobson 1988: 24)

Charles Darwin's theory of natural selection itself required almost a century of debate before rough agreement was reached. Darwin had had the kernel of the theory for a good two decades without publishing a word of it, while he compulsively accumulated data to support it. He was finally forced to "rush" his ideas into print when Alfred Russell Wallace hit upon the same theory. *The Origin of Species* was published in 1859 without a mechanism to explain how natural selection works. Today it is common to define natural selection in opposition to the theory of Jean Baptiste de Lamarck (1744–1829)—for instance the notion giraffes gradually "acquired" a long neck by stretching it a little further in each generation. But Darwin did not clearly reject Lamarckism, even arguing that "information flows from the organism to its reproductive cells and from them to the next generation" (Badcock 2000: 38–40). Only with the rediscovery of Gregor Mendel was it realized that the units of inheritance are relatively unchangeable entities (genes). The "modern synthesis" of genetics and natural selection was forged between 1918 and 1932 (Plotkin 1998: 27). The final piece of the puzzle was supplied in 1953—nearly 100 years after Darwin's initial publication—when James Watson and Francis Crick established the structure of DNA, and the science of "molecular biology" began.

Thus the foundation that Jung was looking for was finally established when Jung was seventy-eight. Complaints that some of his statements about the inheritance of the archetypes have a Lamarckian flavor, therefore, appear to be unfair in view of the fact that no one was clear on the meaning of natural selection until long after the theory of the archetypes had been promulgated.

Through most of the twentieth century, Jung's primary opponent was the "Standard Social Science Model."[11] The SSSM assumed that biology had a negligible effect upon human behavior. Although animals were moved by inherited instincts, human behavior was determined by culture, alone. Our human mind, the SSSM supposed, frees us from the determinism of matter, but shackles us with cultural determinism. At birth our mind is a "blank slate" (*tabula rasa*),[12] waiting to be written upon by culture. Behaviorists measured cultural inputs (stimuli) and outputs (behaviors) and ignored the mind itself. They thought of it as a "black box," the investigation of whose unfathomable innards would simply be a distraction from inputs and outputs that could be measured. They aspired to a science as clean and hard as physics to free themselves from the stickiness and complexity of biology.

While the Standard Social Science Model insists upon a nature/nurture dichotomy, contemporary evolutionary psychology has found that nature and nurture are interdependent. We inherit the neural and anatomical structures that make our experience what it is and give it a species-specific shape. But these inherited structures can be used only in the particular cultural context into which an individual is born.[13] The structure itself is "empty," and each human culture "fills" it with its own specific adaptations. In the words of Konrad Lorenz, "Nurture has nature; . . . nurture has evolved and has historical antecedents as cause" (Plotkin 1998: 60). Similarly, the archetype is "a biological entity . . . acting . . . in a manner very similar to the innate releasing mechanism much later postulated by ethologist Niko Tinbergen" (Stevens 1983: 39). The maturation of the Darwinian paradigm has restored the continuity of humanity's place within the Animal Kingdom.

In 1973, while the SSSM still dominated the scene, evolutionary biologist Theodosius Dobzhansky set the tone for future studies: "Nothing in biology makes sense except in the light of evolution" (Richerson and Boyd 2005: 237). Today, evolution is the braid in the "cabling" of arguments in biology and the social sciences. During the reign of the SSSM, Jung's theory of the archetypes seemed to diverge from the general course of Western science. Now that evolutionary theory has matured, however, the existence of archetypal patterns is no longer outside the purview of science. All living beings depend on them, and every human archetype has evolved from pre-human precursors. We are not set apart from nature; we are part of it.

The task ahead

Evolutionary psychology was founded in the 1980s by people who saw that psychology was "in trouble." Because, "No general theory of how the mind works was on the horizon," they realized they would have to "make psychology consistent with the other sciences by founding it on evolution" (Aunger 2002: 35). Now it is not only possible but also essential that we finally take up the work Jung dreamed of doing and find the connections between archaeology, primatology, neurology and the rest. A truly Darwinian science of the mind and of culture is beginning to assemble and must have a decisive impact on how we conceptualize the archetypes.

Not Jung, but Robin Fox, an anthropologist at Rutgers University, said: "What we are equipped with is innate *propensities* that require environmental input for their realization" (Fox 1989: 45). Fox insists that no account of the human condition can be taken seriously if it ignores the five million years of natural selection that have made us what we are (Fox 1989: 207). He lists more than twenty human patterns that would be sure to manifest if some new Adam and Eve were allowed to propagate in a universe parallel to ours. These would be archetypal realities, passed on through DNA, and expressed in distinctive neuronal tracts in their brains. Such behavioral patterns would surely include customs and laws regarding property, incest, marriage, kinship, and social status; myths and legends; beliefs about the supernatural; gambling, adultery, homicide, schizophrenia, and the therapies to deal with them (Fox 1989: 22).

Jung said pretty much the same things in the 1920s. He did not do the research, and he did not know many who agreed with him. He just had a damn good hunch. In the end, however, science *works* with its hunches, tests hypotheses, discarding some and refining others. Hunches always lead the way, while testing and refinement keep them viable. A theory of archetypes risks becoming nothing more than a "folk theory of psychology"[14] if its consilience with the other fields in the grand Darwinian synthesis is not tended to.

A "folk psychology" lives outside the mainstream of cultural and intellectual discussion and devotes itself to private, "interior" experience. Often it prides itself on speaking an almost secret language. Historian of psychology and lecturer in psychiatry at Harvard Medical School, Eugene Taylor, has made a strong argument that folk psychology is exactly what Analytical Psychology is: that, in the United States, it belongs to a long "shadow" tradition going back as far as the Great Awakening in the early eighteenth century, and including Quakers,

Swedenborgians, Christian Science, and Esalen. By "folk psychology," Taylor means "a mythic and visionary language of immediate experience . . . usually some form of depth psychology" whose "function is the evolution and transformation of personality" encompassing themes "of deepest, highest, and ultimate concern" (E. Taylor 1999: 15).

Analytical Psychology runs the risk of becoming not only a "folk psychology" but a "mystery religion" as well. There is nothing derogatory in what I mean by a mystery religion. During the Hellenistic period and the early Roman Empire, underground religions kept alive a vast reservoir of wisdom about morality, consciousness changing and the spiritual life. Many Jungian analysts believe they are doing the same thing today, and are very likely not deluding themselves. But adherents of a mystery religion cut themselves off from the mainstream cultural dialogue and agree to speak a different language. They may even delight in the numinosity of that language, and they may be right to do so; for such words and metaphors may harbor a great wisdom.

It seems that Jung foresaw this dilemma in the 1930s when he was trying to "fish out from the ocean of specialist science all the facts and knowledge that are of general interest and make them available to the educated public." He tried repeatedly to contribute to the cultural conversation, to found a Complex Psychology that belonged under the evolutionary tent, talking the language and using the metaphors that the wider world uses. As the twenty-first century began, the time for Complex Psychology had finally arrived.

Archetypal hypotheses may someday become testable; if so, the tests will likely be performed in the laboratories or digs of other academic specialties that work under the umbrella of evolutionary science. "Complex Psychology" will go right on "borrowing knowledge from others." It is the aim of this book to sketch a borrowing program, to bring together a large number of discoveries from several Darwinian specialties and see what they tell us about Jung's ideas.

The borrowing program

Part I of this book attends primarily to archetype as a species-specific behavior pattern. We review Jung's definitions (Chapter 2) and examine language behavior as a model archetype (Chapter 3). The evolutionary roots of language are traced into our primate heritage (Chapter 4), and we discuss two forms of symbolic communication that make our species unique, language and art, in Chapter 5.

Part II examines the relationship between psyche and brain. Chapter 6 provisionally accepts the mainstream opinion that psyche and brain are two aspects of the same reality—where psyche is the subjective dimension, the lived brain, and the brain itself is the objective "substrate." In Chapters 7, 8 and 9 we see that neurobiology supports Jung's theory of the distinction between ego and self and the compensatory role of dreams, and in Chapters 10 and 11 that it actually *explains* his theory of the feeling-toned complexes. Chapter 12 deals with the neurobiology of psychotherapy, while Chapters 13 and 14 describe the relationship between archetypes, altered states of consciousness and psychological transformation.

Part III takes up Jung's idea that the human psyche itself has been "evolving" over the course of our species' history. Chapter 15 reviews Jung's claims about the history of consciousness, and Chapters 16–20 describe our emergence from our primate roots and the ways we have used our consciousness from the Paleolithic era to the present. We end with the problem Jung identified as the crisis of modernity: the split in our Western psyche between an underdeveloped capacity for altered states of consciousness and a highly developed capacity for technological thinking. Chapter 21 summarizes the results of this study.

Part I

Evolution, archetype and behavior

When psychologist Noel W. Smith, whose findings are very useful to our argument, discovered striking similarities between the rock art of the California Native Americans and that of our Ice Age ancestors in the caves of Europe, he felt required to make the following disavowal: "'Archetypes' are the mystical concepts invented by psychoanalyst Karl [*sic*] Jung. There is no objective evidence for them nor is any possible" (N. W. Smith 1992: 13). It is not unusual for such repudiations to include a misspelling of Jung's name or more serious errors of fact. They reveal that the scholar in question is dealing with Jung's rumored reputation and not with any ascertainable facts. Smith evidently believes that Jung propounded archetypes as inherited *images*, a view that Jung struggled all his life to correct.

We begin our review of Jung's relationship with contemporary science by clarifying the essence of archetype. It is a behavior pattern. No one doubts that animals inherit behavior patterns; and with the advance of evolutionary science in the last few decades, very few any longer doubt that humans do. Although Jung described archetypes in various ways, the strong trend of his views has turned out to be amply supported by the structure of brain-and-psyche as modern science understands them.

After a survey of Jung's claims about archetypes, we shall describe language as a model archetype and pursue its evolutionary roots into primate communication and sociality. We end this section with an investigation into what sets our species apart from other primates.

Chapter 2

Jung on the archetypes

A vague notion of what would later be called "archetype" began to structure Jung's thinking as early as 1909, as he searched for a central "nuclear complex" in the psyche. On the hunch that all humans have a fundamentally similar manner of organizing and interpreting the world, it seemed that mythology would hold the key. For it is ancient, held sacred by entire peoples, and explores the fundamental questions: who we are, where we come from, what our purpose is and the absurdity of death.[1]

Although one reviewer found more than thirty different definitions of *archetype* in a single volume (*CW9i*) of Jung's *Collected Works* (R. F. Hobson 1980), there is at least one stable fact. The archetype is always some sort of structuring principle that lies outside of everyday consciousness and, when it emerges suddenly, exceeds all subjective expectations. Running into such an archaic reality, Jung said in 1911, is like encountering a 2000-year-old Corinthian column on a modern street corner—the last thing we expect, yet disturbingly familiar.

> Just a moment ago we were given over to the noisy ephemeral life of the present, when something very far away and strange appears to us . . . on this very spot . . . two thousand years ago . . . similar passions moved mankind, and a man was likewise convinced of the uniqueness of his experience.
>
> (*CWB*: ¶1)[2]

Sometimes we seem to find "archetypes" outside ourselves as fascinating objects and people, but even so, something *inside* makes the experience possible. Archetypes guide our perceptions and behavior, often without our awareness. Encountering puberty is a perfect example. Every one of us "remembers" the same package of experiences our ancestors have undergone. When it has not yet happened, we are incapable of imagining it. But once it hits us, we can barely remember how things used to be. Falling deeply in love is another. Every time eros invades our life, the experience seems unique and unrepeatable— the first time it has occurred in the history of the world. And yet, it is as old as time.

Lamarckian flirtations

Jung is often at pains to point out that he did not invent the idea of archetypes, that it has a history, including Plato, Augustine, Malebranche, Bacon, Herbert of Cherburg, Descartes, Spinoza, Kant, Lévy-Bruhl, Hubert and Mauss, and Adolf Bastian.[3] In some places, he specifies that it is precisely the imagination that is structured by the archetypes of the unconscious—just as space, time, and the categories structure our Kantian consciousness.[4]

At a time when Darwinian conceptions were still rather fluid and in dispute, Jung borrowed language and imagery that today leaves him vulnerable to the suspicion that he believed an image of great power could somehow cause a precise mutation in one's sperm or ova and thereby be inherited by one's children. Today we are much more conscious of how absurd that notion is than were social scientists between 1880 and 1920, before Gregor Mendel's theory of genetics had been integrated into the evolutionary synthesis.[5]

Thus, in 1920, Jung was using several problematic terms to characterize what later came to be called the archetype, calling it a "primordial image . . . a mnemonic deposit, an imprint or engram (Semon)" (*CW6*: ¶748). Seven years later, he said the unconscious itself was the "totality of all archetypes," and "the deposit of all human experience right back to its remotest beginnings" (*CW8*: ¶339). In 1928, he said our ancestors had "traced these paths," and that every time an experience of that impressive type "breaks through" it opens up "an ancient riverbed" (*CW8*: ¶100). "Endless repetition has engraved these experiences into our psychic constitution" (1936, *CW9i*: ¶99). These passages leave no doubt that Jung is sincerely trying to align his incipient concept of archetype with the process of evolution. But the images imply a Lamarckian rather than a Darwinian process.

Confusingly, however, Jung also sought to disavow the language of these published statements. He insisted that the term "primordial image" (borrowed from Henri Hubert and Marcel Mauss 1909) and the term "collective representation" (borrowed from Lucien Lévy-Bruhl 1922) did not have anything to do with inheriting images or ideas, themselves—but rather "of having the possibility [to generate and entertain] such ideas" (1917/43, *CW7*: ¶101, 104). What was inherited was, he said in an inspired fit of ambiguity, "an organ of psychic energy" (1920, *CW6*: ¶754). Overlooking the inconsistency in his own language, he insisted to the end of his life that his "critics have incorrectly assumed that by archetype I mean 'inherited ideas,' and on this ground have dismissed the concept of the archetype as a mere superstition" (*CW18*: ¶524).

Archetype and instinct: Darwinian glimmers

Our concern, therefore, is to determine what an archetype would have to be if it were more than a "mere superstition," indeed a concept harmonious enough with modern biology to aspire to the status of a genuine "human science." It would have to be inherited with our DNA and give rise to typical brain structures whose employment correlates with the behaviors ascribed to the archetype. Furthermore, it would have to have identifiable precursors in evolutionary history, as seen in primates, mammals, and even "lower" animals. Fortunately a great many of Jung's assertions about human mental inheritance seem very much in tune with natural selection.

As early as 1918, he said, "We receive along with our body a highly differentiated brain which brings with it its entire history . . . that age-old natural history which has been transmitted in living form since the remotest times" (*CW10*: ¶12). More vividly put thirty years later:

> It is more probable that the young weaver-bird builds his characteristic nest because he is a weaver-bird and not a rabbit. Similarly, it is more probable that man is born with a specific human mode of behavior and not with that of a hippopotamus or with none at all.
>
> (*CW8*: ¶435)

We are born with a structured brain and mind, not a "blank slate" (*tabula rasa*); rather the "instincts . . . engender peculiar thoughts and emotions" that express "ever recurring patterns of psychic functioning" (1958, *CW18*: ¶1271).[6]

In 1912, he referred to "vestiges of obsolete functions" that still occur in our minds today" (*CWB*: ¶36). By 1927, however, he had removed the Lamarckian overtones:

> This whole psychic organism . . . preserves elements that connect it with the invertebrates and ultimately with the protozoa. Theoretically, it should be possible to "peel" the collective unconscious, layer by layer, until we come to the psychology of the worm, and even of the amoeba.
>
> (*CW8*: ¶322)

If it had been known at the time, Jung would surely have been delighted to cite the brain-like functions in the *E. coli* bacterium in support of his intuition:

> The mechanisms whereby they [*E. coli*] sense, remember, and move about their environment provide an excellent model for the basic features of nervous systems, albeit in an organism contained within a single cell and lacking a brain in a conventional sense.
>
> (Allman 1999: 3)

It is still true today that *instinct* remains a fairly loose notion. Jung called it "a biological phenomenon of immense complexity . . . a borderline concept of quite indefinite standing" (1932, *CW11*: ¶493). Nevertheless it remains useful to speak of "instincts" or "drives" when trying to describe the archetypes.[7] In 1919, Jung wrote: "Instincts are typical modes of action" (*CW8*: ¶273), while "archetypes are typical modes of apprehension" (*CW8*: ¶280); instinct and archetype "determine one another" (*CW8*: ¶271). The instinct drives the behavior pattern, while the archetype apprehends the environmental and/or physiological conditions under which the instinctual behavior is an appropriate response. No instinctual behavior will be initiated unless its archetype "apprehends" the necessary conditions.

According to his favorite example, every human archetype functions like those primitive and unvarying mechanisms that drive the yucca moth and leaf-cutter ant to perform highly complicated activities to fertilize their eggs and provide for their survival. Because the adult sexual forms of these insects are so short lived, they never have a chance to observe and learn their mating behavior before they have to carry it out. Archetypes shape innate tendencies that predate all learning. An innate releasing mechanism is identical with the archetype and functions *in place of learning*. While an instinct "drives" them to reproduce, a closely related archetype enables them to "recognize" the appropriate season and the specific plants necessary for depositing eggs and feeding future larvae.[8] Insects carry out such behavior patterns with invariable precision, and with nothing like what we would call "consciousness."

Another aspect of the instinct/archetype relation Jung proposed in 1919 is based in this higher complexity, where the archetype "might suitably be described as the instinct's perception of itself or as the self-portrait of the instinct" (*CW8*: ¶277). The reproductive archetype of the yucca moth apprehends the flowering yucca plants as "affording" it the opportunity and necessity of reproducing.[9] It sees, smells, and feels the blossoming plant *as* an archetypal image. This is the trigger that fires the instinctual pattern. An archetypal image gives the instinct direction.

An insect's behavior pattern is automatic and pre-established. But as we proceed "upward" from phylum to phylum, evolution builds increasing complexity, enabling wider ranges of freedom. In the human imagination, instinctual reactions appear in symbolic fashion, "as ideas and images, like everything that becomes a content of consciousness" (*CW8*: ¶435).

Thus it is that not only our "behavior patterns," but also our dreams, fantasies, illusions, hallucinations, art work, religion—all are structured by the archetypes. Although no part of our experience is free of such structuring, and so subtly that we rarely notice it, there are also times when we undergo disturbing changes in our awareness due to a new archetype interrupting our everyday waking lives. A specific emotional charge may enthuse us, disorient us, or put us "under a spell."[10] We may find ourselves hyper-alert, dreamy, overwrought, or in some other "altered" state of consciousness.

Summary

Although Jung was not a systematic thinker and juggled a variety of different images and ideas to sketch in broad strokes what he intuited as an "archetype," he nevertheless provided a clearly discernible core of notions. An archetype is a module of inheritance recognizable by typical patterns and images. It is the instinct's recognition of appropriate conditions and goals. Subjectively, it manifests as a powerful emotional charge that invests what we see with overwhelming significance. Although it manifests in lower phyla as automatic and inflexible patterns, greater brain complexity gives animals increasingly greater freedom in adapting those patterns to individual circumstances.

Chapter 3

Language
A model archetype

We like to pretend that we are not really animals, for "they" have instincts while "we" have language, culture and free will. William James vigorously denied this cultural assumption more than a century ago: "[N]o other mammal, not even the monkey, shows so large an array" of instincts as "the human species" (James 1890: 737). Instincts (archetypes) give us the capacity to learn some things rather than others, to learn some things more quickly and easily than others, and to learn some things at some times and other things at other times. If an instinct is an unconscious tendency, universal in a species, that makes us do things even when we do not know why, language is surely one of them; for it unleashes an amazing cascade of effects quite suddenly around the age of three years. What amazes us about language and tempts us to deny its instinctual nature is the fine instrument we can make of it. But at bottom, it is an instinct and an archetype like any other.

Language is an "innately guided behavior." For just as bees are innately guided to flowers but have to learn the details of their local blooms, so we are innately guided to pay attention to vocabulary, grammar, and syntax (Aitchison 2000: ix). To say that language is an *archetype* rather than an instinct is to emphasize the "apprehending" and purposive aspect of language. From our earliest babblings to our most eloquent rhetoric, we are innately guided to pay attention to nuance. *Pull* is not the same as *bull*; and *cracked* is considerably less than *shattered*, though both are broken.

A model archetype

Steven Pinker, while directing the Massachusetts Institute of Technology's Center for Cognitive Neuroscience,[1] wrote three books (Pinker 1994, 1997, 2003) that reveal how consilient Jung's archetypal theory is with the modern biological paradigm—even though Jung himself is never mentioned. In *The Language Instinct* (1994), Pinker describes how we are innately guided to become linguistic beings,[2] giving us a model for what to expect of an archetype. Every healthy human infant is driven to mimicry and compulsive babbling which gradually sorts itself out into recognizable words. The process is guided by a language archetype that directs baby's attention toward *our* loquacity. And, though the learning of

English rather than Chinese is a *cultural* artifact, the learning of language itself is "a distinct piece of the biological makeup of our brains . . . [much as] spiders spin webs because they have spider brains, which give them the urge to spin and the competence to succeed" (Pinker 1994: 18).

Effortless learning

As children approach their third birthday, they rapidly acquire a vocabulary of thousands of words and the grammar rules to make sentences possible. In contrast, Pinker (1994) says, no other primate has ever learned grammar. Certainly some monkeys have specialized calls—very much like words—to indicate danger from above (an eagle), below (a leopard), or deep in the grass (a snake). And when a single monkey vocalizes one of them, the entire troop will take the appropriate evasive behavior (Dunbar 1996: 48). But such word-like sounds are never strung together. Monkeys have no grammar. Indeed, Pinker says that chimps "just don't get it" (Pinker 1994: 340).

Pinker's judgment is a bit too harsh. Douglas Keith Candland, Professor of Psychology and Animal Behavior at Bucknell University, says that our human-centered judgments underestimate the intelligence and communicative abilities of apes.

> We do not know the meaning of the ape gestures . . . nor do we know very much about the mind of the ape. . . . Our task now is to learn the language of the animal in order to understand its perceptions. Then we may communicate.
>
> (Candland 1993: 351)

Dorothy L. Cheney and Robert Seyfarth, respectively Professors of Biology and Psychology at the University of Pennsylvania, agree. They have been studying the communicative intelligence of monkeys in the wild: vervet monkeys in East Africa and chacma baboons in Botswana (Cheney and Seyfarth 1990, 2007). They report that while baboon *vocalizations* are not "syntactic" (i.e. are not strung together according to rules), the animals' "social knowledge, their assessment of call meaning, and their parsing of call sequences display a number of syntactic properties." Every vocalization is recognized in terms of who made it, what it concerns (care for an infant, announcement of a predator, etc.) to whom it is directed, what it means in terms of the hierarchy of the social order and the motives of the parties involved. The social background and its history (who is friends with whom, who is sleeping with whom, who is fighting with whom and over what) gives each exchange a sort of soap-opera complexity (Cheney and Seyfarth 2007: 268f).

It seems, therefore, that non-human primates know what it is to communicate with others and do so all the time, even though they do not employ a syntactic language to do so. Their communication implies a full background of social knowledge, knowledge of the world, and memory of recent events. Their *knowledge* is syntactic even if their sounds cannot be analyzed in a linguistics laboratory.

As regards the use of human language by animals, Pinker (1994) is right. *Most* trained animals are indeed practicing a sort of stunt for applause rather than acquiring a vital life-tool. Nevertheless, a few chimpanzees and bonobos have learned to participate rather deeply in the spontaneously creative interaction of human language.[3] Creativity is the key, for Pinker says that the language archetype does not simply imitate, it creates language anew: "Complex language is universal because children actually reinvent it, generation after generation—not because they are taught . . . but because they cannot help it" (Pinker 1994: 32). The evidence for such "reinvention" lies in the difference between a pidgin language and a creole.

Pidgins and creoles

A pidgin is a rudimentary language system that develops when adults who have already acquired one language learn to communicate simple notions non-grammatically in another. When, for example, a colonizing community of English traders establishes a base in a far corner of the world, the natives there have to learn a few words and expressions of English (Aitchison 2000: 11). By contrast, a creole is a real language with a large vocabulary and its own complete grammar. Haitian Creole, for instance, is a French-based language spoken by an entire nation. Originally, French colonists and the native speakers generated a pidgin, but as soon as that language was heard by a generation of children, the language archetype in those children *created* a brand new grammatical language. "A pidgin can be transmuted into a full complex language in one fell swoop: all it takes is for a group of children to be exposed to the pidgin at the age when they acquire their mother tongue" (Pinker 1994: 33). The same is true of sign languages.

Universal Grammar?

As a student of Noam Chomsky, Pinker believes evolution has equipped us "with a plan common to all grammars of all languages, a Universal Grammar, that tells us how to distinguish the syntactical patterns out of the speech of our parents" (Pinker 1994: 22). "Huge chunks of grammar [become] available . . . as if the child were merely flipping a switch to one of two possible positions" (Ibid.: 112). This claim looks similar to Jung's idea that the archetype itself cannot be known although it structures everything that we do come to know. It would explain why a Korean patient who dreams of the Buddha and a European patient who dreams of the Christ may be dreaming the same "message," albeit in separate cultural imagery. It implies that there may universal human themes that always appear in distinct cultural garb.

Pinker (1994) goes even further than the notion of Universal Grammar, however, and speculates that we do not think in English or Chinese, as we believe we do, but rather in what Rutgers Philosophy Professor Jerry Alan Fodor calls "mentalese," the "language of thought" which "must be richer in some ways and simpler in others" than any of the known languages. Knowing English, then, would mean "knowing how to translate mentalese into strings of words" (Pinker 1994: 81–2). Pinker creates an unnecessary problem here. Do we inherit a "collective language" like "mentalese," or do we inherit the possibility to *create* language? These are separate hypotheses, and Pinker wants to embrace them both, thereby putting himself out on the limb of claiming that specific mental contents are inherited which Jung tried so hard to saw off.

"Mentalese" looks like an instance of what philosopher A. N. Whitehead called "misplaced concreteness," turning an abstract concept into a thing (Whitehead 1929: 10). Since no one has determined the contents of "mentalese," it is probably sufficient to think that our brains are built to recognize linguistic structures and learn the vocabulary and grammar of a mother tongue. Once set, what formerly was an open potential acquires definite form, say, that of English. After this, the established mother tongue interferes with our ability to adapt to the rules of a second language, as Jung wrote in 1945/54:

> The unconscious supplies as it were the archetypal form, which in itself is empty and irrepresentable. Consciousness immediately fills it with related or similar representational material so that it can be perceived.[4] For this reason archetypal ideas are locally, temporally, and individually conditioned.
>
> (*CW13*: ¶476)

The biology of language

Language and the brain

The anatomy of the language archetype would seem, in principle, to be fairly simple to establish: "If there is a language instinct, it has to be embodied somewhere in the brain, and those circuits must have been prepared for their role by the genes that built them" (Pinker 1994: 299). Fortunately, our present knowledge of the brain allows us to specify precisely where most of the "language circuits" are located (Figure 3.1). In a left-side view of the human brain, the most prominent characteristic is the Sylvian fissure that diagonally divides the frontal lobe from the temporal, running upward and toward the back of the head. Just in front of that fissure in the lower portion of the left frontal lobe is a bump known as Broca's area (identified in 1861 by Paul Broca) that is involved in the motor output of communication and the stringing of sounds together to form words. Broca's area also handles visual information about language, from reading and signing. A little higher up the path of the Sylvian fissure, but behind it on the temporal lobe, is Wernicke's area (identified by Karl Wernicke in 1874) which is concerned with analyzing the auditory input to the brain.[5,6]

On the front half of the language region with Broca's area lies the motor strip that controls the jaws, lips, and tongue, as well as the region that processes

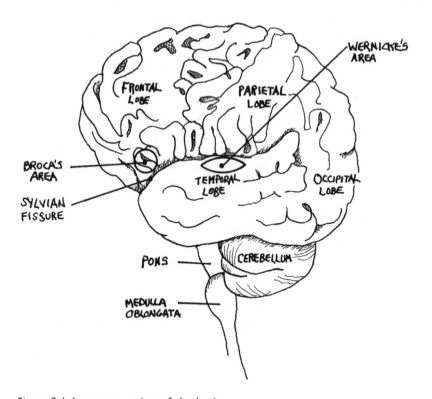

Figure 3.1 Language region of the brain.

Source: original pen and ink drawing by Ann Yoost Brecke.

grammar. On the back half of the perisylvian region, Wernicke's area sits at the crossroads of three lobes of the brain (frontal, temporal, and parietal) where it can integrate information regarding visual shapes, sounds, bodily sensations, spatial relations, and some aspects of meaning (Pinker 1994: 307–13).

The whole left perisylvian region of the cortex "can be considered the language organ," says Pinker (1994: 307) in one place, although elsewhere he says, "No one has yet located a language organ or a grammar gene" (Ibid.: 46). This confusing state of affairs results from the fact that it is not quite true that the brain is "hard wired" for anything: injuries to parts of the brain outside the "language organ" can result in the loss of certain types of language mastery (Pinker 1994: 313ff), and injuries to parts of the left perisylvian are sometimes followed by other parts of the cortex taking over the temporarily lost language function (Ibid.: 309f). Indeed, there are so many exceptions to what has seemed to be established about the brain, that one theory claims, "[M]ental processes are patterns of neuronal activity that are widely distributed, hologram style, all over the brain" (Pinker 1994: 314). Pinker shows his disdain for this model by calling it the "meatloaf theory" rather than the "hologram theory," but it is clearly not a case of one theory excluding the other. The situation seems comparable to theories of light: some experiments justify seeing light as streams of particles, while others make no sense unless light is propagated in waves. Although the two forms of light seem to contradict one another, they are found to be "complementary."[7]

The brain constructs its perisylvian region according to inherited "pre-set preferences" (Aitchison 2000: 46). Later, practice in language builds neural circuits that render our mother tongue easy and resists our learning new languages. The same "practice factor" can create new neural pathways to restore brain function after injuries. Thus it appears the archetype itself cannot be located in the brain in any absolute and once-and-for-all manner. Its patterning is in some sense prior to the brain it structures. Later, practice "wires up" neural circuits in accordance with the familial, local and cultural interactions of everyday life. Thus it seems the archetype may not quite be "in" the brain, rather it *uses* the brain. Perhaps we have to look deeper, into the genes, to find archetypes.

Language and genes

According to the Neo-Darwinian "modern synthesis," the building up of the entire body with all its tissues and organ systems is controlled by the genes, which are stretches of DNA, i.e. strings of four different "bases" (conventionally abbreviated as A, C, G, and T).[8] Contiguous "letters" spell three-letter "words" (AAA, CTG, etc.), each one constituting the code and the template for the manufacture of a single amino acid. A string of such three-letter words on the DNA strand becomes the template for a chain of amino acids, a protein, one of the building blocks of the body.[9] This is the simple part of the theory no one doubts. The genetic foundation of the language archetype, however, still escapes scientific understanding, and may forever.

Popular accounts of genetics sometimes make it seem that there is one gene for each human trait (brown eyes, curly hair) or each human disease (breast cancer, Alzheimer's disease). If such a one-to-one correspondence were the case, as unfortunately it is not, we might hope one day to locate the gene or group of genes that produces the proteins and shapes the cells of the brain's language circuits.

> The grammar gene would be stretches of DNA that code for proteins or trigger the transcription of proteins, in certain times and places in the brain, that guide, attract, or glue neurons into networks that, in combination with the synaptic tuning that takes place during learning, are necessary to compute the solution to some grammatical problem (like choosing an affix or a word).
> (Pinker 1994: 322)

It must be remembered that every cell in the body has the same DNA and that what makes a neuron different from a red blood cell is the individual genes in each that are turned on or off. The on/off "switches" are flipped by "transcription factors," which are proteins, and other molecules in the cell's vicinity. This means that the same genes, and the proteins they produce, are likely to be involved in radically different processes in different parts of the body.

Language, we have to conclude, is an emergent product of millions of simple biological processes that, at bottom, are controlled by the genes. If language is an innately guided behavior, the archetype that guides its acquisition and use does not likely lurk somewhere in a simple stretch of DNA. Rather the guiding pattern itself also emerges. The picture is trickier and more mysterious than we had expected. When we look for the language archetype in the brain, it seems that the archetype must be prior to the brain. When we look into the genome for the language archetype, we again encounter little that is definite. The closer we look, the more diffuse it becomes. Although language surely depends on both brain and genes, there seems to be no kernel of language or even of brain that it can be traced back to. Language comes into being in parallel with the tissues and organ systems of the body. Apparently it is not located in any one place but is everywhere at the same time, like a hologram, perhaps.

Language begins in limbic resonance

Pinker's (1994) account of language is limited by his interest in linguistics and the questionable Holy Grail of reconstructing "mentalese." If we are to grasp the full range of the language archetype's function, however, we will have to pay attention to the wider field of communication within which speech and sign language operate. For example, much of the communicative power of language depends upon the emotional inflection we give to the words we speak. The brain centers that handle emotional coloring are found on the right hemisphere, where the region opposite to Wernicke's area is responsible for understanding *emotional* speech and a right-side counterpart of Broca's area activates the muscles that produce the emotional tone we mean our words to convey (Lewis *et al.* 2000: 59). But the roots of communication go deeper than that, beyond the cerebral cortex to the limbic brain, where the neurons are a different, more primitive sort of cell.[10]

Limbic communication

It is sometimes helpful to speak of a "triune brain," as though our human brain evolved in three neat steps (Figure 3.2). Our brainstem shares much of the structure and function of reptiles' brains; and the ring of tissues around it, the "limbic system" (*limbus* is Latin for "fringe"), first developed among the earliest mammals. A hugely developed "neocortex" has expanded to cover those evolutionarily more primitive structures and handles the higher brain functions. Thus our human brain integrates three levels of neural inheritance: reptilian, paleomammalian (or limbic) and neomammalian (neocortex).

The limbic brain has been insuring the survival of mammals for a hundred and fifty million years. It operates automatically, detecting and analyzing emotional

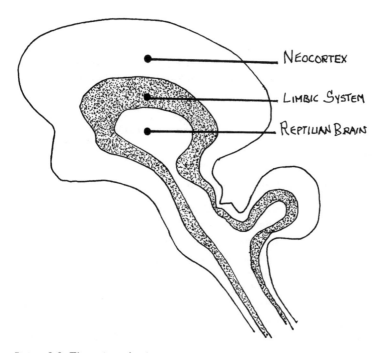

Figure 3.2 The triune brain.
Source: original pen and ink drawing by Ann Yoost Brecke.

cues related to the internal states of other individuals, like a sense organ for *social* meaning (Lewis *et al.* 2000: 62). With our limbic brain, we take special note of facial expression, pupil size, body posture, gait, scent and other factors, and use them to make unconscious calculations to determine the intentions and attitudes of the people we encounter (Lewis *et al.* 2000: 53). It tells us effortlessly whether the person we meet is friendly, aggressive, sexually aroused and so forth. Although our ego-based preference for rational argument often causes us to override the limbic brain's wisdom, it is there whether we want it or not. The limbic system operates so automatically that it forms the foundation of mother-infant communication from the very earliest weeks of life. It is the primitive source out of which the higher communicative functions grow (Table 3.1).

The survival significance of the limbic system can be gathered from the fact that the mammalian archetype of mothering is rendered inoperable without it. Hamsters and monkeys without a neocortex, for instance, can still raise their young, but slight damage to the limbic system renders mothering impossible. Not only mothering, but also every social interaction depends upon the limbic system. After a limbic lobotomy, a monkey will lose all social intelligence and treat its outraged peers as if they were stones or tree trunks (Lewis *et al.* 2000: 32).

Table 3.1 The triune brain

Structure	Phylogenetic origin	Function
Brainstem	Reptiles	Basic plots and actions
Limbic system	Earliest mammals	Emotional influence on the development of plots
Neo-cortex	Higher mammals	Capacity to expand the plots and emotions in as many ways as there are individuals

Source: after MacLean (1993: 40).

Stages in the infant-mother interaction

In the first weeks after birth, mother and infant establish a relationship based on "limbic resonance." Although the mother is surely aware of deliberate efforts she is making to comfort and care for her child, she is probably not aware of the extent to which she is responding to subtle limbic cues. In the baby's case, the appreceptive function of the archetype works as automatically as it does in the yucca moth. By studying mother's face, demeanor, anxiety level and the like, the infant automatically brings its hormone levels, cardiovascular function and other physiological operations into harmony with mother's (Lewis *et al.* 2000: 85).

Stanley I. Greenspan, Clinical Professor of Psychiatry and Pediatrics at George Washington University, and Stuart G. Shanker, Professor of Philosophy and Co-Chair of the Council on Human Development at York University in Toronto, have described the infant-mother interaction in their book, *The First Idea: How Symbol, Language, and Intelligence Evolved from Our Primate Ancestors to Modern Humans* (Greenspan and Shanker 2004). The stages in each infant's development are found to follow the stages traversed by primate evolution, from prosimians to the great apes.

Stage 1

A newborn baby is subject to frequent "catastrophic" emotions, intense global states that involve the autonomic nervous system in fight-or-flight reactions. Distress cries and flailing arms engage the infant's mother, and they stare into one another's face, while mother holds, soothes, cajoles, smiles and caresses her baby. In a deeply archetypal dance, the infant has "his *intent* responded to [and] learns to modulate the intensity of his emotions. He is learning to regulate his mood" (Greenspan and Shanker 2004: 32).

The infant can begin to take pleasurable interest in his sensory experiences, as his catastrophic emotions are tamed and directed toward a social consensus (Greenspan and Shanker 2004: 115). Greenspan and Shanker call this first stage of emotional/gestural interaction, which begins at the infant's birth, "*shared attention and regulation.*" All primate species the authors studied show the same pattern of "regulating emotions." It is an inherited set of expectations, recognitions and responses that the baby misses intensely when it fails. If, for example, a caregiver assumes a still and unvarying facial expression: "The infant typically responds by trying to reengage her caregivers with animated facial expressions, vocalizations, and body movements. When her strategy fails, the infant turns away, frowns, and cries" (Greenspan and Shanker 2004: 46).

Stage 2

A second stage begins when the infant is between two and four months old, the stage of "*engagement and relating*." Here the need for managing catastrophic emotions recedes somewhat and the infant begins to enjoy the relating process and growing sense of intimacy (Greenspan and Shanker 2004: 58f).

Stage 3

The third stage, which is reached at about four to eight months, is characterized as "*two-way intentional signaling*." Here the infant becomes capable of reading and responding to emotional signals from the mother and to initiate new, spontaneous emotional commentary. Automatic limbic resonance has become more conscious and engages the cortex, making cause-and-effect thinking possible. What had been a purely emotional exchange now takes on a logical quality (Greenspan and Shanker 2004: 59f), as the child begins to discriminate the sounds of her own language (*Science News*, April 22, 2006: 246).

Stage 4

From the age of nine to eighteen months, the baby enters a fourth stage, "*problem solving and the formation of a pre-symbolic self*." Now, in "long chains of co-regulated emotional signaling," the child learns the adult's patterns of communication and "to negotiate how she feels herself." In words that might have been taken directly from Jung, Greenspan and Shanker speak of "islands of intentional behavior," that later will be integrated into a sense of ego,[11] a process that conveys a good deal of learning about the baby's own culture (Greenspan and Shanker 2004: 61–5).

Stage 5

Language finally becomes possible at the fifth stage, about eighteen months. This is the phase of "*creating symbols and using words and ideas*." Feelings are now conveyed in words and the child is able to entertain internal images that describe "a sense of 'me' versus 'not me.'" Now the child can say, "Mommy play with me!" or "I don't like that." "Intelligence has reached the symbolic level" (Greenspan and Shanker 2004: 70–2).

The authors distinguish seventeen different stages, taking us all the way to old age. What interests us in this chapter, however, is the process that unfolds out of the deepest mammalian instincts and gradually refines itself into spoken or signed symbolic communication. Pinker's (1994) description of the "language instinct" got us started, but Greenspan and Shanker (2004: 196) have provided a context that reveals the evolutionary roots of language in "the continuous flow of back and forth emotional signaling." In this framework ambient speech sounds are recognized, discriminated and linked up with everyday intentions and experiences.

What gestures represent

The key to the whole process of becoming conscious, according to Greenspan and Shanker (2004), is the interpersonal modulation of emotional states that reveals to the child that emotions are various, that they can be managed, and then that gestures mean something. Interactive signaling takes its first step in the direction of true language when the representational significance of a gesture is appreciated for the first time. The ability to appreciate symbols is the foundational talent and insight that supports language, where every sound stands for something and long interactive chains of sound become a conversation.

Cultural variation in archetypal expression

It may be tempting to think that "mentalese" is the unifying archetype and that English and Hindi are two of its variants, but Greenspan and Shanker (2004) have given us a new perspective. Cultural training begins the moment a child is born and wires the empty form of the archetype with its own variation on the general pattern. Stepwise negotiation of the infant's emotional world through gestural communication with his mother leads by the time he is a toddler to an understanding of more than a spoken language, but the basic themes of the culture into which he was born: the nature of closeness and dependency, the acceptable limits of assertion and aggression, the behaviors that will earn praise or disapproval, and the boundaries of safety and danger (Greenspan and Shanker 2004: 212). The foundations of a culture's kinship system, family structure, mythology, classification system, hierarchy, and socio-economic strata are all embedded in such discourse and learned by every child (Ibid.: 334).

Generations of experience have, indeed, laid down the archetypes

Human beings are always learning from one another; and those behaviors and representations that become "stably recreated in sequential chains of individuals across generations," justify our speaking of "culture" (Tooby and Cosmides 1992: 119). Learning a specific language and culture is the only way to "wire" a brain.

Synapses and neural networks are formed only by *using* the brain. Everyone's brain is wired locally by familial and neighborhood activities.

In this sense, Jung's "Lamarckian" metaphors have been justified by modern evolutionary science. When he says that generations of experience have "laid down" the archetypes, he is right in the same sense that Tooby and Cosmides (1992) are right, when they speak of a "sequential chain of individuals across generations." No experiences are finding their way into the human genome (as Lamarck implicitly believed), but cultural styles and experiences do stamp their imprint upon our brains.

Each Greenspan-and-Shanker stage of emotional/gestural interaction is accompanied by a characteristic change in brain development, culminating in the fifth stage, when the representational value of signals is first appreciated:

> Left-sided neuronal branching becomes denser as the child comprehends, uses, and sequences more words and masters some of the basics of grammar. The visual-imaging parts of the brain grow as the child begins to engage more and more in pretend play. Both sides of the brain are becoming more specialized as language is rapidly being acquired.
>
> (Greenspan and Shanker 2004: 274)

The meaning of archetype

The investigation of the language archetype allows us to list at least nine factors that describe what an archetype is:

1 An archetype is a species-universal pattern
2 of meaningful recognition, imagination and behavior
3 that resembles behaviors in closely related species,
4 allowing us to trace a hypothetical line of inheritance back to a (possibly extinct) ancestor species,
5 and entails identifiable physiological alterations (brain-tracts, hormones, etc.).
6 As a result of hormone and autonomic nervous system involvement, archetypes are usually experienced as powerfully emotional, even numinous.
7 The archetype itself is an "empty program" that needs life-experience to "fill" it,
8 and this filling process "wires" the brain according to local and cultural styles of living,
9 with the result that "archetypal," in the sense of "mythic" images and expectations always take culture-specific forms.

We have also implied a *tenth* trait, namely that the forms of an archetype's expression may be thought of as "nested" within one another (Figure 3.3). Thus the limbic interaction of mother and infant is the more ancient and primitive form of the archetype, the largest nest. As the interaction guided by the archetype becomes more conscious, differentiated and conceptual, it takes on linguistic form. Thus

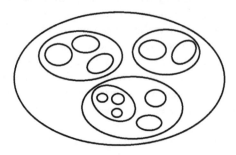

Figure 3.3 A nested hierarchy.

Source: original digital drawing by John Ryan Haule.

speech can be said to be "nested" within the generally mammalian aptitude for reading one another's intentions through facial expression, gesture, scent and the like. It is a more differentiated tool for exploring and sharing information about one another's internal states, and it adds an additional capacity—formulating and sharing detailed information about the world.

Chapter 4

Hundred percent primate

Ten thousand years ago, we were all hunter-gatherers and had been for at least six million years, back to the ancestor we have in common with chimpanzees. Although our brain is rewired in every generation, its basic structure is still 98 percent chimpanzee. Frans de Waal, Professor of Primate Behavior and Director of the Living Links Center at Emory University, reminds us what "talking primates" we are: "People engage in verbal fights, provocative or impressive word displays, protesting interruptions, conciliatory remarks, and many other patterns of verbal activity that chimpanzees perform without an accompanying text" (de Waal 1998: 187).

"How did natural selection prepare the mind for civilization before civilization existed?" asked sociobiology founder, E. O. Wilson (1998: 52). Greenspan and Shanker (2004) have provided a good answer. Natural selection gave us a structured but "empty" brain. As infants, we gazed on our mother's face, tuned our limbic system to hers, and wired our own brain through survival-dependent interactions with a civilized woman. Anthropologist Hugh Brody (2000) discovered something similar when he accepted an invitation from an Inuit named Anaviapik to learn the Inuit language, Inuktitut.

> A lesson I had expected to be about language had also been, or become, a lesson about other things—how to hunt, how to behave when talking, how to use the telephone, how to walk, how to sit . . . how to do and to be *Inuk-titut*, "in the manner of an Inuk."
>
> (Brody 2000: 61)

Wittgenstein (1958: §19) was right: "To imagine a language is to imagine a form of life".[1]

Early primate communication

Recapitulation

Just as there is a non-Lamarckian meaning to "generations of experiences having laid down the archetypes," so the nineteenth century's "recapitulation" theory of embryology. Ernst Haeckel had found that a human embryo has gill slits at one early point and later looks like a fish and then an amphibian. It looked as though every individual passes through evolution's stages one-by-one until it is born in the distinctive shape of its own species. Haeckel's Biogenetic Law therefore states: "Ontogeny recapitulates phylogeny." The similarities in embryo anatomy, however, have proven to be more apparent then real. Furthermore, the recapitulation theory presumes evolution traces out a single "ladder of ascent", whereas it is more accurately described as a many-branched tree.[2]

The Greenspan and Shanker study of mother-infant interactions among primates finds a kind of recapitulation phenomenon, not in the anatomy of the animals but in their capacity for social communication. Table 4.1 summarizes their findings. Tamarins and marmosets never pass beyond the first stage of "shared attention and regulation" that human infants experience in the first two months of life. Adult rhesus monkeys never go beyond the second stage of "engagement and relating," while baboon communication does not advance beyond "two-way intentional-emotional signaling" that human infants develop between four and eight months of age. Chimpanzees, bonobos and (the authors speculate) Australopithecines and *Homo erectus* learn to handle the fourth stage, "long chains of emotional signaling." They make the point vividly in the introduction to their book by providing 300-word descriptions of two nearly identical mother-infant interactions, using only the names of the participants. In the next paragraph they reveal that only one of those pairs was human, the other was bonobo (Greenspan and Shanker 2004: 11f).

Table 4.1 Mother-infant emotional interaction

Human infants	Type of interaction	Primate species
Shared attention and regulation (from birth)	Looking, listening, calming; awareness of outer world patterns	Tamarins and marmosets
Engagement and relating (2–4 months)	Pleasure in relationship, feelings of intimacy	Rhesus monkeys
Two-way intentional-emotional signaling (4–8 months)	Reading, responding to emotional signals; cause/effect thinking	Baboons
Long chains of emotional signaling (9–18 months)	Social problem-solving, start of pre-symbolic self	Chimps, bonobos, Australopithecines *Homo erectus*
Creating representations, ideas, symbols (from 18 months)	Experiences put into words, play, drawing, other symbolic forms	Archaic Homo sapiens (600k–60k years ago)

Source: After Greenspan and Shanker (2004).

Cheney and Seyfarth (2007), experts on vervet monkeys and baboons, say, "To succeed in a social group of monkeys or apes one must understand an elementary form of propositional relations" to manage a hectic social environment. Clearly, natural selection favors individuals who can "form mental representations of others, their relationships and motives," and among baboons this talent has risen to the level of the "language of thought" (Cheney and Seyfarth 2007: 272).

Greenspan and Shanker illustrate what this means with an anecdote about a chimpanzee hunting party. "Through gestures, body movements, head nods, and facial expressions, the hunters coordinate their actions and signal to one another who is to do what and when" (Greenspan and Shanker 2004: 93). In another anec-dote, Greenspan meets three bonobos at the Language Research Center in Atlanta and believes they are indifferent to his presence. Later, when he reviews films of the encounter in slow motion, he is able to see that "a virtual flurry of emotional communication had been going on." The bonobos had been studying Greenspan's every move and "expressing anxiety through fear-grimaces and raised hair," followed finally by acceptance indicated by the slightest of head nods and subtle hand gestures (Greenspan and Shanker 2004: 108).

Perhaps adult chimpanzees and bonobos are capable of performing well above the fourth stage of primate communication skill. For Greenspan discovered that bonobos raised by humans were vocalizing in a high-pitched voice while engaged in emotional signaling with gestures, facial expressions, and body movements. Sometimes he even thought he recognized English words (Greenspan and Shanker 2004: 203).[3] He observed, too, that the bonobo Kanzi and experimenter Sue Savage-Rumbaugh communicated with one another using far more than the 250-icon key-board Kanzi had been taught; they conducted a "gestural dance" that was "centered on the board but not confined to it" (Greenspan and Shanker 2004: 135). Another bonobo took Greenspan by the hand on his first trip to the forest and gave him a gestural lesson regarding which forest plants were edible and which not.

The famous chimpanzee Washoe, raised from infancy in their home by R. Allen Gardner and his wife Beatrice in the 1960s, learned 160 words in American Sign Language (Ameslan). In later life on the "Chimp Island" colony at the Institute for Primate Studies in Oklahoma, she began teaching sign language to other chimps living there. Eventually, Ameslan became "useful to [the group] as a means of communication. Even without reinforcements [from human trainers], they are increasingly using Ameslan to talk to one another" (Linden 1974: 130–4).

Complexities within complexities

As we have gone more deeply into the question of the language archetype, we have found that it is a case of complexities within complexities, much as Jung proposed for the archetypes and all things psychological. Through Greenspan and Shanker (2004) we learn not only that linguistic communication is built upon a limbic foun-dation but also that a large set of interlocking communication skills are related to one another in the shape of a nested hierarchy. Chimpanzees and humans have more "nests" than tamarins and marmosets. But as each of us proceeds through the learning stages of infancy, the skills of one nest are refined into a higher-level set of skills in the next. The language archetype itself is a set of patterns within patterns, each of which is as impossible to isolate as the evanescent "language genes."

The beginnings of language

Greenspan and Shanker (2004) imply that a language comprised of words may have begun as early as 600,000 years ago with one of the Archaic *Homo* species.[4] But other scientists are much more conservative. Many of them, like Steven Pinker and the evolutionary psychologists, make our species an exception, the only one to have "real" language. Jung was suspicious of theories that emphasize the distance between humanity and the rest of the Animal Kingdom. Our Western Christian heritage calls humanity the "crown of creation"—perhaps because Europe is almost the only culture that does not share its world with any non-human primates. If our squirrels had been able to squat on tree limbs and scratch themselves with their fingertips, we might have been more humble. The reality of evolution ought to make us cautious about human exceptionalism, but some of the bitterest disputes in paleoanthropology are waged over this issue.

Singing Neanderthals

Steven Mithen, Dean and Professor of Archaeology at the University of Reading in England, also locates the origin of language in the appearance of our Cro-Magnon ancestors, about 40,000 years ago. Having limited "real" language to our species (Mithen 1996), he conjures up an ingenious and very compelling picture of proto-language in his most recent book, *The Singing Neanderthals: The Origins of Music, Language, Mind, and Body* (2006). He believes that the early hominid communication system consisted in individuals humming to one another. The humming began well before the Neanderthal period (250,000 years ago)[5] but culminated there in the most musical and expressive form of the behavior, which resembles "baby-talk" or "motherese." His argument can be seen as an expansion of the Greenspan and Shanker thesis.

It is the sing-song *tune* of infant-directed speech, not the words, that communicates, for when infants born to English-speaking parents hear a recording of baby-talk in German, Italian or Greek, they respond in the appropriate manner, frowning and smiling to what is being "sung" in a foreign language (Mithen 2006: 72). Even the higher pitch of motherese may characterize the humming of Early Humans, in that the anatomy of the middle-ear canal in fossils where it has been preserved suggests "hominids would have been more sensitive to high-frequency sounds than are modern humans" (Mithen 2006: 129).

Mithen writes "hum" with four or five *m*'s. Before Neanderthals, he says, our ancestors communicated with "Hmmmm" (four *m*'s). The letters describe the communication system in detail. It is *Holistic*, meaning that each sound or string of sounds has a single meaning and lacks meaningful subunits. Nevertheless it carries a variety of *nuances* through pitch, tempo, melody, loudness, repetition and rhythm. The *m*'s in "Hmmmm" stand for multi-modal, manipulative and musical. Hmmmming is used for every sort of situation (multi-modal) and to get people to change what they are doing (manipulative) (Mithen 2006: 138). *Neanderthals* hum with a fifth *m*, mimesis. Mithen (2006) believes they had learned to pantomime and use onomatopoeia to make their Hmmmmming representational: to refer to tracking a bear by acting out both parts while singing a wordless but emotional commentary. Why did Neanderthals not learn to use words and grammar? Mithen says their societies were small and intimate enough that they could understand one another well enough without words; they had not learned to think in signs and symbols; and not much apart from the weather underwent change in their stable culture (Mithen 2006: 228).

Talking Neanderthals

Björn Kurtén, Professor of Paleontology at the University of Helsinki, called by Stephen Jay Gould "one of the world's premier professional paleontologists," expressed his views on Neanderthal lifestyle by writing a novel. In doing so, says Gould, he does not hide from the fact that what all paleontologists do is tell stories to make sense of their findings (Kurtén 1980: xviii).

Kurtén agrees with Mithen's view that Neanderthals spoke with a high-pitched, musical sound which used only two vowels, "ah" and "oh,"[6] and that pitch modulation was essential to their communications. In the novel, Neanderthal speech is heard as "full of uncouth sounds" by the Cro-Magnons. It was neither humming nor a language in which one could whisper. "They gloried in their ancestors, whose exploits and adventures they were ready to tell and retell. . . . who walked unseen by their side, throughout their lives [and to whom] they could turn for advice, encouragement, and precedent" (Kurtén 1980: 30).

A strong argument in favor of story-telling among *Archaic* humans has also been made by Alexander Marshack, Associate in Paleolithic Archaeology at the Peabody Museum, Harvard University. He has studied pieces of bone and antler, most ranging in age from 100,000 to 8,000 years ago, with some examples 230,000 years old. "From the Russian steppe to the tundra, westward to the Atlantic . . . and south to the seacoasts of Spain and Italy, the hunting cultures of the Ice Age have left evidence of notation" (Marshack 1991: 109).

For example, the Blanchard Bone—a flat, oblong piece of bone, about 7½ inches long and 2 inches wide, dating from 34,000 to 32,000 years ago—bears a complex serpentine line of "comma" figures etched into its surface. Close inspection reveals that the marks were made at different times with different techniques and different tools. Marshack (1991: 48) believes that one mark was made each day, that the marked bones were kept as a record of passing time, that the individual who carried the bone and made the marks did so with whatever tool lay nearest to hand on that particular day, and finally that the comma marks are grouped in ways that reflect the phases of the moon. There can be no doubt that the marks were made intentionally and that they are very likely not decorative. Several Native American traditions in North America are known in which sticks are notched for notational purposes and look "exactly like certain Upper Paleolithic notched bones and some Australian message sticks" (Marshack 1991: 139).

Marshack (1991: 25) concludes, "The brain is essentially a 'time-factored' and 'time-factoring' organ." Most vividly, the mastery of fire reveals how pervasive time-consciousness had to be in the everyday life of *Homo erectus*. Wet and green branches will not burn, but they can dry out and be used later. Fire shows signs of life and growth: it must be tended, sheltered from wind, rain, and snow; it must be fed constantly; it "sleeps" in its embers and may "die"; it can be blown back to life with human breath; and its "spirit" can be transported in a burning branch or ember. Fire freed our ancestors to live in new climates and survive the glaciers of the Ice Age, but it also bound them and made them dependent on it (Marshack 1991: 112–15). Marshack makes a strong case that humans who could control fire probably also entertained the first elements of what became mythic narratives, implying that Neanderthals must have told stories.

Grooming and gossip

Assuming that Mithen's humming theory applies to the ancestors of Neanderthals, what tipped the scale to move hominids from humming to language? Robin Dunbar, Professor of Evolutionary Psychology at the University of Liverpool, has outlined a widely respected model of the transition in *Grooming, Gossip, and the Evolution of Language* (1996). His theory is not only simple and plausible, but also backed up with some very interesting statistics.

The evolutionary strategy of primates

Never as powerful as the great predators, primates have had to live in groups to survive. "Indeed, sociality is at the very core of primate existence; it is their primary evolutionary strategy ... based on intense bonds between group members" (Dunbar 1996: 18). Sociality, however, is a problematic refuge. Fear of predation encourages an increase in group size, but overcrowding and competition for a limited food supply, renders groups unstable when they get too large. There is always an ideal range of group size, where the forces of danger from within are in balance with those from without. Even when a group has reached an ideal size, however, primates squabble with one another, trying to steal another's food or settle an old grudge.

Daily life in a troop of primates means keeping a watch for predators while at the same time forming and maintaining coalitions with troop mates. Each animal needs a dependable buffer of reliable relatives and friends it can call upon for defense against bullies inside its own troop (Dunbar 1996: 19). Among monkeys and apes the primary means for cultivating friendship cliques is grooming.

Grooming is essential for health, to keep the skin and fur of one's head and back clean and free of parasites, but it has powerful psychological and social effects as well. It relaxes both parties, reduces their heart rate (Dunbar 1996: 36), and stimulates the pituitary gland to produce endorphins, the natural opiates that suppress pain, elevate mood, and enhance memory (Thain and Hickman 2000). Endorphins like oxytocin also promote strong bonding.

Opiate highs are no doubt the immediate reward that induces primates to spend about a fifth of every day grooming one another. But there is a long-term evolutionary reward as well. For grooming cultivates and cements friendships, and friendly alliances insure that one's day-to-day life will be relatively low in stress. "Only animals that have long-standing relationships groom each other regularly. It is an activity for friends, not for acquaintances" (Dunbar 1996: 68). Lower status animals with fewer grooming alliances experience higher levels of stress, which in females can interfere with ovulation. Poor groomers are less likely to reproduce, with the result that natural selection tends to favor grooming aptitude.

The evolutionary crisis that favored Homo

Somewhere around five million years ago, an ecological crisis forced an evolutionary change upon the apes of the African forests. An Ice Age not only cooled the earth, but also locked up vast quantities of water in the form of glaciers. The sea level dropped and the atmosphere dried out, causing a worldwide drought. African forests shrank and fruit supply diminished, putting the apes at a distinct disadvantage. Monkeys are more nimble climbers and able to eat unripe fruit, whose tannins apes cannot digest. Consequently, apes were forced to the dangerous edges of the forests and into the savannahs, where shade from the equatorial sun was hard to find. There in the tall grasses, upright walking became a distinct advantage: it helped them to see by elevating their eyes above the tops of the grasses and kept them cooler. Upright posture offered a smaller surface area of the body to direct sunlight and opened more of the body to cooling breezes (Dunbar 1996: 106f). "A hairless, bipedal, sweating hominid could have doubled the distance it traveled on a pint of water" (Ibid.: 108).

Risks from predators and other hominids became much greater on the savannahs. Our ancestors had to follow the movement of food-supplying animals and gather fruits and vegetables when they were ripe and where they grew. Nomadic life is inherently more dangerous, as it takes a group into new territories where enemies and predators may lurk (Dunbar 1996: 118f). Thus the pressure to increase the size of the hominid groups grew in order to deal with these environmental threats, and simultaneously the pressure to groom.

Larger group, larger brain

The larger a group becomes, the more individuals there are to keep track of, and the more brain power is required. Thus becoming savannah nomads favored the reproductive success of the largest brained among our ancestors. The idea that there might be a correlation between group size and neocortex size first occurred to Dunbar through studies of bats.[7] Those living in stable groups, like the vampire bat, have a larger neocortex, spend more time grooming, and have special friends who are essential for their survival. Individuals who have failed to find a blood meal are regularly fed by their more lucky companions who regurgitate part of their own meal to help their less fortunate friends. The regurgitator not only preserves the life of a member of its own clique, it also improves the chances that it will profit at some future date when its own foraging has not been successful (Dunbar 1996: 65).

In addition, the ability to use subtle strategies and "exploit loopholes in the social context" depends on the brain's "computing power" and therefore the size of the neocortex. Dunbar (1996: 62) found that neocortex size correlates *only* with group size and not with size or complexity of diet, size of territory, or any of the obvious ecological factors. Extrapolating his figures to include the very large human neocortex, Dunbar calculated that about 150 members would be an average stable group size, a prediction amply supported by anthropological evidence. Put the other way around, human groups tend to become unstable when there are too many members for each to feel comfortably related to each of the others. Our brain capacity is not able to handle the complexities of groups larger than 150 members.[8]

Evolution of language

In an Ice Age hunter-gatherer clan of 150 members, Dunbar (1996) estimates that each member would have been forced to groom 40 percent of every day just to maintain a friendship clique sufficient to insure protection from the inevitable harassment that comes of living in such a large group. This is twice the average of all other primates and simply impossible to sustain in the face of life's other necessities. In fact, such large cliques can only be maintained with language. Gossip, Dunbar suggests, is our human variation on the primate evolutionary strategy of sociality. Assuming that four persons would probably be the upper limit for conversation groups, Dunbar (1996: 121) observes that gossiping can cultivate three personal alliances in the same space of time that grooming can cultivate only one. Dunbar (1996: 110–12) puts the date of the appearance of language at about 500,000 years ago, when group size had reached 115–20 members.

The archetype of sociality

By introducing grooming into our discussion of the evolutionary roots of language, Robin Dunbar broadens the topic. A much larger container for our nested archetypal patterns has come into focus: sociality in general. No doubt the limbic brain makes it all possible, but now we have to consider not only mother-infant emotional interactions and Hmmmming, but also everything that goes on between and among primates—the complexities within complexities that describe the whole field that makes language behavior possible.

Dunbar paints a vivid picture of primate sociality. Primate groups easily distinguish themselves from those of other mammals by their frenetic busyness. At every moment there are significant interactions going on: grooming, squabbling, interventions, trickery, and above all a constant watchfulness, paying attention to who is doing what to whom (Dunbar 1996: 35). The patterns within patterns are difficult to untangle, but we might begin by distinguishing between "empathic" and "aggressive" strategies. Aggressive behaviors have been evident in the Animal Kingdom for upwards of 300 million years—for instance, the "pecking order" of chickens and the way blue jays defend their territory and dogs their bones. The development of *empathic* strategies, on the other hand, is much more recent—Stevens and Price (1996: 49) estimate 10 million years, rather than 300 million for aggressive strategies.[9] These behaviors include currying favor, enjoying and exploring mutual attachments, giving and receiving care—even altruism, perhaps.[10]

While two individuals groom to strengthen their bond of friendship, each may also be checking to see how the other feels about yesterday's fracas, and what effect their grooming has on four or five others who may be jealous or suspicious. Learning to guess what other individuals are thinking becomes a real asset in primate societies. For instance, a rhesus monkey copulating with one of the alpha male's partners will occasionally run to check whether the boss is returning. His mind is in two places at once, not unlike our own (de Waal 1996: 111).

Empathy versus contagion

To some extent the term "empathic strategy" may seem to impute too much consciousness to non-linguistic animals. For instance, de Waal describes a scene in which eight rhesus monkey infants crawl all over a companion infant who is screaming because it had been bitten. These infants are not coming to assist; rather they have been infected with the victim's emotional distress and are seeking to comfort themselves. They represent a case of emotional contagion rather than empathy, for empathy implies the ability to identify with another's emotional state while holding onto the distinction between me and you. Those infants lost whatever identity they may have had, and to emphasize his point further, de Waal (1996: 46) observes that adult rhesus monkeys usually ignore distress in their companions.

Here is a spectrum of consciousness that we have not yet made explicit. The contagion of the rhesus infants implies the kind of emotional connection experienced by a primate infant with its mother—a state of emotional fusion. Still, empathy is not uncommon among primates. Frans de Waal (1996: 52–7) provides a number of instances where monkeys show signs of grief at a companion's demise and make special provision for handicapped individuals. A dying dwarf mongoose is allowed first access to the food, along with the alpha male; and then, because he is unable to climb into his sleeping box, the others join him in sleeping on the floor (de Waal 1996: 80). Dolphins and whales bite through harpoon lines and haul their companions out of nets (Ibid.: 40). Skeletal remains testify, too, that Neanderthals and other early humans took special care of companions afflicted with dwarfism, paralysis, the inability to chew, and other afflictions. The injured individuals would not have been able to survive and grow, and their broken bones would not have healed—as the evidence shows—had their companions not taken special care of them (de Waal 1996: 7).

Theory of Mind

A huge leap has been made in the direction of genuine empathy—as well as a capacity for deliberate deception—when an individual becomes able to make accurate guesses about what another believes. Tests consistently show that human children develop this capacity around the age of four years. For instance, Puppet A gives a cookie to Puppet B, who places it in her pocket. When Puppet A leaves the stage, Puppet B takes the cookie out of her pocket and places it in a box. When Puppet A returns, the children are asked where A will look to find the cookie. Three-year-olds will assume A knows what they know and will (incorrectly) expect A to look inside the box. On the other hand, four-year-olds will be cognizant of A's mentality and will know that there is no reason for A to think the cookie has been moved from B's pocket; four-year-olds are said to have a "Theory of Mind," because they formulate accurate hypotheses about another individual's beliefs.[11] Apes, too, seem to have a Theory of Mind, while monkeys do not.

Mithen (1996) calls Theory of Mind a mental module; Plotkin (1998: 214) calls it "an innate organ of mind." Most discussions of Theory of Mind center on chimpanzees deceiving one another and suspecting one another's motives. Mithen (1996), however, locates it in the evolution of the mind, in that it represents a "second order intentionality": I know not only what I intend, but also what you intend. Fans of television soap operas, he says, demonstrate "third order intentionality"; for they know not only what character A believes but also what character A believes about B's beliefs. Humans are probably capable of five or six orders of intentionality (Mithen 1996: 108) (see Table 4.2). Theory of Mind, therefore, represents the most primitive form of self-conscious sociality, where an individual can formulate and test hypotheses about what others will do and how they will react to developing circumstances.

In *The Human Story: A New History of Mankind's Evolution* (2005), Robin Dunbar says, "The real intellectual work of speech lies in our ability to anticipate how the listener is going to understand—or perhaps *not* understand!" (Dunbar 2005: 119). Theory of Mind, therefore, is an essential precondition for grammatical language. Dunbar uses this fact to argue that apes will never be able to speak, which may be true; but it seems that at least some apes *do* have Theory of Mind and that the bonobo Kanzi can anticipate how the listener will understand his combination of gestures and pointing at icons.[12]

Table 4.2 Orders of intentionality

Orders of intentionality	Description	Animal
0	No awareness at all	None
1st	Aware of own hunger	Fish
2nd	Aware of another's hunger (Theory of Mind)	Chimpanzee
3rd	Soap opera character, A, knows what B believes about C's intentions	*Australopithecus?* *Homo erectus?*
4th	TV viewer of soap opera, above	*Homo sapiens*

Politics and morality

Bees, ants, and termites are social animals, but their social structure is fixed and inflexible; there is no possibility of two individuals changing places in the social order. Politics is about negotiating for position in a hierarchy (Fox 1989: 27), and "chimpanzees never make an uncalculated move" (de Waal 1998: 30). The same is no doubt true of monkeys, who are said to know "not only who is above or below them, but also by approximately how many rungs of the ladder" (de Waal 1996: 101).

When monkeys put down all their challengers and establish prominence, they settle disputes by favoring their relatives and friends. Among chimpanzees, however, it is common for the group leader, the "control male," to place himself above the conflicting parties in a dispute. He often favors the underdog and nearly always places the peace and welfare of the community above his own short-term gains. He must be capable of at least third order intentionality, for mediating disputes surely requires a "soap opera" mind.[13] He exercises not only a Theory of Mind but also an implicit theory of governance. Chimpanzee alpha males, de Waal says, do not dominate but "lead," because they realize that "the privileges of high status [are] contingent upon services to the community" (de Waal 1996: 132).

Chimpanzee politics nearly has a moral dimension. De Waal (1996: 111) believes morality begins "in the primate lineage [with] the evolution of a capacity for guilt and shame." He refers to that little rhesus monkey copulating with the alpha male's consort and repeatedly interrupting his lovemaking to check whether the coast is still clear. Monkeys expect reciprocity, to get what they have given, whether it was food or a thrashing. De Waal (1996: 136) calls this "the first step in the direction of the Golden Rule . . . 'Do as the other did, and expect the other to do as you did'."[14] As we proceed up the primate ladder from monkeys to humans, we see morality emerge as higher orders of intentionality are applied to empathy, internalized social rules, anticipation of punishment, reciprocity, peacemaking and negotiation (De Waal 1996: 211).

The shape of primate society

The archetype of sociality is a set of nested and overlapping patterns (attachment, defense, mother-infant interaction, Hmmmm, Theory of Mind, deception, grooming, gossip, politics, morality), and the roots of these patterns run deep into our evolutionary past. Therefore, if we speak of having an archetype that guides us to form a social order, we know that its boundaries are hard to establish, and that its shape will not likely be fixed. The archetype of sociality, like language, is an empty program. But for our relatives, the great apes, it is less empty. They have considerably less freedom in structuring their societies. De Waal has written a pair of lavishly illustrated books (de Waal and Lanting 1997; de Waal 1998),[15] one on bonobos and one on chimpanzees, that illustrate two rather fixed and opposite approaches to structuring society.

Chimpanzees live in patriarchal societies where shifting alliances between males can bring about major changes in the governance of a group. The males form alliances to control the group and take on the responsibilities of settling disputes and distributing food. There is a great deal of fighting, especially between males who are establishing or challenging alliances, and there are very clear rules for how fights should be pursued. At the end of a fight, the loser is expected to ask for reconciliation. This is generally followed by fervent kissing and embracing and perhaps a lengthy grooming session (de Waal 1998: 27–9).

In contrast to the hot-tempered, burly, and coarse chimpanzees, bonobos are gracile, sensitive, lively and nervous. They rarely threaten one another with raised hair displays and almost never use physical violence, defending themselves when they do by kicking with their feet rather than biting. If a chimpanzee colony is always erupting in violence, a bonobo group resolves its tensions in sexual encounters— between males and females, males and males, and especially between females and females. Bonobos form a female-bonded, female-dominated society where even male rank is determined by the mothers (de Waal and Lanting 1997: 78). Sex has such social importance that bonobo females have extended periods of genital swelling, and sexual receptivity begins at around seven years, long before they are sexually mature. In bonobo society, it is the adolescent females that leave their natal group to visit other bonobo groups and engage in sexual play. Eventually they bond with the females of a new group and make their homes there. In this way unrelated females, through their sexual bonding with one another, form the core of every bonobo society. Because they are not related to one another, continued reaffirmation of their social alliances through sexual encounters is essential.

At feeding time in a zoo, chimpanzees begin hugging one another and rejoicing, while distribution of the food is overseen by the alpha male. Bonobos react to feeding time by displaying their erections and genital swellings. They reduce their competitive tensions by engaging in brief sexual encounters. Bonobo females have first access to the food.

Chimps and bonobos certainly represent opposing caricatures of human social structure: a patriarchy that uses violence to resolve tensions stirred up by conflicting sexual interests, and a matriarchy that uses sex to defuse tensions before they can provoke violence.[16] A sociality archetype that appears to be fixed in one of two positions for our ape cousins is open for wider experimentation and deliberate conscious planning by humans. The patterns within the pattern of sociality, however, reveal our common heritage with the rest of the primate world.

The Cro-Magnon cultural explosion

Just as there are innumerable archetypal patterns nested within and overlapping one another in the realm of sociality, so it is in other areas of life. Steven Mithen (1996) offers a view that it is hard to deny: that humanity possesses at least four "mental modules", language, sociality, physics and biology. Such modules are probably too separate from one another and too much resemble building blocks, rather than the complexities within complexities that Jung spoke of and that appear to be a more accurate description of psychological reality. Furthermore, identifying these four modules as distinctively *human* runs against the whole meaning of evolution, which never starts from scratch, but always builds upon what already exists.

In contrast with Mithen, we would describe an array of archetypes nested in a "physical science domain" by means of which primates and other animals, invertebrate as well as vertebrate, manage their existence in a physical world that obeys dependable laws regarding gravity, the cycle of the seasons and the movement of the stars. Also in the physical realm are the materials from which tools and clothing can be made. We can easily agree with Mithen that our ancestors evidently had an aptitude for recognizing types of stone and wood and how each could be exploited to make sharp tools, straight spear shafts, and so forth. If we speak of a "physical science module," we would argue that it has been there all along and that humans have refined it further than other primates, or indeed than beavers or yucca moths. But we must insist that all animals, however unconsciously, have an innate aptitude for these things—a "universal toolkit," as Marc D. Hauser, Professor of Psychology, Organismic and Evolutionary Biology, and Biological Anthropology at Harvard, describes it (Hauser 2000).

There must also surely be an archetype for sorting out the *natural* world: recognizing species, organizing them by type, discerning the distinctive qualities of a game animal's or a predator's tracks, dung, daily habits and the like. Each of these realms could be described as a pattern within the general archetype that innately suits us for life on Earth. Each is an empty structure. Insects may act upon an innate behavior pattern with rigid predictability, producing very little variation and learning virtually nothing. Birds, mammals, and especially primates fill in the empty structure by learning the flora, fauna, mountains and rivers of their native territory. Humans teach such lore to their children, and very likely so do bonobos, if Greenspan's lesson in edible plants learned from a bonobo at the Language Research Center in Atlanta is any guide.

In addition to these sorts of inherited aptitude, most investigators also speak of a "general intelligence" that can solve problems arising at the limits of a species' specialized archetypes. I am skeptical of this idea, suspicious that it arises from too rigid a notion of a "mental module," one that sees modules as well-defined building blocks rather that as complexities nested within complexities. I believe a conceptual world where the edges between domains are only rarely if ever discernible is more in keeping with experience. Nevertheless, I shall provisionally accept the notion of general intelligence for the sake of simplicity and to follow Mithen's argument. Thus, we can say that the chimpanzees who learned American Sign Language and Kanzi, who suddenly began expatiating broadly with the help of his icon chart, used their general intelligence plus an inborn aptitude for communication to solve problems others of their species had never before faced.

Culture is humanity's survival strategy

Rutgers anthropologist Robin Fox says that two million years ago, our ancestors had a brain only slightly larger than that of a gorilla, and yet they were doing cultured things: building shelters, making tools, treating skins, living in base camps, etc. (Fox 1989: 28f).

> The tool-making animal needed mind to survive; that is, he needed language and culture and the reorganization of experience that goes with these. And, once he got the rudiments and became dependent on them, there was no turning back. There was no retreat to the perilous certainty of instinct.
>
> (Fox 1989: 34)

Human survival became more and more dependent on solving problems one's ancestors had never faced. As new lessons were passed to following generations, a dependable body of cultural lore grew and became indispensable for survival.

Archaeology tells us human culture emerged gradually over the last two million years. A tradition of mentality meandered along, while hand axes were made exactly the same way, millennium after millennium. Here and there in the last half-million years an object of art was made. Around 40,000 years ago, however, a "creative explosion" took place. Cro-Magnon tool making produced notably more varied and specialized products than had ever been seen before. Hunting practices expanded and became more specialized. By 35,000 years ago, stone carvings of abundantly endowed women appeared in great numbers, along with caves painted with well-executed animals, shamans, and vulvas. It is, therefore, evident that those late Ice Age ancestors of ours, the Cro-Magnons who lived in the "Upper" or "High Paleolithic,"[17] had evolved minds that were like ours in every respect. The question is, what happened to make that jump possible?

Mithen's mental cathedral

Steven Mithen has written a well-respected answer to this question in *The Prehistory of the Mind* (1996). According to his view, our modern human mind has been built through three distinct evolutionary steps. First, we had a smoothly functioning general intelligence. Natural selection then added complexity in piecemeal fashion by providing us with specialized mental modules (language, sociality, physical science and natural science). The modules worked pretty much automatically and in isolation from one another and also from our general intelligence, a notion Mithen illustrates by having his readers imagine the floor plan of a cathedral (see Figure 4.1).

The central area of a cathedral is a room with a sanctuary at one end facing rows of pews, a place where a single religious ceremony can take place. To this simple ground plan, the great European cathedrals added "side chapels" so that more than one religious service could be performed at the same time—a solemn Mass celebrating the liturgy of the day at the main altar, for instance, while a small memorial Mass for Aunt Mary is being performed before family members in one of the side chapels. In Figure 4.1, the cathedral floor plan on the left represents the human mind between, perhaps, 500,000 and 100,000 years ago, when language was limited to gossip. Here there are no connections between general intelligence and any of the specialized modules. The modules are open to the outside world but not to one another—except that language and sociality are open to one another, as the nature of gossip requires. Tools were made (physical science module) pretty much as they had "always" been made. No thought was given to

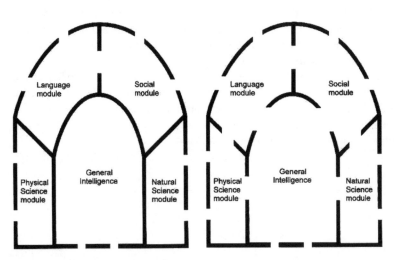

Previous half-million years: Modules have no communication with one another, only directly with the world outside. Language is limited to gossip.

The Cultural Explosion: Modules are all open to one another. Language has become a tool for thinking about and expressing ideas in all domains.

Figure 4.1 The cathedral-floor-plan architecture of the human mind.

Source: adapted from Mithen (1996).

the possibility that different prey (natural science module) might be better hunted with tools of a different design.

The *right* side of Figure 4.1 shows the human mind as Mithen sees it beginning sometime around 100,000 years ago. All the rooms of the human mind were open to each other, and our ancestors first began to realize they could use language not only for gossip but for tool making, hunting, and all the other activities of daily life.[18] An enlarged employment of language, then, opened the walls between our general intelligence and our specialized knowledge, and a cultural explosion was the result (Mithen 1996: 212f). Mithen's model describes a quantum leap in the flexibility and scope of consciousness that does, indeed, make sense of the cultural explosion that archaeology dates to about 40,000 years ago.

Before the explosion, tool making had to be as "unconscious" as driving a car while conversing with passengers. Sufficient attention is directed to the mechanics of driving and the pattern of traffic lights, automobiles changing lanes, and so forth, but there is no deliberate reflection. That is reserved for the conversation we are having with our friends inside the car. Driving consciousness flows uninterruptedly, and we quickly forget what happened a few moments ago as we maintain our place in the stream of traffic. Neanderthals must have had a similar sort of "rolling consciousness" while making tools and foraging. There was no introspection and no critical attention paid to the product, which is why no innovations were produced. It is the reason that tools could be made by identical techniques and achieve identical results for hundreds of thousands of years (Mithen 1996: 148). By the time of the Upper Paleolithic (40,000–10,000 years ago), our ancestors had a brain and mind essentially the same as ours. They knew the phases of the moon, the lore of hunting, told one another stories, and knew the difference between fiction and fact (Mithen 1996: 132f).

There can be little doubt Mithen is on the right track with his cathedral-of-the-mind theory. But another argument may be even more compelling. We need to explore the human mind's capacity for non-ordinary states of consciousness. The phenomenon of the painted cave, the most extraordinary evidence of the Upper Paleolithic revolution, has a lot to tell us about it.

Chapter 5

The archetypes and the numinous art of the caves

Taking language as our model archetype has shown us its genetic, neural, behavioral, apperceptive and hereditary dimensions, and that no archetype can be sharply distinguished from any other. Overlapping and nesting inside one another, archetypes are the complexities within complexities that Jung found to be the best description of psychological reality. One essential aspect of archetype, however, has barely been mentioned: *numinosity*, the fact that archetypal realities are accompanied by an irresistible emotional force that arrests our attention and moves us to do what moments before seemed quite unthinkable. Like the face of Helen that launched a thousand ships or the cosmic intuitions that moved the Egyptians to build the pyramids and the Europeans of the Middle Ages to build the cathedrals, archetypes speak always and everywhere with vital motivating force.

Numinosity derives from *numen*, Latin for "divine command." Archetypes speak with the authority of a god. Jung says, "Zeus no longer rules Olympus but rather the solar plexus" (*CW13*: ¶54). "The archetypes are ... patterns of behavior ... which express themselves as *affects*. The affect produces a partial *abaissement du niveau mental*" (*CW8*: ¶841); this "partial lowering of the mental level" means a loss of conscious energy so that the field of awareness is narrowed down to the archetypal theme. An archetype speaks with the authority of a god because it fascinates us so powerfully that we no longer have the interest or will power to consider everyday matters that concerned us just a moment ago.

When we think of our species' first culture, nothing fascinates us more than the painted caves. The images have not lost their power, for the people who were fascinated enough to make them were just like us. "The brain that painted the caves of Altamira was quite good enough to invent moon rockets; it has not changed in the meantime" (Fox 1989: 133). Our brain is still gripped by those images, and that raises the question as to whether the force that caused our ancestors to integrate their mental modules—to begin using language for physics, biology and politics, and not just gossip; to become revolutionary inventors of weapons, hunting techniques, political alliances and great art—might be connected with those fascinating caves.

Caves with elaborately painted walls have been found at more than 300 sites throughout Europe, from Andalusia to the Ural Mountains. There were probably thousands of them—some not surviving weather or geological changes, some under water since the glaciers melted at the end of the last Ice Age (Clottes and Courtin 1996; Clottes and Lewis-Williams 1998: 59). Upper Paleolithic art appeared as a flood of production, as though what had long been possible and "in the wind" suddenly became irresistible and manifested everywhere (Rudgley 1999: 234–9).

Because we will never recover the meaning of the caves for the people who painted them (Davidson 1997: 127), African rock-art specialist David Lewis-Williams proposes four principles to follow in drawing up a convincing account of the art. No theory can be finally "proved," therefore one must strive for a view that (a) has internal consistency, (b) accounts for diverse fields of evidence, (c) is anchored in verifiable, empirical facts, and (d) leads to further questions and research (Lewis-Williams 2002: 48f). In the end, Lewis-Williams and Jean Clottes base their view—today's most widely accepted account—on three undeniable facts. First, that each cave complex has to be seen as a single, planned unit which makes sense as a whole. Second, that the images themselves have a dreamlike, floating, detached quality. Third, that whatever our ancestors were up to, they were employing the same brain and body that we have today.

Failed theories

Totemism and hunting magic

The first modern guesses as to the meaning and purpose of cave art took their inspiration from anthropologists' reports of totemism among modern hunter-gatherers. The preponderance of painted animals over human figures seemed to recommend the theory that tribal moieties identified with certain animals had made those images as a magical assistance for hunters. The dominant theory between 1920 and 1960 concentrated, then, on the "killing" of the animals painted on the walls and ceilings of the caves and argued that the images played a role in "hunting magic."

Interpreters believed the painted animal in the cave was a potent stand-in for the real animal living above ground; and if the hunter were to enact the hunt in ritual and myth below ground in the cave, he would be assured of success in the hunt for meat to sustain his community. Apparently the ritual involved repeatedly redrawing the animal on the cave wall, an hypothesis that seemed to explain why so many of the painted figures had their outlines retraced many times, possibly over the course of centuries. Once the magic had been invoked, then, the animal in the painting was symbolically killed when the hunters drew "points" on and around the painted image, suggesting their arrows and spears. Slashes were scratched into the wall, as though the animals were being dispatched (Clottes and Lewis-Williams 1998: 66–71).

Eventually, the hunting magic theory had to be abandoned. The spirit of totemism itself argued against the totemic/hunting theory of art, for totem animals symbolize a clan and may not be killed. Furthermore, the walls of most caves do not bear the images of any animals that were hunted for food, but primarily of dangerous beasts—mammoth, rhinoceros, cave bear, cave lion (Clottes 2001: 116).

Structuralism

Between the 1940s and 1960s another far more abstract theory was pursued, namely the "structuralist" notion that primitive people "think" and organize their world in terms of "binary oppositions," such as male/female, right/left. The primary exponent was André Leroi-Gourhan, director of the Musée de L'Homme in Paris, who studied the animal groupings in sixty different caves, and assigned a gender significance to each species, ignoring the fact both males and females of most species had been clearly painted. Jean Clottes, called the "dean" of contemporary cave art interpreters, and David Lewis-Williams, Senior Mentor in the Rock Art Research Institute, University of Witwatersrand, summarize criticism of the structuralist interpretation of cave art:

> Was it reasonable to think that in paintings made over the course of thousands of years, each made reference to others, and that before drawing any new figure the artists took stock of those already in existence? Why would the number of animals have no importance? If they had only general symbolic value, how to explain the fact that they were drawn with details allowing for the recognition of the age, gender, posture, or activity? And finally, the proposed schema were not applicable to many caves, the newly discovered ones in particular; the theories were not confirmed.
>
> (Clottes and Lewis-Williams 1998: 78)

Elements of a more holistic interpretation

With the failure of the structuralist interpretation, anthropology was in a state of shock; and when Leroi-Gourhan died in 1986, anthropologists declared a moratorium on grand theories. David Lewis-Williams describes this policy as "Mr. Micawber archaeology," after the famous character in Dickens' *David Copperfield*, who was always waiting for something to "turn up." Theories will not "turn up" all on their own; they have to be proposed, tested, and either refined or abandoned. Instead of imitating Mr. Micawber, then, Lewis-Williams proposes a few general principles that nearly everyone agrees with: the organization of the space, shamanic themes and the human capacity for trance.

The caves as dramatically organized space

The art of the caves will never be understood unless one takes each cave-complex—all the rooms, passageways, alcoves, basements, and attics—as a meaningful whole. The visitor would take note, for instance, that in the Lascaux cave (Figure 5.1), two

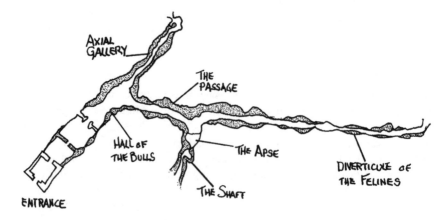

Figure 5.1 Map of the Lascaux cave.

Source: original pen and ink drawing by Ann Yoost Brecke.

lines of animals in red, black, and yellow converge and then seem "to stream into a funnel-mouth, toward and into a dark hole which marks the way into a deeper gallery" (Pfeiffer 1982: 1). Those ancient painters put a lot of time, effort, and vision into decorating the chambers and tunnels. They had a small industry making their paint. They must have devoted a good deal of attention to questions of placement and atmosphere. Which caves should be painted, which walls and ceilings within those caves, what animals in what combinations, which ones depicted realistically and which in distorted or fantastical shapes? They must have considered, too, the routes to and between the chambers, and the effects traversing them would likely have upon their visitors. The caves must have been conscientiously planned (Pfeiffer 1982: 143).

It is not only the cave complex as a whole that is carefully planned, but every nook and cranny as well. In the Cosquer cave, for instance, great attention was given to painting animals and other figures in "secret corners and restricted places, to low areas that one can slip into only with difficulty" (Clottes and Courtin 1996: 124). It seems as though the viewer is meant to be rewarded for spending time in the cave and exploring all its corners, to employ more and more imagination, as though to say: "Spirit-figures fade in and out of the visible realm in this sacred place. Attend!"

Deliberate distortion of the image to produce intensified feelings of awe and mystery in the viewer (*anamorphic* effects) are very common in the caves. Thus in the Tito Bustillo cave in Spain, a painting of a horse with a distorted, elongated neck and snout is wholly transformed when seen from below, and then appears to be a "perfectly proportioned horse" (Pfeiffer 1982: 142). Robert Bégouën, one of the three brothers who discovered the side-by-side caves of Trois Frères and Tuc d'Audoubert, and who is now assisting Jean Clottes in studying the caves, led journalist John E. Pfeiffer through a long set of tunnels and around obstacles in the Tuc d'Audoubert to the point that Pfeiffer had lost all thought of art objects. Bégouën suddenly stopped and whispered, "*C'est ici!*"

> At that moment, and for a moment only, I saw, not two miniature clay bison close at hand but two real-life, full-sized bison at a great distance. They were climbing together up a slope, side by side, every line of mane and muscle sharp and in focus as if caught in photoflash, in a motion-picture frame. My perspective, my frame of reference was transformed. For that moment I was no longer in the dark, underground and enclosed and looking at clay figures, but standing on the edge of a cliff out in the open and looking at animals on a hillside across a wide prairie. A double illusion, because at that distance I would have needed high-power binoculars, plus direct sunlight, to see the bison in such detail.
>
> (Pfeiffer 1982: 132f)

One is advised to spend an hour or two in the caves in complete darkness before attempting to look at the paintings, and then to do so only with a flickering oil lamp, such as the artists used. After fifteen to thirty minutes, the animals seem to become animated in the flickering light (Pfeiffer 1982: 113f). One has to "adjust and readjust one's field of view, in effect to look large, medium, and small," and to change the angle of the light frequently (Pfeiffer 1982: 32). Images seem to emerge from the walls and hold us in their thrall, and then at the slightest tip of our head, "the image retreats into the Stygian realm from which it was coaxed" (Clottes and Lewis-Williams 1998: 91).

Pfeiffer (1982: 124) concludes that the caves were designed to "imprint essential cultural information." He believes that a growth in population density during the Upper Paleolithic made such propaganda necessary, and that cave art provided "highly charged emotional, inspirational settings for the sharing, imprinting, and passing on of new traditions" (Pfeiffer 1982: 195). We might well imagine that the painters, sculptors, and lay-out artists who executed the caves were struggling to give form to vague but imperative inklings and intuitions about the human condition, about life on earth, about the real and the surreal—not unlike the artists of our own time. Furthermore, ritual appears to have been a vital function of the painted galleries, for "resonant areas [within the caves] are more likely to have images than non-resonant ones" (Lewis-Williams 2002: 225).

The shamans

In contrast with the care devoted to the depiction of animals, human images are surprisingly crude. Apart from the cave entrances, there are almost no female forms but many vulvas. Men are few in number, often nearly stick figures, and sometimes having or perhaps wearing the body parts of animals. They usually display an erect phallus. Such figures have been called sorcerers or shamans in light of the worldwide tradition of shamanic practices based upon cultivated trance states. Nearly all scholars agree with this position, and the reason is not hard to find, as Paul Bahn points out: "The phenomenon of shamanism is almost universal among extant hunter-gatherers, and it is virtually certain to have played a major role in the Upper Paleolithic" (Bahn 1992: ix).

In his classic overview, *Shamanism: Archaic Techniques of Ecstasy* (1964), Mircea Eliade collects anthropological reports from every region of the earth, and argues that shamanism is characterized by visionary journeys through the air or under the Earth on the part of an expert, the shaman, who sometimes rides or takes on the figure of an animal for the purpose. Shamanism envisages a three-tiered cosmos in which a shaman is capable of descending to the underworld or ascending to the celestial realm. The shaman-like male figures, therefore, have given rise to the notion that the caves represent the visionary realm encountered in the ecstatic shaman's journey.

David Lewis-Williams explains that the capacity to "shamanize" is probably a feature common to all mammals. It is part of our heritage and a viable candidate to be the source of the massive psychological integration that made the cultural explosion of the Upper Paleolithic possible (Lewis-Williams 1997: 324).

The role of posture in trance

Felicitas D. Goodman (1990), retired professor of anthropology at Denison University, specializing in possession-trance religions, founded the Cuyamungue Institute to study the nature of non-ordinary states of consciousness. She may have discovered important information about how our Upper Paleolithic ancestors were experimenting with trance. She began by organizing workshops of students whom she assisted into altered states by rhythmically shaking a rattle. Up to a point all participants experienced the same set of sensations, augmented heartbeat, elevated body heat, muscle stiffness, shivering, twitching and seeing shapes. Many reported the rhythmic sound of the rattle disappeared or turned into sensations of light. Afterward, they said they were joyously energized in a world that seemed changed and had a distorted sense of time (Goodman 1990: 16). What was *not* the same in the individual reports was the set of visions and beliefs that each experienced as the "content" of trance. Goodman concluded that the trance state must be a kind of empty form that will be filled with whatever belief system the individual brings: "If no belief system is proffered, it will remain vacuous. It is a neurophysiological event that receives content only from signals present in the respective culture" (1990: 17).

Her research took a new direction when she found reports from a Canadian psychologist, V. F. Emerson, that differences in the content of meditation depend upon bodily posture.

> As soon as we controlled for posture, something much more important began emerging. The experiences began falling into place. . . . we found that each

posture predictably mediated not just any kind of vision, but a characteristic, distinctly different experience.

(Goodman 1990: 20)

Hoping to find classic, tried-and-true postures that had been used since time immemorial, Goodman studied ancient art, looking for bodily postures that appeared frequently. One of the postures she selected is that of the bird-headed shaman figure from the Lascaux cave (Figure 5.2). It was nearly exactly duplicated 12,000 years later in Egypt in a painting of Osiris rising to the heavens. Both are lying flat on their backs, but with their heads elevated thirty-seven degrees above their heels. The right arm of the shaman lies next to the body, elbow slightly bent, right hand resting on its outside edge with the thumb pointing upward. The left arm extends straight out from the shoulder, left thumb pointing downward. Summarizing the experience of the participants who entered trance in this posture, Goodman writes:

> [T]he posture prompted such excitation to arise that in the perception of the participants, a flow of energy was churned, the course of which then became controlled, converging on the genitals; hence perhaps the erection of the Lascaux shaman. From there it started streaming up through the body and into the head, and then, as the astounded participants told so graphically, "I was being squeezed out through my head," or "this thing was coming out as an exact duplicate of myself," and "I came out, flying about in the blue." The agreement with countless tales from around the world was evident. In fact, the conclusion was inescapable: We had rediscovered the ancient art of embarking on a spirit journey.
> . . . Put differently, *guided by hitherto unnoticed traditional body postures, these "subjects" of a social-science experiment had taken the step from the physical change of the trance to the experience of ecstasy, they had passed from the secular to the sacred.*

(Goodman 1990: 23, italics in original)

Many of the participants saw birds in their visions or became birds or were taken away by birds, giving a potential reason why the Lascaux shaman has a bird's head or mask and a bird-topped staff.

Goodman found similarly typical themes generated by other postures she attempted. Apparently she has discovered another archetype, a species-wide guiding principle characterized by patterns of bodily energy and visionary content made possible by typical postures the cave painters knew. Perhaps we should not be surprised by this, for we know very well that the yoga tradition has cultivated postures for the sake of producing altered states of consciousness for at least eight millennia.[1] Lee Sannella's (1992) work on the Kundalini experience—which bears some similarities to Goodman's Lascaux shaman experiments—may be an encouraging beginning toward understanding the mechanics of the process.[2]

Figure 5.2 Bird-headed shaman and disemboweled bison in Lascaux cave.

Source: original pen and ink drawing by Ann Yoost Brecke.

Evidence of altered states in the caves

Jean Clottes and David Lewis-Williams (1998) believe the cave paintings reflect altered states of consciousness cultivated by shamans the world over. It "is a function of the universal human nervous system." Entering into a cave, in fact, promotes altered states through social isolation, sensory deprivation, extended exposure to cold temperatures and the uncertain light of a flickering lamp. Without warning, all of our senses "hallucinate" (Clottes and Lewis-Williams 1998: 12, 29, 14).

Stages of trance

The essence of the Clottes and Lewis-Williams (1998) interpretation is that trance is known to manifest in three stages, and that visions characteristic of all three are to be found painted in the caves (Figure 5.3). The stages have been well established and have been used elsewhere to analyze shamanic visions (e.g. Reichel-Dolmatoff 1971, 1975, 1987). The cave's walls and ceilings themselves, then, constitute the evidence for the altered states of consciousness experienced there.

Figure 5.3 The three stages of trance.

Source: original pen and ink drawing by Ann Yoost Brecke.

Stage 1: phosphenes

In the first and lightest stage of trance, one sees abstract geometric forms: grids, rainbows, parallel lines, star bursts, zigzags, dots, and the like. They are brightly colored, flicker, change size and shape, and merge with one another. Such figures occur naturally as "phosphenes" (i.e. objects glowing with light) or "entoptic forms" (i.e. figures internal to the eyes). With the eyes open, one sees them projected on walls. Reichel-Dolmatoff reports that in South America, Native Americans who achieve these effects today intensively discuss the geometric forms and interpret them in line with their mythology. Our Ice Age ancestors probably also made them a matter of community discussion but the point is, they painted them on the walls of their caves. What Leroi-Gourhan interpreted as gender symbols, appear much more likely to be literal representations of the sights people saw when they entered trance. Figure 5.4 compares entoptic forms derived from medical reports (first two columns) with figures painted or engraved on the rocks of southern Africa (middle column) and those on the walls of Ice Age caves (last two columns to the right).

Although the term *entoptic* is sometimes criticized for suggesting the phenomenon is "in the eyes," Lewis-Williams prefers the term because it emphasizes the physiological basis of the experience. Neurons in the visual areas of the cortex are firing independently of information from the eyes: "In other words, people in this condition are seeing the structure of their own brains" (Lewis-Williams 2002: 127).

Some have criticized the entoptic hypothesis on the basis of our not having sufficient evidence for psychotropic drug use among the people of the Upper Paleolithic.[3] However, it is a mistake to think that only potent drugs are capable of producing phosphenes. Noel W. Smith, Professor of Psychology at SUNY, Plattsburgh, NY, lists eleven conditions or behaviors that can generate entoptic forms: waking, falling asleep, fever, photo-stimulation, psychosis, dizziness, migraine, crystal gazing, deprivation of food or water, self-torture and yoga (N. W. Smith 1992: 40). Phosphenes have been observed since Alessandro Volta discovered them around the year 1800 by experimentally applying leads from the

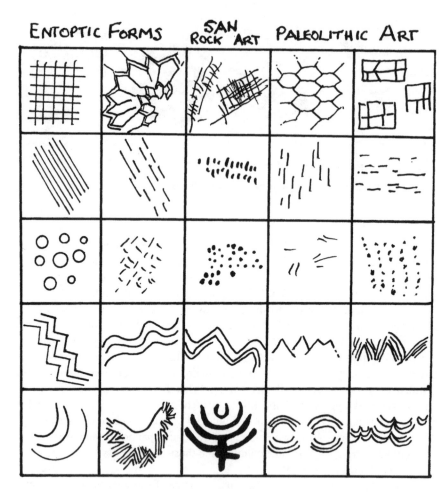

Figure 5.4 A comparison chart of entoptic forms.

Source: original pen and ink drawing by Ann Yoost Brecke.

electrodes of his newly invented battery to his face. About a century later, Jan von Purkinje produced patterns of light in the form of concentric circles using electrical stimulation. Jung (*CW3*: ¶582) believed they were evidence for the archetypes:

> It was the Swiss psychologist Carl G. Jung who first suggested that some of mankind's most ancient symbols might have their origin in these subjective light patterns, and went on to observe that the eight-spoked wheel Purkinje had induced, was also present in South African rock paintings, and that concentric circles and semicircles appeared in Australian pictographs.
>
> (Reichel-Dolmatoff 1987: 15)

Stage 2: ordinary objects

In the second stage, the changing phosphorescent forms seem to coalesce into recognizable everyday objects: baseballs, snakes, etc., as depicted in Figure 5.3.

Transition stage: tunnel

The second stage flows right into the third, as the phosphenes organize themselves into a vortex or tunnel that draws one through into a world of deep trance. The tunnel experience is also certainly archetypal. It is a common feature of near-death experiences and deliberately employed by anthropologist Michael Harner in his efforts to revive shamanism in the modern world (Harner 1980). Lewis-Williams says that the entire "Axial Gallery" in Lascaux cave is a carefully planned and communally executed evocation of the neurological vortex (Lewis-Williams 2002: 252).

Stage 3: mythic world

At the end of the tunnel, one encounters people, animals, monsters, and landscapes that are vividly real, or perhaps intensely dreamlike. Figure 5.5 shows a theriomorphic human from the Trois Frères cave, the shaman or sorcerer as part man, part mélange of animals. His erect penis is feline. Entranced individuals may

Figure 5.5 "Sorcerer": dream-like composite being, from Les Trois Frères cave.

find they can fly or that they become the animals they see or even the geometric forms: "The fretwork is I" (Clottes and Lewis-Williams 1998: 16f).

Themes of death and transformation

David Lewis-Williams came to the Paleolithic caves after a lifetime studying the rock art of the San Bushmen in southern Africa. The parallels and similarities between the two forms of rock art are remarkable—indeed similarities exist worldwide, with the rock art of Australia, North and South America and India. Lewis-Williams' advantage in studying African rock art was that he could inter-view descendants of the people who had made it. It is tempting and hardly implau-sible to apply some of the principles he turned up in those interviews to interpreting the art of the caves.

Trance and death

When an eland is killed In southern Africa, the act of killing, the death of the eland, and the place where it dies are all "filled with power" and may occasion a commemorative dance by the tribal shaman. Furthermore, the blood of the eland may be mixed with the paint to be used in the rock art, in order to fill the paintings themselves with potency (Clottes and Lewis-Williams 1998: 33). Finally, when realistic elands are painted, they may be given "small, easily missed features, such as red lines on their faces, that imply that they are actually transformed shamans" (1998: 34). This does not *prove* anything about the cave art, but it does suggest that many of those "points" and "slash marks" that gave rise to the "hunting-magic" theory might have been intended to indicate that the animals so decorated represent shamans who had been transformed into animals in their trances.

Shamans in North America are said to "die" when they enter trance, the precondition for transforming into an animal (Lewis-Williams 2002: 174). The vortex itself signifies death and transformation (2002: 155), just as in modern near-death experiences. David S. Whitley, archaeologist and internationally known rock art specialist, tells us the association between shamanism and death was so strong among some California Native Americans that the words *shaman, murderer* and *grizzly bear* were used interchangeably. In both death and shamanic trance, the individual collapses, loses consciousness and motor control, his eyes roll back, his vital signs diminish, he may suffer convulsions, and he may bleed from the mouth and nose (Whitley 2000: 110).

The same is true of the San Bushmen; when they enter trance—usually as a result of intense dancing—a supernatural potency is activated, "causing it to boil up their spines until it explodes in their heads and takes them off to the spiritual realms" and sometimes causes them to bleed from the nose (Lewis-Williams 2002: 139–41). Brian Fagan personally witnessed San "medicine men [who] trembled, then sweated, then bled from the nose." He continues with the observa-tion, "Many white hunters have seen dying eland . . . with melted fat gushing like blood from their nostrils" (Fagan 1998: 61). The parallel with the animals and shamans of cave paintings that seem to be passing something from their nose or mouth is too close to overlook.[4]

In general it appears utterly convincing that cave art scenes, like the one in Figure 5.2—where the bird-headed shaman lies beside a disemboweled bison, with its tail up, something the animal will do only to defecate and just before dying— that the death of the animal is linked with the shaman's passing into trance and taking on theriomorphic form. Among the Bushmen, a "dying" shaman may be depicted near an eland dying from a poisoned arrow. The eland's hair stands on end in the rock art, just as it does in reality at death. Meanwhile, the Bushmen speak of hair growing on the back of a man when he is in trance (Lewis-Williams and Dowson 1989: 50f).

Whitley (2000) reports the same theme in California rock art. Bighorn sheep are represented with large and upraised tails, when the natural fact is they have diminutive tails, which they keep between their legs except when defecating or dying (Whitley 2000: 111). They are almost all sexually mature males, and in nearly every case the tail in the painting is made unnaturally large, as though to draw attention to its meaningful position. In the mythology of Mojave Desert rock art, rain falls when a bighorn sheep is killed; and rain-shamans "die" when they enter the three-tiered cosmos of trance in order to cause the rain to fall (Whitley 2000: 59, 91). The San see the eland's death related to the coming of rain (Lewis-Williams and Pearce 2004: 193–5).

The world behind the rock wall

The San believe that behind the painted rock wall lurks a spirit world, and they try to establish a link with that world, not only in their altered states of consciousness but also by means of their blood-powered paint. Just like the Ice Age people in the caves, they blow paint over the backs of their hands while pressing their palms against the rock wall. In this way, they leave the red outline of a hand trying to reach through the wall "into the spiritual realm behind the membrane of rock" (Clottes and Lewis-Williams 1998: 95). Furthermore, the way they have painted many of the animals on the cave walls makes some of the horses and lions seem to be squeezing out through the cracks in the rock, sliding out of the invisible world behind the wall and displaying themselves to rapt initiates (Ibid.: 33). Just as the animals seemed to pass through cracks in the rocks in both directions, so entering the rock wall served as a metaphor for the shaman's altered state of consciousness through which he attained the supernatural world (Lewis-Williams 2002: 161).

That this idea may be universal to shamanism is suggested by archaeologists Miranda and Stephen Aldhouse-Green of the University of Wales, Newport: "Modern shamans, while in trance, persistently experience the sensation of penetrating solid rock or squeezing into cracks" (M. and S. Aldhouse-Green 2005: 99). More remarkably, "In historic western Iberia, Christian saints are recorded as having appeared from fissures [in rock faces] in just this way, and such hierophanies there have led to the Christianization of pre-historic rock-art sites" (Ibid.: 47).

Andrzej Rozwadowski of Mickiewicz University in Poland finds the same theme in petroglyphs east of the Aral Sea in Central Asia. Human and animal figures pecked and scratched into the stone exploit the presence of natural cracks to represent shamanic transformation. The figures are represented as moving into, out of, or becoming transformed as they cross over a natural crack. In this way the artists represent passing between the worlds, changing shape, contacting spirits, and encountering entoptic phosphenes (Rozwadowski 2001: 73–6).

In North America, Noel W. Smith reports that the Ojibwa of the northern Great Lakes drew human-like figures and signs representing life believed to live "behind waterside rock faces, especially those with cracks or shallow caves suggesting an entrance" (N. W. Smith 1992: 51). In California, David S. Whitley reports on a Native American vision-quest dream in which the dreamer attempts to perform cures and in the end enters a rock face (Whitley 2000: 78–81). Each shaman's rock-art site was "his portal into the supernatural: during his altered state of consciousness the cracks in the walls of the site were believed to be open, allowing him to enter the sacred realm" (Ibid.: 74). The California Native Americans knew a coherent mythic narrative describing the structure of the cosmos that makes such transits through rock walls meaningful:

> Another belief was that the power residing in the supernatural underworld spread out, under the mundane surface of the earth, in a web or netlike fashion. Points on the landscape where this supernatural power approached the surface of the mundane world consisted of rock outcrops, including caves, rock shelters and peaks, and the permanent sources, such as springs, lakes, and ponds. Because the supernatural world was inhabited by spirit beings, such locations on the landscape were likewise thought numinous. Indeed, these various locations were the portals into the supernatural . . . [where] it was thought [to be] a perfect inverse of the natural world. Ceremonies, for example, were often conducted at night to correspond to daytime in the sacred; likewise, the ghosts of the dead had no smell in the supernatural whereas a living person, when in this region, smelled as if decayed and rotten.
>
> (Whitley 2000: 24f)

Unified cosmos

Ice Age cave art leaves us with an overall impression of unity. The styles of representation change over tens of millennia, and though we see no unmistakable story being told, what comes through is a numinous vision just the thickness of a rock wall from where we stand right now, where one catches a glimpse of ultimate reality. The empirical world is set within a greater cosmos where beings undergo mysterious transformations and reveal underlying kinships with one another, where death becomes meaningful as finally passing over the barrier that is crossed temporarily by everyone who enters a trance. "Whatever the correct interpretation [of the art of the caves], no one doubts that the paintings reflect close spiritual relationships between the domain of the living and the forces of the supernatural cosmos" (Fagan 2004: 20).

Several theories have been proposed to account for the colossal cultural integration of the Upper Paleolithic. Pinker (1994) sees it as evidence of a neurological mutation that made our brains different from those of Archaic *Homo*. Marshack (1991) says that what looks like a "sudden explosion" of culture is simply an illusion, that the evidence for earlier species of *Homo* achieving similar levels of insight have simply not been preserved. Mithen (1996) says it results from learning to use language in all domains of human life and not just for gossip. I prefer to think the exploration of altered states of consciousness came first, opened up the greater cosmos and brought with it the central mystical insight every tradition everywhere and in every age has discovered for itself: that ultimately all is one and interconnected.

From gossip to social sophistication

David Lewis-Williams (2002) sketches the conscious capabilities of our Cro-Magnon ancestors by comparing them with the Neanderthals with whom they shared Europe for some 50,000 years, right down to the time the first caves were being painted. He says that if Neanderthals experienced altered states of consciousness, they never took note of them, never noticed the range of conscious states at their disposal, never conceived of an "alternate reality," never developed a language of imagery, never learned to communicate their non-ordinary experiences, and never attributed greater power to some individuals rather than others— individuals who had a greater facility for cultivating and using altered states (Lewis-Williams 2002: 93). Brian Hayden, Professor of Archaeology at Simon Fraser University, disagrees. He believes Neanderthals did have the capacity to enter altered states, for although they left behind no images, they did leave evidence of some sort of bear cult practiced in caves. "It seems clear that Neanderthals were exploring deep caves, presumably for the purpose of inducing ecstasy or altered states by at least 50,000 years ago, if not many thousands of years earlier" (Hayden 2003: 118). Probably the spark of cosmological thinking had been smoldering for tens of millennia before it burst into the flame we call the Upper Paleolithic cultural explosion. When it did, all the cultural universals of the human race manifested in visions cultivated in those caves: religion, language, kinship systems, technology, and political organizations (Hayden 2003: 13).

The evidence, however gradual, suggests that our ancestors began suddenly to do everything better. Their hunting showed more strategy; they developed a greater variety of weapons, some with longer range; they carved figures out of stone and in relief on walls; they began to paint fantastic scenes. Very likely they did more than record the moon's phases in notches on bones. They contemplated the greater cosmos of slowly turning star clusters, mostly invisible to city dwellers today, and saw that it is related to what happens here below. They became aware of what they were doing and curious as to its meaning. No sooner did they learn they had a consciousness, they found it could be altered. They could open their outer eyes and see, or their inner eyes and imagine. The cave walls bear witness to what they were attempting.

They probably recognized the parallel between moon and menses, moon and tides, moon and seasons. Primate curiosity took on new dimensions. Millions of years before this, chimpanzees and bonobos became experts in soap-opera thinking and learned to question why their friends and antagonists do what they do. Humans question why the world is the way it is—fourth-order thinking (Dunbar 1996: 104). Science and religion comprise the two fundamental sorts of questions humans ask. We want to know the laws of nature, and we want to know what transcends those laws. Both science and religion were present in the caves. The technology to produce the paints and the scaffolding to reach the ceilings demonstrates what they were capable of doing with science.[5] The themes and executions of their cave paintings demonstrate where their techniques of ecstasy had taken them in the direction of religion.

It is not just that they became "aesthetic." They had to have already developed an ability to "see" images, and that itself required social agreement. There had to be shared values in the forms they painted, and shared conventions as to the meaning of certain shapes, certain animals. "One cannot 'notice' a representational image in a mass of lines unless one *already has* a notion of images. And such a notion must be *socially* held" (Lewis-Williams 2002: 183; italics in original).

Hunter-gatherer societies: simple and complex

Although researchers can surely go too far in making comparisons between our little known Ice Age ancestors and contemporary hunter-gatherers, some things would have to be pretty much the same. For today's hunter-gatherers live in regions where the environment is in some ways as harsh as it was in Ice-Age Europe. Under such conditions, the sharing of food and other resources is absolutely imperative for survival. Private property is virtually non-existent; natural resources must not be exploited competitively; and egotistical behavior has to be suppressed in favor of the group's survival (Hayden 2003: 93). The sacrifice of ego for the sake of communal solidarity is manifest, too, in initiation ceremonies—where, as Hayden (2003) notes, the severity of the initiation increases as everyday conditions become more harsh.

The very idea, however, that some individuals might choose or be chosen to undergo more severe initiations suggests that degrees of personal power and influence were already being acknowledged in the Upper Paleolithic. The immense organization that went into the decorating of the caves implies that Europe at that time was inhabited by *complex* hunter-gatherer groups. They periodically enjoyed an abundance of animals to hunt and developed extensive trading networks and alliances. These things required some specialization and division of labor. Thus our

Ice Age ancestors were not confined to small isolated bands like the Kalahari Bushmen or Australian Aborigines of the recent past, but resembled more the Kwakiutl hunter-gatherers of Canada's Pacific coast, with their large, permanent settlements, substantial division of labor, hierarchical social system, hereditary political rank, and extensive large-scale warfare (Richerson and Boyd 2005: 227). The evidence for this sort of complex social organization in the Upper Paleolithic has been assembled by Hayden (2003): magnificent carvings and paintings, unprecedented wealthy burials, undisputed evidence for elaborate rituals and religious conceptions, beliefs regarding an afterlife, pursuit of altered states of consciousness, animal cults, initiations, shamanism, and ancestor cults (Hayden 2003: 122).

Social complexity and alliance building

In his best-selling overview of the rise and fall of human societies from the end of the Ice Age until the present, *Guns, Germs, and Steel*, Jared Diamond distinguishes four types of society by their size: "bands" with dozens of members, "tribes" with hundreds, "chiefdoms" with thousands, and "states" with 50,000 or more (Diamond 1999: 268f). The organization required to paint the caves must have required the hierarchy of a chiefdom. Someone had to provide the structure by which a throng of specialists from several different fields of expertise were able to cooperate successfully to produce an extensive micro-environment in which the founding myth of the Upper Paleolithic could be entered physically and explored. For the caves were clearly equivalent for their day of medieval cathedrals—architectural embodiments of the myth that guided the consciousness of their builders.

The cathedrals are less enigmatic than the caves only because we know so much more about what those more recent builders of worship chambers had in mind. Hayden's ethnographic experience in Guatemala, Australia, and South East Asia suggests that about 10 percent of a population care nothing for rituals and supernatural beliefs, while another to 10–20 percent have abandoned traditional beliefs for a rival myth. Thus it is not unreasonable to think that a quarter of the Upper Paleolithic population was either indifferent or only mildly convinced. Someone had to "drum cultural conformity into the skulls of their members," and those societies that managed this feat had significant survival advantages over those who did not (Ridley 1996: 189).

A society as large as a tribe cannot function unless someone is able to plan, someone to organize and command, someone to fight, someone to hunt, someone to distribute food and other necessities. There has to be a hierarchy of some kind. And an essential role within a leadership group will have to be the voice of the spiritual world, the one who ties it all together and reveals the transcendent meaning that guides the whole, binds the bands into a tribe, motivates the members to work in new ways, and rewards them with the conviction that they are participating in a process of transcendent significance. This was the job of the shaman, the specialist in entering altered states of consciousness and in mastering them, gaining enough conscious control over one's own ecstatic states as to alter the consciousness of others, heal them, reveal the transcendent world to them, introduce them to the experience of other parts of their brain (Hayden 2003: 66).

Alliances and bonding

No primate other than *Homo* is able to overcome its fear and suspicion of strangers so as to cooperate in joint enterprises. Science writer Matt Ridley (1996) observes that our human capacity to enter into trusting alliances must extend at least as far back in time as evidence of trading networks among Archaic Humans can take us, hundreds of thousands of years. For trade requires a genuine permeability between groups. Chimpanzee troops are closed to emissaries and traders; they have no exchange with one another apart from violence and emigration (Ridley 1996: 201). In contrast, it appears that the principal survival technique of human hunter-gatherer groups has been the establishment of alliances with other bands, both near and far (Hayden 2003: 29).

Emotional bonds stronger than familial ties were necessary. Such was a primary function of altered states of consciousness: to establish and maintain bonds that seem "irrational," for why should virtual strangers assist us and we them? The answer, according to Brian Hayden (2003), is that our human capacity for altered states of consciousness has been naturally selected as a biological adaptation that confers significant survival benefits, namely the ability to form these inter-group bonds. "Groups that had the potential for such religious emotions and used them by holding rituals in which participants entered into ecstatic states . . . would be more likely to survive because of mutual help in time of need" (Hayden 2003: 32). The capacity for altered states may have been what ultimately defines the survival strategy of *Homo sapiens*.

What we have learned about the archetypes

An archetype is a species-specific behavior pattern that recognizes and imagines the settings in which the behavior is an appropriate response. Inherited with our genes as an empty program, it becomes activated automatically when it encounters appropriate stimuli. The details of the inherited pattern are developed and refined through a socialization process that begins in earliest infancy, building neural connections through active engagement with caretakers and the world at large. When an archetype is constellated, our whole body is engaged and its emotional arousal focuses and motivates us with a force that is very difficult to resist.

It is not necessary to go very deeply into the structure of the brain to see that the levels of consciousness/unconsciousness in Jung's model of the psyche correspond very well to how the brain is structured by a combination of inheritance and experience. Table 5.1 can be read from the bottom upwards to describe the archetypal structure of the brain. In the bottom row, we have only the brain with which we are born, prior to experience, as pure an instance of genetic inheritance as can be found. At this point, an archetype like language is an empty form,

Table 5.1 Biology of Jung's model of the psyche

Jung's psyche (levels of unconscious)	Psychic contents	Neural wiring (origin of neural basis)
Personal unconscious	Complexes	Idiosyncratic wiring
Collective unconscious	Mythic images and behaviors (English language)	Cultural wiring (e.g. mother-infant emotional-gestural interaction)
"Archetype itself"	Innate behavior patterns (language)	Biological inheritance (wired by genes)

corresponding directly to what Jung calls the "archetype itself" (*das Archetyp an sich*). At this level of development, the language archetype contains no words or grammar. It is simply the readiness to recognize stimuli that are relevant for the behavior pattern (speech). Later, beginning with mother-infant emotional-gestural interactions, the archetype begins to be filled with patterns of sound, rhythm and grammar. One's mother tongue and cultural assumptions are gradually "wired" into the brain through constant participation in the social life of one's family and neighborhood. Finally at the top row in Table 5.1, an individual's idiosyncratic experiences, traumas and triumphs create expectations along with a self-image and a worldview that are peculiarly one's own. This is what Jung calls the personal unconscious, comprised of habitual, personal patterns he calls the complexes.

Part II

Jung's psyche and its neural substrate

Part I focused on the behavioral dimension of archetype so that we could appreciate what such patterns are, how they are inherited, how they manifest in characteristic ways at characteristic times, how they prepare us to attend to and to work at some things rather than others, how they have evolved through our primate heritage, how they are filled in and completed by culture and how the numinous power of their emotional charge can alter our consciousness and transform us personally, socially and culturally.

Now in Part II we look at the relationship between psyche and its primary physical organ, the brain. In Chapter 6, we consider the relationship between psyche and brain in a general manner, particularly the dominant contemporary paradigm of psyche/brain identity. A Jungian perspective will have some reservations with this paradigm, but we will accept it provisionally so as to more easily demonstrate that Jung's theories are in fact consilient with evolutionary science. Our reservations will be reserved for Volume 2.

Chapter 6

The role of the brain in psychic process

Mind and body seem to be quite different things. We sometimes talk as though the mind gives orders and the body carries them out, or perhaps rebels against a one-sided sort of mind, producing neurotic symptoms. The "machine" of the body—it has often been said—harbors a "ghost" that has a free will, may be immortal, and is probably sullied by its association with matter, instinct and the body's love of comfort.

Some four centuries ago, René Descartes gave voice to this naive body/mind dualism by distinguishing "corporeal substances" that are extended in space from "spiritual substances" that are capable of thinking. When he said, "I think, therefore I am," he identified himself with his thinking soul, which he called "the principle of biological, sensitive, and intellectual life" (Copleston 1960: 129). Along with the vast majority of his intellectual contemporaries, he stayed firmly in the tradition of Western theology, according to which I *am* a soul, which is my eternal identity, and I *have* a body, which is my temporal abode for an earthly sojourn far from my heavenly home with God. For Descartes, therefore, biology deals only with the machinery of organisms. It misses the most important entity, the ghost. Even today, at the start of the twenty-first century, our folk psychology favors a soul like the one Descartes described, but conveniently forgets to worry about how a non-material substance can bring about physical changes. How does a ghost that is invisible to the eye and able to pass through walls, make itself solid enough to pull the neural cranks and chemical levers that move the muscles and steer the body? For: "Anything that can move a physical thing is itself a physical thing" (Dennett 1991: 35).

A matter/spirit dualism like Descartes' is very much with us today. There appears to be a worldwide efflorescence of fundamentalism in religion (Christian, Jewish, Islamic, even Hindu) trying desperately to reassure us that advances in science have not eliminated God and the soul from the world. The new pseudo-science of Intelligent Design is a symptom of our anxiety. If there is no eternal, spiritual substance, no soul, perhaps we just die and cease to exist. Perhaps there is no eternal life, no transcendent meaning, no reward for following the rules or punishment for breaking them. We embrace mind/body dualism because it reassures us. It is part of a mythic narrative, not one that takes us through walls of rock on ecstatic journeys while we are alive, but one that takes us on a never-ending journey far beyond the rocks of this planet when we die.

When we do psychology or philosophy, however, mind/body dualism poses a problem no one has solved. Science has to proceed as though God does not matter to its theories and experiments; for if it had to assume that God can enter the evolutionary process at any moment with miracles, there would be no regularities on which to make scientific predictions and test their validity. Richard Dawkins and others may delight in taunting believers and flirting with atheism; but when they do so, they are not practicing science, only prancing on an ideological stage.[1] Science simply must assume that everything we need to know is in principle right here before us and can be measured. Indeed, much of what counts as progress in science is coming up with new instruments and techniques (electron microscopes, magnetic resonance imaging (MRI) machines) to make perceptible and measurable what was formerly invisible. The problem with a soul like the one Descartes describes is that it is in principle wholly imperceptible to any instrument that will ever be invented.

Four approaches to the mind/body problem

Our folk psychology and Descartes have left us with a "mind/body problem" that has been much discussed over the past three centuries. There are four positions on the issue (see below), each a separate metaphysical stance, a deep claim about the nature of reality. None can be proven. The crucial question is, which most adequately describes the world of our experience.

Dualism

Mind and body are two different kinds of substance. This position seems to do justice to our deep convictions about the nobility of the soul, but we pay a high price for it. Either we deny our soul has anything to do with our body, or we assume they have a mysterious relationship that can never be understood.

Material monism

Monism, the claim that only one principle is involved, avoids the dualism problem. Since it would seem to be foolish to deny the reality of the material world, matter must be the one substance. Therefore, mind must somehow "emerge" out of matter when its organization becomes complex enough, as it is in the human brain. Material monism, the most widely held view today in philosophy and neuroscience, holds that brain and psyche are two aspects of one and the same thing: the psyche/brain identity theory. Psyche is the subjective, first-person brain, the lived brain. Meanwhile the brain itself, the third-person brain, is the object science studies in the laboratory. Scientists look at the brain from the outside, while we inhabit our brain and live "inside" it.

But if matter is inherently devoid of anything resembling psyche, how does it "emerge"? Philosopher David J. Chalmers (1996) notes that the psyche/brain identity theory explains only the *function* of consciousness in solving the problems life throws at us. It ignores what is most important to us about our consciousness, namely what it is like to *be conscious*—the "phenomenological" meaning of consciousness, rather than the "functional" meaning. The proponents of psyche/brain identity are concerned only with the brain's input and output. The Standard Social Science Model of behaviorism returns in a somewhat more subtle form. The "black box" of the brain is now open to inspection, but what we find inside are countless little black boxes, the neurons that handle the inputs and outputs.

Spiritual monism

For this brand of philosophy, the one substance has a spiritual nature. Matter is a sort of necessary illusion concocted by our sense organs. We live in a very impoverished version of a cosmos that is much greater than we know. This is the position of one of the dominant schools in Hinduism, established in the ninth century by Adi Shankara. Consciousness does not need to be explained because it is the one and only constituent of the universe. As absurd as this position may seem to be for most Westerners today, it has been proposed by a few contemporary scientists who take their departure from the fact that quantum mechanics has thoroughly undermined our folk belief in the "solidity" of matter. We now know matter is interchangeable with energy, and that atoms are comprised of subatomic particles that are constantly winking in and out of existence. Amit Goswami (1993, 2001) has intriguingly combined quantum mechanics and Hinduism, and N. C. Panda (1995, 1999) describes how quantum mechanics and astrophysics are generating pictures of the universe that have long been held by Hindu non-dualism (*Advaita Vedanta*).

Matter itself has a psychoid dimension

This position resembles material monism, but denies that matter is inherently devoid of everything related to consciousness. If human consciousness "emerges" from the complexity of neural organization, some primitive form of psychic sensitivity must be present in the parts—in every neuron and every molecule comprising it. This is the position Jung ultimately took when he proposed the idea of synchronicity, that matter has a "psychoid" aspect. We shall examine it in detail in Volume 2.

Jung on psyche and brain

As we saw in Chapter 2, Jung remained consistent throughout his life, arguing that the archetypes are inherited with the structure of the brain, that they represent the results of evolutionary process, and that they are the structural, organizing members of the psyche. He eagerly took up work in von Muralt's laboratory at the Burghölzli, in hopes of learning something useful about the psyche by studying brain anatomy. In a 1906 review of a book by Carl Wernicke, discoverer of the brain's language center, Jung expressed his enthusiasm about finding connections between brain and psyche (*CW18*: ¶891). In 1911/50, he says "the archaic basis of the mind" is related to "inherited brain structures" (*CW5*: ¶38). In 1936/42, he says that the psyche is based on the evolution and anatomy of the brain (*CW8*: ¶234). And most explicitly of all, in 1957: "The collective unconscious is simply the psychic expression of the identity of brain structure irrespective of all racial differences" (*CW13*: ¶11).

There were occasions, especially in the 1940s and 1950s, when behaviorism and the Standard Social Science Model were at their most influential, that Jung insisted on the uniqueness of the psyche vis-à-vis the brain. Possibly the most explicit statement is to be found in the first book he aimed at a general audience, *The Undiscovered Self* (1957), where he said, "The structure and physiology of the brain furnish no explanation of the psychic process. The psyche has a peculiar nature which cannot be reduced to anything else" (*CW10*: ¶488–588). Here, and elsewhere (e.g. *CW11*: ¶14), Jung was battling a notion that had been finding more and more adherents in those days, the idea that the psyche is a mere "epiphenomenon" of the brain—a sort of illusory by-product that has no effects of its own.[2] He said epiphenomenalism makes the psyche "only semi-existent" (*CW11*: ¶769). Significantly, most of today's authorities agree with Jung and reject epiphenomenalism. Philosopher John R. Searle calls it "the view that mental structures exist but are functionally inert [that] consciousness is like the froth on the wave . . . it is there but it does not matter" (Searle 2004: 30).

In one of his most intriguing statements, Jung said of the collective unconscious that it is theoretically possible to peel back the layers of psyche, one by one, until we get to the psychology of a worm or even of an amoeba (*CW8*: ¶322). If an amoeba has a psyche, the evidence would surely be in the fact that every protozoan, like every higher animal, strives constantly to survive and to enhance its life processes. Psyche expresses itself in its holistic striving (intentionality), a process that guides even animals that lack neural tissue. In a letter to American analyst Alice Rafael, September 16, 1930, Jung wrote:

> It is surely a very interesting problem, the question of the relation between the brain and consciousness. Everyday experience tells us that consciousness and brain are in an indispensable connection. Destruction of the latter results in destruction of the former. Bergson is quite right when he thinks of the possibility of relatively loose connection between the brain and consciousness, because despite our ordinary experience the connection might be less than we suppose.
>
> (*Letters, i*: 76)

Jung never seems to have conceived the psyche as a separate substance in the manner of Descartes, but rather a "psychoid" capability lurking in the nature of matter itself.

In this first volume, we go along with the psyche/brain identity theory that most scientists and philosophers agree upon, for here is where the work is being done that supports Jung's astute intuitions of nearly a century ago. We take the position that the psychoid dimension of matter is a fact that science has not yet discovered. When it does make the discovery, it will not need to throw out any of its accomplishments. It will simply understand them better.

Mind as an emergent phenomenon

Francis Crick, who made his reputation in the early 1950s for his part in determining the structure of DNA, went on in the last stage of his career to tackle the question of how consciousness and mind arise from electrochemical events in the nervous system. He argues that the process is emergent, and calls it "The Astonishing Hypothesis," the title of his 1995 book. In doing so, however, he is careful to point out that the notion of emergence has two quite different meanings. Both meanings agree that the whole (consciousness) is greater than the sum of its parts (interacting neural networks). Those inclined to see wonders take "emergence" to be a marvelous process that "cannot in any way, even in principle, be understood." Crick rejects this "mystical" tack,[3] and places his work within the *scientific* tradition: "Although the whole is more than the sum of its parts, it can be understood on the basis of the parts and how they interact" (Crick 1995: 11).

To say that mind emerges from neural events is to claim that "the mind is co-dimensional with the brain; it occupies all the brain's nooks and crannies" (Llinás 2002: 2). According to this view, neural firings are not themselves conscious, and none can be singled out as solely responsible for consciousness; but all of them together cause the specific states of consciousness that we experience. In the words of John R. Searle, Professor of Philosophy at the University of California, Berkeley, consciousness is a "system feature" of the brain, a higher order phenomenon which exists only because neural networks are blinking on and off in their characteristic patterns (Searle 2004: 149). He says, materialism is wrong for trying to reduce mentality to the neural events themselves; and dualism is wrong for claiming that something else exists over and above the physical substrate (Ibid.: 126). He takes a position similar to ours except that he does not question the nature of matter. He somehow believes that "emergence" will do it all without knowing how.

Rodolfo R. Llinás, Professor of Neuroscience and Department Chair at the New York University School of Medicine, calls the brain "a wondrous biological 'machine' that is intrinsically capable of global oscillatory patterns [the composite effect of those blinking networks] that literally *are* our thoughts, perceptions, dreams—the self and self-awareness" (Llinás 2002: 133). He begins his book, *I of the Vortex: From Neurons to Self*, with the neural modules that control well-defined motor functions, such as the movements by which we walk or ride a bicycle—what are called "fixed action patterns." They operate pretty much outside of consciousness, but we can start them up consciously and tune them for specific problems, like keeping our balance while negotiating a rocky path. From our perspective, they are islands of psyche: already psyche-like ("psychoid"), but not yet conscious.

Llinás (2002: 167) concludes that if fixed action patterns are "modules of fleeting, but well-defined motor function," then consciousness consists of "modules of fleeting *focus* in the context of movement". We would say, psyche is the integration of those islands into holistic function. Thus "consciousness" in the sense of ordinary everyday awareness requires the complex arrangement of many elements that have consciousness in a lesser way. "A system with only one or two possible states would not require consciousness." Humans are constantly required to make momentary judgments "which are re-entered into the system for the predictive needs of the organism." Such reentered judgments "*are* the 'ghost' in the machine" (Llinás 2002: 169, 221). In this statement, the ghost has been stripped of its Cartesian nature, as a separate, non-bodily substance and has become the subjective aspect of objective neural events.

Psychic image and brain image

Our everyday experience is filled with images that we seem to watch in our heads, flickering by like pictures on a film strip, or stored in memory banks, as though our brains were living photo albums. Such habits of thought may seduce us into believing that traumatically repressed memories can be restored in all their original accuracy and clarity many years after the events to which they refer. Even scientists and philosophers have until relatively recently spoken of the "registration," "storage," and "retrieval" of memories, as though brains had the capacity to make, hold, temporarily lose, and finally recover cerebral snapshots.

The error lurking in such naive assumptions is to overlook the difference between brain events and conscious experience. Mental images are a different order of being from brain images. Indeed, what scientists sometimes call images in the brain are not images at all, in the sense of pictures of people, objects, and situations. Rather, they are patterns of neural activation. "Blueness doesn't exist in the external world" (Llinás 2002: 100). Blueness is a psychic experience, a universally human mental interpretation of the way certain neurons in the brain respond to wavelengths of light in the 420nm (nanometer) range.[4] Modern neuroscience has abandoned "naive realism" and agrees with Immanuel Kant, just as Jung did: our experience of the world is determined by our human knowing apparatus, while the "thing itself" can never be known as it is, apart from our human brain and psyche.

For the time being we do not need to ask what it is like to entertain a psychic image, for every image that has ever entered our consciousness is a psychic image. It is a matter of everyday experience. What we need to look at more closely, however, is what sorts of things are going on in the brain when we entertain a psychic image.

Having an image in the brain

An image in the brain is "not an objective entity functioning like a picture or other symbol" (Winkelman 2000: 42), but rather is "a simplified representation of the external world written in a strange form" (Llinás 2002: 108). One of the strangest things about that form is the fact that the brain's response to a single being in the external world—say, a bull advancing toward us across an open meadow—activates a multitude of circuits scattered all over the brain in separate regions. In the visual sphere, alone, dozens of separate areas immediately begin analyzing from a variety of aspects the ever-changing shape of the bull's body; and all of these things are being correlated with circuits recently active but now silent, and analyzed for their emotional value; alarms are being sent to the autonomic nervous system to prepare for an emergency requiring flight and to the fixed action potentials in the spinal cord to get our legs churning and headed for the nearest fence. There is no "image" of the bull anywhere in the brain, but the brain allows its energetic configuration to be shaped by the sensory stimuli that impinge upon it in order to mobilize all of the body's systems.

This whole-body response is what it means to have the image of a threatening bull in the brain. Furthermore, essentially the same configuration results when we *dream* of a bull coming toward us across a field. In a dream, the motor response is inhibited by certain centers in the brainstem, but otherwise the whole bodily "set" is the same (J. A. Hobson 1988). This is why, when we speak of psychic images, an entire bodily configuration is implied. Jung was not contradicting himself when he said that "primordial images" are not simply images but typical human situations.

How the brain responds to a stimulus in the outer world is described vividly by Walter J. Freeman, Professor of Neurobiology at the University of California, Berkeley. He asks us to imagine what happens when we grab a coffee pot to fill a mug. The body responds to the sight of coffee pot and mug by shaping itself in a characteristic manner:

> You do not transfer geometric shapes [of those objects] into your brain. Instead you incorporate your body to the forms of the objects by shaping your hands to them, so you can manipulate them. . . . The body . . . changes its own form to become similar to aspects of the stimuli that are relevant.
>
> (Freeman 2000: 27)

In similar manner, but in accordance with the electrochemical nature of its cells, the brain shapes itself in response to the object. When it does so, there is not a single image of a coffee pot anywhere in the brain. Rather, aspects of our sensory response to the coffee pot are fragmented and scattered all over the convoluted cerebral cortex. "Up to thirty-three functionally segregated and widely distributed visual maps in the brain" deal with such separate issues as edges, orientations, color, and movement (Edelman 2004: 44). Much of our cortex is comprised of tiny functional maps, some of the outer world and some of our own body; every-thing is being constantly processed and reprocessed as the activity occurring in one map is relayed to other maps and regions and receives still further inputs itself. The pattern of reactions and mappings that feed into one another always occurs against a background which is the history and goals of the organism (Freeman 2000: 82).

Everything we encounter in our experience of the world activates patterns of similar events we have encountered in the past, and when this happens, "we retrieve not just sensory data but also accompanying motor and emotional data" (Damasio 1999: 161). Every image with historical resonance reconstructs "a tran-sient pattern" that has been mobilized again and again in our lives (Damasio 1994: 105). Antonio Damasio, University of Iowa Professor of Neurology, places auto-biographical sensitivity at the heart of his theory of consciousness. We never experience bare images. Rather, "We are wired to respond with an emotion" when we perceive certain features, such as the size of large animals, the type of motion of snakes, the sounds of aggression (growling), and such bodily states as angina. All these things trigger typical emotional reactions (Damasio 1994: 131). They are archetypal.

The binding problem

In speaking vaguely of blinking networks and scattered maps, we have been skirt-ing one of the major unresolved issues in brain research, the "binding" problem. What "binds" countless psychoid fragments into a single picture of the world? For Descartes the answer was simple, the "thinking substance," the soul, does it all; and does it mysteriously in a manner that, in principle, can never be investigated. But if modern science is right and the brain does it all without a blueprint and without a central control—what makes us function as a unit?

At least three different hypotheses have been proposed to solve the binding problem. Damasio (1999) makes a very convincing argument that whatever we apprehend is grounded in the sensory/kinesthetic sense of our own body at the moment the binding takes place. Our body-sense itself, he says, is the binding element, though he fails to explain what unifies the body-sense. Others have argued that the prefrontal lobes of the cortex, with their many connections across several modes of brain-processing, have a directing function. It is surely plausible that such a brain area that is so important to "final processing" would be crucial for the binding operation, but it is not favored by many researchers (Solms and Turnbull 2002: 74–6). Perhaps the most popular class of theories favors syn-chrony, whereby everything that happens in a given moment is bound together as a single object or scene.

The most frequently mentioned version of the synchrony hypothesis is the 40-hertz pattern. At a frequency of roughly forty pulses per second (40 Hz), a synchronized wave of neuronal firing sweeps across the brain from back to front, and whatever representational processes are "on" at the time of the sweep are bound together (Siegel 1999: 134). Damasio (1999: 126) agrees that "core consciousness is generated in pulse-like fashion." But others point out that there are *many* rhythms in the brain. The neurotransmitter acetylcholine, for instance, acts in a fraction of a millisecond, while a neuromodulator like luteinizing hormone-releasing hormone (LHRH) reaches a peak only after sixty seconds and its effects last over ten minutes (Quartz and Sejnowski 2002: 25). Harvard dream specialist J. Allan Hobson agrees:

> Binding via synchronicity occurs in milliseconds to seconds. Binding via chemical modulation occurs in minutes to hours. We need both, and we must make the best of both until we understand the mother of all questions: how does [all this] result in conscious experience in the first place?
>
> (J. A. Hobson 2002: 137)

The emergence of psyche: an analogy

The binding problem would also apply to a protozoan. How does an amoeba act as a unit, always maximizing its opportunities in an ever-changing environment; how does it get the countless chemical reactions that comprise its life to act infallibly in concert? This appears to be pretty much the same binding issue.

Functional magnetic resonance imaging (fMRI) shows networks of neurons "lighting up," as blood delivery is increased to the most active neural populations, giving us static snapshots of the brain at work. Much can be learned this way, but the brain's incessant activity is left out of the picture. A shift in focus from neural networks to brain waves is more than a "step back," for the electromagnetic activity seen in the waves actually governs and shapes the course of cellular chemistry, much as the life process of an amoeba shapes its chemistry.

Neural chemistry and electromagnetic waves

Chemical activity at the level of cells generates electromagnetic waves, the same sorts of waves that are recorded by electro-encephalographs (EEGs). Refined techniques have enabled researchers to train their attention on several different levels of wave propagation: individual neurons, neural populations in small patches of cortex, and so on up to the whole brain. These provide a far more dynamic, "real time," set of observations of the brain at work than do MRI snapshots.

Chemical reactions and wave generation are two aspects of the same process. In what follows, a material description of neural chemistry will be followed by an account of wave patterns. Not only do the waves originate in the activity of the cellular, chemical substrate, but also they exert control over that activity, unifying it, and giving it shape. These two levels of interrelated brain dynamics stand as a compelling analogy for the emergence of a unified psyche from the psychoid elements of brain dynamics. Emergence means that there are two entangled levels of being operating simultaneously. The chemistry of the brain's gray matter and the EEG waves represent one and the same phenomenon, as seen from two points of view.

Neurons talking to neurons

Conscious experience emerges as the highest order of meaning from a plethora of patterns nested within patterns that comprises the brain's activity. At the very bottom of these layers is the single nerve cell performing a variety of chemical reactions. It grows a bush of dendrites to receive impulses from other neurons at one end of its body, and at the other end, it extends a single long axon through which it transmits electrical impulses. A neuron "fires" when its many dendrites combine more-or-less simultaneous inputs to produce a large enough charge to cause channels arranged along the sides of its axon to open. Positive ions are pumped in through these channels, and negative ions out, in a wave of positive charge that moves down the axon to produce a similar excitation in downstream neurons. The information carried by an axon depends upon the frequency of its firing as well as by the rate of change in that frequency (Rose 2005: 158).

The active pumping of ions all along its length shows us that neurons are much more active than a copper wire which conducts electricity from a wall outlet to a reading lamp, and the impulse travels more slowly. When the impulse reaches the synapse, where the axon of neuron number one connects with a dendrite on neuron number two, electrical transmission is converted into chemistry. At the end of the axon, vesicles filled with the neurotransmitter glutamate release their contents into the synaptic space,[5] and the glutamate molecules drift across to the dendrite of the post-synaptic neuron, where further chemical reactions are required before channels are opened and the pumping of ions can begin in the second neuron.

Neurons are bound into networks according to the principle of Hebb's Law: "neurons that fire together wire together."[6] Frequently employed pathways are strengthened when genes in the nucleus of post-synaptic neurons are induced to produce proteins that return to the synapse and alter its chemistry. Sometimes, too, "gap junctions" are formed where there is no synapse at all, but the ions in one axon feed directly into the axon of another neuron, bypassing the complex chemical interactions that occur at the synapse. Gap junctions allow "widely scattered and perhaps distantly located neurons [to achieve] a concise and synchronous signal pattern" (Llinás 2002: 90).

Because each neuron is connected with dozens to thousands of other neurons, networks are extremely complex, and must be so just to keep neurons active; for "only if the postsynaptic cell is bombarded with transmitter molecules from many different presynaptic terminals at about the same time—within milliseconds—will an action potential result" (LeDoux 2002: 47). The brain's operation depends on populations of neurons, organized in networks: all firing with distinctive frequencies, all feeding into one another, sometimes exciting one another, sometimes inhibiting.

The sensory information that enters the brain from the retina of the eye when we notice that bull advancing toward us, sets off some combination of neural signals that rapidly fire up networks that have fired many times before and that have been "wired" to fire as units. Small differences in the color, size, and speed of the bull result in different combinations of networks firing simultaneously than would have fired if the animal moving in our direction were a fawn or a kitten. Some of the most compelling theories of consciousness depend upon the simultaneity and inevitable differences between the multiple drafts of reality being entertained, compared, and contrasted within the brain by means of these networks (e.g. Dennett 1991; Edelman and Tononi 2000). We shall take up this topic at greater length in Chapter 7, when we consider what an ego might be.

Electromagnetic waves

Discussions of neural networks leave much out of the picture, beginning at the most fundamental level—the stuff of the brain itself, neuropil. Neuropil (or "nerve felt") is made up not only of matted axons and dendrites, but also of glial cells that form the brain's organizing skeleton, clean its debris, and assist at its synapses; and of the capillary networks of blood vessels that supply oxygen and nutrients; and finally of intercellular fluid. All of these together (neurons, glia, capillaries, and fluid) make up the "gray matter" of the brain (Freeman 2000: 47). Neuropil is by no means inert. The path that current takes inside a neuron is only part of the electromagnetic picture of the neuropil's activity. For as ions pass into and out of the neuron, those charged particles are drawn out of and returned to the surrounding neuropil. When an axon becomes positively charged, the neighboring neuropil gains a negative charge, and vice versa. As a result, the neuropil is everywhere in a constant state of electromagnetic oscillation. Tiny potential differences, over microscopic distances, dance everywhere on the brain's surface, and deep within it as well.

As a component of the neuropil, every neuron—even when it is not firing—is in a constant state of oscillation, with frequencies between one and forty per second (Llinás 2002: 9). In consequence, electromagnetic waves are generated over tiny millimeter-square patches of cortex—just as electric wires generate a magnetic field about themselves which may influence the flow of electricity through a parallel wire. In similar fashion, the peaks and valleys of the brain's electromagnetic waves have an "entraining" effect upon the neurons below them, which tend to fire on the crests of the waves. Thus the activity of neural networks generates the first level of electromagnetic waves at a microscopic level. The sum of these waves, oscillating together in millimeter-square patches, brings about patterns at higher levels of organization.

When a neuron begins to fire on the crests of a local oscillatory pattern, it ceases to act alone and goes through a "state transition." This means it becomes a member of a "neuronal population" whose activity is governed by its collective oscillatory resonance. A group of non-synchronized neurons is merely an "aggregate"; but a "state transition" draws its neurons into synchrony, turning them into a "population" (Freeman 2000: 53). By pulling discordant aggregates into harmonious populations, electromagnetic resonance holds the brain together, organizes it, and makes it coherent (Llinás 2002: 10). Neurons and their networks, however, are always able to switch into and out of oscillatory modes, changing frequency so as to oscillate with one population and then with another (Ibid.: 12).

The cumulative effect of electromagnetic resonance results in a far more holistic picture of the brain's activity than the more fragmentary view pursued by those who study neural networks. Walter J. Freeman (2000) goes so far as to "propose that every neuron and every patch participates in every experience and behavior, even if its contribution is to silence its pulse train or stay dark in a brain image." He says that those who study the minority of neurons that are more active than the average—those that "light up" in fMRI "snapshots"—are putting too much emphasis on too small a sample of the brain's activity. What the brain does involves *all* the neurons and networks in their various stages of activation, for it is the simultaneous patterns of greater and lesser activity that causes mentality (Freeman 2000: 109f).

Experimental evidence

Freeman studied the olfactory bulb of the rabbit's brain, a relatively large and easy-to-observe structure with a clear sensory function in which moments of information input are simply defined: they occur each time the rabbit inhales. He found that the neuropil of the bulb was continuously active with irregular wave forms. With each inhalation, however, there was a burst of activity, instantaneously, all over the bulb. A cumulative wave emerged over the whole bulb, but with a different amplitude at each microscopic location—an AM (amplitude modulation) pattern.[7] And this pattern, he found, was as unique for each rabbit as the individual history of the animal (Freeman 2000: 71–4).

Between inhalations, the neurons in the olfactory bulb are an aggregate in which each responds mostly to its nearest neighbors (Freeman 2000: 76). Each inhalation, therefore, creates a "state transition" that turns the aggregate into a population. As long as odors in the environment remain unchanged, the common wave burst assumes a characteristic shape that is repeated every time. Such a regular wave form is said to have found (or to be governed by) a "basin of attraction." Think of a landscape dominated by a broad hollow or dip. Everything that moves in response to gravity will flow, roll or tumble toward the lowest point in such a basin. That lowest point is called the "point attractor" that defines the "basin of attraction." Every AM wave generated over the rabbit's olfactory bulb will assume a shape that gravitates to a favored "low point"—which means that this is the shape it "prefers" to have. "This is how the neurons in the bulb make themselves similar to the form of the stimulus in the world" (Freeman 2000: 81). As long as the odors of the environment do not change, every inhalation will produce a wave governed by this same basin of attraction.

But when there is a new stimulus, a new odor, "the first event . . . is the failure of a burst to occur. . . . The new odor means that the background fails to occur as expected. . . . . This is a state of, 'I don't know what it is, but it may be important'" (Freeman 2000: 79). The steady state of the neural population is shocked out of its familiar basin of attraction when a new odor is inhaled. The new stimulus causes the AM pattern to "ring" at a new frequency—one that is characteristically different for each odorant. Then, eventually, it "decays" back to the steady state of the usual basin of attraction—a condition that corresponds to the experience of exhausting our ability to respond to a new stimulus (Freeman 2000: 56).

> The state space of the cortex can be said to comprise an attractor landscape with several adjoining basins of attraction, one for each class of learned stimulus. . . . The attractors are not shaped by the stimulus directly, but by previous experience with those stimuli including [emotional associations[8]] and neuromodulators, as well as sensory input. Together these modify the synaptic connections within the neuropil and thereby also the attractor landscape.
>
> (Freeman 2000: 62)

This statement is a strong endorsement of the notion that brain function is in constant process, and furthermore that the criteria for making distinctions lie nowhere but in the individual brain's own history of responses. There is no "photo album" of memories. The present is always some variation on the past, and becomes, with the passage of a moment, part of the past against which the next stimulus is interpreted. The brain *is* its history. In the olfactory bulb of the rabbit, each AM pattern depends on the history of the rabbit's exposure, not merely to the odorant presently sensed, but to every odorant ever experienced. Each new one leads to a change in AM patterns; and it is the changes in these patterns which count, not some a priori constant like a photo in an album (Freeman 2000: 80). Every region of every brain has its own idiosyncratic attractor landscape, always susceptible to change, and having the shape it has for no reason other than its history of "shaping itself to the form [of a lifelong series] of stimuli from the world."

An analogy for emergence

Two rather exciting conclusions can be drawn from Freeman's research. One, to be taken up in the next section of this chapter, is the picture of a brain—and consequently of a psyche—whose identity is its history. Process is everything. Psyche is not substance but process. A single stimulus (the smell of lettuce or of fox) does not result in an identical pattern in every rabbit brain, but rather a pattern idiosyncratic to each individual rabbit. Every brain responds against the history of its own variable patterning, and every emergent psyche is likewise defined by its own process.

The second issue has to do with how the activity of the neural networks is "bound" via oscillatory resonance. Here we clearly have two views of the same brain activity: one as "material" and "mechanical" as neuropil and its chemistry, and the other as "immaterial" and "subtle" as radio waves that pass right through the bone of the skull like ghosts. Both undeniably are real. Each is a separate "take" upon brain activity. Here is a lucid analogy for the way a unified psyche emerges from a plethora of brain dynamics. Surely it would be a mistake to call the waves mere "epiphenomena" of chemical reactions. For the wave patterns are not useless "froth," they order and "bind" the activity of the cells in the neuropil. Freeman (2000) has demonstrated that the cumulative patterning in the waves that emerge out of cellular chemistry entrains the networks themselves and gives them shape. Wave patterns result from but also govern cell behavior. This is precisely the relationship we have imagined between psyche and brain.

Freeman says that "awareness" has its roots widely distributed in a variety of "subsystems" (neural networks) that are up to divergent activities. When the bull approaches, we may suddenly become intensely aware of the call of a chickadee and wonder whether the bird is as worried as we are. We do not want any "renegade state transitions," where our fascination with the bird call and what it may mean distracts us from the matter at hand: the bull. There are a few "fluctuations" that must be "quenched." What does the quenching and focusing for Freeman are the AM waves, specifically their organization into a single, global AM pattern. And this is precisely what we expect of psyche. Given the myriad blinking networks putting information into psyche, some sort of center must be found, and with the right emotional valuation. Freeman may be right. It might be that psyche's decisions amount to choosing among various possible basins of attraction in the AM pattern over a cerebral hemisphere. But even if they do not, Freeman has offered us a compelling analogy for the emergence of psyche from brain.

Psyche as process, not substance

If evolution has taught us anything, it is that "nothing in biology makes sense except in the light of its own history" (Rose 2005: 187). Freeman's study of the AM patterns generated by the rabbit's olfactory bulb shows that a present event makes sense only as a variation on everything that happened in the past. When a new stimulus arrives at the olfactory bulb, the rabbit does not rummage through a file box of signals stored somewhere else in its brain to find a recognizable pattern. There are no stored patterns. Rather the brain's activities find their shape only in the passing moment as complex AM waves that are constantly dissolving and reforming. There are no fixed representations filed away in storage like a photo album. Each new pattern is slightly different from every other. This is true not only at the level of AM waves, but also deeper, in the neuropil, where from day to day and hour to hour, "certain cells will have retracted their processes, others will have extended new ones, and still others will have died (Edelman and Tononi 2000: 47).

The brain, like every living thing, is in constant flux. LeDoux says, "People don't come preassembled, but are glued together by life" (2002: 3). Learning means building new neural networks and establishing new basins of attraction. At the end of its first month of interacting with its mother, the infant's brain is quite a different entity from what it was when it emerged from the womb. The brain's changes, its history, *are* its identity—even in adults. Three months of regular practice at juggling three balls will cause two brain areas to grow 3–4 percent larger. When the practice is stopped for another three weeks, the same areas reduce by 1–2 percent (*Science News*, January 31, 2004: 78; see also Badcock 2000: 23). Thus the brain is always changing, always growing in its capacities, so long as it is alive.

If the brain has no history of experience in a certain area, its capacity to make sense of new stimuli will be severely limited. Adults blind from birth, who have undergone surgery to correct the problem and give them sight, find that they cannot sort out "the chaos of shifting, unstable, evanescent appearances" that assault them through their newly functional eyes (Zeman 2002: 200). Their sight cannot be "coordinated with their other senses" (Shore 1996: 4) because a gestalt-recognizing function usually employed by sight has been taken over by another sense, usually touch. The history of their brain has left no provision for late-appearing sight. One man who had acquired sight for the first time as an adult was unable to appreciate the work of a lathe until he could run his hands over it, eyes shut. "Then he stood back a little and opened his eyes and said, 'Now that I've felt it I can see'" (Zeman 2002: 201). Such incidents tell us that our mode of being in the world, as meaning-grasping and meaning-manipulating organisms, is a function of our entire body-and-mind operating as a unit. Our physical organism allows itself to be shaped by the world:

> The biology of meaning includes the entire brain and body, with the history built by experience into bones, muscles, endocrine glands, and neural connections. A meaningful state is an activity pattern of the nervous system and body that has a particular focus in the state space of the organism, not in the physical space of the brain.
>
> (Freeman 2000: 115)

For Freeman (2000), "state space" refers to the sort of experience made possible by state transitions: moments when a random "aggregate" of neurons becomes an organized "population." That the "whole organism"—"bones, muscles, endocrine glands, and neural connections"—has a state space or an endless series of them, takes us well beyond the mechanics of brain function. The series of state spaces experienced by our whole organism is what we mean by "psyche." Psyche is the rich biographical process by which we have gotten to and come to understand the present moment—both by its facts and in its implications—and simultaneously as springboard for an imagined future. Psyche is both identity and possibility. Who we *are*, as psyche, is both the outcome of our entire history and the governance of ourselves whereby we carve out a future.

Jung's thinking certainly supports the notion of psyche as process rather than substance. In a London lecture in 1924, he urged his audience "to regard the psyche . . . as a fluid stream of events which change kaleidoscopically under the alternating influence of different instincts" (*CW17*: ¶156). Two years later, he wrote: "Psyche . . . would have to be understood as a purposive system, as an arrangement not merely of matter *ready for life* but of *living matter* or, more precisely of *living processes*." In the next paragraph: "The psychic process [is] a phenomenon dependent on the nervous system" (*CW8*: ¶606f). At the end of his life, in his autobiography, he said: "The psyche appears as a dynamic process" (*MDR*, 350). William James also argued that mind is "process not stuff,"[9] and Edelman agrees, "Consciousness is not an object but a process and . . . a fitting scientific subject" (Edelman and Tononi 2000: 9).

In the end, therefore, the mind/body problem appears as the corollary of an erroneous depiction of reality. Our body is not an inanimate machine in need of some other kind of substance to move it and give it life. Our body lives on its own, and the complex processes that comprise the life of its cells, tissues and organs are the psychoid elements whose integration is our psyche. Psyche is not a substance added on, it is the process of the whole.

Chapter 7

Individuation

Jung's phenomenology of psychic process

Individuation, Jung's name for psychic process, describes the development of a human psyche over the course of a life as a person adapts to the demands of the outer world and the "internal" needs of his or her organism. In its simplest form, individuation is an idealized picture of psyche-as-process, a relatively simple model that can be complicated with setbacks, hang-ups, sidetracks and other neurotic phenomena that regularly occur in all of our lives. The individuation process can be put back on track when these very human divergences are overcome, and analysis aims to assist in the reorientation. Individuation, therefore, serves as a kind of ground plan for psychic process. It is the theoretical background against which all psychic phenomena are interpreted. In this chapter, we describe that process and in the two following chapters detail parallel events taking place in the neural substrate, the biological dimension of individuation.

In Chapters 10 and 11, we consider the sorts of disturbances that may disrupt the individuation process, how Jung believes they arise, and how analytic therapy is said to work—always with an eye to the underlying brain dynamics and the central question of whether Jung's psychology is consilient with contemporary biology and therefore built upon a sound basis.

Psyche as individuation process

In sketching a general picture of individuation, we shall follow the historical course of Jung's thinking so as to appreciate the role played by the idea of individuation throughout the thirty or so volumes of his writings,[1] and justify the choice of sources that will be employed for this argument.

Jung's opus

Jung began his psychiatric career in 1902 with a dissertation on the psychic processes he observed in a case of "somnambulism" in a teenaged girl (his own cousin) who had held séances in which she seemed to serve as a mouthpiece for the spirits of several deceased individuals. Spiritualism of this sort was a very popular activity in Victorian parlors a century ago, and the subject of investigation by psychological experts in Geneva, Paris, London, and Boston (E. Taylor 1996). This international "school" of psychological thinking, writing in French and English and conversant with one another's work, described its central preoccupation as "somnambulism," which today corresponds to what is called "dissociation." *Somnambulism* designated a complex of phenomena, including hysteria, multiple personality, susceptibility to hypnosis, and such trance- and reverie-based activities as automatic writing and mediumship. Jung's discussion of his cousin's performances interpreted her spirit-messages as dissociation phenomena revealing internal conflicts in her self-identity. The most original part of the work was his argument that one of her spirit guides amounted to a spontaneous unconscious project whereby she was "dreaming" her way forward into an adult identity. Already the notion of psychological transformation and goal-directedness as a natural capacity of the human psyche was central to his thought (*CW1*: ¶1–150).

Jung was accepted for a residency in psychiatry at one of Europe's most prestigious hospitals, the Burghölzli in Zurich, where his chief was Eugen Bleuler, famous for developing the world's first description of schizophrenia, a perspective that is still influential today. Bleuler set Jung the job of developing the Word Association Test as a diagnostic tool,[2] which led to a slew of papers published over the next five years that caught the attention of psychiatrists worldwide (*CW2*). By asking patients to supply the first word that comes to mind in response to each on a list of 100 everyday words and by measuring the time elapsed between stimulus and response, Jung determined that words which trigger an emotional reaction in the patient will naturally fall into clusters, which he called complexes. Each complex describes something very much like the split-off part-personalities that the dissociation school was studying.

Believing that the tendency to "block" on emotionally charged words—as measured, for instance, by a delay in response times—constituted empirical evidence for Freud's theory of repression, Jung sent the first volume of his *Association Studies* (1906) to the Father of Psychoanalysis, who enthusiastically responded that he had already bought a copy (CW2). There followed the famous seven years of correspondence and collaboration between the two giants of twentieth-century psychology, in which Jung vacillated between his natural allegiance to the dissociation school and psychoanalysis (*FJL*). He tried to integrate the two approaches in a book published in 1907, *The Psychology of Dementia Praecox* (*CW3*: ¶1–319), which contrasts the dynamics of hysteria (Freud's specialty) with that of schizophrenia (known at the time as "*Dementia praecox*," Jung's specialty). A close reading of the text shows that Jung is still closer in his thinking to Paris and Geneva than to Vienna (Haule 1983, 1984). Cooperation between Freud and Jung began to encounter serious difficulties as early as 1909 on a trip to Clark University in Worcester, MA, when they could no longer trust one another with their dreams (*MDR*: 158–65). At that time, they were discussing the idea of a central complex, a sort of kernel of the psyche (*Kernkomplex*) against which psychoanalytic interpretation could find its compass. Freud favored the Oedipus complex. Jung thought sex could hardly be more important in our psychic economy than the drive for nourishment (*CW4*: ¶234–42). Persuaded by the natural splittings in a dissociable psyche, Jung could not be convinced that the sex drive was more important than any other. He began a study of mythology to learn what other phylogenetically significant themes have been uppermost in the psyches of human beings since the dawn of recorded history. His study resulted in the book we now call *Symbols of Transformation* (*CW5*),[3] and that brought about the end of his collaboration with Freud.

In *Symbols* Jung interprets the fantasy material of a young American woman, Miss Frank Miller,[4] by finding mythic parallels to her dreams, visions, poems, speculations, and the like. The *Kernkomplex* appears as the "night-sea journey" of the sun, illustrated with a diagram from mythologist Leo Frobenius in his book dealing with "The Age of the Sun God."[5] In myths of this type, the sun sinks into the Western Sea at dusk and then undergoes a struggle with the forces of darkness all the night long as it transits beneath the earth from west to east in order to rise renewed out of the Eastern Sea at dawn (*CW5*: ¶306–12). For Jung, this describes the nature of psychological transformation. When our stance toward life needs renewal, we must enter into our own unconscious and do battle with the figures we encounter there. What we learn in these encounters will change us. We will have integrated a bit of our psychic process that has been unconscious. Later on, the night-sea journey became Jung's model for individuation.

In a Foreword to the revised edition of *Symbols* (1950), Jung said that writing the book convinced him that we are all living a myth, whether we know it or not, and that, having no idea what his own myth was, he determined to find out (*CW5*: xxiv). In fact, the break with Freud occasioned a "creative illness" (Ellenberger 1970: 39), what some biographers have likened to a psychosis, and Jung began deliberately descending into his own unconscious, which in any event would not leave him alone (*MDR*: 170–99). There, in the mind's eye of his reveries, he encountered horrifying scenes and met figures who instructed him. He returned to ordinary consciousness and subjected these materials—some of which he elaborately painted first—to the same mythological scrutiny he had employed with the fantasies of Frank Miller. While engaged in this "self analysis," he withdrew almost completely from public life during the years of the First World War.

At the end of this process, in 1920, Jung completed a huge volume, *Psychological Types* (*CW6*), whose theme he had been considering since his last Psychoanalytic Congress in 1913, just before his break with Freud, where he presented a paper that argued Freud's theory of love and Adler's of power were irreconcilable because they stemmed from two different types of mind (*CW6*: ¶858–82). After leaving psychoanalysis, Jung continued to explore "the problem of the *existence of two kinds of truth*" through an extensive exchange of letters with his friend Hans Schmidt (Bair 2003: 279). He began to conclude that people pay attention to the world employing one of eight different attitudes.[6] Everyone follows a single, clearly seen course through the world, and most of us pay little attention to the much larger part of the scene that lies out of focus, blurry, and all run together. The larger, blurry part of one's life course can be brought into focus through the employment of neglected psychological faculties ("functions"), if only one has the patience and discipline to learn how to use them.

Types is a discussion of the inevitable imbalance of the ego, whereby only one approach to life is trusted, and other possibilities remain neglected and without focus. Inevitably, however, life provides situations where ego's narrowness is challenged. When forced into blurry, undifferentiated sectors of our human experience, we encounter our "Amfortas wound"—a reference to the Grail King, rendered impotent by a wound that bled unstaunched for 400 years. The Kingdom of the Grail was entirely male and thoroughly chaste. Amfortas had been a hero in that narrow world until his encounter with his undifferentiated side. He tried to save a raggedy wild woman with magical powers, and he was tempted (Haule 1992). His celibate and intellectual idealism was no match for the feeling demands of eros, and his heroic career was brought to a very long halt. Taken together, *Symbols* and *Types* describe the process of individuation; complexes turn it off course.

There are two kinds of psychic process

Symbols says that processes outside of our awareness powerfully influence our experiences, attitudes, and behaviors, and can also be seen in emotions, fantasies, intuitions, and the like, that occur as the background of our conscious attention. They occur as typical, phylogenetic patterns, later called archetypes; and historically, evidence of their existence can be found in myths, rituals and other sociocultural phenomena. Consequently, when fragments of archetypal processes are discernible in an individual's dreams or behavior, their larger meaning can be gathered by tracking down the cultural prototypes. Jung demonstrated the method with his treatment of the Miller fantasies.

While *Symbols* explores the structure of the unconscious, *Types* explores psyche's *conscious* processes, its attitudes. Our conscious standpoint is always a partial perspective on our own identity (introversion) and on the reality of the world (extraversion). Its narrowness appears in the way we structure our personal narrative, the story of who we are, what we remember of the past and how we project our future. Inevitably, there are large areas we have not yet worked out, that we gloss over and tell ourselves are not important. They are our vulnerable spot, where we carry our Amfortas wound. The blurry, undifferentiated material that breaks through this gap challenges our conscious self-image and sets us tasks we may find repugnant, frightening or overwhelming. As off-putting as this material may be, however, it offers completion and balance. By learning how to survive in areas of life formerly ignored, we develop our neglected "psychic functions."

That struggle is our night-sea journey, for our Amfortas wound always leads into the depths of the unconscious. It is as though the sun of our old attitude has set and plunged into the Western Sea. Probably we experience this as depression or a struggle with strange and unwelcome urges. If we succeed in our course through the dangerous "womb of the unconscious,"[7] we will emerge with our approach to life renewed—more effective and more satisfying because formerly neglected capacities will have been discovered and developed.

Although they lay out the foundations of Jung's approach to understanding and working with the human psyche, *Symbols* and *Types* are huge ramshackle tomes comprising more than 1100 pages between them, and the message I have just delineated is not easy to extract. Jung was aware of this problem and had been tinkering since 1916 with two essays that together would provide an easily comprehensible overview of how he understood psyche and how his treatment approach was designed to work. Today these two short works are published together as Volume 7 of the *Collected Works* and ought to be read as a restatement of the most important themes of Volumes 5 and 6, but with an eye to practical application.

Two Essays on Analytical Psychology (*CW7*), therefore, provides Jung's most complete account of individuation, and it was his last attempt to sketch the basic trajectory of his theory. From about 1930 onward, he devoted the majority of his efforts to the study of alchemy, Gnosticism, hermeticism, and other neglected cultural themes that represent a subterranean stream within Western culture. Just as unconscious themes run below the surface of the individual's conscious life, so have these esoteric traditions played counterpoint to the dominant cultural stream. Jung was searching in these out of the way places for naive evidence of the individuation process. For example, alchemical attempts to turn lead into gold were bound to fail, but the alchemists' *fantasies* about what they were observing in their laboratories suggest a great deal about their unconscious psychic process. Jung saw the alchemists as unconscious psychologists, and he mined their work for evidence of the individuation process in medieval imagery (*CW12*: ¶1–43).

"On the Psychology of the Unconscious" (1917/43)

The first of the *Two Essays* begins with a case history in which tracing the meaning of an hysterical crisis back to a childhood trauma (as Freud urged) would have missed the meaning of the event in the present. Neurosis is "self-division" (*CW7*: ¶18) and the evasion of a problem (*CW7*: ¶23); it requires that we look into the "unexamined 'shadow-side' of the psyche" (*CW7*: ¶27). By reducing neurosis to issues of love or power, Freud and Adler undervalue its potential (*CW7*: ¶71). We would be better advised to observe the course of psyche's natural process,[8] and assist it (*CW7*: ¶76–8). "[T]he values which the individual lacks are to be found in the neurosis itself" (*CW7*: ¶93).

Usually the first fantasies to emerge from the neurosis are related to parental authorities, but eventually archetypal imagery will emerge from "the depths of the unconscious" (*CW7*: ¶97–105) "like highly charged autonomous centers of power [that] exert a fascinating and positive influence on the conscious mind" (*CW7*: ¶110). When an archetype appears, there is a danger of *enantiodromia* (Heraclitus), of flipping back and forth from one extreme position to its opposite (*CW7*: ¶111–15). The way to handle such a labile situation is not to repress the matter, but to "put it clearly before [oneself] as *that which [one] is not*" (*CW7*: ¶112). "The point is not conversion into the opposite but conservation of previous values together with a recognition of their opposites" (*CW7*: ¶116).

> The process of coming to terms with the unconscious . . . does not proceed without aim and purpose, but leads to the revelation of the essential man . . . the unfolding of the original, potential wholeness. . . . I have termed this the *individuation process*.
>
> (*CW7*: ¶186)

> The initiative lies with the unconscious, but all the criticism, choice, and decision lie with the conscious mind. If the decision is right, it will be confirmed by dreams indicative of progress. . . . The course of therapy is thus rather like a running conversation with the unconscious.
>
> (*CW7*: ¶189)

When the right interpretation is made, there will be "an uprush of life," while a wrong interpretation "dooms [patient and doctor] to deadlock, resistance, doubt and mutual desiccation" (*CW7*: ¶189).

"The Relations between the Ego and the Unconscious" (1916/38)

The second of the *Two Essays* begins with the case of a woman who sees Jung as her father/lover (personal image), but then dreams of her father transformed into a colossus, rocking her in his arms in a wheat field (archetypal image) (*CW7*: ¶202–15). Such archetypal forces are dangerous for one's personal integrity. Identifying with them leads to inflation, and being overwhelmed by them leads to despair, even psychosis (*CW7*: ¶221–39). "For the development of personality, then, strict differentiation from the collective psyche is absolutely necessary" (*CW7*: ¶240). Know your limits, do not merge indiscriminately.

"Individuation means becoming an 'in-dividual,' . . . [it] embraces our innermost, last and incomparable uniqueness . . . [it is] 'self-realization'" (*CW7*: ¶266). Individuation is not an extreme pose like "individualism" but is one's own personal adaptation to universally human "functions and faculties" (*CW7*: ¶267). Following its course "divest[s one] of the false wrappings of the persona on the one hand, and of the suggestive power of primordial images on the other" (*CW7*: ¶269). In its "running conversation" with the collective unconscious, therefore, ego's knowledge of itself is gradually being adjusted in the direction of appreciating its relatively small role in the "totality of the psyche," which Jung calls the "self" (*CW7*: ¶274). "That touchy, egotistical bundle of personal wishes, fears, hopes, and ambitions . . . has to be . . . corrected by unconscious counter-tendencies"

(*CW7*: ¶275). Such compensation does not follow "a deliberate and concerted plan." It is rather a matter of the natural, organic balancing of complimentary processes (*CW7*: ¶291)—the sort of balance that is found in every organism from the protozoa on up.

In following the course of individuation, we discover our own authentic relationship with the *two* collectivities: first, *collective consciousness*, the public world, the assumptions and pressures of society, for these lie behind "the false wrappings of the persona"; and second, the *collective unconscious*, the phylogenetic propensities that arise from within, "the suggestive power of primordial images." Individuation is thus characterized by two dialogues running simultaneously. See Figure 7.1.

Jung describes each of these dialogues in terms of a mediating figure (*CW7*: ¶296–340). Regarding the *outer* dialogue, we have spoken in earlier chapters of the "persona" as our social strategy. Jung calls persona a "mask" and an inner psychic figure which mediates between the ego and the outer world. It may appear in personified form in our dreams, and Jung prefers to speaks of it as though it were a nearly independent personage, as if to say, I am not my persona strategy, although it is part of my totality (*CW7*: ¶312f). In the *inner* dialogue, on the other hand, the mediator between ego and self is a contra-sexual figure ("anima" in men, "animus" in women). Anima and animus, beginning with their gender, personify everything that is other than the ego. They can be fascinating or fearsome, seductive or repulsive, depending on the ego's attitude and stability. This contra-sexual archetype not only conducts the running dialogue between ego and self, but also plays a significant role in our relations with people of the opposite sex.[9]

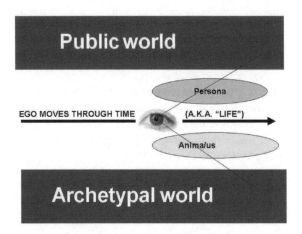

Figure 7.1 The dual process of individuation.

Source: original digital drawing by John Ryan Haule.

Not surprisingly, persona and anima are frequently at odds with one another,[10] and are often at odds with the ego:

> When the anima continually thwarts the good intentions of the conscious mind, by contriving a private life that stands in sorry contrast with the dazzling persona, it is exactly the same as when a naive individual, who has not the ghost of a persona, encounters the most painful difficulties in his passage through the world.
>
> (*CW7*: ¶318)

From this point on in the essay, the emphasis is upon the *inner* dialogue. Jung presents the example of a "spotless man of honour and public benefactor, whose tantrums and explosive moodiness terrify his wife and children" (*CW7*: ¶319). He has developed his persona at the expense of his anima, and Jung proposes "an actual technique" to remedy the situation. The man must stop merging with his moodiness and separate himself from his anima (*CW7*: ¶321). Then he must "listen to the affect" patiently and without criticizing it, hearing its message the way he would listen to the complaints of "a real person." Once heard, however, he must criticize that message as he would that of a colleague, and allow the "discussion" to continue as long as it needs to. This is precisely the method Jung employed for his own night-sea journey during the time of his "creative illness." Later, he calls this technique "active imagination."

"Scrupulous honesty with oneself and no rash anticipation of what the other side might conceivably say are the indispensable conditions of this technique for educating the anima" (*CW7*: ¶323). A variety of examples follow, all exhibiting the same technique. Ego trims away its touchiness and neurotic attachments, while anima or animus is "depotentiated" from its role as inner despot so as to take up its rightful position as "a psychological function of an intuitive nature" (*CW7*: ¶374).

Summary

By the end of the second essay, we understand what Jung meant back near the beginning, when he said, "The values which the individual lacks are to be found in the neurosis itself" (*CW7*: ¶92). Let the neurotic affect "speak" and ego's limitations will be addressed. Engage it in dialogue, and ego will find its rightful place within the totality of psyche's processes.

The self: holistic process

The very idea of "an ego" or "a self" raises the specter of a Cartesian homunculus. We may wish to avoid it, as did Jung's Parisian mentor, Pierre Janet, who preferred to speak of the "real present moment" as it manifests itself "to me." When things happen around me, I have an unavoidable sense that I am involved.

Me-ness, therefore, is not a substance within me but a feeling, *le sentiment du moi* (Janet 1903: 471–7). We must be careful not to conjure Cartesian ghosts, but we cannot ignore the obvious. I am a living personal identity, a body-and-mind, a hungry, itching unity with consciousness. My conviction that I act, that things happen to me, that I have a distinct identity, that I make deliberate choices, and that—deliberate or not—what I do has consequences: aspects of egohood such as these can be investigated at the level of the cerebral substrate. On the other hand, in Jung's comprehensive sense of self-as-totality, selfhood must be something radically different from egohood. The self is other than me; sometimes it even seems to oppose me, and yet it is still somehow mine. It includes everything that belongs to the totality of my being. Unlike ego, the "conscious part," self does not follow "a deliberate and concerted plan." It is nothing separate from the whole, not part of psyche but *all* of psyche. Self is everywhere I am, yet in no specifiable place. Jung loved to say that self is "a circle whose center is everywhere and the circumference nowhere."[11]

Joseph LeDoux, Professor of Neural Science at New York University, expresses himself in nearly the same words as Jung: "When I use the term *the self* I am referring to the totality of the living organism . . . similar to what William James had in mind when he described 'self' as the sum total of who one is" (LeDoux 2002: 26). That totality is later specified as encompassing an animal's physical, biological, psychological, social and cultural being (Ibid.: 31). Self is the expression of an animal's fundamental commitment to life, evident in the way it pulls together all of its component processes in service of the whole. Philosopher John Gray speaks of "a coherent global pattern that emerges from the activity of simple local components, which seems to be centrally located but is nowhere to be found" (Gray 2002: 73). Another group of scholars who will play a large role in our argument, the "Biogenetic Structuralists," distinguish between "our being," described as our "inner operational environment" and "our empirical ego," which is our "inner cognized reality" (C. D. Laughlin *et al.* 1990: 89). All of these people agree on the essential distinction Jung makes between ego and self.

A self *emerges* from the parts of every organism—precisely insofar as it is a single, unitary animal. Self, therefore, in its most rudimentary form is already present in every protozoan, for each of them is so thoroughly "bent on staying alive" that its many disparate forces seem to marshal themselves in the service of that goal. This is so evidently the case that Antonio Damasio says that even the lowly amoeba exhibits "the form of an intention" (1999: 136). In another example, he says: "A brainless creature [a paramecium] already contain[s] the essence of the process of emotion that we humans know—detection of the presence of an object or event that recommends avoidance and evasion or endorsement and approach." A fly, he says, feels angry when we swat at it, happy when it feeds, and becomes giddy from sipping alcohol (Damasio 2003: 41).

If an organism's parts do not pull together, the creature will surely fail in the Darwinian struggle for survival. The "microstructures" that make up every animal—the proteins that test the environment, the neurons that communicate electrochemically—are like evolution's Lego blocks, used over and over again by "virtually every taxonomic group." Each animal combines these microstructures into its own species-specific "macrostructure that has functional consequences" (Plotkin 1998: 167). Therefore, when we speak of the self, we refer to the emergence of a higher order of cooperation—something that can hardly be in doubt for well-functioning animals, but nevertheless a principle we should not take for granted.

Matt Ridley (1996) reminds us that every organism is constantly struggling against mutiny from within. An animal "is merely the sum of its selfish parts; and a group of units selected [by evolution] to be selfish cannot surely turn altruistic" (Ridley 1996: 33). He points out that the fetus frequently behaves like a parasite within the mother's body. Mother and infant, for instance, "churn out escalating quantities of hormones which have opposite effects and simply cancel one another out." Within the mother herself, "the ovaries are parasites on the liver"; for the ovaries cannot survive without the metabolic and detoxifying activities of the liver. But in the end, the ovaries make off with "the jackpot of immortality by producing an egg that carries its genes into the next generation." And this struggle among the parts goes all the way down to the individual cell, whose molecular parts are all pulling in opposite directions (Ridley 1996: 23, 28, 31).

The amazing thing is that, without a plan and without a hierarchy, selfhood emerges. This is perhaps the strongest argument for mind not being a separate substance from the body. Mind does not even dominate the body as we have so long wanted to believe. Mind emerges out of body, out of the totality of its parts. Every organ, every tissue, every cell, and every protein is a partly anarchic, partly cooperating member of a whole; and the principle of holism that emerges out of the potential cacophony of the parts *is the self.* Freeman (2000: 105) attributes this self-organizing evolution to AM waves. In principle, Damasio agrees, when he attributes the process we call self to "a coherent collection of neural patterns which map, moment by moment, the state of the physical structure of the organism in its many dimensions" (Damasio 1999: 154).

We can summarize these findings as a series of three emergent processes. **Self** emerges from the parts that comprise an animal as its *organismic* process. **Ego** emerges from self as conscious, *reflective* process. **Individuation** emerges from the tension between ego and self as *psychic* process.

What Jung means by the self's effects upon consciousness—its capacity to bring unconscious realities to bear on the situation of the present moment—has been nicely suggested in a best seller by Malcolm Gladwell, *Blink* (2005). Apparently innocent of Jung's contributions to the topic, Gladwell has assembled an entertaining collection of anecdotes and experimental results, all designed to demonstrate an idea that happens to be one of the founding principles of Jung's work, namely that we do not create our thoughts, they are given to us. "'Thinking' existed long before man was able to say: 'I am conscious of thinking'" (*CW9i*: ¶500). Self is the ego's benefactor:

The ego stands to the self as the moved to the mover, or as object to subject, because the determining factors which radiate out from the self surround the ego and are therefore supraordinate to it. . . . It is not I who creates myself, rather I happen to myself.

(*CW11*: ¶391)

Although Jung does not want us to forget that the self's role is frequently disruptive of ego's plans, Gladwell (2005: 11) concentrates his efforts on more benign evidence, for what he calls the "adaptive unconscious." He opens his book with an account of experts detecting and failing to detect art forgeries, finding that intensive analyses are far less effective than the "intuitive repulsion" an experienced expert is apt to feel at first sight of a forgery. Similarly bird watchers—who may rarely get to see the whole bird from a good enough angle to allow identification—have to rely on hints derived from the fragmentary shapes and angles the bird presents as it hops from branch to branch behind a curtain of leaves (Gladwell 2005: 44). Fragmentary information is assembled unconsciously and simply handed to the ego. George Soros, to take another example, may be full of theories to justify his stock-trading decisions; but in the end, according to his son, he makes no changes until "his back starts to kill him" (Gladwell 2005: 51). There is a hint of Zen consciousness or Taoism lurking behind the relation between ego and self:

The freest human being is not the one who acts on reasons he has chosen for himself, but one who never has to choose. Rather than agonizing over alternatives, he responds effortlessly to situations as they arise. He lives not as he chooses but as he must. Such a human being has the perfect freedom of a wild animal.

(Gray 2002: 114f)

Such a free individual would be living his life under the direction of an undivided self. Ego would be watching, experiencing deeply, even making all the right decisions because, in some way or other, ego would be in intuitive connection with the wholeness of self. Reaching the point where ego can dependably maintain its harmony with self is the goal toward which the individuation process moves.

Chapter 8

Reflective process

The ego in neural context

Jung did not devote a great deal of attention to the nature of the ego. For the most part, he called it "the center of consciousness," taking it for granted that we all know from everyday experience what having an ego is like (*CW6*: ¶706). His idea of egohood does not include unconscious operations, as Freud's does. He calls ego "the subject of all personal acts of consciousness" that rest on somatic and psychic foundations, mostly unconscious (*CW9ii*: ¶1–3). Ego is responsible for making decisions, the free-will executive functions of consciousness (*CW7*: ¶87; *CW8*: ¶723f); but ego is most frequently described as a complex—that aggregate of ideas, images, and feelings of which we are conscious in any given moment. Jung emphasizes the fluctuating and changeable nature of the ego-complex (*CW8*: ¶611). Ego is therefore a selective synthesis of matters that are important at the moment (*CW8*: ¶614), very similar to what contemporary investigators have been calling "working memory" (e.g. LeDoux 2002: 176). The task of the ego is simultaneously to adapt ourselves to the inner world of the self and to the outer world of physical and social necessity, while at the same time drawing upon relevant memories for guidance (*CW8*: ¶611). Its perspective is narrow:

> The ego has scarcely the vaguest notion of the incredibly important regulative function of the sympathetic nervous system in relation to the internal bodily processes. What the ego comprehends is perhaps the smallest part of what a complete consciousness would have to comprehend.
>
> (*CW8*: ¶613)

General support for Jung's views

Jung's account of ego's ephemeral and fluctuating nature is very much in agreement with modern researchers. Llinás calls it "no such tangible thing, just a particular mental state," a sort of stand-in, like the image of Uncle Sam, who represents the complex reality of a heterogeneous country of some 300 million individuals (Llinás 2002: 127f). T. D. Wilson, in a more popular discussion, thinks that president of the executive branch of government may be too strong a description. On the other hand, presidential press secretary suggests something more like epiphenomenalism. Probably the most accurate image would be of a president like Ronald Reagan, i.e. the entertaining spokesperson for a staff of smart, hardworking powers (T. D. Wilson 2002: 46–8).

I think it would not at all distort Jung's account of ego-function to include a few distinctions made by his more philosophical mentor, Pierre Janet,[1] especially since Jung cites Janet so frequently on the ego's level of psychic functioning.[2] Janet contrasts "immediate belief"—that is to say the *inability to disbelieve* in the truth of what is presented to one, an uncritical attitude that characterizes dream consciousness—with "reflective judgment" which characterizes a realistic and effective engagement with the world. For him, the first characteristic of truly conscious functioning is critical judgment, then the capacity to mobilize one's resources to carry out activities judged appropriate. Consistent and deliberate planning for the future on the basis of an accurately remembered past is also expected of a high-functioning individual, as well as a distinctive style of living that Janet calls "individuation"[3] (Ellenberger 1970: 386–94; Haule 1983, 1984).

Search for a cerebral substrate

Most researchers agree that there is no single area of the brain that is responsible for ego-function. Nevertheless, there is one area which many believe to play a large role, namely the prefrontal cortex (usually abbreviated PFC) located behind the forehead. In making his case for the importance of the PFC, LeDoux points out that it has far more neural connections within itself than it has with other parts of the brain, making it a place where a great deal of "processing" takes place (LeDoux 2002: 188). Furthermore, it has a large supply of axons containing the neurotransmitter dopamine, and the quantity of dopamine in the brain correlates directly with the capacity and efficiency of the PFC. Dopamine biases nerve cells engaged in working memory (the "ego-complex") by "focusing attention on active current goals and away from distracting stimuli" (LeDoux 2002: 189).

Solms and Turnbull (2002) agree with this emphasis on the PFC as an "executive system," but note that the most important work of this brain region may be inhibition, its capacity to "suppress the primitive, stereotyped compulsions that are encoded in our inherited and emotional memory system." The PFC delays automatic decisions in the interests of clear, critical thinking (Solms and Turnbull 2002: 281). This appears relevant to Janet's distinction between "immediate belief" and "reflective judgment." Solms and Turnbull (2002: 27) also link the PFC to another of Janet's characteristics—the ability realistically to plan for the future—for "the prefrontal lobes . . . can check to see whether the imagined solution matches the initial demands of the task . . . by *mentally* trying out actions." Richard Restak (2003) agrees with these arguments and adds that we "lose time" when we switch from one activity to another, and that this corresponds to the PFC shutting down one activity and initiating another. Furthermore, damage to the PFC results in a "loss of restraint and an inability to inhibit aggression and exercise judgment," all indications that ego-functioning is faltering (Restak 2003: 56, 67).

The correlation of PFC functions with ego can be overestimated, however, for the full complexity of ego-function involves wide-ranging patterns in the brain. To illustrate the sort of research that tracks down such patterns and to indicate that there can be little doubt that a neural substrate—however complex it may be—does support ego-function and the emergence of consciousness, we shall consider two different but not necessarily incompatible approaches, that of Antonio Damasio and that of Gerald Edelman.

Damasio's "somatic marker" hypothesis

For Antonio Damasio, the brain was assembled by nature and shaped by culture to generate "somatic states in response to certain classes of stimuli." These somatic states include emotion and are generated in social situations that leave their imprint upon our "adaptive somatic responses" (Damasio 1999: 177). Consciousness, even the implicit sort, involves relating the objects in the surrounding world to a reference point, a "me," which knows of its own existence (Damasio 2003: 184). This "me" is not a homunculus but "a perpetually recreated neurobiological state of our being" (Damasio 1994: 100). It is the whole body-and-mind that I am, but it is not as continuous as I believe. It "pulses." A pulsing, "perpetually recreated state" seems closely to resemble the coming and going of AM waves, but Damasio never refers to such things.

Core consciousness

This transient, pulsing reality is our sense of selfhood in the here and now, the background and foundation of an ego. Damasio calls it "core consciousness" and distinguishes it from "extended consciousness," which, ego-like, is a personal identity "richly aware of the lived past and of the anticipated future, and keenly cognizant of the world beside it" (Damasio 1999: 16). Most of his discussion involves core consciousness, which probably occupies a point halfway between Jung's "self" and "ego." Core consciousness and the emotional disturbances it registers affect the entire range of mental activity. Every act of knowing corresponds to a perturbation in somatic state. The rods and cones in our retinas, for instance, are set into electrochemical activity when light reflects off the world before us. Emotions will be aroused, perhaps the sympathetic nervous system also will be set into action.

When things are quiet, we are deeply unconscious; core consciousness begins with fluctuations (Damasio 1999: 125). Only when slow and constant rhythms are disturbed by spikes and nervous shudders, only when irregularity erupts, is consciousness possible.

> Core consciousness occurs when the brain's reception devices generate an imaged, non-verbal account of how the organism's own state is affected by the organism's processing of an object, and when this process enhances

the image of the causative object, thus placing it saliently in a spatial and temporal context.

(Damasio 1999: 169)

Against the blurry and undistinguished field of our visualization, acting figures stand forth and grab our attention.

Convergence zones and emotional valuation

Consciousness arises from a variety of combinations within the brain. Damasio (1999) refers to "convergence zones," where sensory information from the outer world is combined with memories involving the body and emotion. Before "converging" takes place, the sensory system activates neural maps that analyze the outer-worldly object as well as neural maps of the "proto-self." Both sorts of map belong to what Damasio calls "image space," as though the primary information is merely factual (1999: 170, 220).

The emotional component enters the picture through a third set of neural structures riding the same surge of perturbation that generates images of object and self. This third structure is what Damasio calls a "convergence zone." Such zones are located in the temporal and frontal cortices, but also in such subcortical structures as the amygdala and the thalamus, which are responsible for emotional reactions (Damasio 1999: 242, 221). In contrast to "image space," convergence zones are described as "dispositional space," for they affect the disposition of our body-and-mind. They bring together "implicit knowledge," lurking in neural network patterns often fired in the past, with the situation I face in the present. Memory images color my disposition with the feeling-tone of past incidents (Damasio 1999: 219).

In effect, nothing has meaning without emotion. Emotion is essential to "core consciousness," which disappears during epileptic attacks and other mental states characterized by "absences." "The lack of emotion when core consciousness vanishes may be parsimoniously explained by suggesting that both emotions and core consciousness require, in part, the same neural substrate" (Damasio 1999: 100). Ego, in its broadest sense, emerges from the neural substrate at the moment things become emotional.

Convergence zones pull all three things together: images of object and self together with emotional dispositions based upon previous experience. Each dispositional representation "comes to life when neurons fire with a particular pattern, at certain rates, for a certain amount of time, and toward a particular target, which happens to be another ensemble of neurons" (Damasio 1994: 103f). Multiple, parallel, converging streams of neural signals "never 'terminate' as such, they feed forward and back to create a perpetual recurrence" (Damasio 1994: 92f). There is an implicit narrative here, as the brain represents its own changing state to itself (Damasio 1999: 170). Marshack's (1991) Peking Man could not resist spinning mythic narratives around his experience with fire—how it lives, has to be tended, sleeps in its coals, etc.—because his brain simply works that way. A brain is always in constant motion, and always comparing the present with the past in order to predict the future.

Decision making

Even without ego-consciousness decisions are constantly being made. Damasio (1994) demonstrated this with a gambling game involving two decks of cards. One deck provided an occasional big win, but always offset with even larger losses. The other deck gave no spectacular gains or losses, but produced slow gains over time. The core consciousness of a normal subject was accurately predicting bad outcomes for the more dangerous deck and avoiding it long before the players knew what they were doing. In other words, they began playing rationally long before a conscious ego "clicked in." People with damaged frontal lobes, however, persisted in going for the big win, using the dangerous deck. Even after they knew about the two decks and could rationally discuss the difference, they could not resist taking disastrous chances: they "go for the now rather than bank[ing] on the future" (Damasio 1994: 217).

Somatic marker

The difference between these groups lies in ego's ability to make rational and patient plans. Such a reality function (Janet's *fonction du réel*) works on the basis of what Damasio calls a "somatic marker." The body has to be charged with emotion, a complex reaction generated by a convergence zone. An alarm goes off: this deck of cards is dangerous, avoid it (Damasio 1994: 173f)! A somatic marker, therefore, is an "emotional signal that marks options and outcomes with a positive or negative signal." Emotion "narrows the decision-making space and increases the probability that the action will conform to past experience."

Some of the most important functions of the ego are dependent upon "body states" that can range from the wholly positive (fast, idea-rich thinking associated with pleasant feelings) to the wholly negative (slow, repetitive thinking associated with painful feelings) (Damasio 1994: xiv). The two most important brain areas associated with somatic markers are the prefrontal cortex (analysis) and the amygdala (emotional memory). "[T]he body is engaged by the prefrontal cortices and amygdala to assume a particular state profile, whose result is subsequently signaled to the somatosensory cortex, attended, and made conscious" (Damasio 1994: 184). The essential piece in ego-consciousness is the somatic marker, by which we become aware of the emotional value of what faces us. We are jolted into consciousness by impending significance.

Edelman's "dynamic core" hypothesis

Although he has written several books on "how matter becomes conscious," Gerald Edelman, Chair of Neurobiology at the Scripps Research Institute, is clearly no metaphysical reductionist. He says, "No amount of neuroscientific data alone can explain thinking . . . therefore attempts to reduce psychology to neuro-science must fail" (Edelman 1992: 174f). He agrees with Jung that the ego does not create its own thoughts but is given them:

> When we speak, we know roughly what we want to say, although we typic-ally do not know the words we are going to use. Luckily, however, words seem to pop up when we need them, in the right place at the right time, with the right sound and the right meaning.
>
> (Edelman and Tononi 2000: 182)

Jung would describe this common experience as the ego's being moved by the self. Edelman describes it as "higher order consciousness" drawing upon the activities of a "dynamic core."

Brain organization

Edelman distinguishes three different sorts of organization in the brain. First is the thalamo-cortical meshwork, roughly what we have had in mind with the phrase, "neural networks." Neural impulses from the sense organs lead to the thalamus deep inside the brain and to sensory maps in the cortex. Extensive feedback runs in both directions between thalamus and cortex, resulting in a dense, complicated system whereby "any perturbation in one part of the network may be felt every-where" (Edelman and Tononi 2000: 44). The thalamo-cortical network is respons-ible for analyzing sensory data, and for "generating different patterns of expression in the sensory modalities" through the specific thalamic nuclei that are engaged in feedback loops (Edelman 2004: 21).[4] In this manner, signals from the world are categorized and made sense of (Ibid.: 49).

The second system is not a meshwork but a series of parallel, unidirectional loops that connect the cortex with basal ganglia, cerebellum, and hippocampus. The loops are isolated from one another—just the opposite of a meshwork arrange-ment—making it possible to execute "complicated motor and cognitive routines" (Edelman and Tononi 2000: 46). The third system is described as a "hairnet" or "large fan" of fibers that deliver neuromodulators to the cortex. Edelman calls this arrangement the brain's "value system," for it assigns emotional significance to a complex cluster of brain activities. Large populations of cortical neurons are simul-taneously affected by the release of chemicals such as noradrenalin, serotonin, and dopamine, broadly over large areas of the cortex, as though by a "leaky garden hose" (Edelman 2004: 25) "whenever something important or salient occurs, such as a loud noise, a flash of light, or a sudden pain" (Edelman and Tononi 2000: 46).

Reentry

The most important element in all this complicated and simultaneous analyzing of sense impressions, assigning of categories, and applying of emotional values, is what Edelman calls "reentry," mutual exchange of information. "Functional clusters" of neurons, that is large populations communicating mainly among themselves, also send signals to other functional clusters, which reply. This "ongoing, recursive interchange of parallel signals" is called "reentry." Signals from the same source are entered, returned and reentered into active clusters with the result that selective brain events are altered and signals correlated, leading to "integration of perceptual and motor processes [generating] the ability to discriminate an object or event from a background" (Edelman and Tononi 2000: 48). Surely this is the least we would expect of consciousness—at least of the automatic kind whereby subjects can differentiate between safe and dangerous decks of cards without knowing what they are doing.

The dynamic core

Dispersed processes bound by reentrant circuits into a single functioning unit producing a unified scene is what Edelman calls the "dynamic core." It is a subset of all the neuronal groups contributing to consciousness in any given moment: characterized by (a) strong mutual reentry activity, (b) speed (tenths of a second) and (c) high complexity (Edelman and Tononi 2000: 139). A dynamic core is comprised of a large and diverse group of sub-clusters. If any one of them changes its state of activation, it will have effects upon the whole dynamic core (Ibid.: 148). A unified scene changes as it reflects events in the outer world or within the observing animal (Edelman 2004: 70).

When the dynamic core makes a real-world scenario appear in the psyche of a conscious animal, Edelman (2004: 77) calls this the "phenomenal transform." *Phenomenon* is the English form of a Greek word that means "that which appears." Neural networks blink, and a world springs into view. Electrochemistry becomes phenomenology, inner life.

Edelman identifies the dynamic core with "primary consciousness," a lower-order capability lacking in introspection and sense of time. It is not as comprehensive as Jung's self, which occupies the entire brain. We might visualize its activated meshwork as a glowing, blinking blob with indefinite edges: pulsing, trembling, sending out tentacles and retracting them, bulging this way and that to reflect the scene in the world outside and our state of mind. "The same group of neurons may sometimes be part of the dynamic core and underlie conscious experience, but at other times, not be part of it and thus be involved in unconscious processes" (Edelman and Tononi 2000: 144). Clearly this is a proto-ego rather than a proto-self—but a part of a whole, its contents are in constant flux, like Jung's ego-complex. But it is not the ego; for according to Edelman, there is a "higher order consciousness" we have not yet begun to investigate. "Even before higher-order consciousness appears, a bodily-based neural reference space or body-centered scene will be built up. Such a namable self emerges in humans as higher order consciousness develops" (Edelman 2004: 73).

The vagaries of consciousness

To comprehend the contributions of Damasio and Edelman, we have to take note of the fact that *consciousness* is one of the loosest terms in our vocabulary. Sometimes it designates *any* psychic phenomenon. In this sense, human consciousness supplies the words that just "pop" into our minds. But it would be just as correct to say that "the *unconscious*" supplies those words to the ego. Solms and Turnbull (2002) point out that nuclei in the brainstem control heartbeat, breathing, digestion, wake/sleep cycles, and the like, in a completely automatic manner, for their circuits are "hard wired," shared by all mammals, and inaccessible to cultural shaping. "The mind begins," they say, "where these systems end" (Solms and Turnbull 2002: 275). By this definition, most of what we usually attribute to unconscious functioning (dreams, words that pop into mind, etc.) would be considered part of the activity of consciousness. On the other hand, Damasio says, "We become conscious when [our] representation devices exhibit . . . the knowledge that [our] organism's own state has been changed by an object" (Damasio 1999: 25). In using the term *knowledge*, Damasio may be limiting consciousness to those states in which I know that I know; but it is not clear. For, when I dream of a bull charging at me, does not the imagery and the panic that I experience in the dream imply a certain "knowledge" that my "state" has been altered? Is it important that the bull is only imagined and not seen? Or that I be asleep and not awake?

The unconscious

It has often been said that late nineteenth- and twentieth-century notions of an unconscious have functioned primarily to extend our idea of what *consciousness* entails, for what is unconscious clearly belongs to the realm of the psyche. Unconscious factors may not be explicitly known, but they have demonstrable effects upon our attitudes and behavior. From an evolutionary point of view, therefore, it seems reasonable to conclude with Damasio, Searle, Edelman, and Llinás, that consciousness emerged as a tool to select out of this vast unknown the factors that matter and to decide what they mean. It is a device for dealing with complicated or novel situations, where choices have to be made and strategies laid out.

LeDoux (1996: 19) says, "States of consciousness occur when the system responsible for awareness becomes privy to the activity occurring in unconscious processing systems." But when is that? Our speaking in sentences surely must be "privy to the activity of unconscious processes," for those processes have given us the words. But most people do not realize that they are not themselves consciously inventing the sentences; and those of us who do, know nothing of the process itself. Perhaps LeDoux's statement makes more sense if we turn it around and say, we believe we understand something about processes in the neural substrate when the shape of those processes resembles our conscious experience of thinking, imagining, and feeling.

Our everyday experience exhibits several degrees of unconsciousness. Searle (2004: 240–2) outlines a traditional set. Nearest to knowing-that-we-know is (a) Freud's "pre-conscious" and Jung's "personal unconscious": I know it, but it is not on my mind until the issue comes up. Somewhat more unconscious is (b) personal knowledge that has been repressed: Freud's patient Dora coughs because of her sexual desire (or repulsion) for Herr K. We are deep in the unconscious (c) when we are influenced by matters that have never in any way been consciously thought: a three-year-old acquiring grammar rules. Much further down in the deepest unconscious (d) are neurobiological processes such as neural patterns that never become images,[5] and the firing of sleep/wake nuclei in the brainstem.

"Conscious experience does not just float freely above an ocean of functionally insulated, unconscious processes. Instead, it is constantly influencing and being influenced by [them]" (Edelman and Tononi 2000: 177). This is essentially Jung's position: we know an unconscious exists because it has effects upon consciousness. Searle's layered unconscious has the same structure as Jung's (conscious, personal unconscious, collective unconscious, and psychoid), and his example of language acquisition in a three-year-old reminds us of the archetypes.

Higher-order consciousness

Edelman calls the awareness exhibited by the dynamic core "primary consciousness." It integrates a large and diverse body of information "for the purpose of directing present or immediate behavior" (Edelman and Tononi 2000: 103). This is "the remembered present," for the core cannot gain access to a remembered past or an imagined future. But an ego can "obtain a temporary divorce" from the present moment, and build a world out of images from a relevant past and an anticipated future (Edelman and Tononi 2000: 195). Set free from the emotionally riveting scene of the moment, ego fabricates an autobiography that depends to a large extent upon social and affective interactions with other human subjects (Edelman 1992: 133–5). Higher consciousness is a subtle tool for making choices, selecting courses of action, and steering a nervous system that has "grown too complex to regulate itself" (Edelman 2004: 83f).

Highly sophisticated differentiation appears to be the crucial capacity of higher-order consciousness. Whereas, metaphorically, the dynamic core easily discriminates wine from water, an ego can learn to discriminate between white wine and red, and eventually between cabernet and pinot noir (Edelman and Tononi 2000: 174). Billions of different conscious states, each with its own behavioral outcomes, must be weighed, and selections made. A variety of routines can be tried out by selecting neuronal maps, loops, and circuits, highlighted by values—especially involving the deployment of dopamine, which reinforces desired and effective behavior with the reward of feeling good about it (Edelman and Tononi 2000: 188). With practice each routine becomes more automatic, freeing consciousness to attend to other matters in need of refinement (Ibid.: 59). Edelman demonstrates this last claim with an experiment in which subjects devoted four to eight weeks of daily practice learning the computer game Tetris. At first, PET scans showed an increase of glucose metabolism in certain regions of the cortex;[6] but, with time, these areas of furious activity decreased—showing that conscious control was declining at the same time that game performance was undergoing a sevenfold improvement (Edelman and Tononi 2000: 60). Clearly it was becoming an automatic skill while directing consciousness was being freed for other duties.

It is significant that Edelman has far less to say about the neural processes underlying ego function than he has regarding the dynamic core. It reveals the fairly general and unspecific nature of what neurobiology has been able to determine about the neural substrate behind ego function. What is most convincing about his work is his sensitive and flexible description of proto-egoic function. His work and that of others—such as Damasio, LeDoux, Llinás, and Freeman—is highly consilient with Jung's speculations of a century ago.

Phylogeny and the ego

Edelman is fairly confident that all animals with a cortex have primary consciousness, a form of the dynamic core that can provide "global mappings" that bind sensory and motor systems through reentrant circuits (Edelman 2004: 49). This would include all mammals and birds, possibly snakes, but not lobsters, making consciousness about 300 million years old. Damasio, although less specific in his claims, appears to agree, offering the opinion that chimpanzees, bonobos "and some dogs of my acquaintance" seem to have liberated themselves from Edelman's "remembered present" and gained some notion of a past and a future (Damasio 1999: 198). Edelman is somewhat more specific, saying that it is "likely" that chimpanzees have a form of higher-order consciousness. He says they clearly communicate with one another ("semantic ability") but lack the capacity for syntax. They have sufficient sense of self to be able to recognize their own faces when they see them in a mirror; and they employ a Theory of Mind to predict the behavior of other chimps (Edelman 2004: 98). Llinás (2002: 113) "suspect[s] that subjectivity is what the nervous system is all about, even at the most primitive levels of evolution."

Probably the most convincing evidence we have seen that bonobo consciousness is not confined to a "remembered present" is the behavior of Kanzi on the day that his mother was taken away. Savage-Rumbaugh reports that he immediately began communicating with the keyboard, and described not only what he wanted to be given, but also what he planned to do later on (Savage-Rumbaugh et al. 1998: 25). His capacity to understand his own existence as fundamentally temporal seems therefore to be innate and not to be something humans have taught him.

Frans de Waal has devoted his career to collecting evidence of mental abilities in animals, particularly apes, which are quite capable of recognizing themselves in mirrors, imitating one another and humans, and expressing empathy and intentional deception (de Waal 1996: 78). Mirror recognition, indeed, is sometimes only the beginning of the evidence for a chimpanzee's capacity for a self-concept. De Waal reports observing a chimpanzee checking her teeth and genital swellings in a mirror, an orangutan viewing her reflection with vegetables on her head, and chimpanzees decorating themselves with vines and dead mice draped over their shoulders. Even more impressive, since it expresses an awareness of self-image within a social context, is the chimp who wiped a grin off his face with his hand so as not to telegraph his state of mind. Another young male chimpanzee, when the alpha-male came by, used his hand to cover the erection he had been displaying to woo a female (de Waal 1996: 71, 76f).

There is also evidence of self-awareness in animals lower than the great apes. De Waal (1996) says that monkeys are very much aware of where they rank in their group on the basis of specific skills they have developed. They also have a sense for how far into the canopy their hands, feet, and tail will reach—clearly signifying a very definite and accurate body image which they can apply to everyday situations in the jungle. Bats' capacity for echolocation includes the talent for distinguishing the echoes they themselves produce from those produced by other bats. Finally, it is obvious that dogs recognize their own scent and distinguish it from that of other dogs (de Waal 1996: 68).

To return to the importance of the prefrontal cortex (PFC) for ego function, it is explicitly mentioned by Damasio and Edelman as a significant contributor to the dynamic core—whether in humans or other animals. Monkeys that have had their PFC ablated on both sides are no longer able to maintain normal social relations (Damasio 1994: 74). Quartz and Sejnowski (2002) report on the spindle-cell count in an area of the PFC called the anterior cingulate cortex. The more spindle cells, the more capable an animal is in managing issues related to sociality. Not surprisingly, human adults have a large number of spindle cells, chimpanzees far fewer, and gorillas and orangutans very few indeed. They do not appear at all in the human brain before the fourth month of life (Quartz and Sejnowski 2002: 131). Such correlations of the complexity of neural circuitry with the level of psychic functioning strongly supports the arguments outlined in this chapter regarding the support role played by the neural substrate in conscious abilities.

Ego the storyteller

Temporality—our being always in a present that is the outcome of a remembered and lesson-filled past and an anticipated future—has been a recurring theme in this study. Evolution itself is a story of origins, transformations, and futures in preparation. Marshack's (1991) study of notched bones reveals how long our ancestors had been marking the passage of time as they anticipated the return of specific game animals. His account of Peking Man's mastery of fire was another lesson in time-consciousness: waiting for the wet or green wood to dry, banking ashes around the coals against an anticipated revival of the blaze for tomorrow morning's breakfast. Kanzi the bonobo, when he began communicating, "spoke" of his plans for the future.

Kanzi, and possibly Peking Man, could not talk, and yet they evidently understood themselves and their world in episodic, narrative terms. The continuous working of episodic memory is the foundation of our sense of self, our active construction of egohood within a social world (Siegel 1999: 44). No doubt storytelling precedes language and "is, in fact, a condition for language" (Damasio 1999: 189). We learn to speak because we have stories to tell. Philosopher Daniel Dennett identifies storytelling as humanity's "fundamental tactic of self-protection, and self-definition," comparable in its way to the spider's web-spinning and the beaver's dam-building (Dennett 1991: 418).

Stories full of holes

We like to think that all these stories we tell ourselves are true, but there is considerable reason to doubt our pious assertions. For consciousness is full of holes, and we use our stories to hide them from ourselves. Evolution itself is a story full of holes. Scientists often speak as though they are steadily filling them in. Proponents of the theory of "Intelligent Design" seize on the gaps in evolution's evidence and beg us to let them tell *their* story of evolution—yet another gloss, and a far less useful one. "The conscious brain in health and disease will integrate what can be integrated and resists a fractured or shattered view of 'reality'" (Edelman 2004: 136).

Our primate eyesight is a case in point. We like to believe that we see the world clearly, in good focus, held steady, and full of detail. In fact, however, we have a blind spot in the middle of our visual field, and what we can hold in focus is a relatively tiny portion of that field—"two to three degrees around dead center"—the rest is a blur. We prevent ourselves from recognizing these deficiencies by keeping our eyeballs in constant movement, darting about in "saccades," about five times a second, "an incessant and largely unnoticed game of visual tag with items of potential interest in our field of view" (Dennett 1991: 54). In patients whose cerebral hemispheres have been surgically separated, the left (language) hemisphere is famous for inventing spurious reasons for behaviors or sensations processed by the right hemisphere (LeDoux 1996: 32; Rose 2005: 201f). Morton Prince (1929/39), one of Boston's contributors to the dissociation school of psychology, reports the same of hypnosis subjects who have carried out post-hypnotic suggestions. Unaware they had been hypnotized, they give absurd reasons for doing what they did—reasons they strenuously defend and evidently believe. Our storytelling ego is beset on all sides with its Amfortas wound.

Philosopher John Gray takes a largely Buddhist ("no-self") position regarding the specious stories we tell ourselves. "The *I* is a thing of the moment, and yet our lives are ruled by it. . . . This is the primordial human error, in virtue of which we pass our lives as in a dream" (Gray 2002: 78). But we do not invent these glosses consciously; we are unaware that we are lying to ourselves. The root storyteller is ultimately not the ego but that unconscious proto-ego, the dynamic core. "Our tales are spun, but for the most part we don't spin them; they spin us. Our human consciousness, and our narrative selfhood, is their product, not their source" (Dennett 1991: 418).

Mythic stories

We would be better off if our fictions were not superficial, ad hoc cover-ups for momentary embarrassments, but in some deep sense true to our nature. This is why Jung spoke of discovering the myth each of us is already living. There is a phylogenetic dimension to our life, and we would be better off knowing what it is:

> Myth, says a Church Father, is "what is believed always, everywhere, by everybody"; hence the man who thinks he can live without myth, or outside it, is an exception. He is like one uprooted, having no true link either with the past, or with the ancestral life which continues within him. . . . [Psyche's] ancestry goes back many millions of years. Individual consciousness is only the flower and fruit of a season, sprung from the perennial rhizome beneath the earth; and it would find itself in better accord with the truth if it took the existence of the rhizome into its calculations. For the root matter is the mother of all things.
>
> (CW5: xxiv)

Myth makes sense of life in an ultimate sense and has done so from time immemorial. The ego, however, with its ephemeral nature, is hardly able to invent a narrative of mythic significance. Rather it is, itself, part of the larger story being spun by a dynamic core that tells tales of an archetypal nature, impressing us with their depth of meaning and enduring significance.

Chapter 9

Dreams

Evidence of dialogic process

Individuation is an inevitable dimension of life for a being with a reflective ego. Jung's recommendation of active imagination in *Two Essays* (*CW7*) to deliberately evoke commentary from the larger self imitates nature in order to assist and speed up nature's own process. In everyday life, ego/self exchanges occur whether we want them to or not. Indeed, the foremost source of narratives, mythic and otherwise, spun by our dynamic core and observed by our ego is the theater we enter every night when we sleep. Freud called dreams the "royal road *to* the unconscious." He thought they were designed by a devious unconscious mechanism, the "dream work," to fool us into encountering benign versions of unconscious thoughts that would otherwise be too horrifying to tolerate. Disguised by references to the previous day and subjected to reversals and inversions, heinous thoughts were alleged to slip by their censor as charming absurdities. Dreams constructed a royal road in the form of a riddle for psychoanalytic detectives to unravel in order to reach the real thoughts that lurked in the unconscious.

No doubt Freud's conviction that we inveterately lie to ourselves was not entirely mistaken. But a gappy ego narrative trying to deal with an overabundance of sensations, emotional reactions and internally created fantasies supplied by a dynamic core leaves no place for the sorts of distortion Freud attributed to unconscious imagery. Dream images, as Jung insisted, mean what they say. If there is a "royal road" anywhere for us, it lies in the running dialogue of individuation. Imbalances within our organism as a whole will pull the proto-ego of the dynamic core into different shapes as new brain regions register outer world and inner subjectivity with greater or lesser force. In Jung's terms, the self (in the guise of the shadow)[1] is always trying to reestablish holistic balance—just as every living organism draws its conflicting components into service of the whole.

Dreams constitute a primary source of challenges to the autobiographical fictions we cultivate while awake; and they call us to investigate the inevitable tensions that arise between the reflective process of ego and the organismic process of self. Individuation is the royal road to wholeness that emerges from these tensions.

Jung's phenomenology of dreaming

A careful reading of the *Word Association* papers (*CW2*) and *The Psychology of Dementia Praecox* (*CW3*) will reveal that Jung never accepted Freud's disguise theory of dreaming. Even while Crown Prince of Psychoanalysis, Jung saw dream imagery as transparent. Dreams require "translation" only insofar as they speak in emotionally charged images rather than in words.[2] In 1911, he described "Two Types of Thinking" (*CW5*: ¶4–33): first, "directed thought," usually verbal, outer directed, learned and shaped through social interactions, and tiring to maintain, the foundation of "our modern empiricism and technology"; and second, "non-directed thought" that "lacks all leading ideas and sense of direction" and occurs as an "autonomous play of ideas." Non-directed thought is spontaneously "associative" and "guided by unconscious motives." It is effortless, does not tire us out, and is the source of dreams.

Compensation

In that same chapter, Jung advances one of the strongest themes in all his later writings on dreams, the idea of "compensation," that the imagery and motifs in our dreams tend to reestablish psychic balance and make up for the ego's "one-sided" tendency to avoid its Amfortas wound. Subsequent to the "Two Types" chapter in *Symbols*, Jung makes it clear that he finds the associative thinking in dreams to be organized by archetypes into mythic themes, and these universally human patterns will be secondarily shaped by the dreamer's personal, auto-biographical experience. The "instigator" of the dream is always a powerful affect that has been unconscious (*CW18*: ¶858).

In his 1931 essay "The Practical Uses of Dream-Analysis" (*CW18*), Jung ties dream theory to his claim that the values an individual lacks are to be found in the neurosis; for the dream represents the inner situation of the dreamer, even though the waking ego is likely "to deny its truth and reality, or admit it only grudgingly." Thus the dream describes "the aetiology of the neurosis [and gives] a prognosis as well" (*CW8*: ¶304f). The tension between the dream's truth and the dreamer's reluctance to admit it indicates what is amiss right now in the dreamer's life and suggests what might be done about it.

Support from Hobson

Harvard psychiatrist and neurophysiologist J. Allan Hobson, probably the most respected investigator of the dreaming brain, is wholly in agreement with Jung: "My position echoes Jung's notion of the dream as transparently meaningful and does away with a distinction between manifest and latent content" (J. A. Hobson 1988: 12). He does not find the unconscious to be full of threatening, heinous drives, as Freud did, but sees it as "an ally and a guide to survival and socially sensible reproduction" (Hobson 2002: 134). In the end, Hobson's view fully supports a theory of psyche as individuation process:

I view dreams as privileged communications from one part of myself (call it the unconscious if you will) to another (my waking consciousness). There can be no doubt that our dreams are trying to tell us something about how our memories are organized, that associationism is alive and well, and that dream discussions will continue no matter what we scientists say!

(Hobson 2005: 83)

Hobson lists seven major differences between his findings and Freud's theories, every one of which lines him up with Jung's stance. The energy of the dream process is (a) intrinsic to the brain and (b) the source is neural (Jung's idea that the organismic self is the source of the dream); (c) the sensory images of the dream prepare us for the future and do not represent a regression to the past (Jung's idea that the running dialogue is oriented to present difficulties and future solutions); (d) the information processing in the dream elaborates new life themes and does not disguise unacceptable ideas; (e) the bizarreness of the imagery is a primary characteristic of the dream and not a secondary product of defense mechanisms; (f) the meaning of the imagery is transparent rather than opaque; and (g) themes of conflict are incidental rather than fundamental (Hobson 1988: 220f).

Hobson's explicit support for Jung's theory of dreams is particularly impressive in view of the fact that he seems embarrassed by it. Evidently he fears that association with Jungian ideas may undermine his thesis in the eyes of his readers.[3] He gives bizarre versions of what he thinks "a Jungian would say" about the meaning of a dream, and calls Jung "strongly anti-scientific," while confusing the identity of Jung's chief at the Burghölzli and misspelling proper names (Hobson 2005: 63, 118f).[4] Apparently Hobson believes Jung thought that images themselves are inherited and "intrinsic to the nervous system" (Hobson 1988: 27)— popular misconceptions that we have refuted in earlier chapters.

Dreaming process in the neural substrate

This section summarizes the findings of Hobson and Jaak Panksepp, the authority of whose *Affective Neuroscience* (Panksepp 1998) is widely cited. Panksepp's chapter on the neuroscience of dreaming includes the word "mythmaking" in its title. A footnote explains that the word was included as a tribute to C. G. Jung.

Three states of consciousness

Discussions of the dreaming brain inevitably begin with the explanation that the brain is capable of three quite different behavioral states. The *waking state* is characterized by high-frequency, low-amplitude beta EEG waves, whose irregularity results from the frequent changes in attention that waking life requires. Our muscles are toned and ready for action. We are oriented to the world outside of ourselves. The *dreaming state*, by contrast, is recognizable by rapid eye movements (REM) visible behind closed eyelids. The brain is even more active in

REM sleep than it is in the waking state, despite its unresponsiveness to sensory stimulation and the flaccidity of our muscles. The REM state is intrinsically intro-verted. *Slow wave sleep* (SWS, also called non-REM) is characterized by high amplitude slow waves that perform very little active processing of information (Panksepp 1998: 125).

Although there is evidence for some dreaming in SWS,[5] most investigators have studied REM sleep. Hobson (1988: 205–10) identifies five physiological characteristics of REM: first, REM is "switched on" when neurons originating in the brainstem deliver the neurotransmitter acetylcholine to the cortex. (The waking state returns when different neurons deliver norepinephrine and serotonin to the cortex.) Second, signals from the brainstem deactivate the sensory neurons that respond to events in the outer world, and the brain becomes so busy process-ing information in its internal association circuits that it ignores any sensory data that may get through the sensory blockade. Third, neurons that control motor output (muscle movement) are also blocked. Fourth, the outer world having been shut out, *internal* association circuits and corresponding emotion-managing regions are synchronized by strong regular pulses, "indigenous bolts of neural 'lightning' called PGO spikes" (Panksepp 1998: 129).[6] Finally, the mode of information processing is different in REM: internally generated signals are inter-preted by the brain as though they are of external origin. This is what leads us to experience the activity of the neural substrate as our life in dreamscape. Hobson believes that this change in processing mode explains our habitual failure to remember our dreams.

PGO spikes account for several of a dream's peculiarities. They do not occur during the waking state in normal individuals, but have been recorded in the brains of schizophrenics and those under the influence of LSD (Panksepp 1998: 127). Here is one connection between the bizarreness of dream imagery and that of psychotic and psychedelic experiences.[7] Other parallels will be discussed below. PGO waves constitute what Hobson calls a "startle program." Our con-sciousness is startled by every spike, apparently the cause of abrupt scene changes in dreams. Furthermore, the constantly novel and unpredictable quality of dream-ing probably results from the "uninhibited running of the startle program" (J. A. Hobson 2005: 45).

The evolutionary significance of REM

Research shows that REM is an evolutionary achievement that characterizes mammals (Panksepp 1998: 135). Since it is well established that the amount of dreaming increases when organisms have to face stressful and emotionally chal-lenging situations (Ibid.: 128), it seems likely that REM sleep is a selective pro-cessing device that enable[s] recent memories to be evaluated against 'phyletic' memories" (Fox 1989: 181). In this statement, Rutgers anthropologist Robin Fox suggests that recent personal events undergo a recategorizing whereby they are linked to archetypal patterns of recognition and behavior that have been inherited with our DNA. He believes evolution "freed [us] from the tie to [our] phyloge-netic past to some degree" when it provided us with a huge and complex cortex. This freedom, however, gives us the further burden of having to reintegrate the archetypal with the personal. Here again is Jung's theory that ego strays from its phylogenetic roots in the self and needs commentary from dreams, symptoms and waking fantasies to get itself back in harmony. Panksepp says something very similar: "The REM system may now allow ancient emotional impulses to be integrated with the newer cognitive skills of the more recently evolved brain waking systems" (Panksepp 1998: 135). As Jung puts it, emotional realities of archetypal origin are subsequently "clothed" with associations from our autobio-graphical memory (personal unconscious). Consequently, universal patterns appear in our dreams under the guise of familiar people, settings, and activities.

In Panksepp's thinking, there appear to be two separate systems for informa-tion processing. What we now know as REM sleep may originally have been a form of waking consciousness, in a world where "emotionality was more import-ant than reason in competition for resources." As evolution proceeded into mammals and primates, that ancient form of consciousness "may have come to be actively suppressed" so as to enable a more analytic process of evaluation and planning (Panksepp 1998: 128). At that point in evolution, REM-style processing moved into the "background," where emotional reactions of archetypal shape and intensity remain unconscious until we fall asleep and dream. The integration of these ancient emotional urges with memories derived from waking life brings about a reshuffling of our memories that lines them up in accordance with our inherited tendencies on the one hand and that simultaneously personalizes those archetypal patterns on the other. As archaic patterns are integrated with everyday experience, we come to function more adequately in confronting the challenges of tomorrow and next week (Panksepp 1998: 135). From this point of view, dreams maintain a running dialogue with consciousness even when we do not remember them.

What dreaming accomplishes

Because animals deprived of REM sleep fail to remember from one day to the next new tasks they have been working on, it seems evident that dreams are pro-cessing new memories (Fox 1989: 179). Furthermore, it is known that the sleeping brain manufactures proteins at a faster rate than the waking brain (Lewis-Williams 2002: 191). Thus it appears not only that memories are being organized, but also that synapses are being fortified with new proteins as habitual long-term pathways are constructed. Evidence for such claims comes from rats learning mazes and humans learning video games. Human participants in the experiments report intrusive gaming imagery at the onset of sleep; both human and rat brains show activation during sleep of the same brain areas that had been used in the learning trials the day before (J. A. Hobson 2002: 128). Much of such research from games and mazes is related to learning new motor patterns. But it is also clear that visual discrimination improves after REM sleep, and is best if neither REM nor SWS is disturbed (Ibid.: 124f). Hobson says that dreams enable us to keep track of important relationships and events in our lives through "an emotionally driven shorthand" (Ibid.: 22, 132).

It must also be emphasized, however, that dreaming is a highly introverted activity in which the brain speaks exclusively to itself, and that it will do so even when there are no new outer-worldly experiences to integrate. Dreaming shows that the brain is able to create its own energy and information (J. A. Hobson 1988: 131). The most striking instance of the brain dreaming up its own organization and structure occurs in the human embryo, which at about six months gestation is spending nearly twenty-four hours a day in the REM state. By the day of its birth, however, the infant's REM sleep has declined to twelve or sixteen hours a day. Constant dreaming thus progressively gives way to extraverted sensory and motor operations as an infant matures and gradually learns to orient itself to the outer world (J. A. Hobson 2002: 77). Such findings support the claim that REM develops the brain and helps it structure the mind of a well-adapted animal, preparing it to function as a "prediction machine," deriving conclusions from prior experience to enhance survival skills in the future.

REM activities also support Jung's notion that dreams emerge from our larger being (the self) to compensate for the inadequacies of our waking attitudes. In this sense, they constitute the majority voice on the unconscious side of the running dialogue between ego and self. J. A. Hobson (1988: 291) notes that basic brain circuits that have *not* been used recently in waking life are regularly fired up during REM sleep. He speculates that this is a maintenance operation, on the principle that circuits have to be used regularly or they will be abandoned and die. This is likely true; but in the process circuits neglected by the proto-ego of waking consciousness become parts of the proto-ego of REM dreaming. They achieve balance in the organism as a whole. This is the sense in which Jung's self may be said to "speak" to us in our dreams. Furthermore, if REM tends to "rest the neurons most sensitive to fatigue," as Hobson claims, and "activate[s] non-fatigable brain circuits," Jung's observations of a century ago are supported: "directed thinking" tires us out and is replaced by "association thinking" from the unconscious which does not tire us.

Dreams and the brain's seeking system

Panksepp (1998) ties together a number of the common characteristics of dreaming—its frequently bizarre hallucinatory character, the jumps that occur between "scenes," the similarity of dreams and schizophrenic symptoms, and the importance of emotional values in dreams. In all cases brain activation suggests "seeking" behavior. Panksepp's SEEKING system (he always capitalizes the whole word, we will not) manifests when an animal forages, explores, investigates, or is otherwise curious. It drives an animal "eagerly to pursue the fruits of [its] environment" and has a feeling tone of "intense interest, engaged curiosity, or eager anticipation" (Panksepp 1998: 145, 149). Aroused longing vanishes when the animal finds what it is looking for, but along the way of its quest, the animal will automatically take stock of everything for its relevance to the object of the quest. In the process, stable neural networks are generated in the form of memories that will be useful on future quests (Panksepp 1998: 147).

The brain circuits employed by the seek archetype are principally located in "the extended lateral hypothalamic corridor," a ribbon of neuropil located mostly along the floor and either side of the brain's third ventricle. When in seeking mode, the brain generates highly synchronous theta rhythms in the lateral hypothalamus that are much slower and more regular than the beta rhythms that predominate in most waking states. Because theta rhythms characterize deep meditative states, seeking is a sort of trance state—more focused and avid than ordinary consciousness (Panksepp 1998: 151, 129).

In waking life, the seeking response is triggered by imbalances like hunger, thirst and lust (Panksepp 1998: 145), just as dreams are about sniffing out internal imbalances related to our "Amfortas wound." Developing new neural networks and integrating them with the rest of our autobiography balances the psyche. Dreaming, too, is a quest.

Dreaming and dopamine

Panksepp (1998) says that the seeking system has left an "electrophysiological fingerprint" on our dreaming. Whether dreaming by night or questing by day, dopamine neurons fire two or three spikes, with declining amplitude and growing duration. This pattern keeps the seeking system poised and ready for action at a moment's notice and is so regular that the spikes may well serve as the ticking of an internal clock. Our poised regularity is interrupted by a "bursting pattern" of spikes when some salient object is met. Now the system is aroused, and a rapid series of action potentials promotes dopamine release into the synaptic fields of the neural networks involved in the new discovery. Rapid firing may speed up our internal time sense while it heightens our eagerness, anticipation, and dream intensity (Panksepp 1998: 156).

> The desires and aspirations of the human heart are endless. It is foolish to attribute them all to a single brain system. But they all come to a standstill if certain brain systems, such as the dopamine circuits arising from midbrain nuclei [the extended hypothalamic corridor] are destroyed. . . . Ascending dopamine tracts lie at the heart of powerful, affectively valenced neural systems that allow people and animals to operate smoothly and efficiently in all of their day-to-day pursuits. These circuits appear to be major contributors to our feelings of engagement and excitement.
>
> (Panksepp 1998: 144)

In the REM state, dopamine is not delivered to the cortex in abundance, but the relatively small amount of dopamine contributed by the hypothalamus has a disproportionately large effect in the REM state because in the sleeping brain dopamine encounters no interfering neurotransmitters—such as the norepinephrine and serotonin that keep us awake (J. A. Hobson 2005: 75).

Dopamine is the neurotransmitter that drives the appetitive system; it mediates "wanting," rather than "enjoying" (Panksepp 1998: 155). The eager anticipation with which we greet the people, objects and events that are potentially relevant to our search often causes us to overemphasize their meaningfulness. In fact, when in the seeking mode, we are vulnerable to a "confirmation bias," the propensity to see causal connections everywhere (Panksepp 1998: 145). Paranoid thinking, too, may be due to "overactivation of the mesolimbic dopamine system," for the seeking response facilitates the spontaneous construction of "insights" on the basis of perceived causality. By this mechanism, a paranoid individual will find evidence everywhere that his enemies are after him. The most incidental details in his surroundings will be seized upon as evidence that "They" have been going through his files, tampering with his car, tapping his phone. Evidently his seeking system is out of control; for it will continue to find "confirmatory evidence" even when he tries his best not to worry, not to look for proof, not to see anything suspicious.

Confirmation bias may also lie behind the gullibility we manifest while dreaming (Janet's "immediate belief" and what Jung and Hobson have called the "psychotic" quality of dreaming). Panksepp (1998) notes that a schizophrenic episode usually begins with a night's sleep in which the REM state is markedly elevated. "This suggests that emotional 'energies' that are aroused during the initial florid phase of schizophrenia may be released during the dreaming process." The preponderance of dopamine in the dreaming state bears some resemblance to the schizophrenic brain—and also to the psychedelic brain, for LSD is an excellent serotonin blocker (Panksepp 1998: 127, 142).

Dreaming and mythmaking

Panksepp (1998) believes (although he cannot prove) that schizophrenic process, the emotional discharges of REM sleep, and the electrochemical discharges of seeking behavior are related. They use the same brain tracts, AM wave patterns, and neurotransmitters. Very likely, too, they account for the symbolic character of dream images. Seeing ephemeral things with emotional urgency and fervent conviction lies at the heart of symbol-making; for a symbol, in Jung's view, points to something that is partly known, but mostly unknown.[8] The neural foundation of symbol-making and world construction, therefore, appears to be closely related to the seeking/dreaming/paranoid complex Panksepp has described.

To judge from the dreams we recall upon waking, we make some enormous leaps of faith while in the REM state, as our seeking system imposes a narrative form on the improbable collection of neural networks that fire up when there is no challenge from the outer world to guide them. But ego-baffling associations may bring important insights. Hobson says, "The brain [is] so inexorably bent upon the quest for meaning that it attributes and even creates meaning where there is little or none to be found in the data it is asked to process" (J. A. Hobson 1988: 15). The fact that meaning is sought and will be found is what joins ego and unconscious in the running dialogue of individuation.

Chapter 10

Jung's complex theory

Typically, when Jung described the empirical roots of his psychology, the nature of complexes and how they affect our experience and behavior, he reminded his readers and auditors of the historical background to that theory. In 1924 he wrote, "The psychic double is a commoner phenomenon than one would expect, although it seldom reaches a degree of intensity that would entitle one to speak of a 'double personality'" (*CW17*: ¶227). In 1939, he recommended the writings of Pierre Janet (Paris), Theodore Flournoy (Geneva), and Morton Prince (Boston), so that his readers would understand the premises on which he was working (*CW9i*: ¶490). In 1951, he traced his own heritage from sixteenth-century medical alchemist Paracelsus, through Mesmer, Charcot, Janet and Freud (*CW16*: ¶231). Three years later, he cited cases of double personality, *automatisme ambulatoire*, and the researches of Janet to illustrate what he envisioned the complexes to be (*CW8*: ¶383).

Historical background

Morton Prince's famous account of the Beauchamp case (*The Dissociation of a Personality*, 1905/08) has an honored place as the prototypical American description of multiple personality. The authors of more recent and popular accounts, such as *The Three Faces of Eve* and *Sybil*, have used Prince's book as a guide to observation and treatment—perhaps ill-advisedly. For Prince was not diligent at "keeping his cultures pure," as Janet recommended; he failed to notice that his words and actions might be suggesting the course of his patient's behavior and shaping her memories. But he understood the main point:

> The dissociated and multiple personalities are not novel and freak phenomena, but are only exaggerations of the normal and due to exaggerations of normal processes, and it is for this reason that they are of interest and importance. For, being exaggerations, they accentuate and bring out into high relief certain tendencies and functional mechanisms which belong to normal conditions and they differentiate mental processes, one from another, which normally are not so easily recognized.
>
> (Prince 1914/21: 562)

Complex theory is founded upon this natural dissociability of the human psyche, whereby the parts may act like alternate personalities, seemingly complete in themselves and frequently unaware of other "subpersonalities" inhabiting the same skin. Jung's idea of a human psyche comprised of a number of "complexes" closely resembles the dissociation school's "alternating personalities," but without the amnesia for one another that the warring identities of multiple-personality patients display.

People with multiple-personality are just like the rest of us, except that there is little or no connection between their complexes—little or no recollection of what was happening minutes or hours ago when another part-personality was in charge. But even with us, each complex remembers better and more vividly the episodes comprising *its* part in our autobiography than it does the life stories of other complexes.

The philosopher Frédéric Paulhan wrote a very influential phenomenology of the dissociable psyche in 1889, *L'Activité mentale et les elements de l'esprit*, which was read and cited by Janet, Alfred Binet, and Jung. It introduces three laws to describe the characteristics of dissociation:

1   The Law of Systematic Association: each image and memory tends to associate with others "which are able to be harmonized with itself," work toward "compatible goals" and "comprise a system" (Paulhan 1889: 88).
2   The Law of Inhibition: every such psychic element tends to interfere with and deny "the phenomena which it cannot assimilate in the interests of a common goal" (Paulhan 1889: 221).
3   The Law of Contrast: contrasting and opposed psychic states tend to alternate with one another and may sometimes function concurrently (Paulhan 1889: 315f).[1]

In his *Principles of Psychology* (1890), William James discusses such "Mutations of the Self" (1890: 240–59) and the laws of association (Ibid.: 360–95). One of his more interesting examples concerns "co-conscious" part-personalities in a congressman from the state of Connecticut in the late 1850s, Sidney Dean.[2] Dean had the recurring experience of watching in amazement and some horror, as his own hand wrote out a philosophical treatise that challenged his own long-held beliefs:

> When the work is in progress I am in the normal condition and simply two minds, intelligences, persons, are practically engaged. The writing is in my own hand but the dictation not of my own mind and will, but of another, upon subjects of which I can have no knowledge and hardly a theory; and I, myself, consciously criticize the thought, fact, mode of expressing it, etc., while the hand is recording. . . . There is in progress now, at uncertain times, not subject to my will, a series of twenty-four chapters upon the scientific features of life, mortality, spirituality, etc. . . . These were preceded by twenty-four chapters relating generally to life beyond material death, its characteristics, etc. . . .

From my standpoint of life—which has been that of biblical orthodoxy—the philosophy is new, seems reasonable, and is logically put. I confess to an inability to successfully controvert it to my own satisfaction.

(James 1890: 235)

The opposition between Congressman Dean's conscious philosophy of life and that of his alternate personality is more conscious and full of detail than that found in most "somnambulists" of a century and more ago. More typically, the patient was a young woman, timid, pious and poorly adapted to her social environment, who one day turned up pregnant and had no idea how such a thing could have happened. Subsequently, hypnosis would then uncover the simultaneous existence of another personality, more bold, less respectful of conventions, more adept in social encounters, and sexually independent. Such typical examples of *dédoublement* did not think their way through a separate philosophy of life; they simply lived it, acted it out. What their alternate personalities share with Dean's is the fact that they are "compensating" for the narrowness and inadequacy of the "first" personality.

Contemporary views

The very possibility of a psyche comprised of alternating part-personalities prompts a second look at Edelman's dynamic core—the proto-ego that supplies us with the words we need to express our thoughts. For the instinctual, impulsive and less effete subpersonality of Prince's Miss Beauchamp and Janet's Lucie must have their own dynamic core, one that has separate memories, places its values in different areas of life, and strives for different goals than those of the first personality.

Edelman himself is open to this possibility. In his book, *Wider than the Sky* (2004: 142ff), he speaks briefly of "alternations of the core and its interactions with non-conscious substrates." To "somnambulistic" phenomena like hysteria, hypnotic trance and multiple-personality, he adds some organic conditions: severing the corpus callosum (disconnecting the brain's two hemispheres) as well as "blindsight, prosopagnosia, hemineglect, and anosognosia."[3] In all these cases, one part of the brain can be shown to act as though it "knows" what remains unknown to the conscious personality. Edelman speculates that "the core can split into a small number of separate cores, or even be remodeled constructively."

Damasio, too, is aware that these phenomena offer a challenge to his notion of core consciousness. Generally he seems defensive about them, reminding us that multiple-personality is "not considered normal" (Damasio 1999: 142) or suggesting "that their proto-selves and core consciousness may be anomalous" (Ibid.: 216). In a lengthy endnote, however, he treats the issue more seriously:

It is possible that instead of having one single set of rallying points for the generation of identity and personality, . . . such individuals manage to create, because of varied circumstances of their past history, more than one master control site. I suspect that the multiple master control sites are located in the temporal and frontal cortices and that the switch from one master control to another enables the identity/personality switch to occur.[4] . . . In such patients, to a certain extent, it is reasonable to talk about more than one "autobiographical memory."

(Damasio 1999: 354f).

In reading this, I was disappointed that he did not mention his central hypothesis, that of the somatic marker. For there is no doubt that each part-personality has its own anxieties, its own skills, and its own relation to the body. Sometimes the patients described by Prince and Janet had different allergies when they were in one subpersonality rather than another. If there is an emotion-based somatic jolt that organizes the consciousness of a healthy ego and "binds" its sensory processing into a single scene, each complex must have its own somatic marker. For although each alternate personality knows only a part of the autobiography of the afflicted individual, each lives in an organized scene that is anchored in an experience of its own body.

Jung's complex theory

Around the time Jung changed the name of his psychological "school" to Complex Psychology, he addressed two rather different audiences with an overview of his mature thoughts on what he had learned thirty years earlier conducting Word Association tests at the Burghölzli. At the inaugural lecture (1934) for the chair he had endowed at Zurich's Federal Institute of Technology (ETH), he presented "A Review of the Complex Theory" (*CW8*: ¶194–219). The next year, he devoted the third of his five-lecture series at the Tavistock Clinic in London to a summary of the same theory, illustrated by the dreams of a self-made man, an overambitious school headmaster whose dreams revealed strong unconscious opposition to his conscious plans. When he ignored them, he suffered a severe psychological crisis (*CW18*: ¶145–227).

When he speaks of a "complex," Jung always means to describe a relatively independent and autonomous part of the unconscious psyche—one of "an indefinite, because unknown, number of . . . fragment personalities" that "have a tendency to move by themselves, to live their own life apart from our intentions" (*CW18*: ¶151). In the same lecture, he goes on to enumerate the following characteristics of a complex: first, it has a sort of body with its own physiology so that it can upset the stomach, breathing, heart; second, it has its own will power and intentions so that it can disturb a train of thought or a course of action just as another human being can do; third, it is in principle no different from the ego which is itself a complex; fourth, it becomes visible and audible in hallucinations; and fifth, it completely victimizes the personality in insanity.

In "A Review of the Complex Theory," Jung thanks Janet and Prince for having discovered the extreme dissociability of the human psyche (*CW8*: ¶202). When he says, "Complexes are not entirely morbid by nature but are characteristic expressions of the psyche" (*CWD*: ¶209), he presumably acknowledges that, by the Law of Association, repetition and habit-formation cause certain helpful behaviors to become automatic and "second nature" to us. For instance, bicycle riding involves a sensory-motor program that is originally learned with effort—even painful trial and error—but soon becomes a skill we perform easily without having to give it special attention. The multiplication tables, too, are an association program. But neurotic or useful, each complex is organized to carry out mundane chores quickly and smoothly. In principle, this would leave our conscious attention free for more novel and unfamiliar challenges.

The *neurotic* complexes are the part-personalities Jung's theory is interested in. They disrupt our individuation process with biased and inaccurate interpretations of events in the world outside and with distorted images of ourselves. Such "*feeling-toned*" complexes "originate in trauma and moral conflict"; their roots extend deep "into [our] biology" and "reveal their character as *splinter psyches*" (*CW8*: ¶203f). Thus, in the Word Association test, when Jung pronounced an everyday word like *bed*, the victim of insomnia, rape, or sexual impotence would react emotionally, stumble, and experience a delay in completing her task of voicing the first word that came to mind. A "disturbance" had occurred, a failure to react smoothly and without effort. A common, ordinary word had been "assimilated" to the intentions and worldview of a single-minded complex, "an insuperable tendency in the psyche" (*CW8*: ¶195f). Furthermore, a complex-reaction like this "also happens in every discussion between two people" when a word is spoken or an image evoked that "constellates" a complex in one of the speakers. Immediately, the conversation "loses its objective character and real purpose"; it gets side-tracked into the same old repetitive nonsense every time (*CW8*: ¶199).

Jung speaks of a complex becoming "constellated" when "an outward situation releases . . . an automatic process which happens involuntarily" (*CW8*: ¶198). The scene before us arouses an emotional response, and the somatic marker of a part-personality jolts us into an alternate identity.

> A "feeling-toned complex" . . . is the *image* of a certain situation which is strongly accentuated emotionally and is, moreover, incompatible with the habitual attitude of consciousness. This image has a powerful inner coherence, it has its own wholeness and, in addition, a relatively high degree of autonomy.
>
> (*CW8*: ¶201)

"It has its roots in my body and begins to pull at my nerves" (*CW18*: ¶148). The ego simply becomes "assimilated" to the intentions of the complex, usually without realizing it has lost its way (*CW8*: ¶207).

Emotions and feelings

The expression *feeling-toned complex* is somewhat unfortunate in that it introduces a confusion in Jung's usual terminology. Some fifteen years after settling on the expression *Gefühl-betonter Komplex* to designate the emotional nature of a complex, while writing out his ideas on typology, Jung hit upon the necessity for distinguishing between "feeling" (*Gefühl*) and "emotion" (*Affekt*). In his writings from 1920 onward, he insists that—unlike emotions—feelings are "rational"; they assess the value of an object or situation. Does it make me feel happy or sad, relaxed or anxious? Am I more or less happy and relaxed than I was yesterday? The fact that we can make such conscious comparisons with our "feeling function" is the reason Jung insists it is "rational." Emotions, however, get down into the body and disturb our physiology; they interfere with rationality and reliable function. Emotion is a condition or state of the whole organism, rooted in the body and restricting psychic flexibility (*CW6*: ¶723–9, 681). Clearly, therefore, complexes are *emotionally* toned. In fact, it might be most accurate to describe complexes as emotion-*driven*.

It is perhaps not surprising that it took Jung fifteen years to appreciate the sharp contrast between *feeling* and *emotion*, since Pierre Janet insisted on pretty much the same distinction and was similarly inconsistent. For Janet, *émotion* described a "shock" to one's conscious integrity that lowered the "mental level" of one's conscious functioning:

> In a state of emotion, we see the disappearance of the mental synthesis, the attention, the will, the acquisition of new memories, and at the same time we see the diminution or disappearance of all reality functions, the feeling of reality and the ability to take pleasure in it, or to have confidence or certitude. In their place we see [neurotic symptoms].
>
> (Janet 1903: 523)

In contrast to *émotion*, Janet used the expression *sentiment* to refer to our ability to make value judgments, what Jung would call "feelings." Janet's German-speaking disciple, Leonhard Schwartz, in what is the only textbook of Janet's psychology (Schwartz 1951), translates *sentiment* as *Gefühl* (feeling). *Sentiment*, therefore, appears to be a relatively conscious recognition of the value of an object or situation—not a shock to our mental synthesis, but a condition of relatedness. Nevertheless *sentiment* is more regularly used to name disordered neurotic feelings that are symptoms of the loss of ego-function, in that they overwhelm the personality. Under "*sentiment*" in the index to one of Janet's volumes, for instance, there are about 100 entries, beginning: "the feeling of discontent, of imperfection, of anorectic euphoria, of shame, of sacrilege," etc. (Janet 1903: 754). Such feelings are excessive and inaccurate views of reality that are at least neurotic if not fully psychotic.[5] Janet's use of the term *sentiment*, therefore, appears to describe the "feeling-tones" that characterize Jung's complexes. The fact that Janet made a point of praising Jung's Word Association papers for their clinical value (Janet 1919: 604f) seems to confirm that the two psychologists were describing similar phenomena.

In any event it is clear when a "feeling-tone" takes over, we are emotionally affected, and our capacities for reality testing and discrimination decline, along with the stability of our attention and the resolution of our will. Our "level of consciousness" (*niveau mental*) drops, and we can no longer criticize the plausibility and relevance of the scene that opens before our eyes. As in a dream, we have lost the capacity for critical reflection and slipped into "immediate belief," the inability to doubt what we think we see.

A trance of unreality

This is the essential trait of a complex having taken over the ego. Some event in the outer world constellates—brings together into a familiar shape—salient elements of the scene before me and retrieves, by the Law of Association, memories of similar scenes from the past. And these memories are charged with a familiar emotion strong enough to drive out reason. When a complex takes over, I fall into a sort of trance, where I cannot accurately present to myself the circumstances that challenge me. Instead I am transported to another scene, nearly a dreamscape whose apparent reality I am temporarily unable to doubt, though I may believe myself to be functioning more or less normally (the Law of Contrast). The emotional atmosphere of the complex blinds me to everything that does not conform to my altered perspective (the Law of Inhibition). "Emotion is a disorder that seems to arise at the moment a situation is perceived" (Janet 1924: 155).

Modern investigators like LeDoux, Damasio, and Siegel agree with the distinction between emotion and feeling, but they reverse the mechanism. Jung believed that a feeling comes first and gives us an opportunity to make a conscious assessment of a situation, and that it *becomes* an emotion if it lingers long enough and is powerful enough to generate physiological effects and "get into the body." Better instruments and techniques of investigation than those available in Jung's day have shown that emotion is generated first as part of the overt bodily response in brain, autonomic nervous system, and the like.[6] Secondarily, when we become conscious of the changes that have already begun in our body, such consciousness of our emotional state is called a "feeling" (LeDoux 2002: 106). Damasio agrees, saying that feeling occurs only after the brain brings together in a "body loop" our sense of selfhood with the object that is bringing about changes in our proto-self. Feeling is the conscious registration of those changes (Damasio 1999: 280).

Ego and complex

Jung has left us with a small conundrum. Part-personalities are "in principle no different" from the ego, which is itself a complex (*CW18*: ¶149). The ego-complex, to make things more complicated, may be "assimilated by" or "merged with" a feeling-toned complex. When this happens, normal ego-function is lost, the level of mental functioning drops, and we become automatons, unable to critically assess the presumed reality that faces us; we cannot escape compulsively repeating ourselves. What in the end is an ego, and how does it manage to maintain a high level of functioning in between episodes of merging?

When Damasio tells us a somatic marker jolts the ego into existence at the same moment an outer worldly scene is "bound" into a unity in our brain and psyche, is it not the emotional significance of the scene that generates that "binding," and its reception by my embodied me? But this is precisely what happens when a complex is "constellated": a scene is bound together by an emotional response; a somatic marker locks me into a world of compulsive repetition. Somehow "true egohood," a high mental level of functioning, is lost when a part-personality takes over.

For the ego to have "merged" with a feeling-toned complex seems to mean that the complex itself *becomes* the ego for a while. Proper egohood—the capacity to think critically about my circumstances, to assess values accurately, to make adequate decisions, and to muster sufficient energy to carry them out—has been lost. I no longer learn from past mistakes or envision a realistic future.

Summary, the phenomenology of complexes

A complex is an organized, automatic response driven by a specific emotional state. It acts like an independent personality that shares my body and mind with me, even though its attitude toward the world and myself is largely alien to the "real me." When "constellated," it takes over my ego and reduces my critical reflective capabilities so that I am limited to a stereotyped and constantly repeated perspective governed by old memories that have a quasi traumatic character. The organizing principle of a complex is its disordered feeling tone, and as soon as the body assumes the physiological state associated with that feeling tone, my consciousness of the world outside and of the me within is narrowed. In this limited condition, I see and respond exclusively to aspects of the world that are salient to the "personality" of the complex. As long as a complex operates unchallenged, each episode of its dominance adds new memories that stabilize its powers and broaden its scope. Any evidence to the contrary escapes notice.

We have already considered Jung's first line of approach for dealing with a complex that brings the individuation process to a halt.[7] He urges us to take the unconscious obstacle seriously as a personality with a perspective of its own that is different from ours. Hence, the spotless man of honor whose temper tantrums frightened his family should, first, stop merging with the moodiness of the complex; second, pay attention to the emotions without acting them out and without criticizing them, as he would listen to the complaints of a real person; third, once patiently listened to, he must criticize these views from his alternate personality as he would those of a reasonable and earnest colleague; and fourth, allow this internal discussion to go on as long as it needs to (*CW7*: ¶319–23). In brief, Jung describes a process of differentiating one's emotional reactions so as to break free of their compulsions.

The first step, to stop merging with his moodiness, is the crucial one; for nothing will help until we realize that we are not ourselves but have been taken over by a complex. It is humiliating to recognize such neurotic behavior in ourselves, and we will defend ourselves against it. Thus, one of the most important functions of Jungian analytic therapy is to identify such a complex, reveal its stereotyped and inadequate nature, and aid the analysand's attempts to catch himself in the act of merging with its compelling emotion. The other three steps amount to an exploration of the Amfortas wound that keeps this aspect of our lives unexamined and its feeling values unclear and undifferentiated. In the end, we escape from habitually acting out the emotional rigidity of a complex by acquainting ourselves with its unexamined value system.

Chapter 11

Complexes and the neural substrate

Daniel J. Siegel of the UCLA School of Medicine describes what he calls a "state of mind" in terms that strongly resemble the characteristics of a complex. It is a pattern of activated brain systems (apparently something like a dynamic core) that are responsible for perceptual bias, a regulating emotional tone, interpretive models, and behavioral patterns. It coordinates brain activity in the moment and at the same time strengthens its own pattern of neural excitation so that it becomes more likely to be activated in the future (Siegel 1999: 211). The brain "wires itself" outside of our awareness, and in doing so creates a condition of "self-fulfilling prophecy." For example, if the amygdala signals "Danger!" the sensory innervations occurring at that moment will "become associated in memory with the feeling of danger" (Siegel 1999: 133). Such a recurringly stable structure filters everything we perceive in accordance with its feeling tone—Paulhan's Law of Association (Ibid.: 43). But on account of its traumatic nature, it remains outside our "narrative memory," the ego's sense of itself—Law of Inhibition—and from this outside position is able to "intrude upon [one's] internal experiences and interpersonal relationships" (Ibid.: 55)—Law of Contrasts.

Not unlike Jung, Siegel (1999) illustrates his position by describing a man whose temper tantrums frightened his wife and daughter. The man was prone to feel that he was "going out of his mind" when he felt rejected by either of them. He would respond by squeezing his daughter's arm or screaming at her in rage. He was too ashamed of his loss of control to be able to discuss his outbursts or to repair his relationship with his daughter. Siegel traced the origin of this complex behavior back to the man's relationship with his alcoholic father, who was prone to outbursts of rage.

> The perception of his daughter's irritation with him induced a shift in his mental state. . . . represented in his mind as a perceptual representation, or engram. This engram became linked with other representations connected with the perception of an irritated face.
>
> (Siegel 1999: 115)

It is interesting that Siegel chooses the expression *engram*, for this is one of the terms Jung claimed as a precursor of his notion of an archetype. The term originated with Richard Semon in Germany in 1904 to designate a memory trace formed by changes in neural tissue and prone to be revived under the right conditions. The great early theorist of evolutionary biology, Ernst Haekel, praised Semon's idea of an engram as the "most important advance that evolution has made since Darwin"; Jung's chief at the Burghölzli, Eugen Bleuler, also championed the term (Shamdasani 2003: 189f). Since an engram is a memory event, it is hardly a good model for describing inheritance according to natural selection. But the fact that evolutionary biologists in 1904 should not notice this discrepancy suggests the reason Jung did not. Although not a good description of an inborn archetype, *engram* excellently describes a complex: a compelling image derived from experience that imprints itself by its emotional charge and frequent repetition. Here is further indication that a century ago Jung's theories were largely harmonious with a biology that was poorly understood then and remains consilient with biological facts that are better understood now.

Joseph LeDoux (1996) also describes a mechanism that resembles the constellation of a complex. He says:

> in order for a memory to appear in consciousness, the associative network has to reach a certain level of activation, which occurs as a function of the number of components that are activated and the weight of each activated component.
>
> (LeDoux 1996: 212)

If he had spoken of "emotional tone" instead of "weight," it would have been clear that he was describing the phenomenon of a complex. Elsewhere, he describes what makes an experience memorable. The brain's amygdala "turns on all sorts of bodily systems, including the autonomic nervous system," resulting in the release of adrenalin from the adrenal glands (LeDoux 1996: 207). An emotional charge activates a network of associations, makes them memorable, and renders their image of the world and what we should do about it nearly irresistible.

The archetypal nature of emotion

Animals most likely to survive and pass their genes on to future generations are those whose inbuilt structures generate the right behavioral patterns without internal debate, making them automatic, swift, unchanging and largely successful. To accomplish such everyday feats, an animal needs a reliable system for evaluating every critical situation that is typical for its species. "Emotions" are what we call these inborn patterns of immediate evaluation. Their corresponding states of bodily arousal and the action patterns they generate "express" the emotion. "Under normal conditions," Llinás (2002: 227) says, "fixed action patterns are only liberated into action by the generated emotional states that precede them."

Damasio has articulated this issue very clearly. He speaks of the constellating event as an encounter with an "emotionally competent stimulus" (ECS). This is what we have been calling the emotionally salient object or situation. Damasio's ECS is detected unconsciously and automatically, before we can direct our attention to it (Damasio 2003: 60), thereby initiating an inherited (archetypal) program that activates specific neural maps of the body. These contribute to the release of neurochemicals that change the state of the body, arousing it physiologically, focusing its attention, preparing it to survive a crisis (Damasio 2003: 53).

> In a typical emotion, then, certain regions of the brain, which are part of a largely preset neural system related to emotions, send commands to other regions of the brain and to most everywhere in the body proper. . . . One route is the bloodstream, where the commands are sent in the form of chemical molecules . . . The other route consists of neuron pathways . . . which act on other neurons or on muscle fibers or on organs (such as the adrenal gland) which in turn can release chemicals of their own into the bloodstream.
>
> The result of these coordinated chemical and neural commands is a global change in the state of the organism.
>
> (Damasio 1999: 67)

Along with the amygdala, which "turns on all sorts of bodily systems, including the autonomic nervous system," the hypothalamus plays a crucial role in triggering archetypal emotions. They belong, with some half-dozen other brain structures, to what is called the limbic system, the brain's emotional center. The hypothalamus sits at the base of the forebrain where it serves as an interface between forebrain and more primitive lower brain areas (LeDoux 1996: 82). It samples the body's internal environment (temperature, sugar and salt levels in the bloodstream, etc.) and orchestrates internal preparations for such things as sex, hunger, thirst and sleep (Zeman 2002: 60f). Llinás calls the hypothalamus the "master switch" (Llinás 2002: 162) that releases into the bloodstream a variety of neuromodulators that alter "the internal milieu, the function of the viscera, and the function of the central nervous system itself" (Damasio 2003: 62). This is the operation of Edelman's "value system," the "hairnet" of neural fibers that "leak neuromodulators like an old garden hose." Emotional changes are initiated by chemical agents, including norepinephrine (noradrenalin), serotonin, acetylcholine, dopamine, histamine, oxytocin, and vasopressin (Edelman and Tononi 2000: 89).

These molecules have a variety of different effects, and act upon a variety of different targets. It seems likely that each emotion involves a different set of circuits, a different combination of neurotransmitters, and a different set of organs (LeDoux 1996: 106). In this way, each emotional pattern is governed by its own "discrete system" (Damasio 1999: 62). Each emotional unit has its own set of "natural triggers," such as certain aspects of a predator's appearance, sound, and smell, as well as a set of "learned triggers" associated with the animal's history, such as locations where it escaped death or found a mate (LeDoux 1996: 127). Emotional experience, therefore, involves associations between these inherited patterns of bodily excitation and the animal's memory of the occasions on which they were triggered. Strengthening such links, as we learned in Chapter 9, appears to be one of the main functions of dreaming.

Donald L. Nathanson, Professor at Jefferson Medical College in Philadelphia and disciple of seminal affect theorist Silvan S. Tomkins, has assembled a set of photographs of infant and adult human facial expressions and bodily postures illustrating the "social displays" that belong, universally, to the human organism and that are generated by value-assigning patterns in the neural substrate (Nathanson 1992). Nothing makes it more evident that inherited brain structures lie behind archetypal behavioral patterns than the cross-cultural similarity of emotional expressions in the human face. We cannot resist "making" faces associated with "limbic resonance." Because they occur unconsciously and immediately, we may be able to play them up or down for social effect, but we cannot eliminate them. They are the same the world over, but the degree to which they may be exaggerated or hidden is very much culturally determined.

In emphasizing the priority of bodily state over conscious feeling, Nathanson (1992: 61) goes so far as to claim that, "It is awareness of its own facial display that tells the infant what affect has been triggered," because the process of learning our typical bodily states occurs within a context of interpersonal communication. He appears to agree with Greenspan and Shanker (2004) but is less interested in language than in the process by which we learn how to feel. He agrees with them that an infant's emotional experience begins with global, undifferentiated states of overwhelming affect that are gradually tamed and interpreted through interactions with parents.

Primatologist Frans de Waal implicitly extends the argument for the archetypal nature of emotions by demonstrating that emotional displays are not only universal within a species, but also often across species. His favorite example compares the behavior of Richard Nixon in the privacy of the White House on the night before he resigned the presidency with that of alpha chimpanzee, Luit, on the day he was deposed from his position of dominance at the Netherlands' Arnhem Zoo. For Nixon's reaction, de Waal cites Bob Woodward and Carl Bernstein's book, *The Final Days*: "Between sobs, Nixon was plaintive. . . . How had a simple burglary done all this? . . . [He] got down on his knees . . . leaned over and struck his fists on the carpet, crying aloud, 'What did I do? What has happened?'" (de Waal 1998: xiii; 2001: 304). The chimpanzee, Luit, was deposed by a coalition of two males, Nikkie and Yeroen, who declared their united intent by ostentatiously "mounting" one another before him:

> Luit reacted by collapsing in a heap, screaming and rolling around in the grass, and beating the ground and his own head with his fists. His two opponents stood screaming in chorus with Luit for a short time, watching his tantrum, but then they walked away together, leaving an inconsolable leader for other members of the group to try to comfort.

(de Waal 1998: 126)

Such parallels between primate species ought to build a foundation for determining which emotions are basic enough to qualify as primary archetypes, matters of pure inheritance. To my knowledge, we have at this time little more than anecdotal evidence for such definable primate patterns. But this has not stopped researchers from attempting to draw up a list of the "basic" or "primary" emotions. While most address the human condition only, it is likely that such archetypal patterns have cognate forms in our primate relatives. Probably most would be shared by all mammals; and, given the primitivity of emotional expression patterns, many may also be shared by reptiles. The earliest such list was made by Charles Darwin (1872) in *The Expression of Emotions in Man and Animals.* Several of the authors cited in the present volume have also ventured a list. On the basis of nine such sources,[1] I find strong agreement on the following six universal patterns of emotion: joy, anger, fear, disgust, sadness, and surprise. Surprise was specified by only five of the nine while all, or all but one, of the authors agreed on each of the other five.

If it were possible to specify the electrochemical dynamics behind each of these six archetypal emotions, it would exceed the limits of this chapter to try to describe them all. In what follows, we shall consider LeDoux's research investigating the dynamics of fear. He has described the universal pattern of fear as it manifests in the neural substrate, and pointed the way toward taming our fear, differentiating it, and rendering it a conscious "feeling" that can be used for accurate orientation to the world outside and to the forces of the greater self within. It need not be "a shock to the psyche" (Janet) but can become a tool in our individuation process.

Fear: an archetypal pattern in the neural substrate

The amygdala is the most important brain structure for producing the subjective feeling of fear and all the bodily changes of state that make that feeling possible. LeDoux says the amygdala has handled fear responses in all animals since dinosaurs walked the earth, making us "emotional lizards" (LeDoux 1996: 174). Artificial electrical stimulation, alone, to the amygdala will generate a sense of foreboding danger; and an epileptic seizure (i.e. an *organic* "electrical storm" centered in the amygdala) will produce an overwhelming sense of fear (Ibid.: 172f). The fear response, however, is evidently not solely about recognizing and retreating from danger; for when an animal's amygdalae are both damaged, it loses the ability "to muster the vehemence required for the initiation and completion of even the simplest of acts" (Llinás 2002: 164). Thus, it appears that the fear response presumes a capacity in an animal unconsciously to choose among a variety of courses of action; and as though to make sure the animal knows how crucial for its survival these choices are, the amygdala generates a powerful state of arousal.

There are two amygdalae, almond-shaped structures,[2] each located below one of the temporal lobes of the cortex and a center of the brain's emotion-generating "limbic system" (see Figure 11.1). The amygdala plays a key role in conditioning an animal to its environment by generating bodily states that correspond to what we consciously recognize as hate, pain and fear. When both amygdalae have been removed, we are rendered incapable of fear and rage, and no longer have any urge to compete or to cooperate, nor do we have any sense of our place in the social order (Goleman 1995: 15f). The amygdala generates affect at an automatic, pre-conscious level of functioning. The fight-or-flight reactions, governed by adrenalin and our autonomic nervous system, are activated so automatically by the amygdala that we are already in a state of bodily shock before we become conscious of the situation and its significance. We "react to danger rather than think about it" (LeDoux 1996: 247).

As is often the case with medical science, the function of a brain structure—in this case the amygdala—was learned by observing the effects occasioned by its removal. A woman known by the initials D. R. suffered from such a severe form

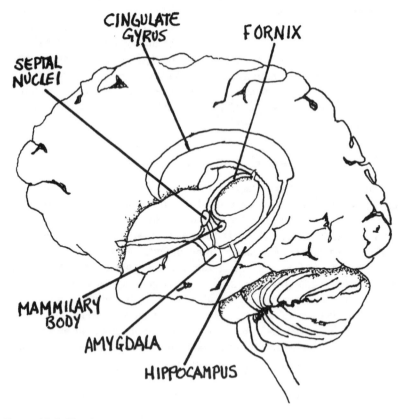

Figure 11.1 The limbic system.

Source: original pen and ink drawing by Ann Yoost Brecke.

of epilepsy that she had her amygdalae on both sides surgically damaged in an effort to relieve her symptoms. The operation was successful as regards the epileptic symptoms, but D. R. lost her ability to recognize fear in the faces of other people and also had some difficulty identifying angry faces. She could recognize people's identity well enough and whether they were sad or happy, but she could not recognize emotions in the range of danger and threat. Thus the amygdala has at least two functions related to the fear response: it recognizes fear in others and mobilizes a set of bodily processes that place our body in a state of fear. It represents a typical top-to-bottom archetypal structure: at the "top," more conscious, end it recognizes and imagines images of danger; at the bottom, "bodily," end it changes bodily chemistry and neural activation.

A third, related, function of the amygdala has to do with fear-conditioning: learning what objects and situations demand a fear response. LeDoux (1996) reports on experiments with rats that have learned a fear response to a non-natural stimulus (a "conditioned stimulus"), such as a tone that is sounded prior to delivering a small shock to a rat's feet through the floor of its cage. After the tone has been paired with the shock a few times, the rat's fear response to the artificial stimulus will be indistinguishable from what it displays before a cat. A cat is a "natural trigger," what Damasio calls an "emotionally competent stimulus" (ECS) that is inborn, while the artificial stimulus is a *learned* ECS and becomes associated with the inborn fear-producing processes only secondarily. In both cases the animal responds to the ECS as though the question of its survival is at stake. A rat's fear response involves "freezing" (complete immobility) along with changes in blood pressure and heart rate. At the same time, the autonomic nervous system is aroused, lowering the pain response, increasing the sensitivity of the reflexes, and elevating stress-hormone levels in the bloodstream (from the pituitary and adrenal glands) (LeDoux 1996: 144). This pattern of activation is universally mammalian—even reptilian. It has been the survival system of choice for about 150 million years; and the human species has not tampered with it, except perhaps to become more conscious of how it feels and how it may be tamed and integrated.

The wheel of fear

The amygdala is not alone in generating fear. LeDoux calls it "the hub in a wheel of fear." It receives (a) information about what threatens through signals from the sensory **maps of the cortex**, (b) sensory information interpreted by the **thalamus**, (c) emotionally toned memories that provide context from the **hippocampus**, and potentially, (d) extinction of the fear response from the **medial prefrontal cortex**. The medial PFC shuts down the fear response in rats when repeated soundings of the "conditioned stimulus" (the tone) are not followed by a shock (LeDoux 1996: 170). The first three structures in the "hub of fear" provide the amygdala with the value-laden life-situation that confronts it. The amygdala says, "Assume the fear-state!" and the body's chemistry changes. Some processes are tuned down, others tuned up; a posture is struck, a facial expression assumed. Only the medial PFC fingers the knob that turns down the volume.

This business of turning down the volume will be crucial when we discuss becoming conscious of our emotional state and learning to differentiate among the situations that have confronted us in the past in comparison with what we face in the present moment. But first, we need to know more about the other three structures in the wheel of fear.

The **thalamus** sits well below the cortex, but its neurons are like cortical neurons in not having their axons sheathed in myelin to insulate their electrical signals; therefore it is "gray" in appearance like the "gray matter" of the cortex. The thalamus constitutes the sides and ceiling of the third ventricle.[3] We are already familiar with a ribbon of neuropil along each side of the *hypo*thalamus (bottom of the third ventricle), for this forms the center of Panksepp's seeking system. The thalamus receives information about the state of the body from the spinal cord, brainstem and cerebellum, and it receives sensory information about the outer world directly from the sense organs and again from the sensory maps of the cortex. In addition, the thalamus shares reentrant circuits with the sensory cortex, so that information is processed, shared, and reprocessed. It is part of Edelman's thalamo-cortical meshwork, the analytic part of the brain that is involved in establishing meanings and relationships.

The thalamus, therefore, is wired between three different structures: the body, the sensory cortex that is oriented to the outer world, and the amygdala. It brings together me, the world, and evaluation—the three components necessary to establish my life-situation in the moment. Filled with Damasio's convergence zones, the thalamus can potentially answer the question, "What confronts me right now, and what should I do about it?" It presents the amygdala with value judgments, "We've been here before, and we better get out!" But it makes them thoughtlessly. As a convergence zone, it is informed only by similarities from the past and functions like a complex or an archetype. When constellated, it does the same thing every time. Because it is so much in the thrall of emotion, the thalamus is the more primitive partner in the thalamo-cortical dialogue.

We should not overemphasize the importance of the thalamus in the wheel of fear, for LeDoux says the amygdala receives "low level inputs" from the sensory regions of the thalamus. In comparison, the **sensory cortex** provides "higher level" information. We need say nothing more about the sensory cortex, since we considered it at great length in previous chapters. But, despite its importance, the sensory cortex does not dominate the amygdala's information system, since the hippocampus provides a still higher level of information that is "sensory independent" (LeDoux 1996: 168). It plays a significant role in the amygdala's decisions.

The **hippocampus** is a small seahorse-shaped structure on the inner part of the temporal lobe of the cortex,[4] found on both sides of the brain, which is essential for the acquisition of new, explicit or "declarative" memories. Because such memories can be "declared," they are at least potentially conscious. Discovery of hippocampal function occurred when brain science stumbled onto another histori-cal lesson. A 27-year-old male patient, generally known only by the initials H. M., had both of his hippocampi surgically removed in an effort to reduce his disabling epileptic seizures. The operation proved successful as far as the epilepsy was concerned, but it left him unable to acquire new memories. What he had known before the operation was retained, but the ablations left his brain unable to create memories of new people, objects, situations and events. He became unable to recognize the post-operative therapists who he worked with every day.

The hippocampus, itself, is not a memory bank but "more like the hub of a spider web" of neural connections, where it works like "a central processor in a computer," as regards the making of new memories (Freeman 2000: 101). The hippocampus' usefulness in the conscious work of assessing the feeling-value of a situation is, therefore, fairly evident; for only if we can compare present circum-stances to past events in terms of their emotional significance can we make good judgments about how to conduct ourselves in the present.

Research on birds and mammals—including rats, rabbits, monkeys, and humans—has demonstrated that "damage to the hippocampus interferes with con-ditioned fear responses." This means that the things animals *learn to associate with dangerous situations* cannot be retained without a functioning hippocampus. The fact that both mammals and birds respond this way to hippocampal damage implies that reptiles must have similarly equipped brains; for they are relatives of the common ancestor of birds and mammals. This seems to be another indication that we are emotional dinosaurs (LeDoux 1996: 171). Humans with hippocampal damage act a bit like Damasio's impulsive gamblers: they know and can discuss the relationship between the decks of cards; but when placed back in the experi-mental context, they do not act as though they recognize the larger significance of their situation (LeDoux 1996: 173).

Thus it appears that the function of the hippocampus is not merely to produce new memories, but also to appreciate the meaningfulness of emotional context and to be able to update contextual meanings on the basis of experience. "The sights and sounds of a place are pooled together before reaching the hippocampus, and one job of this brain region is to create a representation of the context that contains not individual stimuli but relations between stimuli" (LeDoux 1996: 168).

Thus, sitting at the center of the "wheel of fear," the amygdala receives sensory analysis of the scene before us from the cortex, background and context from the hippocampus, and an evaluation of the life-situation from the convergence zones of the thalamus. When all of these things come together ominously for the amyg-dala, it sounds the alarm by initiating sequences of neural circuit activation and neurochemical distribution that prepare the body to face the worst.

Learning to differentiate the fear response

Pierre Janet's distinction between an "emotional shock" that lowers the level of mental functioning and a "feeling" that, accurately or not, evaluates a life-situation has also been made by Joseph LeDoux. He distinguishes a moderate emotional arousal during memory formation, which fosters the development of strong memories, from an excessive emotional arousal that results in memory impairment by inhibiting the hippocampus. It appears, therefore, that when amygdala activation is kept in the middle range, memory retrieval is facilitated because the emotional state generated on previous occasions is recreated, "at least in part" (LeDoux 2002: 222f). Such amygdala participation becomes unnecessary later on when we have learned how to avoid or otherwise handle the specific danger that once threatened us (LeDoux 1996: 251). Malcolm Gladwell (2005) gives us an example of such taming in the training procedures for police officers who need to be desensitized to the shock of facing criminals firing guns. The technique is to create realistic situations in which the officers are actually shot, but with plastic capsules rather than bullets. "By the fourth or fifth time you get shot in simulation, you're OK" (Gladwell 2005: 238). The hair-trigger amygdala calms down when the hippocampus learns to contextualize a situation as manageable.

At the other extreme, it has been found that when conditions of severe stress persist for a long time, the dendrites of the neurons comprising the hippocampus begin to shrivel up. They essentially shut down their capacity to receive new information. In this way the "shock" of remaining under constant emotional stress actually results in a decline in our brain's capacity to contextualize such situations. The hippocampus' decline can even become irreversible and has been found to be associated with post-traumatic stress disorder (PTSD) in Vietnam veterans (LeDoux 1996: 242). Perhaps something of this sort occurred in the brain of Jung's patient, Babette St., who fell under the influence of a single complex and remained there so long that eventually even the coherence of her repeated phrases was lost and her dementia proceeded to the point of "word salad" nonsense.[5]

In between the fully tamed situation, when the amygdala's participation is no longer necessary, and the damaging situation, when the amygdala is in overdrive, we find what LeDoux calls "emotional feelings." Here are feelings in the sense of Jung's "feeling function," accurate evaluative assessments of life-situations. "Emotional feelings result when we explain emotionally ambiguous bodily states to ourselves on the basis of cognitive interpretations . . . about what the external and internal causes of our bodily states might be" (LeDoux 1996: 47). Damasio's position is very much the same: a feeling is a conscious grasp of our emotional state; ideally it makes possible a "flexibility of response based on the particular history of [one's] interaction with the environment" (Damasio 1994: 133). Furthermore, he lists two sorts of benefits conscious feelings give us: first, they permit "integration of large sets of information that can be brought to bear on a current situation," and second, they "prompt the brain to process emotion-laden objects and situations saliently" (Damasio 2003: 177). It seems to me that this is precisely the sort of thing Jung had in mind when he claimed that feeling is a "psychic function," a tool for relating to the world and to ourselves.

How feelings are differentiated

When we apply such findings to the individuation process, we can say that an emotion-driven complex lowers the level of our mental functioning, setting our body into a state of emergency. In this condition, we lose our ability accurately to assess our life-situation and can no longer see that what confronts us right now is in some important ways different from similar past situations. We have very little power of discrimination or nuance. We require *moderate* emotional arousal in order to be engaged with our lives, attentive to what is happening, able to remember crucial facts, and the like. Emotional shock occurs when the amygdala rings an alarm bell that implies we have been in a similar situation in the past and found it traumatizing. We immediately become too scared to think straight.

Jung based his ideas about the nature of the psyche and the process of analytic therapy on the premise that complexes can be handled. At least slowly and gradually, we can become conscious of their automatic interference in our lives, regain our psychic integrity, and return to the path of individuation. We can depotentiate disorienting emotions and derive useful feelings from them. Such is Jung's phenomenological description for differentiating our feelings to free ourselves from autonomous complex-reactions and raise our mental level from "immediate belief" to "reflective judgment."

LeDoux (1996) has found a mechanism in the neural substrate to account for this differentiation as it applies to the emotion of fear. He studied the response to a warning tone (conditioned stimulus) in the brains of rats, first by selectively severing neural pathways until the effective ones were discovered, and then by the use of tracer chemicals that revealed the progress of a neural message in bright colors, when observed under a microscope.

There are two pathways by which the thalamus communicates with the amygdala. The thalamus is the site where the complex-reaction originates in a convergence zone that remembers only similar events from the past and the emotion they inspired. By one route to the amygdala, the automatic complex-reaction proceeds unchallenged, and by the other it is subjected to criticism. Along the direct pathway, the thalamus says: "Here it is again, get ready!" LeDoux calls this the "low road" because it bypasses the cerebral cortex and never rises to the top of the brain. The low road is "down and dirty," but fast and effective. It provides exactly the response an animal needs when a saber-tooth tiger steps out from behind a rock: "Don't think, just run!" The other pathway from the thalamus to the amygdala is the "high road," for it passes through the cortex and makes possible critical reflection and discrimination: "Yes, that is a saber-tooth tiger, but there's no need for panic; it's just a mother carrying her cub. If I stand still, she'll ignore me" (LeDoux 1996: 155–70). See Figure 11.2.

Through its "reentrant" conversations with the cortex, the thalamus derives new information for evaluating the original sensory input, e.g. the tone the rat hears, the saber-tooth our ancestor saw. In this way inputs from two sides to the amygdala are changed; both thalamus and cortex develop new messages. The

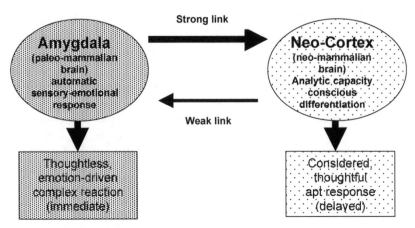

Why complex-possession is so hard to overcome

Figure 11.2 The "low road" (left) and "high road" (right) of emotional response.
Source: summarizing LeDoux (1996: 155–70).

assessment of our life-situation becomes nuanced, meaning is added. This is what differentiation provides. LeDoux puts the matter in everyday terms: "The Beatles and the Rolling Stones (or, if you like, Oasis and the Cranberries) will sound the same to the amygdala by way of the thalamic projections but quite different by way of the cortical projections" (LeDoux 1996: 162).

As we learned in Chapter 8, the pre-frontal cortex (PFC) inhibits primitive, stereotyped compulsions encoded in inherited pathways and in the emotional memory system. The thalamo-amygdala circuits' generation of fight-or-flight reactions are the inherited pathways; the convergence zone in the thalamus is the emotional memory system. Unchecked, such low-road circuits keep us responding automatically with primitive, stereotyped compulsions. Delaying their automatic response leaves room for clear thinking, reflective judgment, and plans for the future; and this is the role of the PFC. The strongest evidence for this is the fact that loss of the PFC results in loss of restraint, the inability to inhibit aggression, and the failure to exercise judgment.

Once the "key 'off' switch" is thrown in the PFC (Goleman 1995: 26), we are provided time and opportunity for careful consideration of similarities between past and present as well as anticipated outcomes for potential choices. Having reached this level of consciousness, we have escaped the compulsions that characterize complexes.

Neurobiology, then, has discovered the evidence in the neural substrate for both complex-formation and complex resolution. Undifferentiated feelings produce complexes on account of LeDoux's "low road" of amygdala activation, a primitive neural design selected by evolution to insure potentially life-saving responses at lightening speed. At the same time, complex reentrant circuits in the thalamo-cortical system, including the slower-moving but more fully analytic PFC, has been evolution's solution for introducing flexibility of response and the multiplication of choices required by primates. For the primate survival strategy of sociality has clearly pushed evolution in the direction of a larger and larger neocortex, as Robin Dunbar's grooming-and-gossip research has demonstrated. Psychic process—a.k.a. individuation—involves overcoming complex-formation through analysis and differentiation; the capacity to do so is equally a product of natural selection.

Chapter 12

Jung's psychotherapy and neuroscience

To this point we have followed the concept of individuation to see that the ideal of psychic process involves bringing consciousness in contact with unconscious needs so as to keep ego apprised of the larger psychic reality within which it operates. Problems arise for individuation when one is sidetracked by complexes, which originate in an organism's automatic responses to crisis-like situations and then perpetuate themselves through convergence zones that see every new emotional situation as another instance of an old pattern. Such automatic and relatively unchanging reactions do not allow for sufficient analysis of one's momentary life-situation to ensure accuracy of perception and adequacy of response. Individuation is impossible so long as an accurate grasp of one's life-situation cannot be formed. Fortunately, emotion-driven complex-reactions can be reduced when an individual learns to restrain automatic responses in the interests of conscious reflection. The brain is wired to make complex resolution possible, and it makes sense to conclude that an effective psychotherapy will introduce techniques to assist in the process of differentiating our feelings and acquiring a more accurate and objective view of the life-situation that confronts us.

Jung: four stages of therapeutic process

From time to time in the course of his career, Jung described psychotherapy as a four-stage process. The earliest version of this argument is to be found in the series of nine lectures, titled "The Theory of Psychoanalysis" (*CW4*: ¶203–522), he gave at Fordham University in September 1912, while the second and last installment of *Symbols of Transformation* was still at the printer. Jung designed the lectures as a new outline of psychoanalysis based on *Symbols* but for a clinical audience. Freud was prepared to find them a radical version of Jung's growing heretical tendencies:

> I am very eager to read your English lectures, I hope they will meet with vigorous opposition on the part of our fellow analysts; my own opposition,

even if it outlives my reading of the lectures, would be too self-evident to make an impression.

(FJL: 532)

In this first version of the four stages, Jung listed confession (*CW4*: ¶431–5), analysis of the transference (*CW4*: ¶436–42), resolution of the transference (*CW4*: ¶443–51) and the prospective function of dreams (*CW4*: ¶452–4). They roughly parallel the stages outlined in a 1929 article he wrote for the *Swiss Medical Journal*,[1] "[The] Problems of Modern Psychotherapy" (*CW16*: ¶122–74), the most complete account. The four stages are now known as confession, elucidation, education, and transformation. A very brief and incomplete version of the four stages was repeated in 1932 (*CW11*: ¶519), and an outline of the first three stages appeared in 1935 (*CW16*: ¶24f). Many of the same phrases are used each time, making it clear that the 1929 version remains the blueprint.

Confession

Jung notes that possessing personal secrets alienates us from our community and that "unconscious secrets"—including the concealment of our emotional reactions—are more injurious than conscious ones. Hiding such personal matters from others and from ourselves, unless motivated by sincere religious beliefs,[2] is bound to lead to bad moods, irritability and over-virtuousness, if not neurotic symptoms. A full cathartic confession is called for, "not merely the intellectual recognition of the facts with the head, but their confirmation by the heart and the actual release of suppressed emotions" (*CW16*: ¶134). Confession of the suppressed shadow, however, is only the beginning: first, because there is also *unconscious* shadow material which people resist discovering; second, because a sincere, heartfelt confession will bind the patient, emotionally, to the therapist; and third, because sometimes the patient will become fascinated with unconscious material "at the expense of his adaptation to life" (*CW16*: ¶138).

The most important of these, to judge from the amount of space Jung devotes to it, is dependency upon the analyst, a natural consequence of the empathy and feelings of mutuality that made confession possible. This is the heart of what Freud called transference. Jung discusses the transference next, but treats it as much in the manner of Pierre Janet as in that of Freud. Janet spoke of the patient's need to be dependent (*besoin de direction*), saying that it is the key to therapy insofar as it makes the patient wish to follow the therapist's guidance. Furthermore, it functions as an index to measure the patient's recovery, for the more the neurosis is left behind, the weaker the need for direction becomes (Haule 1986). Jung says, dependency on the therapist is "a new neurotic formation," but it "brings to light contents which are hardly ever capable of becoming conscious" by way of catharsis. The transference, therefore, "is the cardinal distinction between the stage of confession and the stage of elucidation" (*CW16*: ¶139, 141). When a transference develops, elucidation becomes possible.

Elucidation

"The transference relationship is especially in need of elucidation" through interpretation, particularly of dreams (*CW16*: ¶144f). Jung assumes, here, that since
dreams "compensate" for what is missing in the conscious attitude, they will inevitably have something to do with the patient's former secrets. Furthermore, having
been hidden, they belong to the patient's Amfortas wound. Interpretation of the
dreams will therefore provide a "reductive" explanation of the patient's feelings
and fantasies regarding the suppressed material. The patient is led backwards into
the past and downwards into the unconscious, to the presumed origins of the complexes in question (*CW16*: ¶146). Elucidation must be pursued carefully and
empathically lest it be destructive. Its aim is to loosen the patient's "fixation" on
the worldview of the complex (cf. Janet's *idée fixe*) and to make it "untenable"
(*CW16*: ¶148).

Clearly, Jung is speaking here of the differentiation process we have just
described, or at least its first stage, where the patient has to step back from the
automatic emotion-driven response generated in the convergence zones of the
thalamus so as to provide room for a more considered, nuanced, and accurate
understanding of her life-situation. The stage of elucidation, however, is modeled
on a Freudian reductive analysis of the symptoms and fantasies—finding their
origins in early life. It ends at the point where the patient realizes that the old way
of responding cannot succeed.

Education

Freudian reduction has to be followed by Adlerian education to teach the patient
how to function adequately as a social being, a responsible member of society
(*CW16*: ¶150). Having discovered that the old ways are inadequate, the patient
needs to appreciate "how he arranges his symptoms and exploits his neurosis in
order to achieve fictitious importance" (*CW16*: ¶151).[3] The patient must be drawn
"out of himself and into other paths" (*CW16*: ¶152). During this phase, when
automatic complex-reactions have been discredited, the analyst takes advantage
of the patient's "need for direction" to conduct a discussion of the nature of the
patient's life-situation and what a more adequate "reality function" would reveal.
The aim is evidently the development of a realistic dialogue between the ego and
the social world, the outer half of the dual dialogue that is genuine individuation.

Transformation

The first three stages aim for "normality," which is an appropriate goal "for the
unsuccessful" (*CW16*: ¶161). Jung means that those who have been kept out
of life and away from their Amfortas wound by their neurotic secrets will inevitably have failed to succeed at life in some essential way. But mere "normality" is
not the ultimate goal. Transformation aims beyond, toward "satisfaction and

fulfillment . . . in what [the patient] does not yet possess" (*CW16*: ¶162). There is no way, however, for the therapist to know in advance what the patient needs in this regard. Consequently, the treatment can only be "the product of mutual influence in which the whole being of the doctor as well as that of his patient plays its part." Their two personalities, each with their "fields of consciousness [and] an indefinitely extended sphere of non-consciousness . . . are often infinitely more important for the outcome of the treatment than what the doctor says and thinks." Both parties must be transformed (*CW16*: ¶163). "What happened to the patient must now happen to the doctor, so that his personality shall not react unfavourably on the patient. The doctor can no longer evade his own difficulty by treating the difficulties of others" (*CW16*: ¶172).

Exploration of the nature of transformation became a predominant preoccupation during the last thirty years of Jung's life and was approached in terms of mutual influence between analyst and analysand, as well as through the notion of "experiencing the archetype," an enlarging and insight-providing state of consciousness. We shall, therefore, leave discussion of these matters to later chapters of this book.

The task of the patient

The four stages just presented concentrate on the task of the psychotherapist. Scattered throughout Jung's works, however, are references to what the patient must do. One of the most lucid of these is a letter written in 1945 to Olga Fröbe-Kapteyn, the wealthy Dutch woman who sponsored yearly Eranos Conferences between 1933 and 1988 at her villa overlooking Lago Maggiore in Switzerland. Jung's letter is evidently a response to a cry for help. Frau Fröbe was sixty-four in 1945, and had been a widow since 1916, the year her twin daughters were born (Bair 2003: 412). It seems that one of the daughters, now twenty-nine, had recently complained that Fröbe had been a neglectful mother, more concerned with administering Eranos than with nurturing her. In her pain at this accusation, Fröbe had written to Jung, needing to know what she should do at this late date about her sorrow and her guilt. Here is the substance of his letter:

> The opus consists of three parts: insight, endurance, and action. Psychology is needed only in the first part, but in the second and third parts moral strength plays the predominant role. . . . It is conflicts of duty that make endurance and action so difficult. Your life's work for Eranos was unavoidable and right. Nevertheless it conflicts with maternal duties which are equally unavoidable and right. . . . There can be no resolution, only patient endurance of the opposites which ultimately spring from your own nature. . . . Admit that your daughter is right in saying you are a bad mother, and defend your duty as a mother towards Eranos. . . . The apparently unendurable conflict is proof of the rightness of your life.
>
> (*Letters, i*: 375)

The "opus" is a reference to alchemy, on which Jung was working industriously at the time of the letter, but here he means to describe the lifework of coming to grips with the unconscious. He implies that Fröbe already has sufficient insight and therefore does not need psychotherapy. There is "no resolution" for the sort of internal conflict from which she suffers. She must be unflinchingly honest with herself and not diminish either side of the battle raging within her. He makes no attempt to console her and insists that she admit she has been a "bad mother." What is essential is having the "moral strength" to hold these two painful truths steadily in her awareness.

Transformation, it appears, comes at the end of painful endurance. In the following chapters we shall look more closely at Jung's notion not only that the opposites must be endured, but also that the tension they generate be held steadily in consciousness. Allowing oneself to be pushed to the limit by one's own internal conflict brings conscious and unconscious together, generates powerful autonomic responses, and makes transformation possible.

Parallels in the neural substrate

The heart of any psychotherapy is its ability to help the patient manage emotional states, to rescue awareness from the automatic reactions occurring in convergence zones that bypass analysis and reflection. LeDoux suggests that the reason psychoanalytic work usually takes so long is that neural connections from cortex to amygdala "are far weaker than connections from the amygdala to the cortex," making it easy for "emotional information to invade our conscious thoughts, but hard for us to gain control over our emotions" (LeDoux 1996: 265). The other obvious reason psychotherapy is a slow process is that brain circuits are stabilized through repetition and that existing networks, each driven by feeling-toned associations, fire more easily than new circuits can be built. In this way, "repeated experiences of terror and fear can be engrained within the circuits of the brain as states of mind" (Siegel 1999: 33f).

The earliest, foundational circuits are established in infancy, the likely origin of fearful and confident personality profiles. This is why Freud was correct in his "reductive method." Deeply rooted emotion-driven patterns that are inadequate to current life-situations can be undermined by building new cortical connections, when an individual gains some conscious insight into how her habitual patterns operate and why they are counterproductive. But such changes are frightening to contemplate and not likely to be tolerable unless some degree of security can first be established. If internal feelings of security and trust were not established in infancy, a healthy secure attachment must be built in later life. In therapy, the condition necessary for such confidence-building will take the form of the "positive transference" Jung described in his third stage (*CW16*: 150–60) and that Janet called the "need for direction."

Psychotherapy is truly effective when it can build sufficient confidence in the patient to allow flexibility of response and the capacity to develop new attitudes.

This is the only way we can escape from compulsive fixations governed by thalamus and amygdala. It is the reason Jung insists that a reductive approach to symptoms and fantasies must follow the confession stage of therapy and be followed in turn by a positive transference.

> Therapy is just another way of creating synaptic potentiation in brain pathways that control the amygdala. The amygdala's emotional memories, as we've seen, are indelibly burned into its circuits. The best we can hope to do is to regulate their expression . . . by getting the cortex to control the amygdala.
>
> (LeDoux 1996: 265)

Jung's choice of the word *education* to describe his third stage has not been favored by most psychodynamic theories in the twentieth century. They have preferred more mysterious and compelling phrases, such as "breaking down the resistance," "metabolizing projections," and "structuring a self." But *education* and *learning* may be the most accurate way to describe the process by which "synaptic plasticity" is achieved (LeDoux 1996: 9). "The reason animals can learn is that they can alter their nervous systems on the basis of external experience. And the reason that they can do that is that *experience itself can modify the expression of genes*" (Marcus 2004: 98). Specifically, the genes whose expression is modified (turned on or off) are those that manufacture the proteins which alter the synapses, "hardening" the wiring in some and "softening" it in others.

According to Edelman, learning is "the means by which categorization occurs on a background of value to result in adaptive changes in behavior that satisfy value" (Edelman 1992: 118). The word *value*, for Edelman, refers to feeling-tone and emotion. He means that a rational reassessment of one's life-situation has to be based in feelings that are adequate to the adaptation one hopes to achieve. He does not speak in this regard of transference, but that would be the most likely source of "background values" in the psychotherapeutic meeting where the patient is undergoing the Adlerian re-education Jung describes. Edelman does say that conscious learning requires conscious attention which will employ a considerable percentage of the cortex. Practice will make learning automatic so that cortical involvement will decrease with time (Edelman 2004: 93f). In the course of learning, "the brain constructs maps of its own activities that categorize, discriminate, and recombine the various brain activities" (Edelman 1992: 109).

Learning, therefore, involves perceptual recategorizing, building new memories, and linking the resulting maps with value systems that belong to different parts of the brain than those responsible for the mapping:

> The sufficient condition for adaptation is provided by the linkage of global mappings to the activity of the so-called hedonic centers and the limbic system of the brain in a way that satisfies homeostatic, appetitive, and consummatory needs reflecting evolutionarily established values.
>
> (Edelman 1992: 100)

Edelman describes, here, what might be called the re-education of emotional circuitry through building new neural networks connecting thalamus, hippocampus, and amygdala with the cortex. Furthermore, such re-education proceeds within the limits of phylogenetic (archetypal) patterns.

Ego's narrative

When the work of elucidation and education succeeds, long-lasting changes are effected in brain circuits; but what matters most is having these newly created or organized circuits integrated with the dynamic core (Edelman and Tononi 2000: 176). In effect, psychotherapy will not have lasting effects unless the habitual "shape" of the dynamic core is altered. In Jung's language, this would mean that the contents of the ego-complex and the most accessible sectors of the personal unconscious are altered by psychotherapy. The results may be described in various ways, "integration" (Jung), "global mapping" (Edelman), "cognitive reframing" (Goleman); but the phenomenological/experiential end result of such processes is that we begin to tell different stories about who we are. "Psychotherapy works by changing people's narratives" (T. D. Wilson 2002: 180).

While in a complex-ridden state, I am sure to tell repetitive stories about myself—how people take advantage of me, why no one seems to appreciate my intelligence or my contributions; or perhaps it will be about how thoughtless and selfish people are, how dangerously they drive, how gladly they inconvenience others for their own selfish advantage; possibly it will be about immigrants with strange accents and customs and how they are ruining the country; maybe my stories will all be about how arrogant and autocratic my superiors are, or how stupid and incompetent those placed under my authority. Such whining, raging, and self-exculpating stories are nearly always an indication that I am protecting a narrow, distorted, and vulnerable self-image. My dynamic core is supplying me with narrative material to keep my neurotic sense of self-superiority justified and implicitly unchallenged. There is no chance of my embarking on a real individuation journey, for I tell myself incessantly (and erroneously) that I am already as perfect as I can be.

If I follow Jung's advice and allow the complex to speak to me of everything I hate to hear and then engage it in dialogue (the method suggested in *Two Essays* (*CW7*) or if I submit to the process of confession, elucidation, and education (*CW16*: ¶122–74), I open up these obsessive, narrow and defensive categories that my convergence zones have built and maintained, and bring my cortex to bear on my life-situations. My stories about who I am and my relations to my neighbors, colleagues and rivals—not to mention my parents, children and siblings—change, too. Much more of objective reality enters my stories; my stories themselves become more flexible and original, more open to novelty, more tolerant of challenge. Wisdom may even replace knowledge. No longer knowing all, I become an avid learner. When ego's narrative starts here, psychic process as individuation can be lived.

Chapter 13

Jung on archetypes and altered states

Our discussion of brain and psyche now reaches the realm of experience most readily associated with the name C. G. Jung: the spiritual, numinous, transcendent, and transformative. Because it has earned Jung the disparaging title of "mystic" among "hard-headed" writers from Sigmund Freud to J. Allan Hobson, we have first sought to establish a secure foundation in the discoveries and theories of today's mainstream science for Jung's ideas about the conscious mind and its "penumbra," to use William James' expression, the poorly illuminated and fuzzily defined region of human experience that *might* just as well be conscious. Jung calls it the "personal unconscious"—the domain of the complexes.

The discovery of the complexes guided the early years of Jung's psychiatric practice. He first assumed that therapy might consist in simply *informing* the patient of the nature of her complex and the putative traumatic experiences that lay behind it. Grateful to be informed, although chastened to know the shameful truth about herself, the patient was to end her denials, face up to her obligations, and change the course of her life. This was clearly an overly optimistic plan, but not unlike Freud's first naive and briefly held notion of what therapy ought to be. In his autobiography Jung even gives us some spectacular instances where the procedure seems to have worked (*MDR*: 114–30). Soon, however, he was talking about an "energy gradient" (*CW6*: ¶130). He was thinking of a waterfall, a ball rolling down an inclined plane, or the flow of electrons between the poles of a battery. Movement occurs in the psyche only when there is a natural downhill flow of energy. We are rarely if ever successful at simply *deciding* to change. Something powerful must move us. "Psychic energy is a very fastidious thing . . . we cannot make it serviceable until we have succeeded in finding the right gradient" (*CW7*: ¶76).

In the last analysis, what supplies psyche's irresistible energy gradient is always the archetype with its "distinctively numinous character which can only be described as 'spiritual,' if 'magical' is too strong a word" (*CW8*: ¶405). When an archetype "becomes conscious, it is felt as strange, uncanny, and at the same time fascinating. At all events the conscious mind falls under its spell . . . [it] always produces a state of alienation" (*CW8*: ¶590). By means of its power to fascinate, an archetype can "mould the destinies of individuals [for good or ill] by unconsciously influencing their thinking, feeling, and behavior" (*CW5*: ¶467). Ultimately *experiencing an archetype* is the bottom line in psychological transformation; for only the compellingly emotional downhill flow of instinctual energy is capable of "producing extensive alterations in the subject" (*CW7*: ¶110).

> When [in life] a distressing situation arises, the corresponding archetype will be constellated in the unconscious. Since this archetype is numinous, i.e. possesses a specific energy, it will attract to itself the contents of consciousness—conscious ideas that render it perceptible and hence capable of conscious realization. Its passing over into consciousness is felt as an illumination, a revelation or a "saving idea."
>
> (*CW5*: ¶450)

Clearly "the experience of an archetype" results in non-ordinary states of consciousness. It feels irresistible, numinous, spiritual, magical, fascinating, compelling, transforming, illuminating and revelatory. It carries us beyond the merely empirical, beyond the soberly rational into altered states of consciousness. It reveals our kinship with the cave painters of the Upper Paleolithic. Although Western culture has been suspicious of altered states for at least the last 500 years, relegating them to the realm of the "non-ordinary," the "fantastic" and the "illusory," they are truly normal and necessary for everyday life.

Jung in 1925

To get an idea of the role altered states of consciousness play in Jung's thought, we shall consider some of the highlights from an extremely important year of his life, 1925, when he turned fifty. In January, he had his first opportunity for extensive conversation with an individual living outside the thought-world of Western culture, in Taos Pueblo, New Mexico. Then, between March and July, in a seminar to some of his closest associates, he described a series of altered states of consciousness that had played a determining role in the development of his theories. Finally, the year ended with his famous trip to Mt. Elgon, in Kenya, and another set of non-ordinary experiences and reflections.

New Mexico

Jung describes his non-Western interlocutor, Mountain Lake (Ochwiay Biano),[1] chief of the Taos Pueblos, as an intelligent man, five to ten years younger than himself. Conversing with him was in some ways more satisfying than talking to another European (*MDR*: 247). Mountain Lake observed that white people are always staring, uneasily and restlessly seeking something. He said they act as if they were mad; and most disturbingly, they claim to think with their heads. Jung wondered with what Native Americans did their thinking, and Mountain Lake patted his heart (*MDR*: 248). He evidently linked thinking to his body and emotions—the source of everything the West finds to be contaminating and unreliable. Jung was impressed with the depth and confidence of the Native American's demeanor. He found a stability there, a more secure foundation than anything Westerners knew. Eventually, he got Mountain Lake speaking of mythic matters:

> It was astonishing to me to see how the Indian's emotions change when he speaks of his religious ideas. In ordinary life he shows a degree of self-control and dignity that borders on fatalistic equanimity. But when he speaks of things that pertain to his mysteries, he is in the grip of a surprising emotion.
>
> (*MDR*: 250)

The "Indian," in short, is not ashamed to show the consciousness-altering effects of the archetypal energy-gradient. Sitting on the roof of a pueblo, the New Mexico sun blazing above them, Mountain Lake pointed to the sun and asked: "Is not he who moves there our father? How can anyone say differently? How can there be another god?" Struggling for words, he "exclaimed at last, 'What would a man do alone in the mountains? He cannot even build his fire without him.'" Jung wondered if the sun might not be "a fiery ball shaped by an invisible god." Mountain Lake would have none of it: "The sun is God. Everyone can see that" (*MDR*: 250f).

Shortly, he made it clear that the sun is the central mystery of Pueblo life, for they "live on the roof of the world" and are "the sons of Father Sun." They assist the sun in his daily journey across the sky, not for themselves alone but for the whole earth. Despite this, the Americans foolishly and unaccountably try to prohibit them by outlawing their rituals and dances—the institutionalized activities that foster their altered states of consciousness and the mythic realities that underlie them. The Pueblo people, however, were not about to acquiesce: "If we were to cease practicing our religion, in ten years the sun would no longer rise. Then it would be night forever." Jung was deeply moved:

> I then realized on what the "dignity," the tranquil composure of the individual Indian, was founded. It springs from his being a son of the sun; his life is cosmologically meaningful, for he helps the father and preserver of all life in his daily rise and descent. If we set this against our own self-justifications . . . we cannot help but see our poverty.
>
> (*MDR*: 252)

Here, in the awe shared by Jung and Mountain Lake, lies the ultimate significance of the archetype's emotionally charged "gradient" and the altered state it brings about. It transforms a lifeless, mechanical world into a living cosmological mystery that is not separate from the individual but makes each of us a meaningful participant in the whole. We Westerners like to think that our foundations are rational and fully explicable, and we fear being led astray by misleading superstitions that may arise from less than sober states of consciousness. Our rationality leaves us rootless, restless and searching for we do not know what. By contrast, Mountain Lake was "living his myth," and doing so consciously. His dignity and imperturbable self-confidence bespoke the richness and depth of his lived world. In Jung's view, he had what we have lost. Only the archetypes and the "revelatory" states of consciousness they induce will take us there.

The seminar

Jung makes it clear to his followers in 1925 that he had been searching over the past three decades for a vantage point from which to view the human condition and to reduce the inevitable limitations that history and culture impose on any European academic of the twentieth century. He explored in several directions, especially our nearest cultural relatives in the European Middle Ages, and our most distant in the hunter-gatherers whose way of life had survived into the first quarter of the twentieth century.[2] Mountain Lake was not a hunter-gatherer, but he surely lived closer to that way of life than Jung did. Ultimately, Jung thought, we will not know ourselves with clear objectivity until we have been visited by an intelligent species like our own that has evolved in complete isolation from us, on a distant planet.

Jung's quest to understand the human mind, he told the seminar participants, was first sparked in 1896, when he was twenty-one, and discovered the peculiar talents of his somnambulist cousin, Helly Preiswerk.[3] He thought of Schopenhauer's idea of the will as a blind and aimless urge to create; but there seemed to be nothing blind and aimless about Helly's voices. The unconscious material seemed, rather, "to flow into definite moulds" (*Sem25*: 3f). His second lesson set in when, "after several years," he began to realize that *Symbols of Transformation* was about himself, that the Miss Frank Miller whose fantasies he analyzed had become in the course of the writing his own anima and personified his own "autonomous thinking." She "took over my fantasy and became the stage director to it" (*Sem25*: 27). While writing *Symbols*, he had been unaware that his thinking had been "directed" by an unconscious factor. But a dozen years later, in 1925, he had developed a relationship of trust with an inner advisor of a rather different character.

> [N]ow I have within myself a "man" who is millions of years old ... when we get the view that suits the "old man," things go right. If I am holding views that are out of keeping with the unconscious, they are certain to make me ill, and so it is safe for me to assume that they contradict some main current in the universe.
>
> (*Sem25*: 12)

These things did not happen by chance. Jung practiced "active imagination," which he likened to "yogic concentration." The conscious effort, he insisted, is essential, for archetypes have the ability to withdraw energy from the contents of consciousness (*CW8*: ¶841). In active imagination, nature's "darkening" process is reversed. By applying a strong, steady attention to the images that arose before his mind's eye, Jung focused the psychic energy available to his ego in a way which animated images already active in his unconscious. The consciously applied energy brought them "to the surface," and made them available for observation and engagement. By contrast, daydreaming is a *passive* activity that may continue for hours without effort, whereas one soon finds active imagination tiring (*Sem25*: 35).

When in December of 1913 he first "let [him]self drop" by deliberately imagining a passageway into the depths of the earth—what anthropologist Michael Harner and his students would call a "shamanic journey" (Harner 1980)—Jung encountered a number of disturbing images and events that he struggled to understand by painting them and searching out thematic parallels in world mythology. Paramount among his imaginal encounters was a cast of regular characters who instructed him: a wise old man with a white beard who called himself Elijah, a beautiful but thoroughly untrustworthy blind woman named Salome, and a large black serpent. One of Elijah's most important lessons was what Jung came to call "original thinking." Elijah "said that I treated thoughts as if I generated them myself, but according to his views, thoughts were like animals in the forest, people in a room, or birds in the air" (*Sem25*: 95). By taking it for granted that we are the authors of our thoughts, we maintain the illusion that we are identical with our conscious mind and thereby devalue the *source* of our thinking, which resides in the unconscious. In place of this, Elijah recommended a meditative discipline. By turning our attention onto the thought process itself, we can observe the thoughts as they arise, given to us in a manner that "is immediately convincing [and] comes as a revelation."

"Original thinking" means attending to ideas as they "originate" and before they have been folded into our habitual assumptions. Jung found parallels to Elijah's method in the *Tao Te Ching* and the Upanishads (*Sem25*: 75). But unbeknownst to him, another continental thinker published a similar account in the same year of 1913. In *Ideas: General Introduction to Pure Phenomenology*, philosopher Edmund Husserl (1913) described a meditative discipline to "put out of action . . . the natural standpoint," the naive mode of thinking whereby cultural and other assumptions impose themselves, unnoticed, upon our thinking. Disabling the natural standpoint allows the philosopher to be "free from theory and free from metaphysics by bringing all of the grounding back to the immediate data . . . just as it is in reality experienced" (Husserl 1913: 99f).[4] Husserl called his method the *epoché*, the "phenomenological reduction" or simply "bracketing." He wanted to hold the "natural standpoint" at bay so that he could attend to "the things themselves": ideas and images as they rise into consciousness. Another parallel to this sort of critical-minded introversion may be found in the "insight" meditation of Theravada Buddhism (*vipassana*),[5] where one aims "to apprehend cognition at a stage before it becomes assembled into higher cognitive events . . . directly apprehending the sensory aspect of a moment of consciousness before mapping a cognition upon it" (C. D. Laughlin *et al.* 1990: 25).

A few evenings after his lesson on "original thinking," Jung had a most extra-ordinary archetypal experience. He began his descent into the underworld only after great resistance, and then, he says, "a most disagreeable thing happened." The blind Salome began worshipping him, calling him the Christ, and claiming that he could cure her of her blindness. While Jung was struggling with his reaction to that, he found the snake encircling him several times from the ankles to the chest, while he stood with his arms extended in a crucifixion pose. He does not say whether he was trying to keep them away from the snake or whether his body simply took on that pose. Then Salome rose up and claimed her sight had been restored, while Jung felt his face reshaping itself into that of "an animal of prey, a lion or a tiger." He says he was afraid he was losing his mind, that he was under some evil spell personified by the sinister Salome (*Sem25*: 95–7). In fact, his shape shifted into that of Aion, one of the gods of late antique Persia. The lion-headed, snake-encircled Aion, whose image forms the frontispiece of Jung's book of the same name, *Aion: Researches into the Phenomenology of the Self* (*CW9ii*), was known as the god of Endless Duration, the evil half of a pair of gods. His twin brother represented Eternity, the eternal and ever fascinating Now, against which Endless Duration is torment.

While reluctantly undergoing the deification, Jung was reminded too strongly of his schizophrenic patients at the Burghölzli asylum. But he tells his students in the seminar that if one wishes to become conscious of crucial unconscious facts, one cannot do so without taking the risk, "without giving yourself to them"; and if you do, "then these facts take on a life of their own. You can be gripped by these ideas so that you really go mad, or nearly so." Still it is an awesome mystery, deification. In Jung's case, he became the *leontocephalus*, the lion-headed god with the winged body of an ithyphallic human. He does not tell us whether the encounter with Salome was sexually charged, but he leaves us no doubt that deification, becoming "the vessel of creation in which the opposites reconcile," was of decisive importance for him. "When the images come to you and are not under-stood, you are in the society of the gods or, if you will, the lunatic society; you are no longer in human society" (*Sem25*: 95). When you feel the lunacy, you are bound to be frightened and tempted to try to dismiss the experience as nonsense, whereupon you will derive no profit from it. Alternatively, you may be so swept up in it that you decide you really are some sort of misunderstood god and thereby "become a crank or a fool"—if not an outright schizophrenic (*Sem25*: 99).

The 1925 Seminar ranges over the theory of psychological types and the history of Western culture since the Greeks, but its central message is that the modern European is no longer in touch with the unconscious. "Primitives show a much more balanced psychology, for the reason that they have no objection to letting the irrational come through, while we resent it" (*Sem25*: 105). The way to handle deification and all other "disagreeable" but overwhelming archetypal experiences is to let them be, take them as information that needs to be puzzled out. Neither deny them nor take them literally. Feel how they move you. Accept the reality that life is larger than you have been told.

Africa

From Nairobi Jung's party drove out to see the great game preserve of the Athai Plains, and from a low hill he looked out on a magnificent expanse where great herds of grazing animals moved in silence:

> This was the stillness of the eternal beginning, the world as it had always been, in the state of non-being. . . . There I was now, the first human being to realize that this was the world, but who did not know that in this moment he had first really created it.
>
> (*MDR*: 255)

The whole scene took him back some eleven or twelve months to his conversations with Mountain Lake.

> I . . . had been looking about without hope for a myth of our own. Now I knew what it was, and knew even more: that man is indispensable for the completion of creation; that, in fact, he himself is the second creator of the world, who alone has given the world its objective existence—without which, unheard, unseen, silently eating, giving birth, dying, heads nodding through hundreds of millions of years, it would have gone on in the profoundest night of non-being down to its unknown end.
>
> (*MDR*: 256)

Here was, evidently, the most profound altered state of consciousness Jung had had, or indeed, would have before his near-death experiences some two decades later. This time there was no "induction procedure"—no drumming or dancing, no ingestion of drugs, no existential crisis—just a silent vision of endless duration, Aion's domain, the slow crawl of blind evolution suddenly illumined by conscious reflection.[6]

No doubt this answer to his deepest longing was the last thing Jung had expected from his trip to Africa, for his aim had been to bring back information from the natives. He hoped to find unspoiled hunter-gatherers happy to share their dreams and mythic narratives. He learned a bit of Swahili in hopes of communicating with them, but found that it only helped in his conversations with his porters, who were generations removed from hunting and gathering. He did learn, however, that they distinguished between "big dreams" and "ordinary dreams." Ordinary dreams were personal and held little interest. Big dreams, on the other hand, had mythic significance; they were infrequent but impressive, and tended to occur at decisive moments in the life of the dreamer or the group; they gave guidance, and they always had a collective meaning (cf. Burleson 2005: 147). Jung seized upon this distinction and made it part of his Analytical Psychology, but he heard no big dreams from the Elgonyi, the remote tribe of herders (not hunter-gatherers) he stayed with on the side of Mount Elgon.

They told him that in the old days before the English had taken charge, their medicine men had had dreams and knew when war, sickness or rain would come. But now there was no need for that, since "the English know everything" (*MDR*: 265).

It meant a great deal to Jung that big dreams could show a people the way to go and that some individuals were more likely than others to get the message; for it was his own experience that when it was crucial to know something, the unconscious came to his assistance. Furthermore, this fact was perfectly coherent with the possibility that a people's dreams might go silent when they no longer had charge of their own destiny—for then there would be no crucial need that could constellate an answer from the unconscious. The biographer of Jung's Africa trip, Blake Burleson, accepts the possibility that Jung's understanding might not have been wrong on these points, but he adds that the Elgonyi were far more politically astute than Jung. The Swiss psychiatrist had showed up at the head of an English-commissioned and English-equipped safari, with the approval of the English colonial authorities. Furthermore, it bore the name of their traditional enemies (The *Bugishu* Psychological Expedition), and Jung began his formal palavers "by setting forth the *shauri*, that is the agenda of the palaver" (*MDR*: 264). Burleson points out that *shauri* was a politically charged term that meant bringing a matter before the colonial authorities. The Elgonyi would have had every reason to think Jung had been sent as a spy for the English (Burleson 2005: 143f).

Very likely Burleson is right, and that may be why Jung got nowhere asking the Elgonyi about their religious beliefs and practices. But it may also be that, like most cultures outside the Christian sphere, they had no concept of a separate domain that corresponds to "religion." If they had a "religion" of some sort, it was so thoroughly commingled with every aspect of daily life that they could not tease it out, nor could Jung clarify his questions sufficiently to make himself understood. Instead, he had no choice but to catch them in the act, and he managed to do so because he himself liked to be up at dawn. He liked to take a campstool and sit on the edge of the mountain under an acacia tree, where he could watch the "dark, almost black-green strip of jungle" below him gradually turn to "flaming crystal." "At such moments, I felt as if I were inside a temple. It was the most sacred hour of the day. I drank in this glory with insatiable delight, or rather, in a timeless ecstasy" (*MDR*: 268). Evidently the Elgonyi were familiar with this sort of altered state, because it was in response to the same holy dawn that Jung caught them in the act of practicing the religion they did not know they had. Every morning they would blow or spit into their hands and then hold their palms out toward the rising sun. Remembering Mountain Lake, Jung asked them if the sun were God and learned that the sun is God only at the moment when it rises (*MDR*: 269). Jung understood this to be a case of mystical participation: the sight of the rising sun and the overwhelming emotion of an altered state of consciousness occur simultaneously. The encounter with God is the coincidence of these: a cosmic and a psychological event.

Sunrise and his own feeling of deliverance are for him the same divine experience, just as night and fear are the same. Naturally his emotions are more important than physics; therefore what he registers is his emotional fantasies. For him night means snakes and the cold breath of spirits, whereas morning means the birth of a beautiful god.

(*CW8*: ¶329)

A passage like this might be read as evidence that Jung looked upon the "primitives" of Mt. Elgon with colonial disdain, but he did not hide his own "timeless ecstasy" when the forest and mountain become "a temple." Furthermore, he found a troop of baboons a little further up the mountain from where he sat on his campstool, sitting quietly every morning at the edge of an east-facing cliff. The noise, commotion and constant energy of the baboons' day evidently waited for a reverent greeting of the rising sun. Baboons, Elgonyi, and pith-helmeted Swiss were all moved by the same transcendent experience—the very definition of an archetypal pattern. Moreover, it was evident that such moments had been occurring, morning after countless morning, as long as those nodding herds had been grazing on the plains. Jung obtained partial evidence of such timelessness when he steamed down the Nile on his way out of Africa. There he passed the eastern wall of the ancient Egyptian temple of Abu Simbel and saw on its facade a line of sculpted baboons, facing the rising sun side-by-side in the same attitude of reverence he had seen on Mount Elgon (*MDR*: 268f) (see Figure 13.1).

Figure 13.1 Carved baboons worshipping the sun at Abu Simbel.

Source: photograph provided by Gary Grundy, taken at Abu Simbel, Egypt, August 2006.

Lévy-Bruhl

When Jung says, "Sunrise and his own feeling of deliverance are for him the same divine experience," he is citing what is one of the most common types of altered state of consciousness to be met with in human life. Usually he names it *participation mystique*, a term borrowed from Lucien Lévy-Bruhl. Jung's allying himself with Lévy-Bruhl has not helped his efforts to explain himself, for Lévy-Bruhl is—if possible—even more poorly understood and unfairly dismissed than is Jung. Since "mystical participation" is such an important category of experience for Jung, a short explanation is in order.

Lévy-Bruhl has a reputation for being an "armchair anthropologist," one who writes about pre-literate peoples whom he has never visited but only read about in the publications of others. Even anthropologists see him that way. But he was a philosopher, not an anthropologist, and held the chair in History of Philosophy at the Sorbonne. After a book on Germany in the time of Leibniz, his interest shifted to moral philosophy, where he wished to publish an unimpeachable account of human ethics. Lévy-Bruhl began with a book on Auguste Comte, the man who coined the term *sociology*, and then became fascinated with the Durkheim school of sociology, which inspired his *Ethics and Moral Science*.[7] Lévy-Bruhl feared his views in the book were too theoretical and too much limited by European cultural assumptions. Like Jung and Husserl in the same second decade of the twentieth century, he wanted to transcend his parochial limitations and decided he had to get as far away from the European mind as possible.

This is what led him to become an expert in the published reports of missionaries and colonialists working among pre-literate peoples in Africa, Australia, the Americas, and Oceania. He read critically, very astutely pointing out the prejudices that prevent Europeans from understanding the natives. He found case after case of breakdowns in communication that were rooted in cultural differences. For example, a certain Mr. W. B. Grubb in America was accused of stealing pumpkins from a Native American's garden. Grubb defended himself by pointing out that it was well known that he had been 150 miles away at the time the pumpkins were stolen. The Native American acknowledged this fact but asserted that Grubb was nevertheless guilty because he had been *seen* stealing the pumpkins in a dream. This argument is absurd to the European mind, but makes perfect sense to the "primitive." Conflicts like this were what Lévy-Bruhl seized upon to make his case that there is a way of "thinking" that Europeans do not appreciate. "He [the primitive] will put up with two incompatible certainties and unlike the white man will not believe himself obliged to choose" (Lévy-Bruhl 1945: 6). Jung made nearly the same point to his 1925 Seminar when he extolled the richness of primitive thinking in being more like "original thinking." He said the primitive is not disturbed when irrationalities appear, while the European "resents" them.

"Everybody knows" that Lévy-Bruhl was a bit of a racist for holding that "primitives" were "pre-logical," that he held stubbornly to his errors for three decades but finally renounced them in notebooks where he was working out the ideas for what would have been his seventh book on primitive mentality. He died without writing the book, but the notebooks were published posthumously (Lévy-Bruhl 1945). "Everybody" is as wrong about Lévy-Bruhl as he is about Jung. The *Notebooks* renounce nothing, but obsessively search for a way to convince his critics that his observations are correct. He does make it clear that his choice of "pre-logical" in the first book (*How Natives Think*, 1910) had been the obstacle. But he had already made that argument in his second book (*Primitive Mentality*, 1922). Indeed, the last sentence of the much-maligned *How Natives Think* already makes it clear that the object of his critique is as much Western thinking as it is the mental habits of primitives: "If it is true that our mental activity is logical and prelogical at one and the same time, the history of religious dogma and of philosophical systems may henceforth be explained in a new light."

In retrospect, it is clear that Lévy-Bruhl was trying to articulate a point of view in which mystical states of consciousness were taken as legitimate sources of personal and cultural information, alongside and in tension with what we Westerners consider to be "ordinary" states of consciousness. By the publication of his third book on pre-literate mentality, *The "Soul" of the Primitive* (1927), he had begun to identify *emotion* as the critical factor in a mystical state of consciousness like *participation mystique*. Furthermore, this capacity for mystical thinking is "not limited to 'primitive peoples' but is present in every human mind" (Lévy-Bruhl 1945: 101). He refers to Western folklore and the concept of "consubstantiality," the theological concept that describes the Christian Trinity.[8] By the time of his *Notebooks*, he has adopted a language very similar to Jung's:

> In the *affective complex* which is created as soon as the primitive man believes himself in the presence of an act of witchcraft, it is the [imperceptible . . . supernatural force] which is by far the most important and, as a result, the most certain.
>
> (Lévy-Bruhl 1945: 43, italics added)

As an "undeniable" instance of *participation mystique*, he describes a primitive's corpse lying in his hut while his ghost is alive, listening in on the conversations of the living, and in need of food and warmth. There is some mysterious identity between the empirical corpse and the invisible ghost. The connection is to be found in "the emotion caused by the death," so that "participation is essentially feeling" rather than thinking (Lévy-Bruhl 1945: 3).

Jung was aware of the academic disfavor Lévy-Bruhl had suffered and defended him in several of his writings.[9] He found the philosopher to be an astute observer who had aptly named a universal characteristic of human psychology, and believed that the criticism he had received was due to "rationalistic superstition" (*CW11*: ¶817, n. 28). As an affective complex, *participation mystique* is essentially the same phenomenon that we discussed in Chapter 11. A habitual emotional reaction occurs so rapidly in the hypothalamus and amygdala that the cortex is left behind. Our body, and especially its autonomic nervous system, is placed into an attitude such as awe. What then stirs in our memory is the complex of associations that has been linked with that emotion throughout the course of our life. In the case of a personal complex, the topic of the last chapter, the associations are very likely to be idiosyncratic to the individual and her personal history. But in the cases discussed by Lévy-Bruhl, the associated images and concepts are typical and culture-specific. He aptly describes them as *répresentations collectives*. They are archetypal images generated by inherited brain structures and shaped by culture.

*   *   *   *   *

Lévy-Bruhl's naming of the crucial emotional factor in *participation mystique*, therefore, ties up the loose ends. An archetypal emotional reaction occurs when a human being "apprehends" a situation that "constellates" a neural-hormonal reaction that is partly inborn and partly learned through the enculturation process that begins immediately after birth. The constellating situation itself constitutes a "collective representation" on account of this combination of inheritance and enculturation. And it occasions an altered state of consciousness on account of the effects of the neuro-hormonal whole-body reaction. The image, the altered state and the cosmological flavor of myth all imply a numinous archetype that has the power to transform.

Chapter 14

Altered states and transformation

In the last paragraph of his *Varieties of Religious Experience* (1902), William James says that "the whole drift" of his education persuades him "that the world of our present consciousness is only one of many worlds of consciousness that exist, and that those other worlds must contain experiences which have a meaning for our life also." Altered states of consciousness are what have given us access to those other meaningful worlds—at least since the cave painters of the last Ice Age. Over the past 500 years, however, Western culture has not been receptive to the idea that there may be anything of value in mystical or other altered states, even though a genuinely "scientific" spirit ought to be open to investigate every sort of phenomenon.

Altered states of consciousness: an overview

The ancient texts of Hinduism identify four fundamental modes of consciousness, each radically distinct from the others and universally available to humans. We have already discussed the first three in our chapter on dreaming. They are waking consciousness, dream and dreamless sleep; the fourth is called *turiya* (the "fourth"), a "super-conscious" mode of illumination (Fischer-Schreiber *et al.* 1989). In his book on the neurobiology of shamanism, anthropologist Michael Winkelman of Arizona State University specifies the same four modes, each physiologically distinct from the others. He calls the fourth state the "transpersonal or integrative" state of consciousness and finds that it has been employed in a striking variety of ways in different cultures (Winkelman 2000: 113). Some of those cultural forms are fairly familiar: the cosmic journey of the shaman's soul, the trance characterized by the spirit-possession of mediums who experience themselves as vessels of spirits or gods, the vision quest of Native Americans, and the experience of samādhi or enlightenment in various traditions from India to the Far East. According to Winkelman's research, the neurobiology of all these activities is pretty much the same, while each cultural tradition varies from the others and thereby gives a different shape to the experience.

Altered states of consciousness are by no means rare. Although mystical virtuosos are few and far between, we are all capable of altered states, and most of us in the West experience them far more often than we believe. All across the modern world, however, they are very well known. In the early 1970s, Erika Bourguignon, an anthropologist at Ohio State University, reviewed 488 societies from all continents and island groups, and found that 90 percent of them "have one or more institutionalized, culturally patterned form of ASC" (Bourguignon 1973). We in the West like to believe that altered states are exceptional, bizarre, absurd distractions from "real life," even pathological addictions. The fact that humans everywhere are capable of and regularly employ altered states, however, strongly supports the proposition that they are universal capabilities of our human organism and that we would be better off knowing them. Winkelman is right in calling them "fixed structures of consciousness that reflect latent human potentials" (Winkelman 2000: 117). Archaeologist Brian Hayden (2003) believes such powers have been available since hundreds of thousands of years before the cave painters.

> It seems certain that concepts of an "other world" were firmly in place by the time burials first occur, some 150,000 years ago if not before, as indicated by the use of red ochre in general rituals and the defleshed skull from Bodo, Ethiopia, some 600,000 years ago.
>
> (Hayden 2003: 118)

The ubiquity of ASCs

Researchers from all the fields we have been drawing upon agree that one of the hallmarks of human intelligence is the capacity to imagine how things might be if they were different from what we see before us. We owe our survival, in fact, to our talent for momentarily leaving behind the literal, the empirical, the present moment in the outer world, in order to find useful information within. We "drive" our consciousness into altered states in order to comprehend our life-situation more adequately than "bare facts" can represent.

"Ordinary consciousness" is difficult to delineate. If we pay attention to our states of mind, we have a hard time finding anything that is purely "ordinary" about our awareness. We might well agree that balancing a checkbook, driving a car, and contriving an experiment in physics all belong to ordinary consciousness (or "directed thinking," in Jung's language), even though the differences between these three activities are enormous. But consider any one of them more closely. The motorist may be well aware of and appropriately reacting to everchanging traffic conditions while never forgetting his destination, staying in touch with current clock-time as well as the time of his next scheduled appointment. All these details belong to ordinary consciousness. At the same time, however, our driver may be carrying on an imaginary argument with his boss, wonder what his therapist might have to say about the argument, and sporadically singing snatches of songs as they come up on his radio. The motorist, therefore, is simultaneously present to and absent from his task at hand, and the physicist's situation is doubtless more complicated still. Thus the idea of "ordinary consciousness" is hardly more than a convenient fiction.

While the ordinariness of any state of consciousness is difficult to define, it is not hard to find characteristics that most people will agree are definitely *non*-ordinary. Perhaps foremost among them is the sense an image or idea was not consciously invented, but merely "given" to me—even thrust upon me. Another agent seems to be involved. I may feel as though I have lost control over the contents of my consciousness. In extreme cases, I may suffer wide emotional fluctuations, possibly even oscillating between elation and despair.

ASCs may be characterized by a change in our sense of passing time. Athletes often speak of the game "slowing down" when they find themselves in a "groove" or "zone." Many who will never be proficient enough to consider themselves athletes have had the same sort of experience while playing a neighborhood game of basket-ball or softball. Anyone who has been involved in, or closely managed to avoid, an accident on the road or on the ski slope will be aware of time "slowing down" and the extreme clarity of the thinking processes just before the potential impact.

Altered states of consciousness may also be attended by disturbances in thought process and perception. Certain images or thoughts may become more vivid while others fade out; susceptibility to suggestion may be heightened; images may become so energized that we find ourselves hallucinating. We may experience distortions in our bodily perceptions as our performance miraculously seems to improve or deteriorate.

Many who report altered states of consciousness claim that what they have experienced can never be adequately expressed in words; something ineffable has happened; a window has opened onto another world of great significance. Such individuals will likely feel renewed or transformed.

Several of the authors we have been citing list a variety of common ASCs. Brian Hayden (2003: 70f) mentions joggers' highs, anorectic highs, childbirth, and the rush associated with workaholism, states of terror, and sexual orgasm. David Lewis-Williams and David Pearce (2005: 46) list the hypnagogic state that initiates sleep, near-death experiences, intense rhythmic dancing, drumbeats and flickering lights, fatigue, hunger, sensory deprivation, extreme pain, and intense concentration (as in meditation). Dreaming, itself, is perhaps the most common altered state, and always expresses an ego-alien tendency. For dreams "desire" a reality that corresponds to "a neurocognitive structure" within the individual, that is an unconscious neural network (C. D. Laughlin *et al.* 1990: 285).

Storytelling fosters altered states by organizing a narrative stream of images that engages with our cultural expectations and oral heritage. Storytellers take their listeners on "spiritual journeys" (Brody 2000: 130). We in Western culture tend not to notice the altered nature of our conscious states or to devalue them with a trivializing label.

> Many people in our society smoke marijuana for "kicks" and the experiences produced are generally coded . . . as entertainment. Rastafarians, however,

imbibe the drug as a sacrament, which leads to experiences imbued with sacred meaning within the context of their worldview.

(C. D. Laughlin *et al.* 1990: 230)

Thus, those who grow up witnessing shamanic healings, listening to rhythms and chants and dancing to them are "far more likely to enter into a sacred ecstatic state, than if they grow up in an industrial middle class environment" (Hayden 2003: 73).

Athletes who have known "the click of communality," when their team gels into a radiant high-performance unit, come to know "for a while at least, a higher level of existence: existence as it ought to be" (M. Murphy and White 1978: 11).

A well-known long-distance swimmer . . . who prefers to be anonymous, [said] that whenever his physical body is exhausted . . . he relaxes it by float-ing overhead in his double while continuing to swim. When he reenters his body, he feels refreshed and can go for quite a while without fatigue.

(M. Murphy and White 1978: 65)

Stories of a similar extraordinary nature have been gathered from explorers who have been pushed to the limits of their resources. Shackleton's memoir of his 1916 South Pole expedition provides this example:

During that long and racking march of thirty-six hours over the unnamed mountains and glaciers of South Georgia, it seemed to me often that we were four, not three. I said nothing to my companions on the point, but afterwards, Worsley said to me, "Boss, I had a curious feeling on the march that there was another person with us."

(M. Murphy and White 1978: 67f)

Altered states and transformation

These two stories and hundreds like them, collected in a volume called *The Psychic Side of Sports* (1978) by Michael Murphy, cofounder of the Esalen Institute, and Rhea White, reference librarian and parapsychologist, tell us several things. First, altered states of consciousness can be enormously improbable, but so supportive and useful that anyone blessed with such an experience will hardly dare to doubt it. The narrators of both stories, however, are very uneasy about sharing them. They know the events are "too weird" for most people to accept, so they refuse to speak of them, unless they feel they have found someone excep-tional who is likely to understand or at least not dismiss what they have to say. For this reason the swimmer has refused to allow his name to be used, and it is clear that Shackleton dares mention his experience only because it had been mentioned first by someone else. He goes out of his way to let us know that Worsley volun-teered the information without prompting—that he was an independent witness.

In a society like ours, this is the only sensible way to proceed, for those like Jung and Lévy-Bruhl who suggest that altered states are normal and valuable have been marginalized—even though the breadth of their scholarship and the depth of their education is never questioned.

Ninety percent of the world's societies may have institutionalized the cultivation of altered states of consciousness, but their attitudes toward such states and what people can do with them varies enormously. Charles Laughlin, John McManus, and Eugene d'Aquili in their book, *Brain, Symbol, and Experience* (1990: 293–5), have addressed this issue by suggesting a typology of societies based on their openness toward altered states. They refer to our own society as "monophasic." We admit only one "phase" of information gathering. Only ordinary states of consciousness may serve to provide reliable information. We hold that the real is always concrete and material; and we see the world as inanimate and soulless.

Shackleton and the swimmer, however, no longer subscribe to the logic of a monophasic society, for they have found that altered states may be quite valuable aids to success in challenging endeavors. They would feel quite comfortable and be quite willing to speak openly in what C. D. Laughlin *et al*. (1990) call a "minimally polyphasic" society. This clumsy expression describes a society that admits the existence and even endorses the use of altered states of consciousness, but does so in a "small" way. The authors mean that the linear conscious planning and materialistic assumptions of a monophasic society are not seriously challenged. Altered states are encouraged insofar as they are capable of enhancing the aims and achievements of ordinary consciousness. Shamanism, for example, may be an accepted means of healing diseases and interpreting dreams. It is admissible as an aid in the pursuit of goals that are barely distinguishable from those of a monophasic society. New Age movements in our own society are largely polyphasic in a minimal way. Their members want us to be open to altered states such as aura reading and channeling, and they would no doubt change us in small ways, by raising our eco-consciousness and promoting various tolerance programs to make war less likely; but, otherwise, they share our mainstream goals.

"Maximally polyphasic" societies, on the other hand, encourage and promote altered states much more vigorously. Indeed, they value them in many ways *more* highly than they do ordinary states. Altered states of consciousness are not mere helpful adjuncts to life-as-usual, but rather resources for a radical critique. A society is "maximal" in promoting multiple phases of consciousness when it strives to use non-ordinary states to induce transformations in the attitudes and personalities of its members. Jung, in 1925, was primarily concerned with a revolution in the European consciousness of his followers and patients that can only be described as "maximally polyphasic." He found Western culture to be failing in contrast to the Pueblo society Mountain Lake described. Because the story of the incarnate, crucified God of Christianity no longer functioned as a meaning-giving myth for the West and because no replacement had yet appeared, the white man had become an anxious, hollow-eyed searcher who no longer knew what he wanted. Logic and materialism were no substitute for mythic roots. Mountain Lake and the Elgonyi had such roots; and now that Jung had experienced his dei-fication as Aion and his revelatory transformation into "the second creator of the world," he, too, had mythic roots. He envisioned his practice of Complex Psychology as a subversion of ordinary Western values—or perhaps a rediscov-ery of them. He encouraged his patients to pay attention to their dreams and other altered states and deliberately to take up the practice of active imagination with an eye to psychological transformation.

C. D. Laughlin *et al.* (1990) describe a *fourth* type of society, one that is of less interest for our purposes, for it is probably best exemplified by a monastery. The "polyphasic void society" also uses altered states to transform its members, but this time the goal is highly specialized. Ultimate mystical states such as absolute union with the godhead, the experience of the void, the blown-out candle of nirvana, and other such descriptions define the central concern of the void society.[1]

Examples of transformative states of consciousness

Before exploring how it happens that altered states of consciousness can bring about significant and long-lasting, if not permanent, transformations in an indi-vidual's attitude toward self and world, we shall take a look at a few auto-biographical accounts: three individuals whose published writings have had an influence on this volume, a philosopher, an archaeologist, and Jung himself.

G. William Barnard

G. William Barnard (1997) paints a vivid portrait of a philosopher/psychologist who had a strong influence upon Jung in *Exploring Unseen Worlds: William James and the Philosophy of Mysticism*. He does not neglect the wider thought world shared by the American, Swiss, English, and French pioneers of the early twentieth century who took altered states seriously. A year after the publication of *Unseen Worlds*, Barnard wrote a chapter for a book devoted to mysticism as an "innate human capacity" (Forman 1998), in which he described James' views on the nature of mysticism and illustrated his argument by telling the story of his own mystical experience. The reader can hardly escape the conclusion that Barnard's momentous experience changed the course of his life and formed the foundation of his professional interest in William James, a writer who strove to expand the boundaries of what we take to be the legitimate scope of academic investigation. Indeed, it is likely that whenever one comes upon a scholar who has devoted a lifetime to trying to persuade our monophasic society of its blindness, biographi-cal inquiry will uncover altered states of consciousness of a transformative nature.[2] Barnard's experience occurred when he was only thirteen years old:

> I was walking to school in Gainesville, Florida, and, without any apparent reason, I became obsessed with the idea of what would happen after my death.

Throughout that day I attempted to visualize myself as not existing. I simply could not comprehend that my self-awareness would not exist in some form or another after my death. I kept trying, without success, to envision a simple blank nothingness. Later, I was returning home from school, walking on the hot pavement next to a stand of pine trees less than a block from my home, still brooding about what it would be like to die. Suddenly, without warning, something shifted inside of myself, as if I had been expanded beyond my previous sense of self. In that exhilarating and yet deeply peaceful moment, I felt as if I had been shaken awake. In a single, "timeless" gestalt, I had a direct and powerful experience that I was not just that young teenage boy but, rather, that I was a surging, ecstatic, boundless state of consciousness.

(Barnard 1998: 170)

If there is anything typical in this story of transformation, it is the fact that a process began in Barnard's young mind that seemed to come from elsewhere. As in "original thinking," the agent directing this process was not Barnard's ego. He just "became obsessed" for no apparent reason, and his consciously directed thought processes were incapable of working out the problem posed by that unconscious "other." He could neither visualize nor comprehend what had been put so ineluctably before him. It is by no means incidental, of course, that the conundrum that took possession of his mind for some seven or eight hours happens to be the ultimate existential issue of human consciousness: the absurdity and inevitability of death. Finally, the solution to the crisis also came from elsewhere. Without warning, something "shifted," and he was awake for the first time. His ego was overshadowed by a vast ecstatic reality that was also William Barnard. This is apparently the experience of the Archetype of archetypes, what Jung calls the "self."

Timothy Taylor

Timothy Taylor also confronted death as a young man. The English archaeologist wrote *The Prehistory of Sex* (1996) which argues that conventional notions of what is "proper" in sexual relations have had far too great an influence on the conclusions scholars have drawn about the sex lives and burial practices of pre-historic peoples, where the evidence is necessarily limited to whatever grave goods have been unearthed, and sometimes how the skeletons have been arranged. Taylor believes that humans have always and in every society down through the millennia explored every possible variation of sexual experience. Our so-called perversities are part of our nature, too, and archaeology would be well served to beware of puritanical assumptions. In *The Buried Soul* (2002), he wants us to see the shadow side of souls and ghosts, and wants us to appreciate the uncanny altered states that are inspired in humans by the deaths of friends and relatives, the compulsive speculations on the possibility of life after death that accompany those states, and the reasons why our ancestors for tens of thousands of years insisted on burying their corpses twice.[3] Taylor has his antennae up for the most unsettling motives in our ancestors, and often makes a convincing case.

His transforming experience occurred while he was on an archaeological dig in Austria in 1982 (T. Taylor 2002: 249–58). He had just received word that he had been admitted to the doctoral program at Oxford but had not been granted any financial aid, and he feared that he would not be able to continue his studies. On that July night in Vienna, he found himself surrounded by death: the seeming death of his academic hopes, the corpses in the medieval Christian cemetery he had been helping to exhume, the eighth-century skeletons in Hungary where he would be working a week later, and above all the recent death of his grandfather from a heart attack. His family had put the blame on young Taylor for the last of these deaths, and, inexplicably, he had fully accepted it.

On the night of the incident, Taylor was staying with friends in their apartment. There had been much talk and some wine drinking. When his friends went to bed, Taylor remained awake, sitting in his chair, listening to the sound of the trams passing by in the street. Then, apparently without forethought and certainly without rehearsal or even having imagined such a thing, he stripped off his clothes, spread a bath towel over his chair to protect it, folded out the smaller blade of his Swiss Army knife and began making incisions on his arms, legs and ribcage. It appears that he was already in an altered state and directed by an agent foreign to his ego; for he began without debate and without decision. He says, "I was calm to begin with and, as I proceeded making incisions, I became even calmer." Off and on, he felt a sting of pain, but that was only the surface of his consciousness: "I was somewhere deep inside myself untouchably strong . . . I felt fond of myself, perhaps for the first time. It was a miraculous feeling."

He says the endorphins took over, the body's natural painkillers, and he was "floating" peacefully as he began to go over his body a second time, filling in the gaps between the wounds, when he began to be alarmed at the bleeding. His friends found him in the bathtub and cleaned him up. By then he was embarrassed before them, but he insists that the cutting "made me feel better, *not just at that time, but ever since*" (italics added).

> I have never since felt the same intense calm as in those midnight hours when by some grace I found that I had the courage to act. The moment I started to cut, I began to draw my inner mental world and the outer physical world—symbolized and most directly exemplified by my body—closer together. What was needed was a physical act, one that revealed to me the immediate possibility of my own death.
>
> (T. Taylor 2002: 256)

A week later, as he was freeing a 1200-year-old skeleton from damp sand in Hungary, he realized that the inner psychic drama of his self-imposed transformation had had a powerful effect upon his attitude toward archaeology. "My experience helped me to break down an academically formalized, suspiciously bourgeois view of antiquity and forced me to start thinking in an emotionally engaged way about past states of mind" (T. Taylor 2002: 257).

Much more than Barnard's experience, Taylor's was a sort of ritual, not one that he had learned, but one that has been enacted countless times by Westerners who have found themselves to be without meaning in their lives and without hope. Unlike those, however, who end up in hospitals and cut themselves over and over without reaching any goal or finding any solution—people whose only hope seems to be to find a way to stop doing it to themselves—Taylor has never needed to do it again. He found something permanent, and his life's work has been defined by this meaning.

Jung

Jung experienced a number of transformative altered states. We have briefly considered the apprenticeship to Elijah (later called Philemon) which he underwent in his late thirties and illustrated in his *Red Book*. More than a decade later, when he was about fifty, his meetings with Mountain Lake and the Elgonyi resulted in the experience and formulation of his "personal myth." In his sixty-ninth year, 1944, he suffered a heart attack and lived for three weeks in another world, stripped of his "earthly existence," floating in his "primordial form" a thousand miles out in space over Ceylon.[4] He was reluctant to accept the verdict that he must return to this black and white, two-dimensional "box world." His nurse said he had had the "bright glow" she associated with the dying. He spent his days "weak, wretched, and . . . gloomy" with the thought that he had to return. In the early evening he would fall asleep and wake about midnight in a radiant ecstasy that he thought was "eternal bliss." Then, while awake in this blissful altered state, he had visions of the wedding of the gods, the ultimate union of the opposites: Tifereth and Malchuth from the Kabala, the Marriage of the Lamb in Jerusalem, Zeus and Hera. Sometimes *he* was the one being wed. Sometimes he was the wedding (*MDR*: 289–98).

Once recovered, he entered a fruitful period of writing.

> The vision of the end of all things gave me the courage to undertake new formulations. I no longer attempted to put across my own opinion, but surrendered myself to the current of my thoughts. Thus one problem after another revealed itself to me and took shape.
>
> (*MDR*: 297)

The visions "corrected" his attitude, made him tolerant of his mistakes and able to "affirm [his] own destiny." He learned to accept unconditionally "things as they are" and to live his own life without compromise. He now believed he had experienced the truth behind the hundreds of pages he had written on medieval European alchemy, the mystical experiments undertaken by our closest cultural relatives. He had experienced the *mysterium coniunctionis*, the union of the opposites that produces the Philosopher's Stone, the goal of the work, the life of conscious wholeness. Now he dared to edit those articles and have them published.

Statistical support

Each of these men underwent a confrontation with his own death that was vivid enough to be felt as a crisis, and each emerged from it with an enlarged sense of his own personal reality, the meaning of life, and the value of his professional efforts. Only Jung's may be seen as a "near-death" experience.

Although popular discussions of near-death experiences often revolve around the question of whether they demonstrate the reality of a life after death, sober reflection will find no evidence for drawing such metaphysical conclusions. By definition, they are "near" to death: death is approached but not experienced. What they do point to, however, is the possibility that an archetypal experience of such monumental importance and existential immediacy may function as an integrative/ transformative event and therefore benefit the lives of those who undergo it.[5]

Kenneth Ring, Professor of Psychology at the University of Connecticut, has done extensive statistical studies showing that those who have had the "core [near-death] experience" usually find themselves profoundly changed by it. The "core experience," as outlined by Moody (1975: 19–83), includes traveling out of the body, passing through a tunnel, meeting others including a "being of light," undergoing a life review, coming to a threshold that is not crossed, and then returning to this world (Ring 1982: 23f). Some of these experiences are shared by shamans in their soul-journeys to other planes of reality and probably by our ancestors who planned and painted the Ice Age caves. Jung's account does not include passage through a tunnel, but all of the other elements mentioned here were part of his experience.

Ring's research shows that the near-death experience is "largely independent of the means that brings it about" (illness, accident or suicide) and also has no relationship to the religiousness of the subject (Ring 1982: 130, 135). These and similar facts support the view that the near-death phenomenon is a universal human capability and not merely a cultural "suggestion." The long-term effects, however, are the main point, for they make it clear that a near-death experience is powerfully integrating and transformative. Ring summarizes the results of his questionnaires and statistical analyses:

> The typical near-death survivor emerges from his experience with a heightened sense of appreciation for life, determined to live life to the fullest. He has a sense of being reborn and a renewed sense of individual purpose in living . . . is more reflective and . . . adjusts more easily to the vicissitudes of life. . . . He becomes more compassionate toward others, more able to accept them unconditionally. He has achieved a sense of what is important in life and strives to live in accordance with his understanding of what matters.
>
> (Ring 1982: 157f)

Ring (1982: 237) concludes that "the core experience *is* a type of mystical experience that ushers one into the holographic domain. In this *state of consciousness*, there is a *new order of reality* that one becomes sensitive to." Here, by his italics, he seems to mean that the individual who has this sort of transforming experience comes to feel that she herself is a living part of the whole universe: "a gradual *shift* of consciousness from the ordinary world of appearance to a holographic reality of pure frequencies." The language suggests the vision of the goal in non-dualist Hinduism (*Advaita Vedanta*) or the universe of quantum mechanics.[6] Sometimes it seems as though Ring (1982) takes these images literally, while at other times he refers to them as "teachings" and "revelatory experiences," much as Jung does. This latter interpretation appears to be supported by the expanded horizon of Ring's second book, where he identifies the near-death phenomenon as belonging to a "family of related experiences" which includes the Hindu and Buddhist cultivation of kundalini (Ring 1984: 227).

The transformation process

Most evolutionists agree with Brian Hayden that altered states of consciousness "are incomprehensible unless they also confer advantageous survival benefits" (Hayden 2003: 21). William James had already hinted what those benefits might be when he said that every phase of consciousness provides its own "world" of information. In a "minimally polyphasic" sense, altered states make us feel better. Robin Dunbar, for instance, notes: "Religious people in general do suffer less frequently than non-religious folk from both physical and mental diseases; moreover, when they go down with something, religious people recover more rapidly from both the disease and any invasive treatment" (Dunbar 2005: 172).

By contrast, Jung's efforts imply a maximally polyphasic perspective. Altered states are valuable less for supporting the world of ordinary experience than for opening the way to unexpected depth and engaged meaning. Jung sought a mythic depiction of reality, a world in which the irrational is not "resented." He found that altered states of consciousness can make it possible for us to live in a richer world, more comprehensive, mysterious, and compelling. His dissatisfaction with European culture grew by stages. In his somnambulist cousin he found a will independent of the conscious mind but by no means formless. From Elijah, he learned to pay attention to the subtleties of what the unconscious was giving him and to tolerate the irrational. Mountain Lake made him realize that the ultimate gift from the unconscious would be a livable myth. In Africa, he found his own myth, the one that made him (and potentially every one of us) the second creator of the world. His near-death experiences brought him the "holographic" experience of being simultaneously both part of the cosmos and his individual self.

The capacity of the human psyche to rise above its imprisonment in the ordinary world of matter and logic Jung calls the *transcendent function*. He wastes no time speculating on how it might work, but merely notes that when we actively tolerate a conflict of interests, rational contradiction, or some other incompatibility, the self, our wholeness, somehow hands us a clue in the form of a symbolic solution to the problem (*CW6*: ¶828; *CW7*: ¶121; *CW8*: ¶131–93). The transcendent function is set in motion when we maintain steady attention on the conflict and feel how it pulls us in two directions at once. There is nothing more the ego can do but hold to the unsatisfying truth of the situation—not in a spirit of resignation, but with aroused attention. *Somehow* in that charged atmosphere, the transcendent function generates an energy gradient and a compelling course of action is revealed.

Toward a phenomenology of transformation

Recent researchers have identified subsidiary processes that help us understand that mysterious *Somehow* that lies behind Jung's transcendent function. Transcending the ordinary for the sake of personality change becomes less mysterious when the process is broken down into its parts. Utilizing such analyses, this section will describe what happens in more-or-less experiential language. It will be a phenomenology of transformation. The next section will take the objective point of view and consider the neurobiology of the same series of developments.

Not all altered states of consciousness effect major changes in the organization and integration of a psyche. The majority of non-ordinary experiences may easily be co-opted by ordinary consciousness as healings, sources of alternate perspectives, or simply entertaining "kicks." By contrast, transformative or integrative states cannot be so co-opted, for they decommission the ordinary and bring about a radical reorganization of brain and psyche.

Lesser altered states, however, play an important role in the process, for when they are valued and cultivated, they tend to call our ordinary assumptions into question. The more seriously we take them, the more likely they are to "destabilize" our habitual waking attitude toward self and world. This, in turn, opens the door to more dramatic effects, more serious self-questioning, as well as the re-evaluation of life-goals and practices. In short, by "destabilizing" normality they play a permissive role in the "manifestation of integrative potentials" (Winkelman 2000: 115). First the habitual world of experience must be rendered fragile, overloaded with non-ordinary information that splits the seams of our ordinary assumptions. The evidence points to the wisdom of the East, whose mystics say that enlightenment cannot be reached through the efforts of the ego, alone. Rather, fruit falls from the tree the moment it is ripe. When the disciple is ready, any sound, sight or blow from the master's staff can be the occasion of enlightenment. The accumulation of experiences that conflict with consensus reality is what "ripens" the psyche for change.

It is not always easy to accumulate enough destabilizing information to split the seams of our habitual attitudes, because brain and psyche function automatically to reduce conflict. The linear, logical, left-brain tendency to find consistency readily suppresses and judges invalid conflicting information—particularly the "irrational" bits that Westerners so much "resent." All of our cultural training resists transformation. Therefore any practices that encourage tolerance for the non-ordinary will surely assist the process of transformation. Jung, for example, might urge a patient to become curious about disturbing images and feelings, even to paint them or write poems about them, in a process akin to active imagination.

A process like this occurs naturally in REM sleep, that "basic mammalian memory process for evaluating experience and forming strategies" (Winkelman 2000: 136). It is the reason our dreams seem so ordinary and matter-of-fact while we are dreaming and so absurd when we wake up. "During dreams we find access to the activity and content of the oppositional infrastructure upon which ego consciousness rests. This activity . . . never pauses . . . [and behind it] are the fundamental neurognostic organizations often referred to in Jungian terms as *archetypes*"[7] (C. D. Laughlin *et al*. 1990: 268).

C. D. Laughlin and his associates, McManus and d'Aquili, are unusual among scientific investigators in having a fairly accurate understanding of what Jung meant by the term *archetype*. What they do not emphasize, however, is the *energy gradient which makes attractive and compelling* the new set of images and ideas and the new course of action. In the last analysis, it is always fascination or emotional attraction that makes psychological change possible. Splitting the seams of our old certainties, by itself, will only produce confusion and discontent, and in its extreme form, terror. The introduction of an energy gradient sets us rolling downhill toward new ways of thinking and being. This is the implication of Ring's work on the near-death experience. The realm of light at the end of the tunnel and the beings of light that seem to live there personify the gradient in that they represent an after-death existence of far greater scope and meaning than the two-dimensional, black-and-white "box world" the individual has left behind. By analogy with Ring's near-death experience, transformation unfolds "according to a single pattern almost as though the prospect of death serves to release a stored, common 'program' of feelings, perceptions, and experiences" (d'Aquili and Newberg 1999: 122).

Unconscious, unintegrated material will appear to the ego as non-ordinary, even absurd. An altered state as comprehensive as the near-death experience, however, introduces a new energy gradient which changes the organization of the mind. A simultaneous presentation of the familiar and the non-ordinary occurs in an "integrative mode of consciousness . . . [that is] analogous to Jung's transcendent function" (Winkelman 2000: 265). Then conscious and unconscious meet revealing a mysterious and compelling compatibility (Ibid.: 194). Subjectively, such a "revelation" demonstrates incontrovertibly in the form of direct evidence that not only is there more to one's being than the empirical ego but also there is more to reality than what can be known through ordinary states of consciousness (C. D. Laughlin *et al*. 1990: 227).

The neuropsychology of transformation

If neural processes in the brain and the experience of a conscious psyche are two descriptions of the same phenomenon (the psyche/brain identity theory we are provisionally accepting), we should expect that transformative/integrative states of consciousness will show up in the brain as harmonious, holistic forms of neural functioning. The brain ought to be as unified as the transformative state of consciousness that it supports, and that is precisely what we find.

Such unified brain states are exceptional, for as the chapter on the complexes describes, most everyday conscious activities involve specialized portions of the brain operating with relative independence from one another; sometimes they are even in conflict—as when a complex is constellated and an emotional over-reaction interrupts sober, confident, well-adapted behaviors. In such a situation, the "emotional brain" overwhelms the more "rational" cortex. That "emotional brain," also called the "limbic" system, includes the structures we discussed in Chapter 13: thalamus, hypothalamus, amygdala, and hippocampus. The limbic system is responsible for, among other things, maintaining altered states of consciousness characterized by alpha and theta brain waves, which are slower and more regular than the beta waves we employ in ordinary waking consciousness. Alpha waves characterize reverie states and dreaming, while the still-slower theta waves characterize the deepest states of meditation.

The first major pair of opposed brain structures in the ordinary waking state, then, are the limbic system and the cortex. The second pair are the two hemispheres of the cortex. The dominant (usually left) hemisphere is responsible for linear, linguistic, logical, and conceptual understandings, while the less dominant hemisphere recognizes patterns and shapes, and generally views its situation in the world as a matter of generalized wholes (gestalts). The third opposition is that between neurocognitive structures (neural networks) that are conscious and those that fall outside of the conscious field. In integrative states of consciousness, the entire brain enters into a hierarchic unity: the limbic system "drives" the frontal cortex, normally unconscious networks enter a widened conscious field, and the two hemispheres are synchronized (Winkelman 2000: 129). In its integrative state, the brain is as unified as is the "self" in Jung's conception. To understand how this state is achieved, we shall proceed one step at a time.

Tuning the autonomic nervous system

Standard descriptions of the nervous system divide it into two parts, the central nervous system (CNS) and the autonomic nervous system (ANS). The central nervous system includes the brain, spinal cord and most of the nerve net that branches out from them to innervate the "voluntary" striated muscles that move our skeleton and that also gather sensory information to bring back to the brain for processing. Nearly all that we have said so far about the nervous system has been limited to the functioning of the CNS. The autonomic nervous system, on the other hand, innervates the "smooth," involuntary muscles and glands of the internal organs, which operate for the most part outside of conscious control. The autonomic nervous system can be "tuned" because it actually comprises two opposed subsystems, called the sympathetic and parasympathetic (Figure 14.1). Because

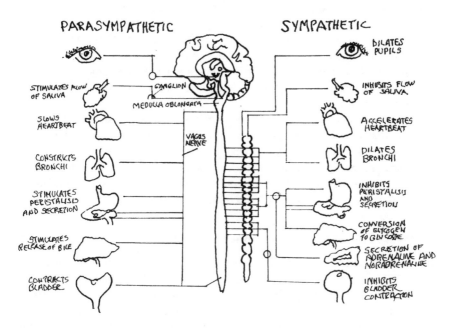

Figure 14.1 The autonomic nervous system.

Source: original pen and ink drawing by Ann Yoost Brecke.

the sympathetic nervous system *arouses* the body for emergencies, it is often called the fight-or-flight system. The parasympathetic system, by contrast, is often called "*quiescent*" because it regulates digestion, growth, relaxation, and sleep. To "tune" the ANS means to regulate the balance between sympathetic arousal and parasympathetic quiescence. "Manipulations of the autonomic nervous system . . . are the basis for experiences of higher phases of consciousness" (Winkelman 2000: 166).

Several high-energy states of autonomic tuning have been found to underlie significant types of altered states of consciousness. In the following paragraphs, I rely largely upon the work of C. D. Laughlin *et al.* (1990: 319–21), d'Aquili and Newberg (1999: 24–6, 90f) and Winkelman (2000: 127–45).

Hyperarousal of the sympathetic system

This "tuning" is typically achieved by vigorous activity, including rituals done to rapid drumbeat and singing, extended periods of intense dancing, long-distance running, and other extreme athletic feats extended over long periods of time. Because they all involve pushing the body to its limits, these techniques of achieving high arousal are known as "bottom-up driving." Brain and psyche (the "top") are affected by high stresses placed on the body (the "bottom"); or perhaps only upon the sensory organs in the case of rhythmic drumming or flashing lights. The sympathetic system can also be driven to high arousal "from the top-down," by intense mental activities, as when Francis of Assisi deliberately placed himself in a condition of shame and terror before "the Lord of the Whole Earth" (cf. Haule 2004). Practitioners of "left-hand Tantra" employ a similar technique when they "heroically" violate the five taboos in order to induce a powerful state of arousal (cf. Haule 1999b).

The effects of stimulating the sympathetic system to a high state of arousal are keen alertness and concentration, much as we know through experiencing moments of impending disaster, when everything slows down and our thought processes are strangely clear and vivid. One has the feeling of being able to channel vast quantities of energy without special effort. One feels oneself inside of and traveling along with a powerful impersonal "flow."

Hyperarousal of the parasympathetic system

Probably "hyperquiescence" would be an appropriate description of this condition, if it were not for the fact that the term seems self-contradictory. What is meant is that the parasympathetic system goes into overdrive, affecting portions of the limbic brain and the endocrine glands that produce hormones to reduce breathing, heart-rate, and waste-product collection, while engorging the erectile tissues and increasing salivation. Bottom-up driving includes fasting and other austerities that cause the body to conserve its resources; slow, sedate rituals; or extended sexual foreplay accompanied by intense concentration. Top-down driving involves most forms of sitting meditation when pursued with prolonged intensity.

The effects of extended high levels of arousal in the parasympathetic system are described as oceanic tranquility and bliss. All burdens and stresses fall away. Probably this is what Jung referred to when he said that his humanity was stripped away and he was left in his "primal form" during his near-death experience. The movement of time that characterizes ordinary consciousness dissolves into an eternal now. The individual is free of intrusive thoughts, feelings or bodily sensations. It is a state of relaxation usually associated with sleep, except that in this case it is illumined by heightened awareness.

ANS spillover phenomena

In the extraordinary situations that produce the integrative/transformative state of consciousness, the halves of the autonomic nervous system—although they usually inhibit one another—experience simultaneous overdrive. In the first case, when the quiescent system is pushed to its limits, eruption of the arousal system can sometimes break through. At this point, the state of oceanic tranquility opens onto the state described in yoga manuals as "absorption in the object." The meditator loses awareness of the usual separation between herself and the object of her one-pointed attention, and she seems to become one with it. When this happens, she feels a tremendous release of blissful energy.

In the other direction, the sympathetic system, when pushed to its limits for an extended period of time, becomes exhausted. The synaptic vesicles in the brain, which are responsible for the synthesis, storage, and release of the primary neurotransmitter of the sympathetic system, noradrenaline, have a limited lifetime. When they become exhausted, the sympathetic system collapses and the parasympathetic takes over. This results in an orgasmic, rapturous explosion of ecstasy in the midst of the "flow" experience that had been in effect before the spillover.

Spillover in either direction results in what d'Aquili and Newberg (1999) call activation of the "holistic operator." This is the capacity of brain and psyche to experience a union of the opposites, a blurring of the usual cognitive boundaries, and an ecstatic sense of belonging to the whole: internal union, union with all of humanity, and union with the cosmos.

The integrative state of consciousness

Contemporary research shows that the brain functions as a series of systems nested within other systems (d'Aquili and Newberg 1999: 69); it is coherent with Jung's 1935 conception of Complex Psychology, according to which it is not ultimate building blocks that we should be looking for, but rather for patterns within patterns. Still, some patterns conflict with and inhibit others, which leads to our everyday experience of our consciousness being fragmented. Such fragmentation is largely "a by-product of both the evolutionary specialization of the left [temporal] lobe for language and serial sequencing of movement and the capacity of consciousness to be canalized [by] . . . conditioned entrainments" (C. D. Laughlin *et al.* 1990: 133). "Conditioned entrainments" may be exemplified by the complexes.

Ordinary consciousness, therefore, seems to lock us into a world that is filled with objects, events, and processes that entrain the same neural networks whereby we recreate for ourselves the same experiences over and over again. Within such a lived-world, it is hardly surprising that humans, as far back as we can see into our evolutionary past, have sought "to release the stranglehold that the conscious rational mind has on our thoughts and experiences" and "to open up channels of communication and experience to other parts of the brain such as the right hemisphere and the older emotional parts" such as the limbic system (Hayden 2003: 66). All altered states of consciousness have the capacity to reduce that stranglehold, and all point to and give us a taste for a larger and more satisfying world of experience. All of them have the effect of exhausting the dominant hemisphere, which is responsible for what Jung calls "directed thinking," for it "fatigues more rapidly and releases control to the right hemisphere" (Winkelman 2000: 194).

Nevertheless, it is only the integrative state of consciousness that is capable of completely transforming our experience of brain and psyche. Spillover from a highly aroused parasympathetic nervous system entrains the frontal cortex, which usually works on behalf of the ego. This entrainment from within (as opposed to the complex-reaction which entrains via events observed in the outer world) is achieved by "highly coherent and synchronized slow-wave discharges emanating from the limbic system and related lower brain structures." What results is an "integration of information processing across all three levels of the brain and the two hemispheres" (Winkelman 2000: 114). By the three levels of the brain, Winkelman means, from top to bottom, the cortex, the limbic system, and the brainstem.

As a consequence of this unified brain operation, neural networks that normally remain unconscious become accessible in the form of "[objective] content rather than as self" (Winkelman 2000: 129). This peculiar expression corresponds to Jung's observation that individuation cannot begin until an "other" appears in the unconscious with which the ego can enter into dialogue (e.g. *CW14*: ¶753; *CW18*: ¶1171). Winkelman (2000) means that in ordinary consciousness we take the feelings and notions that occur to us as part of ourselves. We lack the perspective provided by "original thinking" and have no distance from them. We are thus apt to conclude that I am the type of person who has such lofty or nasty feelings. In the integrative state, however, this unconscious material appears as other than me and therefore contains information I can learn how to use. This gives me "greater flexibility and conscious control [over my] biological and mental systems" (Winkelman 2000: 129).

The integrative/transformative state of consciousness is an archetypal pattern in the sense that all humans are capable of experiencing it. It is something we have in common with all our ancestors going back at least as far as the Upper Paleolithic, and very likely much further. Insofar as everything biological and psychological is comprised of patterns nested within patterns, the process of integration/transformation is the Archetype of archetypes, the largest pattern within which all the others are nested. An archetypal behavior pattern like communicating in language, for instance, has nested within it patterns of sound recognition, gesture and body-language responsiveness, concept formation, and many other contributing faculties. But linguistic understanding has to slide out of the driver's seat for transformation to occur. It is not that language can play no part in the transformation, for we will be able to articulate aspects of the process while it is going on and after it has ended. But the language archetype will become just one of many nested means of understanding when the entire brain and psyche are synchronized by coherent slow waves from the limbic system that integrate all of the information processing regions of the brain. This unified constellation of brain activity *is* the integrative/transformative state. It is how our physical substrate behaves when the "self" operates as "transcendent function."

When an individual finds the "personal myth" that gives his life transcendent meaning, it will appear in this exceptional state of consciousness. Unquestionably, near-death experiences are a form of the integrative state. Winkelman seems to suggest, too, that "big dreams" are related to the same phenomenon, for they reflect "transpersonal and cross-modal potentials" that imply "limbic-frontal integration," though in more limited form (Winkelman 2000: 142).

Part III

History of consciousness

Part I has demonstrated that Jung's concept of the archetype as a species-specific pattern of behavior is harmonious in good detail with the various evolutionary sciences. Part II has demonstrated that when Jung's model of the psyche is interpreted along the lines of the psyche/brain identity theory which dominates today's discussions, it is strongly supported by contemporary neuroscience.

Another essential dimension of Analytical Psychology is Jung's diagnosis of our current socio-cultural situation as an unhealthy psychological environment for the modern Western individual. For Jung, the twentieth century represented the culmination of a long historical development in the West, whereby a strong and well-defined ego has gradually been achieved at the expense of losing organic rootedness in our species nature. We act as though we have no foundation in our collective unconscious, believing that our identity as conscious agents is sufficient. This is why we come across as hectic, lost and hollow-eyed searchers to outside observers like Mountain Lake, the Pueblo spokesman. Jung concludes that we need a myth that gives depth to our lives, and that this will never be found so long as we continue to "resent the irrational." We have to open our culture to polyphasic living, cultivate altered states of consciousness and allow our perspective to be transformed.

Part III will begin addressing these issues. We will consider the history of consciousness from monkeys and chimpanzees through the modern humans of the West. We begin with Jung's views on that history and then follow with what the evolutionary sciences have been able to discover about it. The evidence is quite strong that we have slowly extricated ourselves from a sleepy embeddedness in myth to the point of believing ourselves to be identical with our empirical egos and their monumental accomplishments through science and technology. But we have been left longing for what seems no longer to exist, the sort of meaningful discoveries available in a maximally polyphasic environment such as is common among simple hunter-gatherers. There is much we have to recover.

Chapter 15

Jung on the history of consciousness

The shamans of the Paleolithic are close relatives of the often-maligned "urban shamans" of the late twentieth century. The social context has changed but not our organism's capacities. The same autonomic nervous system has been "tuned" for at least 50,000 years—if not 600,000 or perhaps two million. Several authors have asserted that the capacity for generating altered states of consciousness over such a timescale proves that non-ordinary states of consciousness have long been important survival tools for primates. Natural selection would have eliminated such faculties if they had been jeopardizing rather than enhancing of our evolutionary fitness. Every talent, however, can be used for a variety of purposes. Over time, our ancestors gradually moved from living in tiny isolated bands of hunter-gatherers to herding, agriculture, towns and cities. Artisans, traders, and industrialists have changed the human landscape. In the course of all these changes, different social classes learned to use altered states of consciousness in different ways and for different purposes.

Today we can sketch in broad strokes a history of human consciousness that draws upon evidence from archaeology and anthropology while not forgetting the larger context of what has remained the same in human neurobiology. Doing so will show that Jung's suspicions about our contemporary rootlessness are well founded. This chapter and the ones that follow will take up the progressive story of what we have done with our psychological capacities by paying special attention to the evidence for how our ancestors used rituals. As our first step, however, this chapter will review Jung's arguments regarding the history of consciousness.

Throwing off unconsciousness

The most persistent theme in Jung's writings is that it requires a great effort to "throw off unconsciousness," something that can be accomplished only with "regular work," for that is the force that "has made our humanity," and it first appeared when primitive humans engaged in their "ceremonies" (*Sem25*: 30). Consciousness-altering rituals have performed a great deal of the work required in our species' throwing off its unconsciousness, and hard work is still required of us moderns, "For the strongest thing in man is *participation mystique* . . . stronger than the need for individuality" (*Sem28*: 63).

In this formulation, Jung expands the meaning and application of Lévy-Bruhl's (1922) concept of mystical participation. Lévy-Bruhl means that empirical objects and events "participate" in an invisible world of collective representations. Thus the inert corpse participates in the reality of the dangerous, demanding but invisible ghost that hovers near it; and the crocodile that killed a villager on the bank of the river mystically participates in the identity of the witch who is believed to bear ultimate responsibility for the death (Lévy-Bruhl 1922: 51–7). Without denying Lévy-Bruhl's understanding of the term, Jung emphasizes that *participation mystique* is an everyday experience for every human being. It is a way of remaining unconscious and therefore requires being "thrown off." For example, individual family members are regularly submerged in a collective family identity. "[R]elationship is only possible where there is separateness. Since *participation mystique* is the usual condition in marriage . . . one sinks into that bottomless pit of identity and after a while discovers that nothing happens any longer" (*Sem28*: 63).

Clearly, the tendency to merge and become unconscious stays with us, so that each individual has to wage a constant battle against slipping back. Nevertheless, the hunter-gatherers of 40,000 years ago began a project with their rituals that lets us moderns start off at a higher rung of consciousness. For over a much smaller stretch of time, Jung observes that the effort to throw off a stultifying unconsciousness "is the principle underlying the history of the West in the past two millennia" (*Sem25*: 30). We start off today with much less to throw off than our ancestors had at the time of Christ. In making such a statement, Jung is aware, too, that his own perspective inevitably shares in an unconscious *participation mystique* characteristic of the twentieth century:

> Unfortunately we cannot see into the future, and so we do not know how far we still belong in the deepest sense to the Middle Ages. If, from the watch-towers of the future, we should seem stuck in medievalism up to our ears, I for one would be little surprised.
>
> (*CW15*: ¶179)

The ancients

Since Jung acquired most of his information from the writings of people like Lévy-Bruhl who studied present-day "primitives," he assumed, as most Westerners seemed to do in the first half of the twentieth century, that the hunter-gatherers living on the margins of our modern world, protected by terrain and climate from predatory industrial entities, give us a pretty good idea of what our Stone Age ancestors must have been like. He thought they had "no trace of individuality," but only the collective identity of *participation mystique*. Individuality, in fact, "is a relatively recent acquisition in the history of the human mind and human culture" (*CW6*: ¶12).

As might be expected of a European who acquired an upper class education,[1] at a time when archaeology was in its infancy—a field that fascinated him but promised no income—the "ancients" for Jung were primarily the people of classical antiquity, the Hellenistic world. He did not idealize them. In fact, he held that they had "no control over themselves and were at the mercy of their affects" (*CW5*: ¶644). He illustrates this claim with a passage from St. Augustine's *Confessions*, where poor Alypius, who had sworn off the bloody entertainment of the circus, allows himself to be dragged along with his friends to watch the gladiators. He vows to conquer himself despite temptation, even closes his eyes and covers his ears, but eventually he is drawn in by the roar of the crowd and becomes more dissolute than ever (*CW5*: ¶102).

For Jung, late antiquity represented the end of an era, "full of sickish sentimentality" because "the spark had gone out of the conscious standpoint" (*Sem25*: 69). Those who did overcome "the world of the senses" did so though a rarefied "type of thinking [that was] independent of external factors." They were fascinated by the "sovereignty of the idea" (*CW5*: ¶113), and although they knew mathematics and physics and had master craftsmen, "they never got beyond the stage of inventing amusing curiosities. . . . What they lacked was training in directed thinking. The secret of cultural development is the mobility and disposability of psychic energy" (*CW5*: ¶17). Because it never occurred to them to apply their ideas to achieve practical results, they did no real "work." Hunter-gatherers with their rituals were superior insofar as they had learned to focus their energies on the practical demands of life.

The upper classes got their work done by enslaving the masses. The slaves and downtrodden embodied the unconscious in late antiquity, overlooked and forgotten forces which finally transformed the world. They were easily attracted to the mystery religions, Gnosticism, and Christianity, all of which strove to reverse the value system of the larger culture by idealizing and cultivating mystical states of consciousness, and devising and following training programs that led initiates through a series of spiritual attainments. Participants in these movements "transferred power relations inward," that is, they suppressed their own instinctual life much as they themselves were suppressed by the upper classes (*CW6*: ¶108). Many of them fled to the desert to live as anchorites. Their "libido went over into spiritual values" which brought about an "enormous change in human mentality in [the space of only] 300 years" (*Sem25*: 68f).

The Middle Ages

Christianity suppressed instinct and the material world by idealizing "the imperishable value of the human soul" (*CW6*: ¶8). "Though unfree and tyrannized by superstition, [medieval man] was at least biologically nearer to that unconscious wholeness which primitive man enjoys in even larger measure, and the wild animal possesses to perfection"—closer, that is, than we moderns are (*CW8*: ¶426). By the time of the Gothic period, Christianity was in complete control, and there was a single "language and belief from north to south" in Europe. The people of Gothic culture were completely convinced of a single set of truths, "all doubt [was] excluded" (*Sem25*: 56).

The implication is that by Gothic times people had been cut off from the primitive roots of local traditions, which may have been superstitious but nevertheless carried hints of unconscious wholeness. Gothic people, therefore, had traded an unconscious rootedness in the self for a consciously articulated doctrine, a set of dogmas that may have had a certain archetypal form but was an "unnatural" product of "directed thinking" and, far from growing out of our human roots, was imposed from above by a well-organized Church. They knew everything in advance. Theological certainty imposed from without had silenced the voice of the self within, and the nature spirits fell silent.

Fascinated with this development, Jung began collecting portraits made between the thirteenth and nineteenth centuries, and found that after about the middle of the sixteenth he felt he knew the people who had been painted. Their individuality was unmistakable, as they twinkled with opinions, quirks and the awareness of their differences. Before that, "Gothic man" appears as a stranger: "His eyes are stone-like and inexpressive; none of the vivacity to be seen in our eyes is in them." They were not "individuals" as we are, but they shared a commonality of mind that Jung found symbolized in the smile of the *Mona Lisa*. It is "the smile of a man who meets on the street the woman with whom he is having a secret liaison. There is understanding in that smile—'We know,' it seems to say" (*Sem25*: 55).

The Renaissance

The central theme of Western civilization underwent a sea change with the Renaissance, when Europe exchanged a heavenly goal for an earthly one, and the verticality of the cathedrals gave way to the horizontality of the voyages of discovery. Contrary to general opinion, the spirit of antiquity was not reborn, rather "the spirit of medieval Christianity underwent strange pagan transformations" (*CW9ii*: ¶78). Thus, when the great pioneer of the new cultural vision, Francesco Petrarch, climbed Mt. Ventoux in the fourteenth century,[2] he found the earthly panorama overwhelming, and instead of enjoying it—for he showed greater self-mastery than Alypius a millennium earlier—he opened his constant companion, St. Augustine's *Confessions*, and read:

> "And men go forth and admire lofty mountains and broad seas, and roaring torrents, and the ocean, and the course of the stars, and turn away from themselves while doing so." His brother to whom he read these words could not understand why he closed the book and said no more.
>
> (*CW5*: ¶21, n. 21)

Why he said no more, Jung thought, was that the antique feeling for nature was breaking through in his own mind and endangering the Christian Gothic principles in which he had been raised. In a vague but accurate sense, he seemed to know that, "The more successful the penetration and advance of the new scientific spirit, the more [the newly won rational and intellectual stability of the human mind would become] prisoner of the world it had conquered." The Renaissance represented not that Christian spirituality was about to be "incarnated" in the newly discovered material world but that it would be submerged as "the descent of the . . . Nous into the dark embrace of Physis" (*CW5*: ¶113). The occluding embrace of spirit by matter (Nous by Physis) is the theme underlying the European alchemy that Jung studied for so many years. In Jung's interpretation, Spirit had gone underground again in the Renaissance, and the alchemists tried to free it through their laboratory work. Unlike us, they projected their unconscious intimations of spirit into the mercury, sulfur and salt of their experiments. They saw with their imagination as well as with their physical eyes, and they did not know the difference. Very much as Lévy-Bruhl's primitives mixed up empirical objects and events with collective representations, the alchemists operated in a material world enriched with archetypal significance, making it far more mythic and mysterious than ours.

The great schism

By the sixteenth century a real split had taken place, and the world had lost most of its mystery and wonder. There was no longer any reason for a young Petrarch to shield his eyes from a magnificent vista, for he had nothing left to lose. Alchemy was abandoned because the scientific spirit it had helped to generate no longer had room for collective representations. Scientists had to attend to their empirical measurements, only, and banish emotion and imagination from their work. They knew what "ordinary states of consciousness" were for the first time. The materials with which they worked were less mysterious and thrilling, once "the great schism" had separated perception from imagination (*CW14*: ¶101). In fact, there were a great number of schisms taking place: between science and philosophy, between Protestant and Catholic, between nation and nation, between science and experience. The world of everyday life became much poorer, while technology flourished. Three and a half centuries ago, we finally learned to work with directed thinking, and this forced us to separate ourselves from one another. Our modern sense of individuality had begun to develop.

The modern world

Today, we are far more concerned with a strident and superficial "individualism" than with genuine "individuation" (*CW7*: ¶267). We look outward to the rest of the world for guidance, but we need "to apply some concentration and criticism to the psychic material which manifests itself not outside, but in our private lives (*CW6*: ¶317). Christian truths have become "mystical absurdities" (*CW11*: ¶56) to our "sham enlightenment. . . . Most people are satisfied with the not very intellectual view that the whole purpose of dogma is to state flat impossibilities" (*CW5*: ¶113).

We never imagine the sort of altered state that would produce a dogma which does not resent irrationalities, for our monophasic culture values only the results of directed thinking.

The modern individual, therefore, has but a "veneer of civilization" covering "a dark-skinned brute" who has no interest in self-development and self-criticism (*CW7*: ¶156). Disunity is our "hallmark." "The neurotic is only a special instance of the disunited man who ought to harmonize nature and culture within himself (*CW7*: ¶16). To harmonize like that, though, we need a living myth, as powerful as that of Mountain Lake, but adapted to each of us, individually. Only a "living religion ... allows the [inner] primitive man adequate means of expression through richly developed symbolism" (*CW7*: ¶156). The modern individual has an ego, finally, but not much depth. In the huge impersonal societies of today, our individuality is submerged in a collective "mass" identity. It must learn to recover its instinctual and archetypal roots.

In his 1925 Seminar, Jung seems to have had a genuine hope that some sort of progress along these lines might be on the horizon, for he used the same words to describe European society prior to the First World War as he did the upper classes of late antiquity: "We lived in a world of sickish sentimentality" (*Sem25*: 53). If sickish sentimentality means that the spark has gone out of a civilization's consciousness, as it had two millennia ago when it set the stage for the spiritual revolution that Christianity and her sister religions provided—a revolution that still needed an ego to solidify its gains—perhaps the sickish sentimentality of the *fin de siècle* and the violence to which it led might yet be setting the stage for another revolution. Maybe we can finally use the coherence and stability of a dependable ego to integrate instinct with social adaptation and thereby find the track of our personal myth.[3]

Erich Neumann on the history of consciousness

Discussion of Jung's views on the history of consciousness would not be complete without including the classic work of the man who, in his short life, was arguably Jung's most promising disciple. Erich Neumann (1905–60) was thirty years Jung's junior and studied with him in the early 1930s before emigrating from Berlin to Tel Aviv. He published *The Origins and History of Consciousness* in 1949, and Jung warmly praised it in a Foreword, in which he says that the book "begins just where I, too, if I were granted a second lease on life would start to gather up [the fragments and unfinished thoughts] of my own writings ... and knead them into a whole."

There is some question in my mind, however, as to whether this claim is accurate, for *Origins* contains none of the history we have just discussed, devotes no attention to how people lived their lives, and sketches no series of ages, each with its distinctive attitude toward the world. Furthermore, Neumann makes no attempt to enter into "pre-history," the much larger piece of our past, when our species and those that preceded us were unable to write, or possibly even to speak. Those people were surely conscious, however, for they left behind substantial evidence. Neumann's sources do not go much further back than 6000 years ago, when cuneiform writing began. Even then, however, he is not careful to organize his materials in a strictly historical manner.

Origins tells the history of consciousness as though our race were born about 6000 years ago with the mentality of an infant. We then went through infancy, childhood, adolescence, heroic adulthood, and transformative middle age. In fact the book has two parts in each of which the same development is described, once as "mythological stages" in the evolution of the human race, and again as "psychological stages" in the development of the individual. Like Freud in *Totem and Taboo*, Neumann uses the development of the individual according to theory as the template that gives shape and meaning to history.[4] It is an idealized history and a work in which theory takes precedence over evidence. But he does agree with Jung on the fundamental point: that the central theme of our history is our ongoing attempt to throw off unconsciousness.

Uroboros

The central image of *Origins* is the ancient Greek symbol of the snake biting its tail, the uroboros, the unconsciousness of not knowing the beginning from the end, that constantly cycles and has no sense of time. If the uroboros represents mythic consciousness devoid of any sense of individuality, then it could well stand for those many hundreds of millennia when the same hand axe was made by generation after generation, their "heads nodding" through the "rolling consciousness" of manufacture, going through the motions of chipping off the same flakes in the same way it had always been done.

If we take this approach, Neumann's language about the difficulty an infant has in separating itself from its mother and establishing its own identity, the overwhelming pull back toward the womb of total nurture and protection, would describe how hard it is too extricate oneself from making the same old hand axe and telling the same old stories that had "always" been told to the same nodding heads around the same campfire, back almost to the African savannahs before fire had been controlled or axes sharpened out of stones that were picked up just when they were needed, used unattended and then dropped and forgotten.

If this is what uroboros means, then arriving at the stage of the Ice Age caves might well correspond to Neumann's age of the son-lover of the great mother, as in the myth of Adonis and Aphrodite or of Tammuz and Ishtar. The son longs for his mother sexually. He believes he wants her as wife; he wants to merge with her without losing his individuality and independence. But he never succeeds. Every one of those myths ends with the death of the son, his sacrifice. He lives on impersonally in the pine tree or the stalk of wheat. He never escapes from the eternal mythic round of the uroboros, but he does see it for the magical, consciousness-changing, eros-charged world of longing that it is. The painting of the Ice Age caves would have required such recognition and longing. Those Ice Age cathedrals represent a sort of adolescence of the human race, even as they remained pretty much unchanged for some 30,000 years.

Only some time after that comes the age of the hero, of lasting discovery, of a relatively independent sense of identity. This was the age of the Sun god who descends into his mother's womb in the Western Sea every night to fight with the treacherous uncertainties of his Amfortas wound and rise renewed out of the Eastern Sea every morning. Only with this sort of personal identity and conscious need of renewal was it possible for the hero to become the "Lord of the Two Worlds," as Joseph Campbell calls him in *The Hero with a Thousand Faces* (1949). This is the hero Jung describes in *Symbols of Transformation*, moving back and forth from the empirical world to the mythic world and always applying what he had learned in the other world to solve the problems of this one—doing the work, in short, that the twentieth century shirked in its superficial satisfaction with technology and the ordinary consciousness that makes it possible.

The new ethic

Neumann's *Depth Psychology and a New Ethic* (1949a) is also, implicitly, a history of consciousness.[5] He describes three stages of ethical development: first, the old ethic as practiced by the masses, second, the old ethic as practiced by the "elite," and third, the new ethic. In every case, the source of an ethic comes in the form of prescriptions handed down by a "voice." In the case of the old ethic, the voice is the authority of divinity or its spokesperson: Moses, Christ, Muhammad, etc. The new ethic's voice comes from within the individual as the requirements of the self. The new ethic, therefore, describes the path of individuation.

When the masses follow the old ethic, they obey prescriptions laid down by their tradition's founder to the letter of the law. They are prone to feel righteous when they do so and to project onto non-practitioners the shadow of their resentment over the limitations the rules impose upon their freedom. This situation corresponds well with fundamentalist religionists who try to force everyone to follow the prescriptions of their tradition and condemn those who do not.

The "elite" follow the old ethic in an entirely different way. They are the "saints" of their traditions. Rather than follow prescriptions slavishly as externally imposed requirements, the elite use the prescriptions to examine their own shadows. Instead of accusing others of sin, they accuse themselves. They find themselves guilty of gluttony, for instance, when they allow the very thought of food to distract them from their worship of God. Instead of creating social strife by shadow projection, they look within and become more conscious of their own motives.

Practitioners of the *new* ethic look to the dialogue between ego and self for their prescriptions. Traditional external pronouncements regarding right and wrong are for the new ethicists not self-evidently true, but are respected for having long served a noble purpose. Although anything that has been universally accepted for centuries must be worthy of respect, in the last analysis it is the dialogue with the self that has the final word. One may certainly be mistaken in following what seems to be the requirements of the self. Caution and self-examination are essential. But the new ethic represents the Jungian ideal: to integrate the rational with the irrational, the achievements of ordinary consciousness with the insights provided by altered states of consciousness, to relinquish linearity for wholeness.[6]

The three stages of Neumann's argument, therefore, appear to be a schematic depiction of what might be hoped for in the history of the human psyche. First come rules applied within the context of a mythic narrative and behind it the threat of punishment. In the second stage, the rules are internalized and the individual begins to become truly conscious of her own motives while remaining under the influence of an authority figure's altered states of consciousness. Third, one learns to rely on one's own altered states to find the path most deeply one's own. This last stage is, in fact, the only option in a world where the traditional religions have lost their force and the mythic source of meaning no longer comes from without but only from within.

Chapter 16

History of consciousness
Primate rituals

In this chapter and the ones that follow, we will trace the phylogenetic story of psyche's evolution as progressively more elaborate brains designed ever more complex societies and the ritual behaviors to maintain them. We begin in this chapter with monkeys and chimpanzees, and will also entertain some speculations on Australopithecines and Archaic Humans. In every case ritual has been used to strengthen and differentiate social structure and to prepare the group as a whole to meet future tasks. Before making this argument, however, we will need to discuss how we are approaching our central unifying theme, ritual.

A comprehensive approach to ritual

When Jung cited primitive rituals as the sort of "work" primitives do to "throw off unconsciousness," he meant that "ritual actions bring about a spiritual prepara-tion . . . to direct the libido towards the unconscious to compel it to intervene," in short to alter their consciousness. "Magical ceremonies, sacrifices, invocations, prayer, and suchlike" create an energy-gradient with an emotional charge that persuades participants to engage in activities they might otherwise resist (*CW5*: ¶450). One of his favorite examples comes from Australia, described in an article by K. T. Preuss (1904) on the origins of religion and art. Men of the Wachandi tribe dig a pit in the earth, surround it with bushes to make it resemble a woman's genitals, and dance around it all night with their spears held before them like erect penises, shouting: " 'Pulli nira, pulli nira, wataka!' (Not a pit, not a pit, but a c—!)" (*CW5*: ¶213). Jung understood this ritual as a means to mobilize their sexual energy and direct it toward the earth, where—unlike the pleasures of the hammock—the process of fecundation requires hard work: planting, weeding and harvesting.

Such an argument is not out of favor with many anthropologists and archaeolo-gists, but Brian Hayden warns us not to take it too far. He doubts "religious monuments requiring huge amounts of labor such as Stonehenge or the Pyramid of the Sun in Mexico were built because of religious fervor" (Hayden 2003: 18). Religion may have been a motive, but so were economic interests and political power. It appears to me that Hayden is in the mainstream of scientific opinion today regarding the role of ritual. It must be understood within the entire context of a people's life, and that means psychology, neurobiology, economics, politics and history must all be taken into consideration.

Our aim is to sketch a history of consciousness by tracing the one behavior pattern that is widely accepted to be the sort of "work" that our ancestors have done, age after age, to "throw off" their unconsciousness, the one Jung identified in his 1925 seminar: ritual. We wish to braid a rope of several strands—evolution, ethology, archaeology, anthropology, neurobiology, and psychology—just the sort of collaborative effort Jung dreamed of. Fortunately, there exists a group of scholars that has been collaborating in just this way since the late 1970s. They call themselves "biogenetic structuralists."

Biogenetic structuralism

The central concern of biogenetic structuralism is that interpretations of behavior have to be consistent with the evidence for how our intelligent organism works, as discovered by the neuro-sciences (McManus *et al.* 1979: 343). They address our thesis, whether a scientific foundation exists for the behaviors Jung called "archetypal." Biogenetic structuralists accept the psyche/brain identity theory: *mind* is the name we give to the brain's experience of its own functioning, while the brain provides mind with its structure (C. D. Laughlin *et al.* 1990: 13). They hold that the evolution of the genome—to some degree—determines the brain's structure, and a brain so structured generates the characteristic activities which *are* our behavior. When they say genes determine brain structure "to some degree," they describe it as "*the biogenetic law*": behavior is always a function of the nervous system interacting with the environment (C. D. Laughlin *et al.* 1990: 5).

Most of the principal authors who call themselves biogenetic structuralists have already been met in previous chapters. They are, in alphabetic order: Eugene G. d'Aquili, until his death in 1998 Clinical Associate Professor of Psychiatry at the University of Pennsylvania; Charles D. Laughlin, Jr., Professor of Anthropology at Carleton University in Ottawa; John McManus, independent scholar of psychology and the cognitive sciences; Andrew B. Newberg, Clinical Assistant Professor of Radiology and Instructor in Psychiatry at the University of Pennsylvania; and, finally, a man who has not collaborated with the others, but cites their work as foundational for his own, Michael Winkelman, Senior Lecturer and Director of the Ethnographic Field School in the Department of Anthropology, Arizona State University. There are at least seventeen other scholars who have contributed to the cross-disciplinary project.[1] In addition to the work of the biogenetic structuralists, and particularly their classic, *The Spectrum of Ritual* (d'Aquili *et al.* 1979), our account of the history of consciousness through the millennia of ritual activities conducted by our ancestors will draw upon the work of several archaeologists.[2]

This group describes its work as *biogenetic* to emphasize their contention that behavioral patterns are inherited, the archetypes biologically generated. To ignore neural networks and rhythms is to risk perpetuating the confusion of having two separate theories (psychology and biology) and two separate data collections with no bridge to connect them (C. D. Laughlin *et al*. 1990: 83).

Structuralism was the name of the dominant school of anthropology when the biogenetic group formed. Claude Lévi-Strauss and André Leroi-Gourhan sought to find the "deep structures" of a society's behaviors by examining the imagery of its myths and social conventions. "Semiotic structuralism," as our group describes the effort, studied symbols to find "the unconscious in culture."[3] Our biogenetic collaborators agree that deep structures should be found, but they look to genes and neurons for the deepest and most dependable foundation. They have no argument with the likelihood deep structures will manifest in a society's imagery, but they look first to neurobiology to avoid contributing to irreconcilable theories. In addition, they criticize Lévi-Strauss's approach for being unrealistically based upon a timeless view of unchanging social structure ("synchronic"), while their own school presumes the constant change that societies everywhere manifest ("diachronic").

They claim an illustrious set of precursors for biogenetic structuralism: C. G. Jung, for his theory of inherited archetypal patterns,[4] and the philosopher A. N. Whitehead, for his process metaphysics, wherein reality's building blocks are events rather than objects, and events comprise "organismic systems within systems" rather than "basic units." Other precursors include Jean Piaget, Teilhard de Chardin, Henri Bergson, and the early anthropologist E. B. Tylor, who introduced the term *animism* (C. D. Laughlin *et al*. 1979: 3–6).

The biogenetic structuralists hold that any adequate theory of consciousness must begin from "neurognosis," the fact that everything we know (*gnosis* = knowledge) is a function of the neural activity of the brain. Probably their most useful assumption is that the neocortex is constantly driven by a "*cognitive imperative*," an "impetus to apply cognitive operations" to every bit of information arriving from the outer or inner worlds in order to construct a comprehensive understanding of the whole domain of our experience (d'Aquili and Newberg 1999: 196). Ordinary consciousness is not enough. The cognitive imperative that drives our neurognostic apparatus relentlessly searches in the direction of a polyphasic mentality for broader understanding and generates "theoretical entities" to account for what the raw data do not supply. This never-sleeping drive within every organism to organize a world is the origin of the universal human tendency to invent "spirits, powers, gods, black holes, viruses, photons, and libidos that operate to 'cause' events or to inhibit them" (C. D. Laughlin *et al*. 1979: 12).

The nature of ritual

Ritual is perhaps the only universal human activity that leaves evidence behind that can be dated, and "understood in the same terms as the genesis and development of the human intellect" (McManus 1979a: 183). Because ritual is employed by a society to alter its members' consciousness, the artifacts, monuments and grave goods it leaves behind can be used to sketch a history of consciousness.

The mere fact of "being conscious" is something we humans share with chimpanzees, macaques, foxes, and sparrows. What sets us apart is our ability to manipulate consciousness deliberately. We can turn our awareness back on itself to reflect upon our feelings and behaviors. We can contemplate alternate realities and use them to transform our self-identity. Thus, while the wild bonobos of today live lives that are essentially identical to those of their ancestors six million years ago, our lives are quite different from those of cave painters who lived a mere 30,000 years ago. Our mental capacities are surely the same as they were in the Upper Paleolithic, but what we have learned to do with them has changed. Ritual has always been about changing consciousness and changing identity.

If we consider, for example, a puberty ritual, some may argue that boys are not really turned into men but that the ritual only creates the illusion of such a change (e.g. Boyer 2001: 255). Probably it is true that, with their painted markings washed off and their hair unshaven, the boys who exit the ritual will appear to an outside observer to be indistinguishable from those who entered it. But their minds will have been changed; they will have had numinous experiences; their autonomic nervous systems will have been tuned. In their world, in the world of their society, they will have become—in a real sense—new people. They will feel differently about themselves, and their relations with everyone in their village will have been irrevocably changed. This is no illusion, for it will have become a fundamental fact of everyday life.

Rituals are both symbolic statements and society-changing events, for they articulate a culture's basic values and dramatize the obligatory conditions of social life. Those boys who have been made into men will have a whole new set of duties, perhaps live in different dwellings, address their fellow villagers in new terms. They will experience themselves as having a new moral and social identity. Ritual, in effect, tunes the consciousness of everyone in the village to make such immense transformations possible.

The biogenetic structuralists have been careful to define ritual in a manner that does not blur the evolutionary continuity that obtains between humans and our non-human relatives. Ritual behavior, therefore, is the "subset of formalized behavior that involves two or more individuals in active and reciprocal communication." It is always structured, stereotyped, and repeated over time; and it "results in greater coordination of conspecifics toward some social action, purpose, or goal" (C. D. Laughlin *et al.* 1979: 29). The key feature in this definition, the recurrent pattern, when observed among non-human animals, shows up most conspicuously in courting displays. On this basis, we can verify that butterflies, fish, birds, dogs, and wildebeests all engage in formalized interactions that manifest intention, influence upon one another's responses, and coordination in the interest of procreation (W. J. Smith 1979: 66–8).

Displays are, in effect, declarations of an animal's intentions. Therefore, both the execution of a stereotyped series of actions and the capacity to recognize the pattern when another performs it are inherited tendencies, reducible, in the final analysis, to genes. The advertisement of sexual availability in an individual of the opposite sex produces an affective state of sexual arousal, and the molecules of arousal—neurotransmitters, hormones, endorphins—set off a cascade of discrete actions in a precise sequence that together constitute the mating dance. But even though these behaviors are the same from generation to generation, millennium to millennium,[5] they are not as rigid as they might seem to be. They depend upon the context in which they are performed and the tiniest variations in their execution (W. J. Smith 1979: 63). Intense attention paid to subtleties in the partner's movements produces tiny differences in emotional response and corresponding variations in posture and execution. When we humans participate in a process like this, we claim we have been in conscious control, that our "ego" was responsible for the nuances in our behavior. No doubt we do exercise more conscious control than do geese or elk. But our displays, too, are inherited patterns. We know something of what it feels like to engage in a mating dance because we, too, approach attractive individuals while charged with interest and lust mixed with the fear of rejection; and we, too, carefully watch our potential partner for subtleties of gesture and posture that we use as clues for how to conduct ourselves.

Biogenetic structuralist W. J. Smith (1979) describes human "salutation displays," which are behaviors related to courting but generally carry a smaller emotional charge. Although they admit some variation, their general form is as genetically structured as that of any animal. When two humans approach one another from a distance, we toss our heads, raise our eyebrows and smile, but then avert our gaze. When quite close, we glance at one another and again avert our gaze while smiling and vocalizing. Physical meeting involves a handshake or embrace, an exchange of verbal greeting formulas that may contain more or less information. Finally, we move apart and change our bodily orientation with regard to one another (W. J. Smith 1979: 69).

Smith's description of human salutation displays adds further evidence to support Dunbar's thesis that human gossip is a verbal variation on primate grooming behavior. "The evolution of linguistic behavior began in a primate that already had displays and formalized patterns of interacting . . . We can greet, court and challenge, for instance, entirely with glances, eyebrow raisings, fist waves, growls, and other displays" (W. J. Smith 1979: 73). Ritual, therefore, is a traceable, archetypal link between ourselves and our cave-painting ancestors; but it is also a link to our primate cousins, who have their rituals as well. The biogenetic structuralists cite one of their mentors, Elliot Chapple (1970), on this point:

> The actions the human animal performs may appear to be capable of almost infinite variety, but they are more properly regarded as variations on a set of action "themes." These are probably little more in number than the repertoire of fixed action patterns of the nonhuman species.
>
> (C. D. Laughlin *et al.* 1979: 11)

Ritual: monkeys to archaic humans

Regardless of species, rituals are largely about changing consciousness. Even the human salutation display has to do with stating one's intentions and divining those of one's partner, putting one another at ease, and reducing the likelihood of aggression. Usually when we think of ritual, however, we imagine a much larger change in consciousness. A puberty ritual really does change the mind of the initiate and also the collective mind of the group. Altered states of consciousness may be induced by fasting, strenuous rhythmic activities, isolation in an uninhabited sector of the countryside. But a permanent change is effected, too, insofar as the villagers have altered their relations with one another. Human rituals usually also have a "religious" dimension, in which alternate worlds are encountered in altered states and alternate senses of oneself are generated. In all such cases, our cognitive imperative is stimulated to see the objects and events of our empirical environment in a larger context. Some sort of ultimate, even cosmic, vision of the world and our part in it becomes available. Ritual plays a significant role in shaping society: in establishing relations between its members, in giving them an identity and a meaningful place in the cosmos, and in carrying the society through dangerous times, as when food is scarce or people have died.

Monkeys

Primate grooming behavior serves as a tuning ritual for the autonomic nervous system by establishing parasympathetic dominance. This inhibits the sympathetic system governing aggression and fear that would otherwise predominate when two or more individuals come into close proximity (C. D. Laughlin et al. 1979: 93). Parasympathetic dominance—including the endorphins that reinforce grooming rituals with pleasurable feelings—is probably related to the increased size of the cerebral cortex in primates, compared with other mammals, for this is what gives us an ability to differentiate our affective responses. Primates are capable of the broadest range of affective states and the most subtle discriminations among them. Chimpanzees are more accomplished than macaques, and hominids more accomplished still (C. D. Laughlin et al. 1979: 91).

Perhaps because it is a more dangerous issue in primate societies, intragroup aggression rituals tend to be much more highly structured than grooming behaviors. Indeed, C. D. Laughlin and McManus (1979) argue that such rituals are a primary means by which monkeys re-enact "the cognized social ordering of [their] group," remembering and reinforcing the social hierarchy. Intragroup aggression rituals are more than empty drama and more than conceptual rehearsals, as their primary function is to tune the autonomic nervous system in the direction of sympathetic dominance. Those monkeys who play the roles of the main aggressors in such rituals are "coordinating crucial neural subsystems in order to maintain the social fabric" of the troop. Even animals who only watch and whoop undergo autonomic tuning and network reinforcement.

In one such aggression ritual, called "mobbing" or "line formation" behavior in Cayo Santiago rhesus monkeys, the animals form themselves into two parallel lines facing one another. Then individuals occupying the lines lunge, swing their arms menacingly and growl across the divide at the opposing camp, while mostly restraining themselves from making physical contact. Meanwhile, a second rank of monkeys stands behind each of the "front lines" like tiny companies of reserves, and individuals from this group of "seconds" lunge through the line and then retreat quickly to the rear. Most of the participants are adult females and younger males between two and five years old. Older males pace back and forth behind the lines. "Each animal participating in the line formation alternates between making threatening gestures at the opposite 'camp' and turning his head to watch what his fellow group members are doing." The actions taken are archetypal in form, that is, based in fixed action patterns common to all primates; but exercising these archetypal behavior patterns in the context of an aggression ritual works to coordinate the brains of individual monkeys to engage in effective activity as a social group. Each animal must exercise its neuro-endocrine tuning, and the group must be tuned, as well, so that all can find their place in the social hierarchy (C. D. Laughlin and McManus 1979: 89–93).

Chimpanzees

Laughlin and McManus (1979) also discuss chimpanzee rituals of two sorts. The first type they describe as "danger rituals," and base their remarks on accounts of a chimpanzee "rain dance," as observed by Jane Goodall in the wild, three times over the course of ten years, and a quarter of a century earlier among captive chimpanzees by Wolfgang Köhler. A second instance of the danger ritual is the "war dance" elicited by the appearance of a dangerous enemy. Experiments by Kortland and Kooij in the mid 1960s used an electrically animated leopard to generate the "war dance" response.

In the "rain dance," it appears that thunder and lightning stimulate the males of a troop, one-by-one, to run down hills, grabbing tree trunks with one hand to swing around them, breaking off branches, and throwing or brandishing them. When they reach the bottom of the hill, they plod back up to begin all over again. Meanwhile the females and immature males climb trees and watch. In the "leopard dance," chimpanzees "mob" the predator by forming a semicircle line before it and threaten it with "synchronized individual charges, the animals stamping the ground, screaming in unison, and brandishing (or throwing) uprooted trees, broken branches and other 'clubs' at the leopard" (C. D. Laughlin and McManus 1979: 104). Laughlin and McManus justify their general designation of a chimpanzee "danger ritual" by reminding us that when our human "cognitive imperative" encounters uncanny and disturbing mysteries—a "zone of uncertainty" in the cognized world—mythic explanations emerge from unconscious processes in our brains and psyches. Without the linguistic benefits of our human storytelling abilities, chimpanzees enact rituals that express their fear and readiness to react with aggression in dance-like behaviors that are driven by an aroused sympathetic nervous system.

By contrast, the second type of chimpanzee ritual, meat exchange, tunes the ANS in the direction of the parasympathetic system. The emotional tone of a troop eating shared meat is relaxed, leisurely, uncompetitive enjoyment. Frequently, individual animals will interrupt their gnawing and chewing to beg for more food from other chimpanzees, and about half the time they will be successful. Aggression and thievery are clearly against the rules, and any chimpanzee who gets out of line will be corrected by the group. Not even higher social rank justifies taking another ape's meat. "It is not entirely unreasonable to hypothesize that the meat itself . . . takes on the conceptual status of symbol for chimpanzee participants" (C. D. Laughlin and McManus 1979: 107).

Australopithecines

Although there are no records of *Australopithecus* rituals in the literature, Laughlin and McManus (1979) draw some tentative conclusions based on the shapes of fossilized skulls which show that the frontal lobe had reached hominid proportions in chimpanzees. What has changed by the time of the Australopithecines is in the parieto-occipital region, where neural information is compared across sensory modes (hearing, sight, etc.) and where conceptualization, logic, and mathematical functions are located in *Homo sapiens*. The authors take the rather extreme position that *Australopithecus* might have had speech. Surely, they are not wrong, however, in affirming that these pre-*Homo* ancestors communicated in gestures, for we have already seen evidence in previous chapters that bonobos and chimpanzees have that capability (C. D. Laughlin and McManus 1979: 108f).

On the basis of such evidence, the biogenetic structuralists conclude that the Australopithecine worldview had a "zone of uncertainty" that was much larger than that of chimpanzees. They had to have been more aware of the threat posed by illness, death, the distribution of scarce resources, and the maintenance of group relations. Their memories had to have been more "time-bound." If so, they were capable of modeling a world that extended beyond the merely empirical, into the future—that is into a set of imagined possibilities for what might come to be.

Their affect has to have been more differentiated than that of the apes, and that must have enabled them to have more complex societies, possibly with recognized stages of life and corresponding rites of passage. Intragroup aggression must have been a much smaller problem for Australopithecines than for their ape forebears. An increased memory capacity together with a more nuanced spectrum of affects would have enabled them to remember their relations with specific individual troop mates in greater specificity so that they would not have had frequently to re-enact the hierarchy of the group in the aggression rituals we have considered among monkeys and chimpanzees (C. D. Laughlin and McManus 1979: 110f).

Archaic humans

"Archaic *Homo sapiens*" is a widely used phrase that conveniently lumps together all the many (sometimes disputed) species of our human ancestors that emerged between *Homo erectus* (ca. 1.6 million years ago) and Modern *Homo sapiens* (ca. 50,000 years ago). Very little can be said about the consciousness of these species unless we enter into further speculations of the type employed above in our sketch of *Australopithecus'* mentality. But there is one momentous fact: about 600,000 years ago a few of our ancestors began burying some of their dead. Never before in the course of evolution had a species devoted enough thought to the phenomenon of death to have considered burial or any rites that might go with it. Apparently no previous species had been capable of wondering what might happen to an individual *after* death, the capability for which would imply a greatly enlarged "zone of uncertainty" within their worldview. Archaeologist Timothy Taylor (2002) says, in the subtitle of his book, that "Humans *invented* death." He means that our *Homo* ancestors were the first species to steadily contemplate the uncanniness of death and to devise rituals to manage their emotions.

Archaic humans, however, were not the first to notice death or to find it disturbing. Brian Hayden (2003: 184) notes that "chimpanzees exhibit innate fear of deathlike appearances in other chimpanzees"—although they are not, of course, disturbed by the deathlike appearances they cause in the monkeys and other animals whose meat they treat so ceremoniously. It is safe to say, therefore, that beginning at least with chimpanzees, primates show an increasing capacity to see the deaths of their conspecifics as a problem for which solutions have to be imagined. As their ability to contemplate future possibilities and invisible worlds evolved with their ever enlarging brains, they were able to devise rituals, graves, grave goods and monuments. Such artifacts are our main source of evidence to indicate what they were doing with their consciousness. They are our primary data for the evolution of consciousness between the time our line split off from the common ancestor we share with the chimpanzees, about six million years ago, and the invention of writing about 6000 years ago.

One further fact must be noted. The evidence seems to be that relatively few archaic humans were buried. Before burials occur at all in the archaeological record, it is reasonable to assume that *Australopithecus* and *Homo erectus* left their relatives lying where they fell to be scavenged by other animals, their bones gnawed, "scattered, then shattered and powdered by wind and rain" (T. Taylor 2002: 30). This does account for the fact that whole skeletons are extremely rare until about 26,000 years ago. Cannibalism, however, is a likelihood that cannot be ignored, for human bodies are no less nutritious than those of deer or wooly mammoths. In a world where starvation was a constant threat, eating dead members of the troop and even hunting the humans of other troops as game cannot be ruled out.

Furthermore, for a species that is beginning to be struck by the uncanniness of death, the "endo-cannibalism" of relatives would have been considered a mark of respect and remembrance, while "exo-cannibalism," the eating of one's enemies, could be seen as an appropriate insult (M. and S. Aldhouse-Green 2005: 27). Because the issue is repugnant for us to consider, Taylor (2002) cites the Greek historian Herodotus, on Darius the Great of Persia, who asked some Greeks in attendance at his court what price they would take to eat their dead fathers. They said that no price would be high enough. Then he called before him some members of the Callatian tribe of India, who *do* eat their parents, and asked them what price it would take to cremate their fathers. "They shouted aloud, 'Don't mention such horrors!'" Herodotus closes his remarks by quoting Pindar, who said, "Custom is king of all" (T. Taylor 2002: 82f). Endo-cannibalism, where it existed, may have been incorporated in rituals that did not involve burial and left no archaeological traces behind. But in the Chasm of Bones (*Sima de los Huesos*) in Spain, thousands of bones from *Homo heidelbergensis* (300,000 to 200,000 years ago) reveal systematic butchering by archaic humans, "the earliest unequivocal evidence of a death ritual anywhere in the world" (T. Taylor 2002: 77–9).

We may conclude then that the work to throw off unconsciousness through ritual enactments served first, among monkeys and chimpanzees, to bind their troops in a common purpose, to remind each member of his place in the social order, and to rehearse aggressive responses toward enemies. Ceremonial rituals, such as chimpanzee meat eating, enforced the safety and comfort of a group whose members could trust one another, even that the strongest would respect the rights of the weakest.

As the primate brain increased in complexity, less attention had to be paid to reinforcing group hierarchy, although reinforcing group solidarity remained a major goal. Burial practices, however, imply that rituals were being used for mythic purposes, that is for exploring matters of life, death and ultimate meaning. We may not be able to guess what they thought about those things, but there can be little doubt that Archaic Humans were conscious enough of their "being-toward-death" to try to understand it in ritual enactments.

Chapter 17

Ritual and consciousness in the Paleolithic

Modern human consciousness began around 50,000 years ago, perhaps earlier. Caves were being painted by about 36,000 years ago. The ice began to retreat by 10,000 years ago and by 7000 years ago, "the foundations of the modern world had been laid and nothing that has come later has ever matched the significance of these events" (Mithen 2003: 3). The achievements of the European Upper Paleolithic include magnificent ivory carvings, masterpieces in flint, and undisputed evidence for elaborate rituals and religious concepts. The first reverential burials occurred, implying religious belief and the corresponding intellectual development (T. Taylor 2002: 31). The people of the Upper Paleolithic explored concepts of an afterlife, practiced ecstatic rituals in connection with animal cults, initiated one another to positions of prestige, discovered shamanism and established ancestor cults (Hayden 2003: 122). Because they were the first of our ancestors to have left so much evidence behind, they are the first we can discuss at length.

What was different about the Upper Paleolithic that enabled it to support such an explosion of cultural development seems to come down to feats of conscious "integration" or "mastery" on two levels. First of all, evidence from earlier in prehistory indicates art objects, graves and the like had been produced on and off for tens, even hundreds of millennia. What was different about the Upper Paleolithic was that humans who had long had the *capacity* to do these things now employed their talents habitually and repeatedly. The social and cultural context had begun to support such determined "performance" as efficacious and meaningful (Soffer and Conkey 1997: 6). They had begun the "steady work."

Probably prior to such steady work was "the explosive fusion of language and imagination [so as] to pursue a new type of dialogue" (Harris 2000: 195). We have already considered Mithen's metaphor of the human mind patterned like a cathedral floor plan and his idea that when our ancestors learned to use language for more than gossip everything came together for them, and they became creative and flexible in all areas of thought and culture. Paul L. Harris, Professor of Developmental Psychology at Oxford University, suggests that, in addition to the conceptual, empirical thinking that Mithen (2003) privileges, there was a recognition of the possibilities inherent in imagination so that conceptual thought could be applied to "the distant past and future, as well as the magical and the impossible." In short, the modern minds of the Upper Paleolithic were driven by their "cognitive imperative" to explore an enlarged "zone of uncertainty," and to do so habitually and compulsively.

Ritual and consciousness in the Upper Paleolithic

The mind of the Upper Paleolithic conceptualized and imagined in the same way ours does and made sense of things at the local level, where specific images had shared social meanings (Harris 2000: 185). Just as monkeys and apes maintained and refreshed the shape of their societies with their aggression rituals, "caves were active instruments in both the propagation and the transformation of society during the Upper Paleolithic" (Harris 2000: 229). They "worked out their relationship with the land and each other through this 'art'" (Davidson 1997: 125). Like the boys who become men in puberty rituals, people were "transformed mentally and socially by their experiences [in the caves], questers returned to the level of daily life [and] entered into new kinds of social relations with other members of their community" (Lewis-Williams 2002: 234).

Ritual and myth in the caves

Evidence that the caves were used for ritual performances begins with the fact that very few of the painted caves contain any signs of habitation and those that do reveal only that people may have lived in a space near the entrance—usually nowhere near the most arresting artwork. In addition, there is a strong correlation between those areas of the caves that produce the best resonance—and therefore would be best for drumming and singing—and those where walls and ceilings are the most likely to have been painted (Bahn and Vertut 1997: 199; Lewis-Williams 2002: 225). "Sometimes 80% of the art was located in areas with resonant stalactites and draperies" (M. and S. Aldhouse-Green 2005: 58).

Several kinds of evidence suggest that the caves represented the underworld of shamanic journeys. Phosphenes have been painted on the walls alongside the animals. Many of the half-man, half-animal figures that have been called shamans or sorcerers are depicted with erections, which suggests ecstatic states with strong parasympathetic contributions. Composite beings, masks and costumes also suggest a universal theme whereby the shamanic journeyer becomes his animal familiar. A further theme links the apparent death of the shaman with the death of an animal and the transformations experienced in trance. Finally, the small, hidden "diverticules" in the caves suggest locations for vision questers to seek seclusion a short distance from richly painted chambers (Hayden 2003: 148–50).

Shamanism is an important factor because it implies an active engagement with the spirit world. As in "original thinking," the symbolic world appears on its own terms, unbidden and autonomous. Thus, cave artists first "saw" animals emerging from the surface of the rock and then assisted that process of emergence with their scrapers, charcoal and paints. "With the rise and development of shamanistic practices, we cross the threshold marking the beginnings of systematization of the preternatural world" (Ripinsky-Naxon 1993: 127). Taking active possession of that invisible world is one of the major developments of the Upper Paleolithic. "Ritual is the *engine* of shamanic ecstasy and symbol is the pilot" (C. D. Laughlin *et al*. 1990: 276–8). The repetitious behavior of ritual "turns off the conceptual mind," while the symbols that manifest in altered states entrain neural networks that are normally unconscious and make them visible.

Shamanic practices imply a unified cosmos that allows journeying between its planes and is organized around the changing seasons of the year with their visible rhythms involving animals, vegetation, and the stars (Fagan 1998: 4–8). Unquestionably, some narrative tied all these elements together to answer ultimate questions. "[R]esearchers see caves as 'mythograms.' The strong suspicion is that caves are the visual/experiential accompaniment to verbal narratives concerning such matters as group origins, history, and cosmology" (White 2003: 117f).

The growing complexity of Paleolithic society

In a series of drawings depicting the changes over time on a very interesting cave wall—what is now known as the Panel of the Horses in the most ancient Chauvet Cave—Jean Clottes and collaborators show how the artwork accumulated over perhaps 15,000 years (Clottes 2003: 107). First, a cave bear standing on its hind legs leaves claw marks that slice though the yellow veneer on the wall, leaving white gouges. Later humans have engraved a wooly rhinoceros and mammoth over the claw marks (see Figure 17.1).

Then, humans "prepare a surface" by scraping off a large area of the yellow veneer on the rock to uncover a "canvas" of white "moon milk" at about the height of a human chest and shoulders.[1] Black outlines of rhinoceros, elk and bison are painted on the white surface. In a fifth stage, the black outlines of dueling wooly rhinoceroses appear lower down on the wall, directly on its yellow oxidized veneer. Next aurochs are painted on the white surface, partially overlapping some of the earlier paintings; and this time the outlines are shaded in with black paint. Finally, three stages of horse paintings are made on top of everything that was painted earlier, tying together the white and yellow portions of the rock surface and giving the impression of a massive herd of animals moving mostly upward and to the left, with a couple of them bucking traffic and lending the whole scene a sense of dynamism (see Figure 17.2). This one panel gives us a suggestive account of how the artwork in the caves developed from the early work of individual artists to the collective work of organized artists. Human society in the European Upper Paleolithic underwent a similar development.

The caves have been called Ice Age cathedrals for good reason. An entire complex of galleries and passageways was carefully planned. Scaffolding had to be built to reach ceilings and high wall surfaces. Pigment had to be obtained in such large quantities that extensive trading networks had to be established. A group of talented artists and other workers had to be inspired to engage in an organized

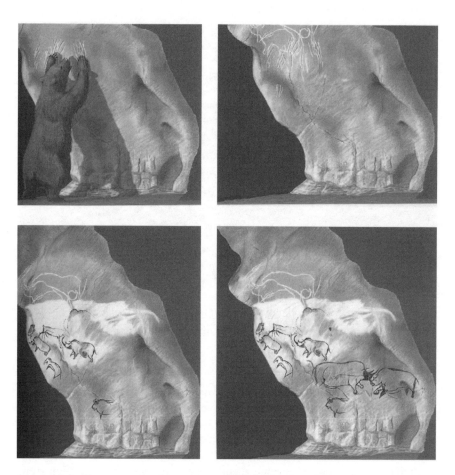

Figure 17.1 Chauvet cave, Panel of the Horses (early stages).

Source: statements and photographs by C. Fritz and G. Tosello, in Jean Clottes *et al.* (2001) *La Grotte Chauvet: L'Art des origines*, Seuil.

project and be relieved of hunting and gathering while they did the work. Such an enterprise resembles in its complexity what their descendants of the Gothic period achieved during the centuries when Europe's great cathedrals were built.

These facts have forced archaeologists to distinguish between simple and complex hunter-gatherer societies. A simple hunter-gatherer society entails a fairly small group of individuals enjoying no private ownership who are entirely dependent upon one another because life is so bare and subsistence so precarious. They have to be constantly on the move, and everyone is equal with everyone else. Their lifestyle allows them no valuables, no rich burials, no permanent campsites, no storage of resources.

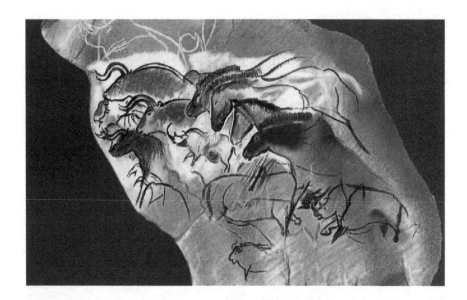

Figure 17.2 Chauvet cave, Panel of the Horses (final stage).

Source: statements and photographs by C. Fritz and G. Tosello, in Jean Clottes et al. (2001)
La Grotte Chauvet: L'Art des origines, Seuil.

Before the "cultural explosion" of the Upper Paleolithic, our ancestors lived exclusively in such simple societies. But over the course of perhaps twenty millennia, they gradually made the transition to *complex* hunter-gatherer societies. What made the transition possible was the production of abundant, stable resources and improved weapons and hunting techniques. They could settle down for part or all of a year and begin to accumulate private possessions. The population grew, small bands joined forces with one another, and permanent architecture became possible for the first time. They became involved in economic competition, trade, warfare against other groups, and slavery

History was being made at the end of the last Ice Age, not in placid contentment, but through struggle and contest (Lewis-Williams 2002: 181). "Image-making played an active role in the evolution of social relations," not for the sake of beauty but for social discrimination. "Social competition drove a spiral of social, political and technological change." Even "the shapes of one's stone artifacts (rather like a car today) signaled one's social group" (Lewis-Williams 2002: 95f, 76). It was private ownership and the need to impress that drove the explosion of art and the elaboration of ritual (Hayden 2003: 132). Simple hunter-gatherers could have a feast only when the hunt was spectacularly successful, and then everyone, hunters and non-hunters alike, participated equally. But among complex hunter-gatherers, the ability to produce food surpluses on a regular basis gave some families the ability to call a feast whenever they wished to compete for labor and power with other families (Hayden 2003: 137). For this reason, "rituals and [their attendant] beliefs benefited some people more than—and often at the expense of—others" (Lewis-Williams and Pearce 2005: 79).

Secret societies and initiatory rites limited to wealthy and influential families became the means "to consolidate economic, social, and political control." Rites involving altered states of consciousness and acquiring animal guardians were well suited to the painted caves, which were not used regularly and whose spaces were usually too cramped for anything but small segments of a complex society to use at any one time. The "great art" of the caves required skill and organization which only the wealthy could afford to sponsor, and this allowed them to produce rituals of high drama and feasting—for which there is evidence in some of the caves (Hayden 2003: 142–5). Iain Davidson, Professor of Archaeology at the University of New England in Australia, reaches a similar conclusion: "The marking of places through symbols painted and engraved on cave walls might [have been] involved with the identification of the manner of corporate ownership of territories" (Davidson 1997: 150).

The neurobiology of ritual in the Upper Paleolithic

Ritual can effect enormous changes in personality and social structure. We begin with a powerful image of this process from one of Jung's friends and correspondents, the great German Indologist, Heinrich Zimmer:

> Dancing is an ancient form of magic. The dancer becomes amplified into a being endowed with supra-normal powers. His personality is transformed. Like yoga, the dance induces trance, ecstasy, the experience of the divine, the realization of one's own secret nature, and, finally, mergence into the divine essence . . . .
>
> Pantomimic dance is intended to transmute the dancer into whatever demon, god, or earthly existence he impersonates. . . .
>
> The dance is an act of creation. It brings about a new situation and summons into the dancer a new and higher personality. It has a cosmogonic function, in that it arouses dormant energies which may then shape the world.
>
> (Zimmer 1946: 151f)

Dance is a rhythmic, repetitive activity that alters our physiology, and it lies at the heart of most human rituals. Barbara W. Lex, one of the collaborators in the biogenetic structuralism project, defines ritual as a "precisely performed emotional-interactional form" that entrains biological rhythms and enhances survival. She says that whereas ordinary events produce "dysphasic emotional responses" among a group of individuals, ritual events ensure uniformity of emotional state and behavior among participants. Patterned repetition acts upon the mammalian nervous system to produce altered states of consciousness (Lex 1979: 120, 117).

The neurobiology of ritual

C. D. Laughlin *et al.* (1979) say that the simplest forms of ritual achieve their effects by releasing "fixed action patterns" (what might be called "motor-archetypes") and entraining neuro-motor subsystems that coordinate an array of physiological processes within the individual and also stimulate cohesive social forces within the group. Ritual is therefore "necessary for coherent, cooperative responses," that have a "common motive and drive" (C. D. Laughlin *et al.* 1979: 33–5). Brian Hayden (2003) implicitly connects such observations with the theological tone of Zimmer's description of the dance when he says, "Any act can be performed in either a profane or a sacred fashion. If it is done in a sacred fashion, the connection is made and the world lights up. We feel euphoric" (Hayden 2003: 54). The larger cosmos thus revealed is experienced as "invigorating," while the rest of our life fades into dull unreality devoid of genuine interest. The difference reminds us of Jung's declaration that he had to return from his near-death experience to the gray, two-dimensional "box world."

The simplest sorts of rhythm—even drumming and flashing lights experienced without dancing—have been shown to have significant effects upon the brain. Lex (1979) reports that lights flashing near the frequency of alpha brain waves increase the amplitude of those waves, as demonstrated in EEG studies. Furthermore, such "entrainment of brain rhythms is quickly established and spreads throughout the brain" to the point that those who are seizure prone may experience an epileptic attack and "even normal individuals can experience unusual jerks." These effects also occur for people who only stand and watch at rituals (Lex 1979: 122f).

D'Aquili and Laughlin (1979) provide more specific information. Auditory and visual repetitive stimuli "can drive cortical rhythms and produce intensely pleasurable, ineffable experience" through "simultaneous intense discharges from the sympathetic and parasympathetic systems." When the dancing is prolonged, the autonomic discharges stimulate the median forebrain bundle, "generating not only a pleasurable sensation but, under proper conditions, a sense of union or oneness with conspecifics" much the way orgasm does in a pair of lovers. The rhythm itself produces discharges from the limbic system which result in a decrease in the sense of distance we feel from one another and an increase in a sense of social cohesion. Because observers are strongly affected by the rhythms, too, infants and children present at rituals undergo a socialization process that causes them to value ritual and cohesive social action in their later years (d'Aquili and Laughlin 1979: 156–9).

Charles Laughlin reports on his own experience of dancing with Mevlevi Sufis, the "whirling dervishes." He learned to spin with arms out "while visualizing a central crystal-form axis running up the center of his body and colorful streams of energy flowing out of his palms." As he persisted in whirling to the music in a structured format with others, he eventually found that "the entire world of phenomena appeared to be spinning around the center of consciousness, which was the axis." The cosmic state of consciousness abruptly ended when his ordinary awareness inadvertently broke through and began to talk about the extraordinary things that were happening to him. At this point, his left hemisphere regained its dominance, and the religious experience was only a memory (C. D. Laughlin *et al.* 1990: 300).

Some of the most important factors in producing altered states of consciousness through ritual depend upon tuning the autonomic nervous system, as we saw in Chapter 14, leading to spillover or reversal phenomena between the sympathetic and parasympathetic systems. Lex reports that such reversals sensitize certain centers in the *central* nervous system. The rhythmic "driving" behaviors of ritual (drumming, dancing, and the like) "evoke a greater accentuation of right-hemisphere activities than usually prevails" (Lex 1979: 130). This can lead to "oceanic feelings, ineffability, or pseudo-perceptions emanating from the right-hemisphere preeminence, evoked by the stimulation of subcortical and cortical centers." These phenomena, which are also associated with increased alpha-wave activity, "may also underlie such concepts as 'mana,' 'faith,' 'power,' and other labels for both personified and impersonal forces" (Lex 1979: 128). These are the phenomena that Jung frequently cites as characteristic of "experiencing an archetype," "numinosity," and becoming a "mana personality."

Such language applies equally well to episodes of spontaneous religious states of mind, like near-death experiences, and to trances deliberately provoked through prolonged participation in rhythmic rituals. In either case, the powerful experiences "begin with unusually high stimulation of hypothalamic or limbic structures" (d'Aquili and Newberg 1999: 103). In ritual behavior, "feedback from proprioceptors [the body's sensation system that keeps us oriented in space] as in singing and dancing, seems to evoke new patterns of affective response in hypothalamus, limbic system, and neocortex" (Lex 1979: 143). Among these brain parts, the limbic system functions as the "seat of motivation and affect" (C. D. Laughlin *et al.* 1979: 30). The limbic system acting in concert with the hypothalamus and reticular formation integrates purposive, foresighted behavior when acted upon by a "tuned" autonomic nervous system (Lex 1979: 135). D'Aquili and Newberg add to this picture the component of religious awe, generated when human ceremonial ritual activates the amygdala and makes it more than normally responsive (d'Aquili and Newberg 1999: 101).

Ritual and human survival

Most sorts of externally imposed emergency that modern humans and their ancestors have had to face are economic. Climate change, for instance, generates a variety of economic crises for hunter-gatherers: sudden loss of food, clothing, tools and shelter; sudden threats from neighboring groups of conspecifics who need to expand their hunting range and eliminate competitors for dwindling resources; greater difficulty in dealing with large predatory animals who may be inclined to see human meat as a supplement to their shrinking diet; and greater danger from hungry scavengers when the hunt has been successful. When such crises persist, the social order will break down, leading to new instabilities, including damage to trading networks. All these factors threaten group survival.

"The principal technique that hunter-gatherers throughout the world developed to cope with such recurring [economic] crises was to establish alliances with other bands, both near and, especially, far" (Hayden 2003: 29). When dealing with other bands of conspecifics, there are only two ways to proceed: making war upon the neighbors to eliminate competition and acquire slaves, or making friends and cooperating with them. In the long run alliances provide longer-lasting benefits. They are "the unique survival characteristic of humans," a strategy that requires overcoming the xenophobia natural to all primates. This is the fundamental reason why "virtually all hunter-gatherers have had strong ritual relationships"; for bonding with strangers requires "earth shaking emotional experiences created in ecstatic religious rituals that were adaptive in this respect" (Hayden 2003: 31).

Emotional bonding is the ultimate "glue" for alliances based in ritual, but image and narrative are also important. Ritual must protect and maintain the story that links the empirical world of ordinary consciousness with the greater cosmos revealed in altered states. A society cannot survive unless its members share most of the features of an effective and single vision of the world (McManus 1979b: 224). What distinguishes us from other primates lies in the flexibility by which we can "learn to use alternate meanings of the same stimulus and to develop different patterns of interrelationship within the same set of meanings" (McManus 1979b: 216). It is primarily ritual which establishes this flexibility and harmony, and it is the reason anthropologist Anthony F. C. Wallace (1966: 102) famously declared, "Ritual is religion in action; it is the cutting edge of the tool."

Ritual and transformation

There are three stages in every ceremonial ritual. First, by entering the ritual space and beginning the sacred invocations, songs and drama, a community separates itself from the activities of normal, or profane, life. Then, in a second stage, the repetitive behaviors of ritual enact a cosmic worldview that replaces the old profane perspective with a new sacred vision and anchors it in the aroused emotional state of the participants. This cognitive/affective condition is the altered state of consciousness that ritual generates by tuning the autonomic nervous system and reversing the usual balance between the two cerebral hemispheres (McManus 1979b: 227). The third stage integrates the cosmic perspective of the myth with the activities of everyday life (Ibid.: 211). In the puberty ritual, for example, the third stage is accomplished when the former boys have been reintegrated into society as men. By this time, everybody's mind has been changed, and the reality of village life has undergone a transformation.

Ritual is the cutting edge of religion because it transforms the lived world. In the first stage, joining in the ritual challenges the profane perspective and causes the participant to *believe* in visionary experiences. In the second stage, direct experience confirms elements of the mythic worldview and helps to replace belief in the cosmic perspective with *understanding*. Finally, in the third stage, one enters into full participation in the mythic cosmos. The myth is *realized*, becomes fully real

(C. D. Laughlin *et al.* 1990: 228). By repeated participation, members take possession of a new model of reality characterized by "entirely new sensitivities to events in the operational environment previously not perceived" (McManus *et al.* 1979: 228). The same outer world will now be seen differently, aspects of it that formerly were overlooked will now be noticed and accorded new significance. As we become habituated to the new worldview, we see evidence for the new cosmic vision everywhere, and this gives us conceptual certainty and the feeling that this is the way things necessarily are. Such "redundancy" in our experience is supported by redundancy in our brain. New neural networks are established and their wiring "hardened," and this gives rise to our increasing confidence (McManus 1979a: 196–200).

Lest we think that hunter-gatherers and churchgoers are activating inferior brain processes in opening themselves up to such alternate worlds—for this is surely what our monophasic society wants us to believe—the biogenetic structuralists, following Thomas Kuhn (1970), admit that they, too, and all scientists, live in a world confirmed by repetition and habituation. A scientist "remains in a cycle of repetitive action and confirmation of the model until expectancy is violated." When this violation affects "structural expectations," the scientist stops trying to fit discrepant data into his model, and, after struggling through

> a phase of more or less severe alternation in interpretation and behavior . . . there emerges a reorganization of the structure of expectations that leads to a new structure of knowledge . . . a new reality model . . . characterized by entirely new sensitivities to events in the operational environment previously not perceived.
>
> (McManus *et al.* 1979: 352–4)

Ritual and myth

There is an old debate about which came first, ritual or myth. On the one hand, ritual always enacts a perspective on the world and our place in it. Since it is the business of myth to tell the story of how and why we came to be, it seems self-evident that myth came first and that ritual dramas were subsequently devised to illustrate it and thereby to focus the energies of participants in socially useful ways.

Our *evolutionary* approach to ritual, however, calls such logic into question. For, as our ancestors evolved through primate stages, the only thread to be followed is comprised of repetitive species-specific behavior patterns. Because for millions of years no primate could say why these things were enacted, the most likely scenario is that our distant ancestors found themselves acting out rituals that had been handed down through countless generations before their cognitive imperative began to concoct rationales for why they had "always" done such things and why they continued to do them. Anthropologist Pascal Boyer says, "We have gods in part because we have the mental equipment to make society possible, but we cannot always understand how society functions" (Boyer 2001: 28). Gods, the protagonists of myth, arise as our cognitive imperative struggles with a zone of uncertainty surrounding questions of who we are and why we do the things we do.

John McManus says ritual *maintains* our cognitive imperative by the enactments we and our ancestors perform because they are "both adaptively efficacious and phenomenologically satisfying" (McManus 1979a: 184). In performing our rituals, we satisfy ourselves but do not know why. A large zone of uncertainty is uncovered. "Myth provides solution to the ambiguity"—seemingly on the basis of the story it tells, but actually "by its effect on the limbic system and the autonomic nervous system" (d'Aquili and Laughlin 1979: 162). The problem the myth articulates is "vividly felt to have been resolved" (d'Aquili and Newberg 1999: 85).

Generally, the monophasic West believes that myth belongs to its past, that directed thinking and double-blind experiments have taken us well beyond such narrative ventures into the unknowable. But the need for mythic explanations is universal. Jung felt it at Taos Pueblo and the Athai Plains. "This need is an inescapable condition of human existence, pervading all areas of interactions: from techno-mechanical and sexual to highly symbolic and creative" (Ripinsky-Naxon 1993: 10).

Myth and the union of opposites

Jung says that the numinous power of every archetype stems from the tension between opposites which the archetype contains: good and evil, divine and animal, spiritual and instinctual, nurturing and devouring.[2] God, the archetypal image *par excellence*, and symbol of the self, is always described in Jung's works as the *coincidentia oppositorum*, the abiding together of the opposites, in the phrase made famous by the medieval philosopher Nicholas of Cusa (1401–64).

The biogenetic structuralists have taken up this theme in their discussion of myth, arguing that the human capacity to mythologize requires three faculties: the ability to conceptualize, the ability to think in abstract causes, and the ability to think in terms of pairs of opposites. The first two seem fairly obvious. The third quality, handling "antinomies" or pairs of opposites, is the most interesting and characteristic. For the biogenetic structuralists, "The ultimate union of opposites" is the union between "the contingent and vulnerable in man and a powerful, possibly omnipotent force" (d'Aquili and Laughlin 1979: 162). Myth and ritual "existentially unite opposites to achieve some form of control over what appears to be an essentially unpredictable universe" (d'Aquili and Newberg 1999: 87). Myth articulates "supraordinate goals . . . that are compelling and highly appealing to members of groups in conflict and that cannot be achieved with the resources and energies of the groups separately" (C. D. Laughlin and d'Aquili 1979: 297).

But alliance building is only possible on the basis of what happens within the psyche of each group member, where the ultimate "glue" lies in "the ineffable, positive affect associated with the resolution of a crucial antinomy" (d'Aquili and Laughlin 1979: 172). We must recall Hayden's report:

> about ten percent of the people simply did not care about rituals or supernatural beliefs, while another ten to twenty percent had abandoned their traditional

beliefs ... and most ... did not have a working knowledge of their own religious doctrines or myths, even though these were accessible.

(Hayden 2003: 15)

But Hayden (2003) refers to reports from ordinary consciousness. Alternation in states of brain and psyche occur for the most part unconsciously, where "a structure greater than the ego is gradually integrated into a wider consciousness" (C. D. Laughlin *et al.* 1990: 281). This position is quite similar to Jung's notion that the whole personality gains when the ego begins to experience its relationship with the greater reality of the self.

Myth and neuropsychology

Biogenetic structuralism proposes an easily understood model for what occurs in the brain when we enter altered states of consciousness and encounter a numinous solution to mythic conundrums. Tuning the autonomic nervous system is the key, for the cerebral hemispheres are each associated with one of its antagonistic subsystems. The rational, linear and linguistically oriented dominant hemisphere (usually the left) is closely connected to the energy-expending sympathetic system, which deals with emergencies. Meanwhile, the gestalt and pattern-recognizing non-dominant hemisphere is closely connected to the relaxed and energy-conserving parasympathetic. Driving either to the spillover effect can lead to an ecstatic state in which both systems are intensely stimulated. Most characteristically, such states involve the satisfaction of feeling that "polar opposites as presented in myth appear simultaneously, both as antinomies and as unified wholes . . . [what Christian theologians have called] *conjunctio oppositorum*" (d'Aquili and Laughlin 1979: 176). They may also "yield ... an intense awareness that death is not to be feared, accompanied by a sense of harmony of the individual with the universe" (Ibid.: 178).

Tuning the autonomic nervous system is essential for the production of altered states of consciousness that explore and unite antinomies, even as the brain's regions and tendencies are harmonized by slow rhythmic waves. Over the course of phylogeny, the nervous system has increased in anatomical elaboration and complexity in ways that enable: (a) making conceptual and affective connections between experiences separated by larger gaps of space and time, (b) making more elaborate and diverse associations, (c) finding more flexible ways to apply such associations to our intentions, (d) ordering larger arrays of priorities within a hierarchical structure, (e) detaching logic from emotional inclination, and (f) developing more extensive and nuanced behaviors. All of these increased capacities have been made possible by the "elaboration of prefrontal, parietal, and temporal association [regions of the] cortex" (C. D. Laughlin *et al.* 1990: 181).

As a shorthand notation, the biogenetic structuralists have given these interconnected regions of the brain a collective name, the *causal operator*; for the neural networks connecting these areas automatically search for and concoct causal rationales. Data presented in Chapter 4 on the inheritance of a "physics module" indicates that all mammals have some sort of causal operator. Ours is simply more elaborate and complex, and it has the advantage of language. On account of the causal operator inherited with the human brain and developed through cultural and personal experience, "human beings have no choice but to construct myths to explain their world . . . codifications of unexplained reality in terms of antinomies and causal narratives" (d'Aquili and Laughlin 1979: 171). The causal operator "automatically generates gods, powers, spirits, and personified forces." It lies, too, at the foundation of Western science, although the scientific disciplines have "imposed restrictions on the causal operator" to keep it in line with experimental evidence. Nevertheless, the history of science celebrates numerous instances in which theoretical breakthroughs have occurred through the dreams, visions and other altered states in scientists (d'Aquili and Laughlin 1979: 170).

Symbolic penetration

Just as rhythms in sound and light entrain our neural networks and tune our autonomic nervous system, even when we just stand at a ritual and watch, so mythic symbols in narrative, icon, and drama "penetrate" beneath the conscious field and activate unconscious processes in our brain and psyche. The biogenetic structuralists refer to this process as *symbolic penetration*: "Symbolic penetration created by ritual can evoke ['infra-egoic'] structures and their intentionalities and can operate on them, mediating and transforming them outside of awareness" (Winkelman 2000: 244).

When Jung argues that images can "constellate" an archetype in the unconscious and begin or carry forward an important unconscious process, he is describing what the biogenetic structuralists call symbolic penetration. Occasionally, our authors say so straightforwardly: "All religious systems in the world use symbols to penetrate to and activate intentionalities that are either neurognostically present in all human brains (i.e. archetypes) or that have been developed through programs of enculturation" (C. D. Laughlin *et al.* 1990: 195). Because symbols point to meanings that are, in the words of Jung, "partly known but mostly unknown,"[3] they act upon neural networks that lie outside of the conscious field, and these networks "exercise effects . . . upon other neural, endocrine, and physiological systems within the being." Instances of such penetration, since they occur outside of awareness—even if we are conscious enough to find the images strangely interesting—"bypass [our] inhibitions" and thereby "transform, elaborate, and even integrate with the conscious network previously suppressed models [i.e. networks]" (C. D. Laughlin *et al.* 1990: 190, 196).

Along with rhythm, symbolic penetration—achieved through words, costumes, choreography and the like—probably constitutes the first and most important effect of any ritual upon its participants and observers. It begins the process of producing altered states of consciousness in human beings, certainly, and very likely in all primates. For as "a complex of standardized activity . . . ritual may operate to *amplify* a symbolic penetration technique" (C. D. Laughlin *et al.* 1990: 196). Therefore the drama of ritual generates a "theater of the mind," entraining neural processes that in the best of cases bring about psychological and sociological transformation (Ibid.: 213).

Consciousness in the Upper Paleolithic

When wishing to characterize human consciousness in the Upper Paleolithic with a brief phrase, we have mentioned the cave paintings, for they are monuments to the awareness of the earliest members of our species. As statements about a civilization's consciousness, they correspond to the pyramids and Sphinx of Egypt, the Cathedrals of Gothic Europe, and the North American effigy mounds. Mute and enigmatic as they are, they tell us a people was gripped by an idea and disciplined itself to "steady work" for generations in order to produce such enormous, well-planned and decisively executed statements. Death was a central concern for the cave painters and evidently understood on analogy with trance. Losing ordinary consciousness, our ancestors entered an invisible cosmos somewhat similar to the "kingdom of light" encountered in near-death experiences.

The relationship they had with the rock walls was similar to what Jung discovered in "original thinking." Images were given to our ancestors in subtle hints, images constellated by the cracks and bumps. Jung did the same thing with the rock walls of the "medieval tower" he built on Zurich's Upper Lake. He saw animals and human figures in the uneven surfaces of the carved and mortared blocks and helped them to emerge with hammer and chisel (Figure 17.3).

Figure 17.3 Jung's carvings on the walls of his Bollingen tower.

Source: A. Jaffé (1979) *C. G. Jung: Word and Image.*

Images so constellated inevitably belong to mythic narratives that give meaning to existence. Neural networks stabilized through frequent repetitions reside in the brain as pre-assembled wholes, "cultural archetypes," ready to fire preferentially any time some associated shape or sound occurs in the empirical world. Such "symbolic penetration" is roughly the same principle we described in connection with the constellation of complexes.

Ritual and the control of society

The layout and painting of the caves was a function of a new sort of hunter-gatherer society. Alliances between bands of ever growing size and surpluses made possible by mass killings of animal herds enabled certain families and clans to commission such huge "public works" projects as the painted caves. Because the new populations were far too large to permit everyone inside cave galleries at the same time, it seems only reasonable to agree with Brian Hayden, Steven Mithen, David Lewis-Williams, John Pfeiffer, and other authors we have cited, that the rituals performed in the caves must have had political and economic significance. Rituals and feasts must have been employed, as so often in human history, to gain control of laborers, to promise rewards for services not yet rendered—rather the way political fund raisers and pancake breakfasts are used today. The biogenetic structuralists agree. In the Upper Paleolithic context, mythic symbols could become persuasive tools in the hands of the families who controlled the surpluses, allowing them to gain control also of the mental states of the economically less fortunate (C. D. Laughlin *et al*. 1990: 176).

At this point in the history of consciousness, the free individual-centered exploration of the greater cosmos through shamanic altered states of consciousness was falling under the control of political and economic elites. This trend grows when the ice melts and the Middle Stone Age, the Mesolithic, begins.

Chapter 18

Ritual and consciousness in the Mesolithic

We are constructing a history of consciousness in order to ascertain whether Jung's intuitions of a century ago were correct. He looked back two millennia into our European past and saw that we have spent the past 2000 years building an ego and divorcing ourselves from our collective unconscious. In doing so, we have created a new task for ourselves: finding a way to integrate our conscious rationality with the "irrational" (unconscious) wisdom of our race, to which we can gain access through altered states of consciousness. Recent discoveries in archaeology allow us to go further back into the past, even into primate evolution, to paint a more complete picture than the one Jung had at his disposal. Thus we are able to place the question of ego-development into a much larger context than he knew.

Evolution and the psyche

As organisms increase in complexity from protozoa to mammals, psyche evolves as well. We have begun our "history of consciousness," however, with primates— finding that monkeys and apes use rituals to change their consciousness in ways that strengthen and differentiate their social bonds and prepare for future crises. With increasing neocortical development, more recently evolved primates have a larger memory capacity and power of differentiation. This has made it possible for *Australopithecus* and *Homo erectus* to use rituals for more and more specialized and far reaching purposes. By the time of *Homo neanderthalensis*, deep caves were being used, probably for consciousness-changing rituals involving a cave-bear cult.

Over the billions of years of feeding, reproducing, dying and mutating that occurred before *Homo sapiens* arrived with a reflective ("co-creating") awareness, changes in consciousness were accomplished only through phylogeny. Evolution produced ever more powerful nervous systems, culminating in the expanded cerebral cortex that primates have found essential for their society-based survival strategies. In 50,000 years, our own species has experienced no changes in the neural apparatus we inherit. Rather we have spent all this time learning how to take advantage of the potential built into our brains and psyches.

Imagination, altered states of consciousness, and directed thinking can be used in so many combinations and toward so many different ends that our psychic explorations are ongoing even today.

Evolution increased the capacity and complexity of the cerebral cortex, making it possible for apes to live in larger bands than monkeys, and *Australopithecus* in larger, yet more nuanced social groups. When gossip began to take over the grooming function, societies emerged at human levels of size and diversity. Another Rubicon was crossed, when we learned to talk about biology, physics, tool design and flavors of meat. Rituals were performed by all primate species, but the flexibility of language accelerated the process of change for *Homo sapiens* and addressed also the issue of *why* we were dancing and singing. Our cognitive imperative compels us to come up with explanations for the apparently irrational and absurd things we find ourselves doing.

Physics has achieved its successes by honing the cognitive imperative and forcing it to couch its explanations in mathematical language that conforms to experimental evidence. But it still reveals its mythic and metaphorical origins. Nobel Prize winning physicist Robert B. Laughlin, for instance, describes how mathematicians, visionaries, and computer modelers work together to define, simplify, and solve crucial problems (R. B. Laughlin 2005). Each is a specialist in a different human faculty, and their cooperation achieves results that none could achieve on his own. Discovering how to integrate our personal psychic faculties is what each of us has to learn to do in our own life, and it is the central theme of the history of consciousness from the Paleolithic caves to the present. Contrary to the delusion of our monophasic society, imagination and altered states are essential parts of our psychological armamentarium. Robert Laughlin and his associates in science "throw off unconsciousness" when they use them. They make these faculties part of their "steady work."

The biogenetic structuralists allude to the integration of such faculties when they say, "The evolutionary course has been from reliance on the perceptual field as frame, to reliance upon intentionality as frame" (C. D. Laughlin *et al.*, 1990: 183). They mean that millions of years ago *Paramecium* oriented itself entirely by its "perceptual field," i.e. what it perceived in the ambient water in which it swam. By the time monkeys evolved, we find individuals going beyond the perceptual field to "intentionality." For example, they deliberately misdirect one another's attention (an aspect of intentionality) to steal some food or a moment of orgasmic bliss with a forbidden partner. Among chimpanzees, alpha males need to have third-order intentionality, what we have called a "soap-opera mind," in order to manage their troops with fairness. As we move further up the "phylogenetic ladder," societies get larger and the range of difference in personality, temperament and role playing increases proportionately. These more recent and sophisticated developments belong to the "frame" of intentionality. Humans are concerned not only with what we intend, but how we intend it. Manipulations of the intentional frame have characterized the human project for the last 50,000 years, and become more and more prominent as we approach the present.

As we resume our survey of the history of consciousness, we will limit our attention to the Near East and Western Europe, the source of the Western heritage that Jung's theories address, the most intensively studied region of the world. It is unfortunate that we will largely ignore Asia, Africa, Australia and the Americas, but some limitation of focus is essential to prevent this section of the book from growing too large and distracting our attention from the main issue, which is the relationship between evolution, history and the archetypes.

The transitional nature of the Mesolithic

The "Old Stone Age," the Paleolithic, was characterized by the lifestyles and social strategies of hunter-gatherers; and the "New Stone Age," the Neolithic, saw the wide-scale introduction of agriculture. But there was a long, uncertain transition that took our ancestors from a hunting lifestyle that was thoroughly egalitarian, precariously subsistent, and dependent upon harmony with the cycles of nature, to a farming lifestyle that was hierarchical and distinctly inegalitarian, depended on stored surpluses, and championed the conquest of nature. For some 5000 years, humans learned elements of cultivation and domestication and then abandoned them as the climate changed, only to take them up again later on. This period of transition is called the "Middle Stone Age," the Mesolithic.

The most obvious change that brought the Paleolithic to an end was the gradual retreat of the ice—back to the Earth's poles and mountain tops. The first effects of the global warming process, however, were far less evident at the southern edge of the glaciers than they were hundreds of miles further to the south, where rain began to fall more abundantly. As the glaciers melted, they released water that had been bound up as ice. This raised sea levels and filled in lowland areas with lakes and swamps. Thousands of square miles of liquid water was free to evaporate in the newly elevated temperatures, thereby supplying the atmosphere with rain clouds to soak the arid earth and cause it to bloom abundantly with grasses and trees. The Near East moved on to the Mesolithic while people in the north were still living in the Ice Age.

Consciousness in the Mesolithic

When the climate began to change, not long after the last of the caves had been painted, complex hunter-gatherers began founding "Natufian" villages in the Middle East (ca. 14,300–12,800 years ago). At 'Ain Mallaha, north of Lake Tiberias in what is now Israel, wild cereal grains were being ground into flour with stone mortars as large as boulders, and nuts were stored in plaster-lined pits. Evidence shows that the Natufians had extensive knowledge of the plants in their vicinity, not merely those with economic value. They were evidently curious and payed close attention to the details of the world around them. They learned to grow plants from cuttings, and exchanged them with friends and relatives. Mithen believes the exchange of cuttings and the cultivation of "wild grasses" was symbolically associated with their origin myths (Mithen 2003: 29–37).

Cultivation versus domestication

Although they *cultivated* plants, they had not learned to *domesticate* them. They kept "wild gardens." Real domestication involves producing a new variant of a species of plant food through "artificial selection." A plant in the wild may have variants of a single gene (called "alleles"). One of them may produce a plant that is economically more useful than the other. In such a case, a farmer who is a real domesticator will find a way to plant only seeds that have the favorable allele.

The way this worked out for our ancestors who learned to domesticate grain may be illustrated with the example of wild and domestic wheat. The ripe seeds of wild wheat have a brittle connection with their stalks. This means the slightest touch—much less the swipe of a sickle—causes most of the grain to fall to the ground and be lost. Wild wheat is efficiently adapted to a world in which it has to reseed itself, but inconvenient for farmers. Domesticated wheat, in contrast, has a tighter, less brittle bond between stalk and grain so that nearly all the ripe seeds can be gathered and brought home. Under ordinary circumstances, since the grain from the most brittle plants is the hardest to gather, humans will inevitably bring home more seeds from the plants with the least brittle attachment and plant them in their gardens. The ripe seeds from these plants will be more tightly bound at harvest time, when again the most brittle seeds will be lost. "In ideal circumstances, as few as twenty cycles of harvesting and resewing in new patches would have transformed a wild brittle type of wheat into the domesticated non-brittle variant" (Mithen 2003: 38).

By this very natural and unconscious process, the planters would have selected the plants whose genes most tightly bound their grain, and thereby produced a real domestic variety. But the Natufians did not. The Mesolithic is defined in part by "wild gardens." The Natufians frustrated the domestication process ingeniously by harvesting the wild wheat when it was not quite ripe and before it became brittle. They were observant enough to see the problem and work out a solution, but it was less satisfactory than genuine domestication. For that, the world had to wait another 3000 years.

As our ancestors began to leave the Upper Paleolithic behind, therefore, they began expanding their awareness in a new direction. The cave painters produced and exploited altered states of consciousness in an introverted manner. The Mesolithic people, however, expanded their consciousness in a more extraverted manner, as they learned to explore and exploit the natural world in new ways. They may not always have hit on the most efficient solution, but they were clearly studying nature and learning new techniques. For example, to provide ever greater, more impressive feasts, families learned to capture wild animals and keep them alive, well-fed and ready for a slaughter and feast that was essential to their rituals (Hayden 2003: 174).

The theme of pursuing familial aggrandizement by controlling surpluses, as we have seen, was already a main characteristic of complex hunter-gatherer societies in the Upper Paleolithic. The same principle applies to trade and to burial practices among the Natufians. They conducted a vigorous trade in dentalium shells collected along the Mediterranean coast and used them in jewelry for personal adornment and the advertisement of personal and familial wealth. The shells could also be traded to groups further inland for other items. But luxury goods could maintain their status as signifiers of wealth only as long as they remained relatively rare. Thus,

> the key to maintaining [wealth and power] may have been to ensure that limited shells were in circulation within their village. The most effective way of doing that was the regular removal of large quantities by burying them with the dead.
>
> (Mithen 2003: 33)

Burial was, therefore, taking on a dual symbolic role. It evidently had spiritual and cosmic significance related to notions of the soul and afterlife, and also a profane meaning as a political and economic statement concerning who had power over whom.

Here we see that myth and ritual serve two roles. On the one hand, they satisfy our human "cognitive imperative" that wishes to make sense of mysterious realities by telling cosmic stories that interpret the meaning of human life. This is the religious/mythic/cosmic meaning of extravagant burial practices and rites. On the other hand, it has a pragmatic, manipulative and greedy economic meaning as a way for those in charge of the jewelry surpluses to artificially inflate the price to stay in power.

The Younger Dryas

Between 12,800 and 11,600 years ago, the climate turned colder and the rains diminished, drying out the Middle East. This 1200-year-long period is referred to as the Younger Dryas. "Later" Natufians had to move 700 miles north and east of 'Ain Mallaha to the foothills of the Taurus and Zagros Mountains. They built villages like Hallan Çemi Tepesi in what is now Turkey with the most elaborate architecture yet seen, lived on nuts and fruits they gathered in the forest, and hunted goats, deer, and wild boar. The climate forced them return to a more strictly hunter-gatherer lifestyle, mobile and egalitarian, but far less wealthy. They buried individuals, now, rather than families, and the burials were temporary. After an interval sufficient for the corpse to be reduced to a skeleton, the graves were dug up and the bones carried—all jumbled together in baskets, often missing parts, especially the skulls—back to the deserted village of their golden origin, 'Ain Mallaha, a "sacred site existing in the nether world between history and myth," where they were reburied (Mithen 2003: 46–51).

Here we see the realm of myth receding. The holy location where everyday life and the mythic realm meet is no longer here, but 700 miles away, back there, and associated with another era when our relationship to the land was different, a golden age inhabited by our ancestors, blessed by their memory; for they were the protagonists of our myths, and our recent dead will not rest easily except in the company of those heroes.

Contemporary with the late Natufian village of Hallan Çemi Tepesi in Turkey was Abu Hureya on the banks of the Euphrates in what is now Northwest Syria. Changes in Abu Hureya over the course of the Younger Dryas give us a convenient model for understanding the adaptations Mesolithic people had to make as the climate swung back and forth. About 11,000 years ago the village was built right on the edge of a forest, making it convenient for the people to stroll out every day to gather fruits and nuts. Resources were abundant and the gardens were wild. But as the extended cold spell took effect, the forest retreated due to strongly reduced rainfall. Fruit and nuts became more scarce and the trip to gather them more burdensome so that the people had to rely on their wild grasses for a significant proportion of their nourishment. By 10,000 years ago, the drought had become so severe that the site of Abu Hureya had to be abandoned. Three centuries later, however, the mini Ice Age had come to an end, the rains began to fall, and the people returned to the site of their ancestors' village with new skills. They had domesticated wheat, rye, and barley (Lewis-Williams and Pearce 2005: 21).

Precisely what must have happened in those 300 years will be discussed in Chapter 19 when we get to the Neolithic revolution; but for now it is enough to observe that dry conditions had evidently forced them to master the art of domestication (Mithen 2003: 53). This was characteristic of the Mesolithic Age in general. The Upper Paleolithic, with its fairly stable conditions of drought and ice, had placed a premium on knowing where to be and when, so as to intercept herds of animals that migrated with the changing seasons, and kill large numbers of them. Vegetation was scarce and unreliable. But with the coming of the Mesolithic, mass killings of animals herds were no longer necessary; the warmer weather was less conducive to storing surpluses of meat; and with the new flora and fauna made possible by the rains, it was no longer necessary to be precisely at the right place at the right time. Life had become more variable, and the rules could be rewritten as the situation demanded. The world had become less predictable and less harsh, and human consciousness adapted and became more flexible, too (Mithen 2003: 148f).

Ceremonial burial sites

Lepenski Vir (8800–7800 years ago), which Steven Mithen (2003) calls "the first hunter-gatherer village in Europe," was built beside the Danube River, "the Mesolithic Highway." The remains of canoes and fishing nets have been found there, and the Mesolithic Age is characterized by the exploitation of fish and other sea foods (Mithen 2003: 161). Indeed, Mesolithic villages near the seacoast are often identifiable by the huge mounds of discarded shells they left behind.

Brian Hayden (2003) does not agree with Mithen that Lepenski Vir was an everyday residential village. He thinks the evidence points to intermittent use, that it was "a cemetery for the veneration of ancestors." He points to the large, carved boulders, elaborate hearths, and numerous prestige items. They are not what one would expect for day-to-day domestic tasks, and must have had, rather, a grander, more ceremonial function. The fact that small structures resembling homes are found there does not necessarily mean that Lepenski Vir was a village, for such structures appear in various parts of the world in the form of cemeteries where rituals are periodically held—e.g. Maya sites in Mexico, Vanuatu in New Hebrides, and modern Vietnamese lineage houses (Hayden 2003: 205).

Most convincing for Hayden's argument is the fact that the Mesolithic site on the Danube resembles cemeteries on the Northwest Coast of North America, still used by Native Americans as feasting locations where the living descendants of the dead honor them from time to time but do not reside. Another trait the Pacific sites share with those of the European Mesolithic, despite their being separated by nearly nine millennia, is the large number of individuals who died a violent death, which "likely indicates high levels of competition over resources and wealth" (Hayden 2003: 162). Steven Mithen may disagree about the function of Lepenski Vir, but he agrees, in general, that there were such ceremonial burial sites during the Mesolithic, and that they were used as places of ritual to maintain societies and exchange gossip, tools, furs and luxury items (Mithen 2003: 168f).

The end of the Mesolithic

By 8000 years ago, Mesolithic hunter-gatherers living in the general vicinity of the Danube were hearing rumors of a new people who lived in great wooden houses and controlled the game. Soon they found their neighbors using polished stone axes, firing clay vessels, and herding cattle (Mithen 2003: 178). Evidence from mitochondrial DNA ("mt-DNA") shows that the Mesolithic people were not slaughtered by the farmers or driven away.[1] Their mt-DNA survives in the Europeans of today, proving that they had to have intermarried with the newcomers and become Neolithic people themselves.

Thus, the distinctive remains left by Mesolithic hunter-gatherers—deer and wild boar bones together with tiny split-stone blades ("microliths") used for weapon-points and scrapers—gave way to the Neolithic package of timber-framed houses, pottery, polished stone axes, and domesticated crops and cattle. The Mesolithic people gradually became farmers. First by trading fur, game, and women for prestige items, and then by selectively adopting a few Neolithic practices. Eventually, there was no longer room for semi-nomadic hunters in a land occupied by farms, and Mesolithic culture collapsed completely (Mithen 2003: 189).

Chapter 19

Ritual and consciousness in the Neolithic

The Neolithic represents a major change in human consciousness and in the orga-nization of society. It is truly an *archetypal* development in the full sense of being a species-specific response in human behavior that produced strikingly similar solutions in the form of imagery and architecture as well as social organization. For in the West, alone, we are privileged to have archaeological evidence of two rather separate "Neolithic Revolutions." The first took place in the Near East, beginning as early as eleven millennia ago with agricultural discoveries that were dependent upon the plants, animals, topography and climate proper to the region. Agriculture then migrated up the Danube and around the coast of Europe and began all over again some 5000 years later in the British Isles, where the plants, animals, topography and climate were different. Two different regions, two differ-ent times, two different sets of circumstances, and yet the solutions are remarkably similar. There is both archetypal similarity and cultural difference, and this dem-onstrates unmistakably that the Neolithic Revolution in human consciousness was an organic response of the human psyche. It is almost *evolutionary* evidence for the development of human consciousness through history.

To come to grips with what human consciousness was doing in the Neolithic Age, we will first need to describe what archaeology has uncovered. To this end, we will discuss a few sites from the beginning of the Neolithic in the Near East, and then a few more from the end of the Neolithic in the British Isles. After establishing the facts on the ground, we will be able to consider what was occur-ring in human consciousness by looking at the process of domestication, the arrangement of funeral rites, and the tensions that arose between hierarchical political organization and shamanism.

The Neolithic in the Near East

A shift in diet away from seafood is one of the characteristics of the Neolithic Revolution, but reverence for the past retained fish as an offering to be buried with the dead—as though to nourish the soul of the departed in the afterlife, but perhaps as a guide to show the dead the way to the sea. For, "The Neolithic dead were frequently placed in rivers that, of course, eventually find their way to the sea. The sea seems to have become part of the underworld in a way that earlier Mesolithic people did not accept" (Lewis-Williams and Pearce 2005: 284). Such facts strongly imply that the agricultural revolution was in the first instance a change in consciousness. The impetus for changes in lifestyle seems to have been led by changes of a mythic nature. In their book, *Inside the Neolithic Mind*, David Lewis-Williams and David Pearce (2005: 23) argue that the Neolithic was a "symbolic revolution" in which "changes in thought (superstructure) *preceded* changes in subsistence (infrastructure)."

The "domestication revolution," that is the turn to agriculture using domesti-cated plants and animals, began around 11,000 years ago in the Near East. It ended about 5500 years ago when bronze tools began to replace stone. The first wave of the new way of living, called "Pre-Pottery Neolithic-A," brought the practice of burying the dead twice ("secondary burial") and the creation of the first substantial cemeteries for permanent disposition—neatly laid out, in contrast to the random arrangement of Mesolithic graves.

We have already seen one form of secondary burial in connection with the Mesolithic Natufians who had to leave 'Ain Mallaha on account of the drying of the climate, but who periodically returned baskets full of their ancestors' bones to the village of their mythic/historical origins for reburial. In the Mesolithic, a secondary burial may have been as much practical as it was mythic. But the practice seems to have taken on a new and rather uncanny meaning for the earliest Neolithic people. In the second wave of cultural change ("Pre-Pottery Neolithic-B") skull and ancestor cults had become a key feature of the symbolic revolution along with bull imagery (Hayden 2003: 169–201). Much of the imagery from this period is rather disturbing.

Nea Nikomedeia

One of the first farming villages in Europe was Nea Nikomedeia in Greece 9500 years ago. Remains of the village reveal that it was comprised of separate, self-sufficient households, all arranged around common outdoor fireplaces. Having devoted themselves entirely to farming family-owned land, the tendency to distin-guish themselves as families grew stronger in the Neolithic than it had been among their hunter-gatherer ancestors. The village lasted about 2500 years, and was finally abandoned apparently because the soil had been exhausted (Mithen 2003: 167).

Village residences were built of reed bundles, plastered with clay and fastened to a framework of oak saplings. One larger building, about thirty feet square, apparently served a ceremonial function.

> Clay figurines sit upon wooden tables. Most are of women—moulded to have thin cylindrical heads, pointed noses and slit eyes. Arms are folded, with each hand grasping a breast made from a tiny knob of clay. Their diminutive size is compensated for by enormous, near-spherical thighs.
>
> (Mithen 2003: 164)

Plastered reed figurines are common in the first Neolithic villages. Precisely what they mean may be hard to specify, but they are uniformly associated with the earliest agriculture in the Eastern Mediterranean area and surely point to a new symbolic/mythic understanding, a new stage in the history of consciousness.

The eyes of 'Ain Ghazal

Two or three hundred years after the founding of Nea Nikomedeia, the largest of the Neolithic towns, 'Ain Ghazal, was built at the outskirts of what is now Amman, Jordan (Mithen 2003: 83). The structures were a good deal more substantial, having rectangular stone walls and lime-plastered floors. Evidently people no longer knew one another's business, as they had in hunter-gatherer settlements, for here much took place behind thick walls (Mithen 2003: 76). Again, clay statues constructed on reed armatures were found, but this time they have "eerily large eyes outlined by black, oval ridges," and they are not arranged on tables but buried under the floors of long abandoned houses (Figure 19.1). One figure depicts a woman thrusting her breasts forward with her hands—reminiscent of the knobby breasts at Nea Nikomedeia and of wall decorations to be mentioned below, found at Çatalhöyük (Mithen 2003: 84f).

Figure 19.1 The eyes of the 'Ain Ghazal statues.

Source: Professor Gary O. Rollefson, Department of Anthropology, Whitman College, Walla Walla, WA. Photograph by John Tsantis.

A minority of the dead were buried beneath the floors—undoubtedly the skeletons of the powerful whose soft tissues had been removed in an earlier burial (Mithen 2003: 101). Furthermore, the practice of burying big-eyed statues together with the bones of powerful ancestors suggests something about how the dead were regarded. "Their ability to 'see' was beyond anything that ordinary human beings could experience. They were frighteningly omnipercipient" (Lewis-Williams and Pearce 2005: 75). The souls of the dead must have had the perceptive powers of the most powerful of shamans who traveled through the invisible planes of the cosmos. Lewis-Williams and Pearce (2005) quote Waldemar Bogoras, the great pioneer in collecting anthropological evidence of shamanism in Siberia a century ago. He found that the eyes of a Chuckchee shaman were universally said to be so striking that one destined to become a shaman could reliably be recognized by his gaze.

[T]he eyes of a shaman have a look different from that of other people, and they explain it by the assertion that the eyes of the shaman are very bright, which, by the way, gives him the ability to see "spirits" even in the dark.
(Lewis-Williams and Pearce 2005: 70)

The eyes of the living were also important to the citizens of 'Ain Ghazal, for the shrines all had a focal point. The earliest ones had an apse and a screen-wall to direct the gaze of participants in ritual. Later, when the shrines were built as round buildings, orthostats ("standing stones [to] emphasize the vertical dimension of the three-tiered cosmos") were used to focus attention. The theme of shamanic transformation appears as well. For there is evidence of human and animal sacrifice; under the floor human skulls, their flesh replaced by carefully molded plaster to make them resemble living people, are buried with the bones of gazelles, a juxtaposition that suggests both translation between cosmic planes and the transmutation of entranced human souls into animals (Lewis-Williams and Pearce 2005: 100). 'Ain Ghazal means "Place of the Gazelle."

'Ain Ghazal lasted about a millennium and ended in ecological disaster around 8300 years ago. The soil had been exhausted through overuse, and lost through erosion; fuel had become scarce; the river had become polluted with human waste; and infant mortality had reached catastrophic proportions. The same fate befell all of the Pre-Pottery Neolithic-B towns of the Jordan Valley. Surviving citizens were required to return to nomadic pastoralism (Mithen 2003: 87). It appears that the Neolithic farmers quickly lost the trust in and respect for the natural world that had served their hunter-gatherer ancestors so well only a few generations earlier. Neolithic efforts to control nature seem to have ended in the people coming "to fear and despise the wild" (Mithen 2003: 96).

The model cosmos of Çatalhöyük

Contemporary with 'Ain Ghazal and Nea Nikomedeia is the most famous and spectacular of all the early Near East Neolithic towns, Çatalhöyük, in south-central

Turkey (9000–8000 years ago). It was a wealthy and elaborately built town surrounded by fertile land and abundant game, and engaged in a lucrative trade in
high-quality obsidian acquired from the nearby Taurus Mountains. Again there
were burials under the floors (Hayden 2003: 188). A layout of the town shows forty
or fifty more-or-less rectangular rooms and four or five courtyards, all built as a
single structure, without hallways or windows, and accessible only by ladders
leading down from openings in the roof (Lewis-Williams and Pearce 2005: 103,
Figure 22).

In the view of Lewis-Williams and Pearce (2005), the town of Çatalhöyük
represented a deliberate recreation of the three-tiered cosmos of the Ice Age caves.
The roof represented a "new land surface," the middle plane of the cosmos under
the sun and the rain, where the crops grew and the animals roamed, the sphere of
empirical consciousness (Figure 19.2). But to enter the roof openings and climb
down the ladders was to enter a "*built* underworld," a maze of structures in which
homes were not distinct from shrines, and traveling through them was equivalent
to moving through the chambers of limestone caves. Indeed, there were limestone
caves nearby in the Taurus mountains, and the people had brought home stalactites to place in the artificial underworld they had created (Lewis-Williams and
Pearce 2005: 102–12). Also reminiscent of the caves are small unpainted chambers behind the walls of richly decorated rooms, as though for the isolation of
vision questers. The authors believe it likely that as people moved through and

Figure 19.2 Çatalhöyök, roof level.

Source: original pen and ink drawing by Ann Yoost Brecke.

between the rooms of the town, they "made statements about their social statuses, in the same way that a Christian priest makes a statement about his status when he moves into the sanctuary of a cathedral."[1] Furthermore, the walls of those rooms bear some of the characteristic decorations of the Paleolithic caves, especially geometrical ("entoptic") imagery and hand prints (Lewis-Williams and Pearce 2005: 112, 119–22).

Jutting out from the walls disturbingly are large plastered heads of rams and bulls and the breasts of human women—some with their nipples split open and the skulls of vultures, foxes and weasels looking out. One thinks again of the native art of the Northwest coast of North America (Kwakiutl, Haida, etc.), with its fierce, teeth-bared, nostrils-flaring, eyes-wide-open depictions of animals and humans inside one another. Through anthropological study with living practitioners, we know that the Pacific coast Native Americans meant their art to portray a cosmic process of hunting, devouring and renewal in which humans cooperated with the sacred cycles of Nature by eating animals appropriate to the season and recycling their remains so as to maintain the world order (Lévi-Strauss 1982). In contrast, the art of Çatalhöyük remains enigmatic and mute.

Wall paintings, which were periodically plastered over and renewed, depict a mélange of dancing and hunting, with human figures in leopard skins or naked or headless. A repeating theme of vultures—some with human legs—appears to refer to the town's practice of *excarnation*, that is, of exposing corpses to have their flesh devoured by vultures before their bones were buried under the floors of the houses (Lévi-Strauss 1982: 110–19; Mithen 2003: 92–6). The practice of excarnation has occurred here and there throughout the world, most famously by the Parsees in ancient Persia (now in India); and it is usually believed to free the soul, which may fly like a bird from the flesh that has held it earth-bound in life. Çatalhöyük is the earliest clearly documented site where excarnation was practiced. Later it became central to the megalithic tombs of the Neolithic Age in Western Europe (Hayden 2003: 191). In addition, it may also be associated with the death/trance analogy that occurs widely in shamanism (Lewis-Williams and Pearce 2005: 119).

The Neolithic in Western Europe

The argument for a history of consciousness that shows distinct "ages" through which our ancestors progressed is powerfully supported by the fact that we can see great similarities from one Neolithic society to another—even when they are separated by thousands of miles and several millennia. By the time Western Europeans had undergone the domestication revolution and begun building their mounds, megalithic tombs, passage graves, and henges, Çatalhöyük and 'Ain Ghazal had been abandoned and buried under the sand for perhaps 3000 years. No one from Western Europe had visited those places or been taught their rituals and mythic narratives. The monuments they left behind were quite different, yet there is deep similarity. Again there is a fundamental tension between economic and political forces on the one hand and a neurologically based shamanism on the other; again their enduring structures are where the powerful are buried; and again each monument is a model cosmos, an artificial underworld that repeats many of the themes already encountered in the Ice Age caves.

Bryn Celli Ddu

The oldest of the Western European megaliths date from about 6800 years ago. There is a progression of architectural styles of monument construction that generally holds true. The West European Neolithic began with huge burial mounds that covered a stone chamber at the center containing the bones of the ancestors. Later such mounds were built as "passage graves" so they could be entered for seasonal rituals. In a final stage, the monuments were built as henges, arrangements of huge standing stones. One of the most interesting examples, however, the one we have chosen to illustrate many of the themes involved in megalith constructions, Bryn Celli Ddu, on the Welsh island of Anglesey, was built first as a henge which was later buried and incorporated into a passage grave. It dates from perhaps 5000 years ago (Figure 19.3).

Bryn Celli Ddu ("The Mound in the Dark Grove") is now a famous megalithic monument, though it passed unnoticed for millennia. As is true of nearly all the monuments of the European Neolithic, it is surrounded by a ditch and earthen bank, inside of which fourteen huge standing stones were erected in a circle, without any identifiable celestial alignment. At the base of some of the stones are

Figure 19.3 Bryn Celli Ddu, entrance.

Source: original pen and ink drawing by Ann Yoost Brecke.

deposits of burnt human bones and shattered quartz crystals. One contains the nearly complete cremation of a fifteen-year-old girl. At the center of the henge was a ritual pit.

These details suggest that from the beginning the henge was conceived as sacred ground, set apart for ritual purposes. Cremation, possibly sacrifice, and quartz crystals all belong to the shamanic death/trance complex for acquiring extraordinary powers through altered states of consciousness. Anthropologists believe that the henge served social functions of a wide variety, including trade and the cementing of alliances. "As in the Near East, economic and religious activities were probably not clearly differentiated. Religion was an integral component of daily life, not a gloss on it. Neolithic people could not imagine life without religion" (Lewis-Williams and Pearce 2005: 175).

Before the henge was buried in the soil that makes it a mound, an inner chamber was first created directly to the east of the ritual pit, employing broad standing stones placed side-by-side to form walls, and roofed by similar stones resting on their tops. A passageway some twenty-five feet long was formed with similar, somewhat smaller stones functioning as walls and ceiling, and running out to the bank and ditch on the eastern side of the henge. Once a mound of earth was heaped up to nearly twice the height of the standing stones, it was ringed about with curbstones whose arc bends inward at the eastern side to emphasize the entrance to the passage. Outside the ditch, directly across from the entrance, most passage graves have been sanctified by the burial of a cremated human being and an animal. At Bryn Celli Ddu, an ox is buried there. All of these details suggest that the passage grave is a transition zone, a place where ritual is performed, where the dead are transmuted by fire, where the dead and those in trance make the transit between cosmic planes.

The role and function of megalithic monuments

Brian Hayden (2003: 230) states what may seem to be obvious when he says that the megaliths "were megalomanic monuments to the dead." They surely had to do with the honoring of ancestors rich enough to afford the immense planning and labor required. In the British Isles, that wealth came primarily from owning cattle, and "societies that depend on herding tend to have hierarchical political organizations" (Hayden 2003: 237).

Hayden notes there is plenty of evidence that the tombs—especially if they were passage graves—were "constructed to induce or enhance altered states of consciousness." There are entoptic forms inside and at the entrances of the passageways, and evidence for the use of psychotropic substances such as Amanita mushrooms and opium has been found (Hayden 2003: 235). Hayden backs up his interpretation by describing an amazingly similar treatment of the death of the elite, including the erection of megaliths and extensive feasting in the highlands of Sulawesi, Indonesia (Hayden 2003: 238–45). Acoustic tests done inside the passage graves have found a resonance capacity somewhat like that of the painted galleries of the Paleolithic caves. The mounds therefore appear to have been constructed for conducting rituals designed to alter consciousness. The passage graves were

> far more than symbolic or metaphysical gateways to other dimensions. Rather, their structures permitted the creation of extraordinary experiences that could have been understood as the physical manifestation of those powers—venues where other worlds were actually brought into being.
>
> (Watson 2001: 189)

Although no celestial orientation has been discovered for Bryn Celli Ddu, most of the passage graves and henges do have such a connection, which makes it appear that they were deliberately built to send the souls of the elite ancestors on their journey toward the sun (as Hayden found among the Indonesians). It has recently been discovered, for example, in the passage grave at Newgrange in Ireland, that a "fake lintel" was constructed over the entrance (Figure 19.4). A lintel is the horizontal crosspiece that forms the top of a doorway. In the case of Newgrange,

Figure 19.4 Entrance to Newgrange Mound, lintel removed.

Source: original pen and ink drawing by Ann Yoost Brecke.

quartz blocks were made to be removed from the lintel, and scratch marks indicate that they *had* been. At sunrise on the shortest day of the year, direct sunlight enters Newgrange through the slit that is opened by removing the blocks; and for seventeen minutes a shaft of light illuminates carved triple spirals in the cruciform chamber at the end of the passage (Lewis-Williams and Pearce 2005: 229–31). Thus, spirals and ancestors were conceptually connected with the cycles of the sun (Hayden 2003: 245).

Hayden (2003) points out that the same spiral design is carved into Indonesian monoliths. The design has also been found decorating a mace head uncovered in the megalithic grave at Knowth. In all probability it was a ceremonial mace, not a tool but a symbol of its owner's power.

> The owner . . . exercised political power over other people, and that power was posited in a particular cosmology and the continuing influence of the dead. There was, the Neolithic maces tell us, a close relationship between access to spiritual realms and control of people. Politics and religion went hand in hand.
>
> (Lewis-Williams and Pearce 2005: 221)

The agreement between Hayden, Lewis-Williams and Pearce over the importance of the spiral motif suggests another feature of passage graves—that they were designed to "send off" the souls of the departed. The ritual route followed by the body of the deceased as it is carried in for its final disposition goes first one way and then the other—just like the spirals drawn with a single line. This route is most evident at Knowth, also in Ireland, where the central chamber has been built as a large dome, suggesting that "after the 'descent' into a 'cave' there is a view upwards to a realm above." Lewis-Williams and Pearce (2005: 218) find this to be an architectural replica of "the mental vortex that leads from the second stage of our neuropsychological model into the third stage of hallucinations as another existential realm . . . The 'cave' in the tomb replicated the cave in the mind." They seem to have discovered the myth of the soul which Jung has identified as the individuation process, the Sun's Night-Sea-Journey. It stands as the primary interpretive model in *Symbols of Transformation* (*CW5*), *Psychology and Alchemy* (*CW12*) and his seminar on Kundalini (*Sem32*).

Consciousness and altered states in the Neolithic

Whether we talk about the residences and shrines of the earliest agricultural villages in the Near East, or the mounds and henges that were built when the same revolution reached the British Isles, the central characteristic of Neolithic consciousness appears to be the active involvement and creative control they exercised over the relationship between the empirical world of survival and the greater three-tiered cosmos they visited in their altered states. In the Old Stone Age, people accepted nature's layout of the caves. Imagination was *guided* by

Nature. By contrast in the Neolithic Age, consciousness shaped elements in the empirical world to bring them into line with the visionary world. Imagination *shaped* Nature.

> Neolithic people eliminated the variable labyrinth [of the caves] and replaced it with more predictable and simpler structures of their own design. In doing so they gained greater *control* over the cosmos and were able to "adjust" beliefs about it to suit social and personal needs.
>
> (Lewis-Williams and Pearce 2005: 85)

The transcendent ideas that Neolithic people mapped onto the landscape were cultural adaptations of the neurologically generated three-tiered cosmos we have inherited with our brain structure. From the beginning to the end of the age of domestication, they found symbols to unite the two realms through architectural forms "that still have an effect upon the imagination" (Fagan 1998: 124). Lewis-Williams and Pearce (2005) agree. They walked along the avenue of standing stones that forms a processional entrance to the henge at Avebury and found that they could "appreciate, though perhaps not understand, the vastness and subtlety, ingenuity and technical brilliance, socio-political labyrinth and conceptual intricacy of the Neolithic world" (Lewis-Williams and Pearce 2005: 202).

Shamanism and domestication

In discussing the developments of the Mesolithic Age, we noted that the people of Abu Hureya disappeared for a mere 300 years and returned as farmers. We wondered what had happened to change their conscious behavior from frustrating the domestication process by harvesting their grain before it became ripe and brittle to domesticating the grain by manipulating the natural evolutionary process of selection.

Lewis-Williams and Pearce (2005) believe they have an answer to this question. They note that the first uses of molded, hardened clay were those big-eyed statues buried beneath the floors in Neolithic towns of the Near East. Only later did it dawn on people that they could use clay to make pottery vessels. Clearly, therefore, spiritual inspiration came first—ideas and images gathered in altered states of consciousness and were then woven into new mythic narratives. Practical applications followed (Lewis-Williams and Pearce 2005: 77).

Mithen (2003) found another instance of religion coming first and practical invention following. At Göbekli Tepe (Figure 19.5) in southeast Turkey, seven-ton limestone pillars with "shoulders" were erected on a hill around 11,500 years ago—all carved with male animals plus one human figure with an erect penis—the sort of imagery associated with hunter-gatherers; 11,500 was the turning point between the Mesolithic and the Neolithic in the Near East. As Mithen stood there on that hilltop, knowing that genetic analysis has shown the earliest strain of domesticated wheat came from the very region that had produced the carved

Figure 19.5 Göbekli Tepe.

Source: photograph by Professor Klaus Schmidt, Deutsches Archäologisches Institut, Berlin.

pillars, he realized that gathering the vast amounts of wild grain that would have been required to feed the workers had to have taught the people the principle of domestication.

> [S]ome may have carried bags of grain to sow in their own wild gardens. As they did so, they were spreading not just the new seed but also a new way of life to the hunter-gatherer-cultivator villages.
>
> (Mithen 2003: 67)

Lewis-Williams and Pearce (2005: 144) pursue this idea into the question of how animals became domesticated and find the secret to lie in the "shifting relationships between spirit-animals and real animals, an important part of the way in which shamans build up their status." Shamans the world over have spirit familiars who teach them, aid them in their work, and carry out their wishes. They become familiar with and transform themselves into spirit-animals, thereby learning to control them. In the Neolithic, therefore, it seems they started out by domesticating spirit-animals, later on found spirit-aurochs were indistinguishable from fleshly aurochs, and finally learned that real aurochs could be controlled like their spirit doubles.

There is no literature from the Neolithic to prove these hypotheses, so Lewis-Williams and Pearce (2005) rely on the same two pillars of inference that Jean

Clottes and others have used in making sense of cave art: the fact that the human neuro-psychological apparatus is everywhere the same, and the testimony of contemporary shamans in traditional societies who are engaged in related activities. Thus, the Barsana people of Colombia are a shamanic society that models its longhouses after the structure of the greater cosmos. Their shamans are said to "become" jaguars, eagles and anacondas, each of which is the primary predator on one of the cosmic tiers (land, sky, and water/underworld). By transforming into one after the other of these predators, a shaman can move between the cosmic planes (Lewis-Williams and Pearce 2005: 88–94). Other anthropologists (e.g. Reichel-Dolmatoff 1971, 1975) have found that many native South American shamans have a special relationship with jaguars and eagles and are particularly feared for their ability to become jaguars. Lévi-Strauss has shown that it is a universal characteristic of South American mythology that jaguars are wild people and people domesticated jaguars (Lévi-Strauss 1969). Therefore, "As Barsana shamans *are* jaguars, Çatalhöyük shamans may have *been* bulls." The Barsana even "say their shamans . . . 'domesticate' spiritual jaguars" (Lewis-Williams and Pearce 2005: 137, 139).

The /Xam San use a single word, /ki, "to mean both supernatural possession of a spirit animal and ownership of real flocks and herds."[2] "Wild animals became akin to domesticated animals through the notion of shamanic /ki in a way comparable to that in which South American Desana shamans kept spiritual jaguars" (Lewis-Williams and Pearce 2005: 143). The most important game animals for the /Xam San were springbucks—as were aurochs in Çatalhöyük and gazelles in 'Ain Ghazal. The shamans of the game wore caps made from the scalps, including the ears, of springbucks; it was believed that real springbucks would follow anyone who wore such a cap. One such shaman, a woman named Tãnõ-!Khauken, said:

> She kept a castrated springbuck "tied up" . . . so that it did not wander about. She said she could untie the springbuck and send it among wild springbucks so that it would lead the herd to the place where her people were camped.
> (Lewis-Williams and Pearce 2005: 142)

She called it her "heart's springbuck," which the authors interpret to mean that it was her animal helper, her spirit familiar (Lewis-Williams and Pearce 2005: 142).

The whole shamanism/domestication complex is contained in the shaman's story: shamans get their power, in part, from spirit-animals; spirit-animals give the shaman some control over game animals; spirit-animals sometimes mingle with and are indistinguishable from real animals; and the appearance of incarnated spirit-animals seemed to prove the shaman's power (Lewis-Williams and Pearce 2005: 144). Something new was occurring in Neolithic consciousness. People were learning to apply non-ordinary experience to everyday life. If spirit-animals could be domesticated, then perhaps game animals could, as well. The imaginal world of altered states of consciousness was becoming more useful and employable, and the experts in this department, the shamans, were showing the way.

Dangerous souls and Neolithic funeral rites

Over at least seven millennia, from the Mesolithic inhabitants of 'Ain Mallaha to the passage graves of the British Isles—and even much further into more recent times that our survey has not yet reached—we find a variety of funeral practices, all of which involve at least two ceremonies for the disposal of the deceased's remains. In the late stage of 'Ain Mallaha, dual interment seemed to make both practical and mythic good sense. Having been driven some 700 miles north of their original home, the Natufian people remembered the site of their glorious beginnings with special reverence, and wanted the bones of their relatives to reside there permanently. By the time of Çatalhöyük, serial funerals had become a necessity for a different reason. Bones were buried beneath the floors of their homes, and this required that the soft tissues be removed first.

Progress of the deceased's soul

It seems clear today that over a period of ten or eleven millennia, our ancestors found it necessary to practice dual funerals. Wealthy and influential people decided which corpses should be honored by ceremonies that articulated the mythic foundations and cosmology of their societies. Shrines like the elaborately decorated rooms of Çatalhöyük and the passage graves of the British Isles were built at great effort and expense to make such rites possible.

Clearly, there were several stages of post-mortem existence, and the rites were designed for the living to help the dead get safely through them (Lewis-Williams and Pearce 2005: 79). The biogenetic structuralists articulate the widely accepted three-stage process behind those multiple funeral ceremonies. In the first stage, the deceased is *separated* from the living through a first funeral, when the body is removed from the village to a place of burial or excarnation. In the second stage, the living members of the community (and in his isolation, the deceased as well) go through a *transition* period, where they learn to carry on in the new circumstances introduced by the death. Then, in a third stage—when the bones are buried under the floor, the skull plastered with artificial flesh, or the passage grave entered for the final rites—the dead are reintegrated into the life of the community with new identities and new roles as ancestors, and the living adopt a new reverence for them (McManus 1979a: 195).

Pascal Boyer (2001) finds this same structure manifested in two examples of double funerals he observed in the Philippines. Such dual funerals have essentially the same structure as any rite of passage. Like puberty rituals, they involve removal from the community, seclusion for a time, and reentry into the community with a new status. Therefore, at the time of the first disposal, the dead body is dangerous and must be removed. After a period of seclusion, a second disposal deals with the skeleton or skull, which is a more proper, stable, and less dangerous entity (Boyer 2001: 208f).

Corpses, Boyer (2001) reminds us, induce dissociation. They present all of our inference systems with contradictions they cannot handle. We cannot get used to the fact that everything we know about this person has ceased, all our familiar expectations frustrated. The body looks recognizably the same, but everything has changed. We wonder, "How she would have wanted" things to be taken care of. Does she still "want" in her new condition of being; does she listen in on our conversations; is she jealous of our vitality; does she bear resentments over the slights she bore while she was alive due to our actions? The time between the funeral of separation and the funeral of incorporation allows our anxiety and dissociation to subside (Boyer 2001: 224).

Dangers of the disembodied soul

Archaeologist Timothy Taylor—whose youthful cutting ritual (described in Chapter 14) brought him face-to-face with his own death, induced a transformative altered state of consciousness, and gave him a sense of professional purpose—wants us to stop romanticizing the past and our ancestors. Altered states may surely be transformative and potentially wonderful, but they also shake us to our foundations, expose us to existential dread, and can be abused for selfish and destructive purposes. The uncanny shock of a relative's death has been universally disruptive to our personal and social stability. It gives rise to the idea that the deceased are still with us in the form of a soul that moves about invisibly, has preternatural capabilities, is "omnipercipient" like the reed-and-plaster statues of 'Ain Ghazal, and must be defended against with rituals powerful enough to reorient the thinking of both the living and the dead.

Taylor (2002) believes that as the Ice Age ended the idea became common that people buried at the back of caves "were still somehow there" in the form of souls, permanent haunting beings. "It became important that this disembodied soul should find a place to live, and the idea of this place being a new body, magically constituted on some other plane of existence, took shape." In Europe around 15,000 years ago, fetal burials began, suggesting the idea of the earth as a great womb for some sort of resurrection (T. Taylor 2002: 225).

Jung encountered the idea of the souls of the departed as dangerous entities during his trip to Africa. He tells fragments of the story in several different places. Putting some of the details together, it seems that one of his safari bearers was a pregnant woman who one morning had a miscarriage that led to a severe infection that threatened her life. A shaman was called for, and he determined that the cause of her illness lay with the souls of the woman's parents, who had died young and wanted to draw the soul of their daughter into the other world to be with them. The shaman then built a tiny hut of stones, complete with a bed and other amenities to give the souls of the parents a comfortable place to stay so that they would leave their daughter alone. Jung says that "to everyone's surprise," the young woman recovered in two or three days (*CW8*: ¶575n; *Sem28*: 320f).

Jung described the little hut as a "ghost trap": "Occasionally the souls of the natives wander off and the medicine man catches them in cages as if they were birds" (*CW10*: ¶128). Clearly the great danger is that the souls of the dead can

snare those of the living and draw them, too, into the other world. Jung appre-
hended the sinister power exerted by the souls of the dead, as understood by the
natives. The biographer of his Africa journey seems to miss the point, however;
for he takes Jung to task for speaking of a "ghost trap," when a more accurate
translation of the native expression would be "ancestral shrine" (Burleson 2005:
157). Perhaps so, but it is a well-known phenomenon that the most dangerous
realities are typically given euphemistic names.

Lévy-Bruhl (1927) tells several such stories, most interestingly, perhaps, an
account from the same Mr. W. B. Grubb who was once accused of stealing a
Native American's pumpkins on the strength of someone's dream. Grubb's "ghost
trap" story recounts an incident from Chaco Canyon in which "witch doctors"
were planning to kill him, but first took the precaution of setting up little huts at
suitable distances along the route he was used to traveling, so that his soul would
be attracted by them after his death and his killers would be safe from his restless,
vengeful ghost (Lévy-Bruhl 1927: 262f).

> The desire of the disembodied soul [to repossess its property and spouse] is
> viewed as dangerous by the living, who had by all means to enchant, cajole,
> fight off, sedate, or otherwise distract and disable it . . . only as long as the
> flesh lay on the bones.
>
> (T. Taylor 2002: 27)

Funeral rites during the Neolithic, therefore, appear to have had a double purpose:
not only "to keep the unquiet soul zoned off" from the living, but also "firmly and
finally to incorporate the deceased into the realm of the ancestors" (T. Taylor
2002: 27).

Efforts to manage dangerous souls

Taylor (2002) advances four analogies to back up his interpretation of the souls of
the dead as dangerous agents. The earliest of these comes from the Greek historian Herodotus, writing about 2500 years ago (ca. 484–425 BC), reporting on
events in Iron Age Scythia, around 600 BC. At a first burial, the Scythian king was
interred with servants, food and horses. All the bodies, including those of the
horses, were given a temporary embalming, their bodies cleaned out and filled
with herbs. The purpose of this action was to preserve the body in a form that
would be attractive to the soul, "encouraging it to remain close to its own corpse"
(T. Taylor 2002: 126). Doubts about the historical accuracy of Herodotus' account
were put to rest in the 1950s when a Siberian burial was discovered. Grave robbers
had allowed freeze-drying Arctic air into the grave preserving everything in
perfect parallel to what Herodotus had described.

After the first burial, a dangerous transition period began, when normal rules
were suspended and the king's closest servants could be strangled in preparation
for the final burial, the rite of incorporation of the king and his retinue into the

world of the dead. In that final burial, the king was provided with a mounted army. Fifty young men were strangled, cleaned out, stuffed with herbs and sewn up again. Then they were set astride similarly stuffed horses, all held up with stakes and horizontal rods running through the bodies. Thus, at the final rite, the king enters the world of the dead at the head of an army, manifesting all his earthly glory (T. Taylor 2002: 124–35).

An amazing parallel to the Scythian example, and from the same area of the world, is the multiple burial of Vladimir Ilich Lenin. After a first embalming, his body was displayed for a week in the center of Moscow and then buried in the permafrost for a three-year transition period. At the end of that time, he was permanently embalmed by immersion in a chemical bath, and given a "secondary burial," with viewing platform, that constituted a "ritual of incorporation." He was moved again six years later, in 1930, to a black granite mausoleum. Only then, after the apparently final disposition of Lenin's body and soul, did Stalin begin the reign of terror to establish his own hold on power (T. Taylor 2002: 136–43).

But there is a great ambiguity in this unburied body that still requires constant work to make it appear natural—including a laboratory with 100 scientists, each with a human body on which to experiment. As recently as 1998, the Patriarch of Moscow, Alexis II, "stated that, if Lenin's body was not buried, 'his malign soul would go on hovering over the country to its great detriment' " (T. Taylor 2002: 143). Thus the Neolithic fear of the dangerous soul remaining in this world persists in the human psyche as a compelling pattern of thought.

Taylor's third story comes from tenth-century Russia via the Arab writer Ibn Fadlan, who claimed to have been an eye witness. A Viking king was buried first for ten days in a wood-lined chamber and covered with earth. At this point, "He has died physically but not socially." A great funeral pyre was prepared for the "social death and social resurrection in the world of the ancestors," i.e. the "incorporation" (T. Taylor 2002: 117). For this, the king's dangerous soul is kept near his corpse by the presence of his favorite concubine who is sacrificed immediately before the incorporation ceremony so that she can become his bride in death. Her freshly killed body is designed to persuade the king's soul to reenter his body for his last journey (T. Taylor 2002: 178).

Taylor's fourth argument has to do with European bog bodies, corpses buried in peat bogs to preserve them from decay about 2600–1600 years ago. All bog bodies that have been found bear evidence of execution or torture. In Taylor's plausible interpretation, these individuals were designed to be permanently kept in an unresolved liminal period, their souls never allowed to rest. Assuming the bog bodies all had transgressed social and religious rules—the reason for torture and execution—they could not be sacrificed for fear of offending the gods; they could not be properly buried without offending the ancestors; and they could not remain unburied, for then their souls would wander the earth doing harm to the living. The only solution was to keep them permanently marginal (T. Taylor 2002: 165). Their bodies had to remain recognizable to keep their souls nearby; and the bogs, themselves, were liminal places, for they were watery, and yet raised above dry land, as such bogs always swell up to be. The decomposition process was arrested and time effectively stopped (T. Taylor 2002: 163).

Taylor has exploited the structure that all of our authors accept, namely that the multi-funeral phenomenon has to do with separation, isolation, and incorporation; he has used it to interpret a wide range of mysterious reports. By the end of his book, which includes much that we have ignored, it becomes impossible to believe that the souls of the dead have not been seen as uncanny and dangerous.

Neolithic elites and the decline of shamanism

The single most characteristic development of the Neolithic Age is the emergence of controlling elites, where increasing dependence on agriculture provided extraordinary opportunities for the people Hayden (2003) calls "aggrandizers." Aggrandizers are part of every primate society. Rhesus males who try to gain exclusive control over as many as possible of the highest ranking females or alpha chimpanzees who establish coalitions with other aggressive males to gain control of a troop are well-known examples. Similarly, strong-men played controlling roles in simple hunter-gatherer groups. Complex hunter-gatherer societies provided more opportunities for those seeking personal power. Talents in altered states of consciousness gave some the prestige of being respected shamans, while prowess with weapons gave others hunting prestige. But a new type of power emerged as agriculture made possible the accumulation of huge and fairly stable resources.

Aggrandizers' ambitions are effectively limited during times of scarcity, for the stockpiling of food cannot be tolerated when others are starving. But when everyone has enough, stockpiling is no longer a threat, and aggrandizers will be largely ignored as they indulge their ambitions and use every technique imaginable to draw others into their schemes. Thus, when resources became bountiful after the domestication revolution, aggrandizers were delighted to find themselves at a significant advantage (Hayden 2003: 222).

Control of spiritual resources

Once writing was invented and the ancient world entered the historical period, there is clear evidence that the sanctuaries of public cults have always been under the control of the highest elites. It was true in ancient Egypt as well as in the Inca and Aztec empires of the New World (Hayden 2003: 210). And there is plenty of evidence that it was also true in the Neolithic Age.

By contrast, among simple hunter-gatherers, like the San ("Bushmen") of southern Africa, everyone is free to dance and enter ecstatic states of mind for the purpose of contacting the invisible planes of the cosmos, renewing mythic consciousness and healing one another's ailments. When self-aggrandizing groups gain control of a society, however, they need to control the sources of spiritual power as well as the material wealth. Thus, the success of the "Big Men" of

Oceania, in Hayden's report, is viewed as essential for the group's success; and the Big Men take advantage of this society-wide perception. They grab exclusive control of the ancestral spirits and take over the role of the shaman (Hayden 2003: 223). Indeed, it frequently appears that only the elite "have" souls, for they are the only ones buried with elaborate dual ceremonies. Taylor notes, for instance, that the Neolithic burial mounds in Scotland's Orkney Islands were large enough to have held the bones of every individual who had lived and died on those islands during the Neolithic—"if the bones had been neatly packed, charnel-house wise." Instead, those mounds were treated more like cathedrals than graves, with only a few selected skulls displayed in niches (Taylor 2002: 25).

Mastery of spiritual—that is to say "mythic"—resources was essential if an elite were to have sufficient influence to persuade the majority of a society's members to work for common goals that would also enhance the aggrandizers' own ambitions. They needed to manipulate emotionally compelling symbols which had the power to "penetrate" to the unconscious neural networks of common citizens and move them to join with their neighbors. For it is unlikely they appealed to logic or "the issues" any more than modern politicians do. They needed to generate intense personal experiences that would link the individual's social identity with society's power structure (Hayden 2003: 191). Lewis-Williams and Pearce (2005) agree. Social discriminations and the hierarchical organization of society led to the emergence of elites who manipulated not only a society's surplus wealth but also its sacred images. They "controlled what could and could not be seen . . . within the tiered cosmology" (Lewis-Williams and Pearce 2005: 81).

Eventually shamans, whose power was based on direct personal experience of the invisible planes of the cosmos, became too unpredictable for those who held political power. What they wanted was *priests*, representatives of the sacred who could be counted upon to enact a scripted set of rituals that would have well-known results. The role of altered states of consciousness was reduced. There was no longer a place for spontaneous encounters with the sacred (Hayden 2003: 210). The turn from a society organized around polyphasic principles and wide-open to the sacred had already moved decisively in the direction of a monophasic, control-oriented society.

Struggles to control Neolithic symbols

What seems most likely to those who have closely examined the megalithic monuments of the British Isles is that they were built in the context of religious dissent. Stones from dismantled tombs were reused in new ones built at Knowth and Newgrange. In the process, rectilinear carvings that had been on display in the dismantled tombs were turned to the back and hidden in the new tombs, while curvilinear carvings were made on the newly exposed surfaces to express new cosmological doctrines (Lewis-Williams and Pearce 2005: 198).

We have evidence of similar struggles from largely the same time period in Egypt, where "hundreds of Monopoly 'games' unfolded in prehistoric times"

(Fagan 1998: 292). As the centuries passed, fewer and fewer players remained in the game, while formerly separate domains were acquired and merged. "Players changed—some acquired great influence, then lost it as charismatic individuals died or trading opportunities ended" (Fagan 1998: 292). Successful players were able to combine distinctive ideologies, symbols and rituals to grip the minds of the occupants of newly acquired lands and the workers who produced the surpluses. "These ideologies became an underlying factor in promoting the unification of Upper and Lower Egypt, starting with at least three predynastic chiefdoms that flourished in Upper Egypt around 3500 BC: Hierakonopolis, Nagada, and This, near Abydos" (Fagan 1998: 292).

A millennium later, in England, a 2000-year-long process began of building stone circles, ditches and earthworks, abandoning them, and building others. "Avebury's sacred monuments ... tell a story of changing religious beliefs and rituals, but also of spiritual continuity" (Fagan 1998: 141). That continuity expresses what was common to Neolithic consciousness, while the changes, abandoned sites, stolen dolmens and orthostats that were recarved for new monuments all reflect the way this myth, common to an entire civilization, was manipulated for secondary, local purposes.

Stonehenge was rebuilt three times. The first version, erected nearly 5000 years ago, had only two standing stones and a wooden structure. Over the next 500 years, the site was rebuilt with a new orientation to the midsummer solstice and "a double circle of bluestones set up in the center, but soon removed." The third version was built in three phases between 4550 and 3600 years ago. Stones were set up, moved to new locations, and more holes dug that were never occupied with stones. Finally, around 3600 years ago, the "avenue" was extended nearly two miles to the Avon River (Fagan 1998: 156).

Hayden (2003) makes a similar argument about the "bucrania" (bull skulls) that decorate the walls of Çatalhöyük shrines. Their display was meant to be a constant reminder of the power and wealth of the family whose funerals were held there. He finds a supporting tradition, again among the hill tribes of Southeast Asia, where memorable funeral feasts were sponsored by families whose wealth exceeded that of their contemporaries by a factor of at least ten (Hayden 2003: 192f).

A shamanic underground

As societies become more hierarchically organized, a uniformity of social expectations is imposed. Winkelman (2000: 126) observes that as social complexity grows, altered states of consciousness become limited to the elite, and the use of hallucinogens declines with increasing political integration. Conversely, when the elites struggle with one another, creating social instability, people tend to return to shamans who derive personal power from their familiarity with the greater cosmos and not from any political entity. Piers Vitebsky (1995), one of the better recent surveyors of the shamanistic phenomenon, for instance, reports that the

Achuar of Amazonia and the Baruya of New Guinea, who are governed by so-called "Big Men," or prominent warriors, suffer under "the instability of this kind of 'chieftainship' which fuels their chronic warfare and gives the shaman's magical powers of aggression such prominence" (Vitebsky 1995: 117). By the shaman's powers of aggression, Vitebsky refers to what elsewhere might be called "bewitching" the enemy, casting a curse or magic dart that may result in the illness or death of an individual who is the object of envy or revenge.

Lewis-Williams and Pearce (2005) address this issue by distinguishing two sorts of shamanism, which they call "vertical" and "horizontal." When shamans are themselves the respected elite of a society and when they are closely integrated with a stable ruling elite, their primary orientation is "vertical." Vertical shamans are primarily concerned with journeying through and explicating the *mythscape* of the cosmos. They are familiar with its invisible tiers and know how to draw conclusions from what they find there. They function in a ceremonial way at public rituals, and are respected—not feared.

The situation is quite different for "horizontal shamans." These are individuals who have a talent for altered states of consciousness and trust their own personal experience. Myth may go unnarrated, everybody knowing fragments of it but nobody having the authority or interest to spell it all out. Horizontal shamans journey for specific limited goals: to locate the game, to observe the movement of enemy bands, to restore the health of individuals. Because horizontal shamans act on their own authority and are not integrated into a stable political structure, they are more feared than respected. They may use their powers for selfish ends. They may attack other shamans with their magical powers or hire out their powers to serve the vengeful wishes of others. They may be as dangerous as the souls of the dead during that intermediate period before they have been formally incorporated into the realm of the ancestors. Horizontal shamans are more common in small hunter-gatherer groups, while vertical shamans require the stable hierarchical structure of a more complex society (Lewis-Williams and Pearce 2005: 86f).

When the stability of a complex society breaks down, however, the opportunity for horizontal shamanism grows, and it may be as murderous as struggles between competing elites. Indeed, it may be used by those elites against their opponents. Winkelman (2000) points out that even when political and economic hierarchies take over the control of religion and thereby limit the average individual's autonomy, shamans can function as "mediums" for the invisible spirits.

Summary: consciousness in the Neolithic

The ability to act upon and derive pragmatic benefit from the realm of myth was a major accomplishment of the Neolithic Age. Inspired by alternate worlds visited in non-ordinary states of awareness, our Neolithic ancestors learned to manipulate their environment as no species had ever done before. To find such practical applications, they had to take possession of their visions in new ways. Agriculture and architecture may have been their most outstanding visible achievements, but they are symptoms of the new stage they reached in their mastery of consciousness.

Such mastery opened the door to manipulation; the aggrandizers marched right in and seized the new conscious tool in order to reshape mythic forms in ways that would enrich themselves. The aggrandizers could not challenge the tiered universe—nor were they able to imagine doing so—for it is hard-wired. Nevertheless, myth, like every narrative, is composed of subsidiary episodes, and those episodes could be shaped and rearranged like the orthostats in a Çatalhöyük shrine or an English henge. Furthermore, every one of those building-block episodes was symbolically effective. Each one penetrated to deep neural networks and evoked profound emotion. The aggrandizers discovered a wonderful tool to manipulate the minds of others; this, too, marked a major development in the history of consciousness.

They all lived *in* the mythic world, manipulating aggrandizers as well as laborers, but the fact that they could struggle over which version of the myth was more accurate or effective tells us, too, that the beginnings of skepticism must also be a legacy of the Neolithic. Brian Hayden's (2003) observation that a tenth to a quarter of contemporary hunter-gatherer societies are comprised of people who have no interest in religion and ritual is supported by Peter Lamborn Wilson's experience gained while wandering Central Asia with Sufi-oriented Qalandars:

> A few were con-men and drug salesmen. The majority were amiable lazy wanderers of slight spiritual pretensions, very much like some of the young Westerners on the road in the Sixties. One might accuse them of living off the credulous, of posing as mystics, of social parasitism . . . [but] the bohemian life of the Qalandar is a valuable pressure-valve in a world so rigid and formal.
>
> A small but impressive minority of the Qalandars are—by any fair standard—genuine mystics.
>
> (P.L. Wilson 1988: 202)

Thus the roots of indifference and dissent can be found even in very small, simply organized societies, and they must have been present much earlier, surely in the Upper Paleolithic and very likely as far back as *Australopithecus*. What was new to the Neolithic was the formation of large factions of shifting identity that were openly competing for hegemony. Dissent and politics had become institutionalized. Shamanism as an egalitarian pursuit of self-transcendence had been overshadowed by a sort of priesthood that strengthened the hand of the economically mighty. The power of the individual had been circumscribed. Only the elite were treated as though they had souls.

Surely our Neolithic ancestors were not individuals in the sense that Jung had in mind when he lamented the fact that there were too few of them in the Europe of the twentieth century. But in a world where one could think, "I don't have to be part of the rectilinear-carvings group, I'd rather belong to the curvilinears," a sense of individuality has to have increased over that of the Mesolithic Age, when the graves were not orderly and the bones of the ancestors were mixed randomly together. Furthermore, the use of horizontal shamanism as a source of power for the dispossessed surely served a budding sense of individual integrity, even as it increased the forces of social dissent and undermined the symbolic manipulations of the wealthy.

Meanwhile, the strongest evidence for the vulnerability of the individual in the Neolithic is probably the fear of restless souls that had not yet been incorporated into the society of the ancestors. For the dangers they posed amounted to an immense "shadow projection." Every threat, cruelty and unfair treatment that humans were capable of committing and that might be restrained by the fear of being caught and having to suffer retaliation exceeded all human limits for the unburied souls. They were invisible and unanswerable before any court of justice. Furthermore, in the Neolithic they were the souls of the powerful, who had already been formidable and imperious in life. In death they became magnets for all the insecurities and everyday terrors that people lived with. The apparently consuming fear of restless souls is a testimony to the forces that worked against individuality and suggests how much each person must have been swallowed up in the forces of group identity.

The fear of restless souls closely resembles that of the horizontal shaman, and for the same reason. The issue has been eloquently summarized by Gerardo Reichel-Dolmatoff (1975) in regard to the Tukano people of Colombia's Upper Amazon, whose shamans are believed to be able to turn themselves into jaguars:

> The question is: How like a jaguar does a man become? A [shaman]-turned-jaguar is, for all exterior purposes, a true jaguar: He has the voice of a jaguar, he devours raw meat, he sleeps on the ground, and he has the highly developed vision and olfactory sense of the feline. . . . But in one aspect he is not a jaguar at all: In his attitude toward human beings. In this, he does not behave like a jaguar, but like a man—a man devoid of all cultural restrictions, but still a man. The motivation of revenge and the acts of sexual assault, of attacking from behind and in a pack, and of severing the victim's head are not jaguar but human traits. What turns into a jaguar, then, is that other part of man's personality that resists and rejects cultural conventions. The jaguar of the hallucinatory sphere, the jaguar-monster of Tukano tales, is a man's alter ego, now roaming free and untrammeled, and acting out his deepest desires and fears.
>
> (Reichel-Dolmatoff 1975: 132)

In the Neolithic period, myth taught our ancestors how to manipulate the empirical world, and the resulting surpluses taught the political and economic elites how to manipulate myth. Psyche's shadow, which had already been evident in the monkey anxiously enjoying the sexual favors of his alpha-male's consort, now became painfully conscious. It was flagrantly acted out on the stage of political control and conflict, and it was projected onto the souls of the dead—the most important and dangerous of whose skulls occupied places of honor under the floors and in the passage graves. As society moved from being maximally polyphasic to minimally polyphasic, mythic narratives became the battle ground of the wealthy and the shamans. The "verticality" of Upper Paleolithic mythology was becoming "horizontal" and vindictive, even as the natural world was falling more and more under the control of technology.

Chapter 20

Ritual and consciousness in the historical era

Already our review of the history of consciousness supports Jung's theory about our human tendency away from the eternal wisdom of the collective unconscious and toward empirical, ego-centered obsession with control, and we are only now approaching the people Jung considered the ancients. Attempts by elites to control the content and interpretation of myth did not end with the Neolithic. It became even more pronounced and exaggerated in the Bronze and Iron Ages. The dates for these techno-cultural periods differ by location. Bronze casting was well established in the Near East by 3500 BC, while the British Isles were still building megaliths. But apparently the move from stone tools to metal ones was not accompanied by an immediate change in mythology—surely the gods did not change much. Hayden (2003) notes that the warrior sun- and bull-gods of the Near East and the Mediterranean very likely had their origins in the earliest Neolithic pre-pottery cults. He mentions the Bull of Ugarit, the ancient city on Syria's Mediterranean coast (ca. 1540–1200 BC); the Phoenician Baal; and the Roman Mithras, who was allied with Helios, the sun-god, and whose ritual killing of the bull formed the central mystery of his cult (Hayden 2003: 203). The main feature of daily life that changed was the complexity of the social order and the size of the gap between those in power and those who performed the labor.

From the Neolithic to history

The Bronze Age largely coincides with Proto-Indo-European culture and language, which spread out from its origins on the steppes north of the Black Sea, the region known as Scythia, beginning around 6000 years ago, and lasted about 1500 years. The economy of the movement largely depended on pastoralism; but now a "secondary products revolution" had found tradable value in wool, hides, milk, and cheese. These required transportation to take them from the grazing lands to the markets, and for that domesticated horses were hitched to wagons (Hayden 2003: 271–3).

As societies increased from towns the size of Çatalhöyük to great cities, religious practices diversified, too—more radically than in the Neolithic, but along similar lines. While official religion revered gods proclaimed by elites to support their versions of socio-political hierarchy, the vast majority of laborers revered nature deities and the fertility gods of the woods (Hayden 2003: 291f). Such divisions were exacerbated by the fact that the elite, who derived their wealth from trade and the sale of grazing rights, lived in the towns and cities while many of the laborers were pastoral nomads, moving about with the herds, close to the land and folk beliefs of older millennia. Their mobility favored their independence from the central authorities. Meanwhile, the elites were running risky businesses, where disease and cattle raids could mean sudden losses that might have to be settled by their becoming slaves themselves. They fought one another and needed a class of warriors as well as priests (Hayden 2003: 278–84).

Thus, by 6000 years ago, the classical four-tier social structure—royalty, clergy, warriors and laborers—had been established and would remain fairly stable for more than five millennia, until the industrial revolution. Shepherds and cattle men were not the only class to wander far from the seat of public religion and develop their own allegiances with invisible dimensions of the cosmos. The warrior class, probably taught by altered states of consciousness they induced in themselves naturally by engaging in hand-to-hand combat that released hormones, endorphins and adrenaline, also used herbal drugs to alter their consciousness further. The notion of a drink of immortality that enabled one to partake in the consciousness of the gods was prominent in the Vedic soma, the Persian haoma, and in the later Roman ambrosia and Irish madhu. Symbols of the cup and the bowl (later the Grail) belonged to the Proto-Indo-European tradition. Warriors drank to feed an inner fire of divine possession and magical energy that helped them on the battlefield, while shamans drank to engage in warrior combat on invisible planes (Hayden 2003: 288).

Lewis-Williams and Pearce (2005) agree with Hayden (2003) regarding the symbolic continuity between the simpler Neolithic and the more complex Bronze Age. They cite *The Epic of Gilgamesh*, which dates from the third millennium BC, and describes a three-tiered Sumerian cosmos in which the beneficent Shamash rules in the heavens and the souls of the dead and other frightening spirits inhabit the underworld. The shamanic theme continues in the equivalence ascribed to seeing and wisdom—reminiscent of the big-eyed statues buried under Neolithic floors. The divine/human Gilgamesh, like the divine/human Mithras, kills the Bull of Heaven and takes its horns back to the palace, where he hangs them on the wall, as at Çatalhöyük. Gilgamesh's friend and foil, the primitive Enkidu, whom the gods placed in Gilgamesh's way to limit his power, represents the evolution of human society from its hunter-gatherer origins to pastoralism—that is to say, the process of the Neolithic. The urbanity of Gilgamesh, by contrast, represents the further concentration of the social hierarchy, the mixing of ethnic populations and the systematic management of resources that made Sumerian civilization far more complicated than what we have been looking at in Neolithic villages and towns. Enkidu's death, the great crisis for Gilgamesh, is celebrated with serial funeral rites, as in the Neolithic. Finally, transformations described in the epic allude to an interchangeability of people and animals, that is to the invisible shamanic planes accessible through altered states of consciousness (Lewis-Williams and Pearce 2005: 153–60).

Consciousness becomes more individual

The origin of real individuality through a growing dependence on directed thinking is the theme of Julian Jaynes' famous and very intriguing book, *The Origins of Consciousness in the Breakdown of the Bicameral Mind* (1976). He argues that prior to the great city-states of the Near East, humans knew what to do, where to hunt, how to avoid their enemies, etc. by listening to a voice that emanated from their non-dominant cerebral hemisphere. Why it should have been a *voice* has often been questioned. But we now know the non-dominant hemisphere has been mined for its wisdom at least since the Upper Paleolithic. No doubt a voice was sometimes heard by those who tuned their nervous systems, but that was not all that entered consciousness. Therefore, if we expand Jaynes' concept of the "voice" to include any sort of ecstatic shamanistic knowledge, we are on familiar ground; for we have already seen that architecture, pottery and domestication have all been derived from altered states of consciousness.

According to Jaynes (1976), a change took place in human consciousness around 1500 BC. Before that, carvings and inscriptions from Mesopotamia show the god as the king's confidant, an indication that access to non-ordinary consciousness was wide open and easy to achieve, which was the position that Neolithic elites claimed for themselves. Afterwards, however, carvings and inscriptions show the king begging the god—or, more frequently, the goddess—for counsel. Jaynes concludes the channel through the non-dominant hemisphere had narrowed and life-guiding inspirations had become more difficult as a result of two circumstances. The first is that the new urban environment had become almost unmanageably complex and dangerous. People could not afford to live much of the time in an "open" state of consciousness in which alpha-frequency brain waves predominated. To be safe, they had to cultivate the alert, ever-shifting beta-state that we call ordinary consciousness. Second, with the invention of writing, people began to rely more and more upon language and, therefore, the dominant hemisphere. Our ancestors had begun to set their linguistic hemispheres as the "default" position of their brains. They began to use directed thinking more the way we use it today, and that lay the foundation for developing an ego that more closely resembles ours.

Jaynes (1976) finds evidence for this new sort of ego around a millennium later, sometime before 700 BC, in the *Iliad* and the *Odyssey*. He distinguishes four stages in the use of Greek terms that suggest "mind" to us today: such as a stirring in the bowels, a pounding heart and a panting breath. In the first stage, the body merely pounds and pants. In the second stage, the characters have become aware of these physiological changes as indications of their subjective emotional state. Now the stirring and the pounding belongs to what we have described in Chapter 11 as a complex reaction: "I know I am scared, not just because the other guy is big and carries a club, but mainly because my heart is pounding and my knees unsteady." This describes the effect of the relatively primitive limbic system, LeDoux's rapid-response "low road," which protects us from threats in our environment before we have a chance to think about them. The fact that the characters Homer presents in the *Odyssey* interpret their bodily sensations as evidence of an emotional reaction shows growing reflective consciousness on the part of both the poet and his audience.

In Jaynes' third stage, the mind-expressions become truly "mental" in the sense that they refer "to internal spaces where metaphored actions may occur." Now the heart does not merely pound in the hero's chest but cherishes tender thoughts. The cerebral cortex is involved. Finally, in the fourth stage, these several "mind pieces" come together "into one conscious self capable of introspection" (Jaynes 1976: 260). The product of this Homeric development is the wily Odysseus who negotiates the world's dangers and his own emotions by keeping his own counsel and outsmarting his opponents with trickery.

We have seen tricksters before—as far back as the monkeys and as well organized as the aggrandizers of the Neolithic. If Jaynes (1976) has it right, it cannot be that no one had an "ego" capable of trickery before Odysseus. On the contrary, the breakthrough in consciousness recorded in the *Odyssey* must resemble the cultural explosion of the Upper Paleolithic. It must have been a new consolidation of many small, fragmentary gains that had been stretched out over many millennia. For in the Upper Paleolithic, it was not making art objects that was new; occasional carvings have been found dating tens and even hundreds of millennia earlier. Rather, what was new in the Upper Paleolithic was that artistic conventions and the narratives they illustrated had finally become so much a part of general human consciousness that painted walls and ceilings could be imagined by their creators as a sort of cultural statement, and the general public could be expected to understand the statement sufficiently. In the Upper Paleolithic, the history of consciousness had gotten as far as philosophizing in narratives that asked how did we get here, and what are we doing. These Old Stone Age developments were carried forward into the Neolithic, when people discovered they had some control over how the tale was told. They learned to shape the mythic narrative to benefit themselves, although the story remained a collective one.

By contrast, when the linguistic hemisphere has assumed its dominance, Odysseus is fully an individual from start to finish. Real egohood had become far less exceptional by 700 BC. All hearers of the story identify with the noble Odysseus; all have some inkling of what it means to be constantly "other" than everyone else, and following a different path. For Odysseus, the hero's "shamanic journey" occurs on the three-dimensional stage of earth, and it has become a moral contest. It asks who *we* are by telling a story about who a single individual is, a lone but imposing figure who is guided by a moral compass that brings him into conflict with both the heavenly gods (i.e. archetypal forces of the collective unconscious) and most of the humans he encounters (i.e. demands of the public world). Jung's idea of individuation aptly describes human experience for perhaps the first time in history.

The Greeks and Romans

Somewhat more than a century after Homer, Western philosophy got its start with Thales (ca. 624–546 BC). Thales and the philosophers who followed him, including Plato and Aristotle, used their wily Odyssean egos to liberate their directed thinking from mythic assumptions and tried to establish an understanding of the world and of themselves that rested upon empirical observation and rational deduction. In the next two or three centuries, mathematics and history were established; and after Alexander the Great, by 300 BC, the most ambitious economic and social organization of the ancient world, Hellenistic Civilization, had encircled the Mediterranean, crossed the Near East, and reached into Asia. Later the Roman Empire simply absorbed it and continued expanding northwestward into Europe.

The elites of the empire were well served, the slaves abundant, and the conquered people required to profess formal allegiance to the imperial cult. That the rulers largely had a cynical attitude toward the official divinities of the state is strongly suggested by the case of the god Serapis, who was deliberately created by Ptolemy I Soter, who reigned from 305 to 284 BC, to amalgamate indigenous Egyptian symbolism with Hellenistic ideology. Imperial success at tapping into a symbolism that penetrated to the unconscious neural networks of native Egyptians and strongly motivated them is revealed in the fact that the Serapeum (Serapis Temple) at Alexandria became extremely popular as a place to worship the sun-god Zeus-Serapis, who was also the lord of healing and fertility. Destruction of the Serapeum in AD 391 by the Patriarch Theophilus marked the final triumph of Christianity as the new official religion of the Roman Empire (Doniger 1999).

By and large, however, the imposition of imperial hegemony—with managed surpluses extensive enough to support a huge and far-flung administrative staff and an army—undermined local identities, local gods and familiar rituals. A secular Greek language and philosophy held the empire together but left the cities in confusion, where mixtures of ethnic groups from all across the empire were bereft of their ancestral ways and had no rapport with the imperial cult. To cope with their resulting demoralized condition, the people began to resort again to ecstatic cults that had their origins in the rich shamanic heritage they had left behind in their homelands (Price 2001: 7). These often involved wine, animal sacrifice and the handling of snakes, and they emphasized individual transformation and spiritual fulfillment through personal encounters with the sacred. Religious life in such "mystery cults" involved secrecy, initiations, and private revelations. Well-known examples include the Mithraic, Eleusinian, and Orphic religions, the last of which "invented" the idea of divine retribution after death. And this idea really took hold, completely reinterpreting the notion of the restless soul that had dominated the world for millennia. Religion was linked with morality for the first time (Hayden 2003: 366–77).

The emergence of the mystery cults represents a revolution in the nature of religious life for the general populace because of their focus on morality and because they restored the participatory ritual ecstatic aspects to the religious life of everyone who wished to be initiated into the cults.

(Hayden 2003: 370)

The ideal of personal morality, itself, implies ego development. Myth, which had begun in the Paleolithic as collective narrative about us all and then was taken up as justification of political and economic power by Neolithic elites, now becomes a personal matter. One is responsible for one's own behavior. It represents the kind of development Neumann (1949a) describes when the old ethic is adopted by a religious elite, the saints of the tradition. Morality graduates from merely pleasing the powerful and avoiding punishment to self-examination. Apparently such a concept of personal responsibility was not possible before the late antique period, and an achievement of the mystery cults. Even today, however, this level of consciousness remains a rarely attained ideal.

Other movements that searched for mythic meaning managed to achieve a more universal appeal, while rejecting the impersonality and secularism of the empire. All of them emphasized individual attainment and laid out a program of steps in spiritual advancement. Gnosticism was an eclectic mix of religious movements. Some Gnostic sects were influenced by Judaism, some by Christianity, and others by mystery cults. Central to all strains of Gnosticism, however, was the doctrine that a saving mystical knowledge (*gnosis*) was theoretically available to everyone, even though the truly "spiritual" Gnostics (the "*pneumatikoi*") remained a small elite. Gnostic imagery and theologies were highly syncretic, that is, they drew indiscriminately from other religions and philosophies whatever seemed best to articulate the founders' experience. Improbable myths were constructed describing the greater cosmos and the human soul in such a way as to outline a course of spiritual development together with a catalogue of potential pitfalls that lay before earnest practitioners.[1]

Hermeticism was another esoteric tradition based on writings ascribed to the "Thrice-Greatest Hermes," also identified with the Egyptian god of wisdom, Thoth. There were treatises on astrology, medicine, alchemy, and magic. The greater cosmos was an interrelated unity governed by the laws of sympathy and antipathy whose study and practice was designed to bring about a transformative rebirth of the individual through *gnosis*. Neoplatonism, the final school of Greek philosophy, under the direction of its main proponent, Plotinus, developed a language to describe mystical experience in its personal and cosmological aspects (Doniger 1999).

The Christian era

Out of this ferment of spiritual and magical traditions struggling to find remedies for a highly organized and impersonal economic and political system that stripped ordinary human lives of all meaning, and even led many of the elite to seek guidance from "oriental" prophets and teachers, rose the one entity which came to define the myth of the West for two millennia, Christianity.

The present chapter is part of that new Christian era insofar as it is employing the mythic dating system of BC/AD. In prior chapters it made more sense when many millennia were involved to speak of "years ago," but upon entering familiar historical territory, it seems less confusing to use the more familiar system, one that is as firmly based in myth as anything from the Stone Age. *Anno Domine* (AD), "Year of the Lord," the Christian way of counting the years, is predicated on the belief that the world has become a new place, metaphysically speaking, since the birth of Jesus, requiring the counting of the years to start again from the beginning. Although in recent decades it has become politically correct to avoid reference to this mythic reality by disguising "Year of the Lord" and "Before Christ" with the phrases "Common Era" (CE) and "Before the Common Era" (BCE), we follow the earlier notation to emphasize the fact that our worldviews retain their connection with a greater cosmos described by myth. There is no intention of claiming the Christian view to be superior to any other, only to be sure to remember that even the modern, secular West is deeply saturated with perspectives gained through altered states of consciousness.

Christianity began as a reform movement in one of the local "oriental" religions, Judaism, and appeared as one among the many mystery cults in the cities of the empire. An effective hierarchy, however, prevented it from losing its identity as just another school of Gnosticism and promoted a vigorous theological tradition. In AD 313, when the Emperor Constantine had a vision that he understood to mean that his military campaigns would be successful if he made Christianity the official religion of the empire, Christianity changed almost overnight from a religion of the dispossessed to the religion of the elite. The administrative structure of the Church became so well integrated with that of the empire that when the Roman Empire in the West fell in AD 476, the Church survived as a "spiritual empire," a far-flung administrative entity run by bishops, who functioned more-or-less as local governors.

Dark Ages

Structurally, the Church was the most recent manifestation of an old collaboration of politics and myth, for the Church was both effectively the government and the guardian of the mythic narrative along with its rituals and its moral applications to everyday life. Europe was still the land of barbarians, and though they were gradually converted to Christianity, they lived in an almost Neolithic environment in which certain families ruled over territories and the common people functioned primarily as slaves. The feudal system was mitigated somewhat by the larger ecclesiastical organization of society, which limited the potential for religious strife by making it difficult for the elites to extend their economic prowess by manipulating symbols.

By its universality, its governance of an empire-sized territory, the Church necessarily acted as a moderating influence on local excesses. Theological decisions, with their mythic and political import, were made centrally and by synods of bishops. By this universality, the rationale of religion changed. Life after death was reimagined as a place of bliss that made all the inequities and sorrows of one's earthly existence bearable and potentially meaningful—or else it would be unimaginable torment for those who did not follow the will of God as interpreted by the Church. One had less to fear from the free, vindictive souls of former masters, for they had the same afterlife to look forward to. It was, indeed, possible that the last would be first. Personal responsibility for following the will of God (as interpreted by the Church) was building an atmosphere that implicitly accepted the dignity and value of the individual, even as life became collective and bleak in the Dark Ages. Monasteries, some of which also became economic powerhouses, retained a certain level of scholarship and kept alive a Neoplatonic mystical tradition.

Philosophy, which had sought the ideal of a purely rational pursuit of truth during a millennium of Greek philosophy, from Thales to Plotinus, fell under the influence of Christianity and again asserted mythic (biblical) realities as the ultimate truth. Philosophy became "handmaiden" to the "Queen of the Sciences," theology. Philosophy was understood to be the rational tool that did not question mythic reality (for that had been revealed by God), rather it analyzed the myth and defended it.

Gothic period

By the Gothic period that Jung describes with the help of his portrait collection, a civilization-wide agreement had coalesced based on the conceptual account of the Christian myth that theological directed thinking had been able to devise (roughly AD 1140–1450). One form of this is the "culmination" of scholastic philosophy in the thought of Thomas Aquinas (1224–74), which is still considered the official philosophy of the Roman Catholic Church. It was thought to be the final answer for everything and, interestingly for our purposes, presents an argument that today might be called Intelligent Design that nevertheless remains open to the real scientifically described process of evolution: "God, without surrendering his sovereignty, conforms his government over the universe to the laws of a creative Providence that will each being to act according to his proper nature" (Doniger 1999). Understood against a background of contemporary science, we can interpret this statement as *God's sovereignty and governance evolving along with the universe.*

At the time, however, there was surely a static understanding of the grand agreement that had been reached. Static but enthusiastic. The best representation of their transcendent joy would be the construction of the great cathedrals. The Gothic "broken arch" and flying buttress lend an airy quality to those heavy stone buildings, a spiritual aspiration that seems to have left no place for doubt. Generations of artists and laborers of all sorts worked on these monuments to a cosmic myth. They also bear a certain resemblance to the monuments of the Stone Age and the myths implied by the caves and megaliths. Inside they are dark, pierced by light, decorated with scenes from the mythic narrative, and they are the burying place of the most notable figures from the ecclesiastical elite and the nobility. The cathedrals are the last great statement that the Christian myth was the ultimate description of reality.

Renaissance

The Renaissance, with its rediscovery of pre-Christian high culture and the world as a real and valuable place in its own right, and not merely a testing ground for life after death, prepared the way for empirical studies that sought to understand earthly and cosmic processes in terms of unvarying physical laws. Isaac Newton (1642–1727) exemplifies the transition from the mystical art of alchemy to the empirical science of physics—that is to say the application of exact measurements, the formulation of hypotheses and the experiments to test them. His laws of motion revolutionized European thinking along lines already begun by René Descartes (1596–1650). Descartes had laid the groundwork for the new science with his skeptical style of philosophy, which began with a radically new view of the ego ("I think, therefore I am"). From the middle of the seventeenth century, the West has perceived science and religion as offering opposing views of reality. Even Darwin, as late as 1859, trembled to think that his hypothesis of natural selection would make atheism inevitable.

We would be mistaken to think that a thousand years of medieval submission was the result simply of the ecclesiastical tyranny. People saw evidence for the myth everywhere. They lived in a different cosmos than we do. We could say they "really believed," but it might be more accurate to say they were unable to doubt. A hundred and fifty years ago, Darwin believed, too, but his doubts were overwhelming.

The Church's millennium-long success has to have been due in no small part to the fact that the symbolism of its liturgy, prayers and sacraments penetrated to the unconscious networks of its participants making the spiritual world emotionally relevant, despite life's dreariness. Very little serious dissent appears in the writings of the literate before about 1450. For a thousand years after the fall of the Roman Empire in the West, the people—lords, clergy, serfs—accepted a single narrative describing the greater cosmos and our part in it. They had egos that struggled with sin and hardship, but few that dreamed of great adventures or personal distinctions.

Modern era

All of this changed around the beginning of the sixteenth century, with the great voyages of discovery, the birth of modern science, the Protestant Reformation, and post-Cartesian philosophy. Today, the overwhelming majority of Westerners do not expect certainty from the Christian myth, but from the results of scientific experiment and the marvels of technology. In the past 500 years, we have come to experience our human ego as supreme and isolated. Our feelings and thoughts have become "internal" and private. Myth, imagination, and altered states of consciousness are highly suspect, for what cannot be tested empirically lies outside our monophasic civilization's definition of what is real. We are systematically cut off from what our ancestors for more than 40,000 years took to be the source of transcendent reality.

Summary: the history of consciousness

Our history of consciousness has focused on how primates, including humans, have used ritual to alter their consciousness in order to strengthen and differentiate their societies. From monkeys through *Australopithecus*, rituals define the pecking order of society and prepare for future threats from predators or troops of conspecifics. There are also food-sharing rituals, and rituals having to do with sexual encounters. In all cases, inherited behavior patterns are rehearsed and strengthened. A troop gains confidence in itself as a unit, and individual members become confident of their place in the group. As we move up the phyla, we find progressively greater individuality, greater role-definition, and more complex relationships. The glue that holds societies together and enables them to grasp their relations with one another depends in all cases upon tuning the autonomic nervous system, flooding the body with hormones appropriate to the behaviors being rehearsed, and establishing rhythmic brain-wave patterns that favor holistic perspectives. They are essential to the survival strategies of social animals, and by their nature they involve what modern Westerners call non-ordinary states of consciousness. This describes what Jung refers to as "experiencing the archetypes."

We have no way of knowing how conscious earlier hominid species were of what they were doing in acting out such inherited patterns. Some researchers believe that narrative consciousness began at least 500,000 years ago, and that *Homo erectus* had it, even though his language may have been useful only for gossip. On the basis of comparative brain anatomy, the biogenetic structuralists suggest that these distant ancestors of ours had sufficient memory and narrative capacity that they did not need to rediscover their social structure every time they performed a ritual. They remembered one another's personalities and roles well enough that they could tune their nervous systems to accomplish more nuanced realizations. Their experiences, however, are universally held to have been quite collective; for it was probably only Neanderthals—prior to *Homo sapiens*—that sought out deep caves for individual exploration of altered states of consciousness.

The history of consciousness has been a record of the gradual emergence of individuality in primates, a factor that has depended on the growing capacity of the cerebral cortex. When we get to modern humans, however, brain anatomy has remained the same for some 50,000 years, but during that time we observe the gradual emergence of a real functioning ego out of the "proto-ego" we share with other species.

Ego wonders

It is not until the Upper Paleolithic and the first appearance of our own species that we have indisputable evidence for a highly imaginative, inventive, and narrative understanding of the altered states generated in ritual. The paintings and engravings they left on the walls and ceilings of caves tell us that they had encountered a detailed cosmic vision that provided their lives with a transcendental context. In the Upper Paleolithic, for the first time, we have evidence for *an ego that wonders*—an ego that goes beyond matters of fact in the empirical world and contemplates alternate realms of space and time. They evidently wondered about who they were, where they came from, and what they were doing.

The contrast with chimpanzees is enormous, for we have no way of demonstrating that apes ever know *why* they practice their rituals. Surely they know rituals make them feel better and more confident of their place in the social order, and they are certainly moved by emotions much as we are. By contrast, however, the wondering ego of our cave-painting ancestors had evidently discovered the existence of a "hard-wired" three-tiered cosmos, through which ecstatic journeys are possible. The painted caves themselves reveal that the larger field of awareness opened up by their rituals was of central importance. They had to have talked about it intensively for centuries before developing a universal set of symbols that all would recognize.[2] Furthermore, the overall design and the trading networks required for the painted caves point to a major leap forward in social skills, economic management, planning for the future, and confidence in long-term cooperation.

Ego manipulates

The cave-painting societies of the Upper Paleolithic, however, must have lived in a collective mentality that would appear strange to us today. The group must have been more real for them than the individual was, despite the presence of those diverticules located near the larger painted galleries, where it is believed private vision quests were pursued. Their sense of individuality appears rudimentary in comparison with that of their successors, the Neolithic people. For as soon as we get to the Neolithic Age, we find *an ego that manipulates*. The Neolithic ego manipulated the symbols and narratives that described the greater cosmos, and it manipulated things in the empirical world in quite extraordinary ways, when we compare them to the cave painters.

The cave painters gazed at the bumps on the walls of their caves and wondered at the suggestion of spirit-animals and shamans that seemed to emerge from the rock. But their descendants in the Neolithic Age constructed above-ground "caves" to bring the "temples" where they encountered their visions into line with the visions themselves. Furthermore, they engaged with their visions much more aggressively and made discoveries that were valuable for their everyday sustenance. They found that, just as a shaman domesticates spirit-animals, so could they domesticate certain fleshly animals and grasses.

The building and rebuilding of mounds and henges in the megalithic culture of the British Isles reveals that Neolithic people also discovered that they could alter and reconfigure their myths to gain economic and political advantages. Furthermore, it is evident that the manipulating Neolithic ego was becoming aware of the dangers of manipulation—greed, envy, revenge, and the like—for these are the things that appeared in their anxiety that spirit-beings could be dangerous agents. The phenomenon of the restless soul not yet incorporated into the society of the ancestors means that the Neolithic people had begun to experience the reality of the psychic shadow. They evidently did not yet "own" the shadow as their own sinister capacity, for they projected it onto the souls of the dead, imagining hauntings inspired by envy, acts of revenge, and the like. As soon as they had a manipulating ego at their disposal, they became aware of the shadow of manipulation.

Ego forgets

Just as the Mesolithic Age had been a time of transition between the Upper Paleolithic and the Neolithic, in which certain manipulations had been attempted but not yet mastered, so the Bronze Age was a transition between the Neolithic and history. The elites had become much more organized and successful. City-states made life more confusing and dangerous, and everyday life required constant vigilance to defend against aggressors, thieves and the vengeful—none of whom was bodiless or invisible. Preoccupied by the unpredictable dangers of the empirical world, Bronze Age people developed *an ego that forgot*. At the beginning of the age, people were still primarily dependent upon the transcendent information they derived from altered states of consciousness. The information flowed freely, for they maintained an open stance toward it. But as the centuries rolled by, they had become too busy with the empirical world to keep up their cultivation of ecstatic states, and the greater cosmos began to pull away from the empirical world.

This is one of the "massive facts" in the history of consciousness: our earliest human ancestors lived in a world where the empirical and the transcendental were not distinct; but with the strengthening of an everyday ego, we lost the "garden of paradise" and found ourselves deeply flawed. It had become inescapable that everyone who is an ego has to struggle with shadowy, vicious tendencies. Sociologist of religion Robert N. Bellah, in his famous 1964 article, "Religious Evolution," points out that this was the age when Greek philosophy first tried to establish a purely rational way of thinking, when the first writings of the Jewish Torah devalued the empirical world in contrast with a transcendent God, when the Buddha declared that all of life is suffering, and when Taoism in China urged withdrawal from a human society that had become unnatural and perverse (Bellah 1964).

Ego becomes wily

Odysseus presents us with the image of a lone individual cast upon his own devices to find a path through the difficulties life has set him. But it is not merely a secular task, for his opponents are primarily gods and goddesses. The divine beings have not entirely departed from the world but lurk behind each disaster and fortuitous recovery that makes his serpentine course through a legendary Mediterranean from Troy to Ithaca. Today, we would say that those divine figures with their ambitions, jealousies and resentments are symbols of our unruly unconscious tendencies. In Jung's language, they are archetypal figures; and Odysseus cannot get rid of them or escape their influence. To be a real ego is to live in such a world, where internal tendencies—both shadowy and marvelous—are ever present. In exactly the same way, the gods and goddesses are constantly with Odysseus, having an effect upon everything that happens to him. He has no choice but to live in a world where ego-alien forces of immense power are constantly at work.

Consequently, we can say that Odysseus is the first literary figure to "have a psyche" in the sense of being an ego which is responsible for his own decisions, while at the same time being aware of super-human (i.e. super-egoic) forces, each of which has its own tendencies and predilections—some of which may support his part in today's struggle and others which oppose it. The *wily ego* cannot defeat these forces, but only find a way to live with them. Odysseus must find a way through the difficulties they set him while holding onto his own sense of identity and purpose. His life can never be a straight line from Troy to Ithaca, for his struggle with non-egoic forces repeatedly takes him off the course he might otherwise have taken. This well describes the human project as we know it today.

Ego submits

From one perspective, it may seem as though the Middle Ages represent a massive regression in the history of Western consciousness; for no sooner had philosophers, prophets and wily seafarers pulled themselves out of the collective fog of the Neolithic mind, but they submitted again, this time to ecclesiastical aggrandizers. No doubt the Middle Ages was characterized by theological submission, but it was submission in the sense of "Islam," the religion whose name means to submit: to submit to a reality greater than that of the empirical world, to a divine subject greater than any human ego. To submit in this sense means to see oneself as participating in a myth that makes transcendental sense of every detail of life. It means to belong to and be part of something immense. It is what Jung envied in Mountain Lake and what he discovered on the Athai Plains.

By late antiquity, when Hellenism had the known world in its administrative grip, the anomie and demoralization that was created in people's minds from Persia to Italy and Alexandria to Gaul resulted in great part from the dethroning of local divinities and the relativizing of all myths. An effective myth cannot be invented by the conscious mind—despite the short-term success of Serapis—it has to emerge from the unconscious and represent the point where the forces of the human psyche work together in concert and at the same time depict a greater cosmos that does not contradict essential elements of the empirical world as it is publicly understood. A major reason the Christian myth no longer convinces the majority of Westerners is that a literal reading of the Bible conflicts with the world that science describes. Given its successes, we can hardly afford to contradict the accuracy of science—though we may hunger for something more.

Medieval Europeans did not know the empirical world as we do; their world did not conflict with the ecclesiastical myth. Those Europeans are our closest relatives. We surely do not wish to go back there, but it is important to see that they possessed something we have lost. The medieval ego was able to submit whole-heartedly to a cosmic vision that gave their lives meaning. They had emerged from the chaos and confusion of late antiquity and submitted in joy—despite the day-to-day grind of a serf's life.

Ego becomes heroic

The medieval myth seriously undervalued the empirical world. It gripped the minds of Europeans emotionally, directing their attention so powerfully to the heavenly plane that it denigrated the world about them. When the Renaissance rediscovered the beauties of sunsets and mountain views, it was clear that the medieval myth was losing its grip. The biogenetic structuralists like to quote Claude Lévi-Strauss's *Structural Anthropology*: "Myth grows spiralwise until the intellectual impulse which produced it is exhausted" (d'Aquili and Laughlin 1979: 161). By the four-teenth century, the medieval myth showed signs of exhaustion—at least for the intellectuals of Italy—and the discontent spread northward over the next three centuries.

The spirit of modernity broke out in heroic exploits of investigation. The old rules were violated and retribution dared. Artists exhumed bodied for dissection to learn anatomy so they could paint or carve more convincingly. Seafarers chal-lenged the flat-earth theory. Physicians gave up their theological texts and began to learn from the body itself—even from lowly barber-surgeons (Gottfried 1983). Philosophers argued from experience and empirical observation, daring to ques-tion the accuracy and adequacy of the myth. Throughout Europe a new spirit of physical and intellectual adventure took over. The submitting ego had taken comfort in the universal acceptance of mythic realities. Modern Europe emerged when people became excited to find what had never been found before. They gave up the comforts of the familiar to take risks, to be unique individuals, to find their strength within and no longer to "slumber," as Immanuel Kant (1724–1804) put it, in dogmatic formulations.

No doubt a certain amount of "future shock" accompanies the relentless march of new fads, new technologies and new economic models. Although change always generates anxiety, the heroic ideal is with us everywhere today, from science to sports, to corporate business practices. We believe we are liberated and beyond all superstitions. *Myth*, in popular discourse, no longer refers to the self-evidently true, but to beliefs that are mistaken, even foolish.

Ego becomes receptive

The dissatisfaction of large segments of the modern world with the scientific/ technological assumptions of the official version of Reality may well point to an "exhaustion of an intellectual impulse," very much like what happened when the medieval myth broke down at the time of the Renaissance. It is unlikely that science will be abandoned, but it seems no longer to be *enough*. Altered states of consciousness have become quite popular. There has been an explosion of interest in possession trance religions. Yoga, Buddhism, and a variety of Eastern meditation practices are widely taught. New Age movements are exploring aura reading, spiritual healing, channeling, urban shamanism, and the like. Alternate medical methods are widely consulted—even when insurance companies refuse to pay for them. It appears, in short, that there are huge subcultures that might fairly be described as "minimally polyphasic."

No doubt many of the adherents and sometime dabblers in these traditions are happy to find "authorities" to tell them what is real. But the practitioners of such insight and healing techniques are teaching themselves to *become receptive*. They are cultivating altered states of consciousness in order to support alternate versions of reality, and they are deriving a larger sense of meaning for their lives. Surely many of these people are as gullible as the monophasic mainstream depicts them, and many are merely in awe that altered states of consciousness are achievable at all. But their numbers suggest that the monophasic mainstream of the modern world has widely been found to be inadequate.

Ego seeks mastery

Availing ourselves of altered states of conscious for entertainment and empty speculation will accomplish nothing. In order to move consciousness forward into a new stage, it will be necessary to retain the *heroic ego* which has discovered physical laws and learned how to *manipulate* things for the improvement of daily life. At the same time we must learn to be *receptive* to the polyphasic possibilities that human consciousness offers us. We can well begin by *wondering* at the significance and numinosity of what manifests itself, but we will also have to be *wily* with intrapsychic forces that are more powerful than the ego, and have the wisdom to *submit* to manifestations of wholeness.

Surely, we moderns are as "primitive" in our dealings with our polyphasic psyche as tribal people are regarding science and technology (Hunt 1995: 159). We have become so immersed in the empirical that we have lost a different sort of "science," the learning and the methods that our ancestors specialized in over a period of some 40,000 years. Jung's Complex Psychology envisages our recovering much of what the hunter-gatherers knew, and integrating it with what we have made of ourselves in the last 500 years. We have to learn again to *submit* "to the irrational facts of experience" (*CW10*: ¶505). Only "the evidence of inner transcendent experience" will pull us out of our "submersion in the mass" and make us individuals (*CW10*: ¶511).

A spiritual goal that points beyond the purely natural man and his worldly existence is an absolute necessity for the health of the soul; it is the Archimedean point from which alone it is possible to lift the world off its hinges and to transform the natural state into a cultural one.

(CW17: ¶159)

Chapter 21

Concluding reflections

The preceding twenty chapters have sought to demonstrate that Jung's dream of psychology as an architectonic science—linking the various biological specialties and setting the whole on a reliable empirical foundation—can now, in the twenty-first century, finally be realized. An evolutionary perspective now really *can* undergird a dependable psychology, and we can finally appreciate what Jung meant to accomplish with the idea of "archetype." The research and the writing of this volume has been guided by the aim of Complex Psychology, namely to identify and appreciate the patterns nested within patterns that characterize the data of the human sciences and pursues this aim much the way Jung envisaged in his unsuccessful journal project, *Weltanschauung*—by extracting the leading ideas from the sciences, archaeology to zoology, and making them available to non-specialists. This book has pulled a great deal of material from a variety of specialties in imitation of Jung's own propensity to borrow material shamelessly, like the "accursed dilettante" he confessed himself to be.

The original purpose of all this has been to rescue Jung from his undeserved reputation as an irresponsible and muddle-headed mystic, and demonstrate that he was trying to build psychology on a firm scientific foundation, despite the sketchy nature of biological knowledge a century ago. He did so by making some very astute choices. Archetypes are the intentional dimension of instincts and structure everything we do. They are not images, as is popularly believed; and they are not found exclusively in mythology. They are the products of evolution and evidence of our place in the natural world. They do not reside in some separate spiritual substance resembling Descartes' soul—for that idea is really theological, a claim that we humans stand above and outside of nature by virtue of our immortal destiny in a Christian heaven. We all have psyches, every living organism on earth; and archetypes are patterns in the intentional process (i.e. psyche) by which every organism not only survives but seeks to thrive. Since evolutionarily we are primates, human archetypes are probably 98 percent identical with those of our cousins, the chimpanzees and bonobos.

Although warmly embraced by some, these ideas have proven to be scary for other Jungians who have attended lectures I have given on this material or who have engaged me at academic meetings. If Jung's psychology has a biological basis, some have said, "Where is the magic?" Clearly they assume biology to be as devoid of "soul" as Descartes' machine-like picture of the body. Paradoxically, however, even as they apparently believe they need the hypothesis of a Cartesian soul to preserve the special numinous and magical nature of the archetypes, some also wax evangelical over the romantic idea of "embodiment." Implying that Jung was "too much in his head" (or possibly his "soul") like the mystic of popular legend, they attempt to save Analytical Psychology with techniques designed to assist people to "get into the body." They fail to realize that it is their own philosophical baggage that stands in the way of their discovering the real Jung.

An accurate reading of Jung's intentions does not begin with his brief association with Freud and conclude that he went off the rails on a mystical rampage. On the contrary, it finds his origins where he always said they were, in the "French School" of somnambulism and its investigation of altered states of consciousness. By clarifying the trend of thinking that underlies his more careful definitions of "archetype," an accurate reading of Jung discovers how rooted it is in biology and evolution. Psyche (or soul) is not some esoteric dimension of human nature, it is a universal and essential dimension of every organism. All animals have psyches, even the protozoa. Psyche is the intentional aspect of every living process. Therefore, it is inseparable from the body—inherent in every living creature and dependent upon the complexity of a creature's anatomy and particularly its brain (if it has one) for its higher abilities.

It has been nearly three decades since Anthony Stevens (1983) diagnosed the problem with "Jungians as a group," that we have been "mesmerized . . . by archetypal symbols" and defensive about the biological implications of Analytical Psychology to the point of ignoring the "behavioral manifestations" and the "phylogenetic roots" of the archetype (Stevens 1983: 29). I would go further. We have been mesmerized by *theories* about symbols, as though they have no relationship to the body. Such a perspective fails to recognize the top-to-bottom structure of the archetype and the fact that the constellation of any archetype is above all a typical emotional body state. Those fascinated with symbols and their theories see only the very top of the archetypal configuration, missing the cortical and limbic changes in the brain, the alteration of autonomic nervous system balance, the dispatch of hormones and neuromodulators, bodily posture, facial expression and the like. They call for "embodiment" only because the filter of their mesmerized condition has hidden the larger physical portion of the archetype from their awareness. We have to open our eyes to the fact that symbols are the brain's interpretation of the bodily state itself and include that in our analysis of our patients. In the twenty-first century we can no longer afford to live in the stratosphere of the image alone.

We Jungians have lived, too, in the penumbra of Jung's authority. If that authority has been treated with skepticism in our monophasic society, we have chosen to view that fact with pride. Jung was a misunderstood genius who articulated insights the conventional world is not yet ready for. The effective magic of Jungian jargon—anima, transcendent function, enantiodromia, inferior function, numinosity, ego-self axis—these words and phrases have become the secret language of *initiati* practicing a mystery religion, saving those blessed souls who have thought they were lost because they could not accommodate themselves to the comfortable mainstream. In working like this, we had no authority but Jung's to rely upon. We pulled sentences and images out of the *Collected Works* to justify our claims on the bare evidence that "Jung said so" and that it must therefore be true.

Now, however, that several scientific specialties have uncovered the biological basis for the phenomena Jung named nearly a century ago, we Jungians can begin to find the theoretical foundations of our own therapeutic interpretations, or perhaps discover that they are not as sound as we had long believed. The crucial scientific work is being "extracted" from its primary sources *for* us—not in a convenient single journal as *Weltanschauung* was designed to be—but in an endless series of well informed and well written books, many of them by the very scientists themselves who did the primary work. These are the secondary sources I have relied upon and summarized in this volume.

Widespread support from the biological sciences—as unexpected as it may seem to be—also forces us to shift some of our perspectives. Altered states of consciousness are a case in point. All Jungians surely employ them when we attend to complexes and dreams and when we practice active imagination. Jungians as a group are minimally polyphasic, but we have not recognized the wider implications of these activities—the fact that Jung, in encouraging us not to resent the irrational, has implicitly called for a much more vigorous polyphasic approach to life.

In the last dozen or so years of my practice of Jungian analysis, I have found it extremely useful to attend to the spectrum of conscious states induced in me by the analysand (through limbic resonance) or implicitly reported by the analysand himself as he describes crucial experiences from his childhood or just the past week. For to identify and experience—that is to *feel*—the altered states that our monophasic society denies or denigrates is to be in touch with corresponding body states. Every discrete body state generates or is induced by its own discrete state of consciousness. To feel that state is to be in touch with the archetype, top-to-bottom. Every "symbol" either induces or is the conscious evidence of a discrete state of body-and-mind. The reason for this is that the symbol appears in consciousness as a sort of report from the brain about the state of my body. This is why in the previous twenty chapters I have avoided speaking merely of "unconscious contents," as Jung does. The expression "unconscious content" suggests an image; and the danger is that we will merely speculate about the meaning of the image and ignore the soul-and-body state that it induces in us and in the analysand who reports it. We will be "mesmerized by the symbol," as Stevens (1983) warns.

In turning our attention away from the symbol itself and toward the changes it brings about in our consciousness, we are making what I discovered in researching and writing my book on Tantra to be the essential move in every mystical tradition (Haule 1999b).[1] Here I refer to "mystic" in the other sense of the term—not an irresponsible and muddle-headed way of thinking about monophasic realities—but a serious discipline that learns to use altered states of consciousness for psychological and spiritual development. Mystics in this classical sense are accomplished polyphasic practitioners. This is the sense in which Jung really *was* a mystic. We shall pursue the implications of Jung's mysticism and his challenge to the limitations scientists impose on their investigations in the second volume of *Jung in the 21st Century*, which begins with a discussion of how altered states can be mastered and goes on to explore those extraordinary altered states that prompted Jung to propose his doctrine of synchronicity: not merely a study in psychology but a cosmology as well. He asks the question science has not yet asked: What sort of a universe must this be if organisms and their inherent psyches can evolve in it?

Notes

I The past and future of Jung

1 There have been neurological studies that aim to support fundamental Freudian positions (cf. Solms and Turnbull 2002), though I am not sure they are any more convincing than Dollard and Miller (1950) were a half-century ago, when they tried to reconcile Freud with behaviorism.

2 The word *consilience* was coined by the English philosopher of science, William Whewell (1794–1866), who called consilience the best sort of inductive conclusion on account of its "simplicity, generality, unification, and deductive strength" (Audi 1999).

3 As many biologists today recognize, the modern synthesis is also not the final word. Its main failing is that, a century and a half after the publication of *The Origin of Species*, there is still no agreement on the question of how novelty arises in evolution. This issue will be discussed in Volume 2.

4 For example, Charles D. Laughlin, Jr., John McManus and Eugene G. d'Aquili (1990) *Brain, Symbol, and Experience*.

5 Stevens has been satisfied with the support of his first analyst, the biologist Irene Champernowne, who told him "Archetypes are biological entities ... archetypes evolved through natural selection" (Stevens 1983: 17).

6 The octogenarian Jung said:

> I am the most cursed dilettante that has lived. I wanted to achieve something in my science and then I was plunged into this stream of lava, and then had to classify everything. That's why I say dilettantism: I live from borrowings, I constantly borrow knowledge from others.
>
> (Shamdasani 2003: 22)

citing the "protocols" of interviews and written material that Aniela Jaffé used to produce his "autobiography" (*MDR*).

7 My argument in this section is heavily indebted to Sonu Shamdasani (2003).

8 In fact, Freud fainted on two occasions when Jung brought up such matters. He said (not without cogency) they symbolized Jung's unconscious wish to "kill the father."

9 References to Jung's *Collected Works* will be given as volume number (*CW18*) followed by the paragraph number of the passage.

10 Johan (Gregor) Mendel (1822–84), an Augustinian monk in Brno, who published the results of his pure-bred and cross-bred pea-plants in the 1860s. "His greatest conceptual innovation was to regard heritable factors determining characters as atomistic and material particles which neither fused nor blended with one another" (Thain and Hickman 2000). These "atomistic" particles that neither fuse nor blend are essentially what we mean today, when we speak of genes.

11 Credit for this phrase belongs to psychologist Leda Cosmides and her anthropologist husband, John Tooby, who established the Center for Evolutionary Psychology at the University of California, Santa Barbara, in 1994 (Horgan 1999: 170).

12 The notion of *tabula rasa*, which Jung never failed to ridicule, originated with the philosopher John Locke in the mid seventeenth century, as a deliberate rejection of Plato's notion that we have innate ideas (Plotkin 1998: 172).

13 "There is nothing in the logic of development to justify the idea that traits can be divided into genetically versus environmentally controlled sets or arranged along a spectrum that reflects the influence of genes versus environment" (Tooby and Cosmides 1992: 83).

14 A theory of heredity without genetic data, says molecular anthropologist Jonathan Marks, is "not a scientific theory of heredity, but a folk theory of heredity" (Marks 2002: 91).

2 Jung on the archetypes

1 In what follows, I have not attempted an historical account of how Jung's idea of the archetype developed over the course of his career. Two articles have addressed that material. Gary V. Hartman (2003) gives us a complete but sketchy overview, while George B. Hogenson (2001) discusses Jung's relationship to Larmarckian formulations. Far more thorough is Sonu Shamdasani (2003), who abandons an attempt to present a linear developmental scheme in favor of providing much historical depth for every element in Jung's always confusing and sometimes contradictory claims.

2 *CWB* is Volume B of the *Collected Works*. It is the first version of *Symbols of Transformation (CW5)*.

3 Cf. *CW8*: ¶254, 275f; *CW9i*: ¶5; *CW11*: ¶88.

4 Cf. *CW10*: ¶14; *CW11*: ¶518.

5 Gregor Mendel (1822–84), an Augustinian monk who discovered the principle of the dominant and recessive genes through research on pea plants. His results were published in 1866 and ignored until three separate investigators rediscovered them in 1900.

6 Similar passages may be found at *CW10*: ¶53 (1927/31), *CW18*: ¶1228 (1935), and *CW18*: ¶539 (1961). In one place (1958) Jung distinguishes his approach to the psyche from Freud's in that Freud "would not let himself be taught by the findings of ethologists and historians" (*CW10*: ¶659).

7 The term "drive" (*Trieb*) has entered the language of psychanalysis as a rough equivalent for "human instinct," since both Freud and Jung were careful to follow the German tradition of ascribing "drives" to humans where "instincts" (*Instinkte*) would be ascribed to animals (Shamdasani 2003: 191).

8 Cf. *CW8*: ¶268, 277, 398; *CW10*: ¶547; *CW18*: ¶1260.

9 Cf. Bermúdez (2003) *Thinking Without Words*.

10 Cf. *CW5*: ¶388; *CW8*: ¶405, 841, 590; *CW10*: ¶530.

3 Language: a model archetype

1 Since 2003, Steven Pinker has been the Johnstone Family Professor in the Department of Psychology at Harvard University.

2 Aitchison (2000) comments on the significance of Pinker's work on language. In 1866, the Linguistic Society of Paris refused to accept any papers speculating on the origins of language or the invention of a universal language; for there had been too much unfounded nonsense proposed. In 1990, Pinker and Paul Bloom reopened the discussion and set it on a solid foundation in their paper "Natural Language and Natural Selection."

3 As we will see in Chapter 4, Kanzi, an infant bonobo (bonobos are a chimpanzee-like species) quietly learned the icon-based language that trainers were trying in vain to

teach his mother. When mother was removed for breeding purposes, Kanzi found the icon language to be a vital life-tool. He spontaneously began "speaking" of his future plans to his handlers, using the chart of icons. Apparently, in the absence of mother he found himself with no choice but to ally himself with humans and adapt to their communication system (Savage-Rumbaugh *et al.* 1998).

4 Ernst Mayr (1904–2005), German ethologist, cited in Stevens (1983: 51): The "open programme" of an instinct "enables the organism to adapt appropriately to environmental conditions."

5 Broca's aphasics (those suffering damage to Broca's area) have severe difficulties with grammar, while Wernicke's "fluent aphasics" produce grammatical sentences with little meaning (J. Smith and Szathmáry 1999: 150).

6 There are other such areas in the brain containing the central circuitry for performing specific tasks. The "mathematics circuits" are mostly to be found in another fold of the cortex, the interparietal sulcus, according to "Wired for Math," in *Science News* (June 5, 2006: 286).

7 We owe it to the physicist Niels Bohr to call such apparent contradictory descriptions of nature "*complementary.*" Both descriptions are valid, but they cannot be observed or studied simultaneously (Freeman J. Dyson, "One in a Million," *New York Review of Books* (March 25, 2004: 4–6).

8 The initials stand for Adenine, Cytosine, Guanine, and Thymine. Each base is connected to a carbohydrate molecule bearing a phosphate ion; and the whole unit (base, sugar, and phosphate) is called a nucleotide. Linked nucleotides form each of the dual backbones of the DNA double helix.

9 The smallest protein contains fifty amino acids.

10 Limbic cells prepared for microscopy are stained with dyes that do not color neocortical neurons, and can be destroyed by some medicines that do not damage neocortical tissue (T. Lewis *et al.* 2000: 32).

11 For example:

> It is a fact that in the first years of life there is no continuous memory; at most there are islands of consciousness which are like single lamps or lighted objects in the far flung darkness. . . . Only later, when the ego contents . . . have acquired an energy of their own . . . does the feeling of subjectivity or "I-ness" arise.
>
> (*CW8*: ¶755)

4 Hundred percent primate

1 It is probably not coincidental that Stuart Shanker is one of the world's experts in the philosophy of Wittgenstein!

2 As with Jung's idea of the "laying down of archetypes," the Biogenetic Law also had a Lamarckian quality, insofar as the French naturalist thought the simplest creatures were constantly coming into existence by "spontaneous generation" and evolving upward in a slow "march" toward becoming human (Burckhardt 1995).

3 So did the gorilla expert, Dawn Prince-Hughes (2004).

4 "Archaic Humans" is an umbrella term for all the species that came between *Homo erectus*, who appeared about 1.5 million years ago, and more recent species such as Neanderthal.

5 All mammals sing to their infants: "The limbic brain also permits mammals to sing to their children. Vocal communication between a mammal and offspring is universal" (T. Lewis *et al.* 2000: 26).

6 In this both Kurtén and Mithen cite the linguist Otto Jespersen, who made the argument on the basis of Neanderthal anatomy in the 1920s.

7 By "neocortex size" Dunbar means the ratio of the volume of the neocortex to the volume of the rest of the brain.

8 Dunbar (1996) does not have much to say about baboons, but Cheney and Seyfarth's data seems to have found an exception to the neocortex/group-size thesis, for baboons have proportionately a much smaller neocortex than chimpanzees but inhabit much larger social groups (up to a hundred individuals). Still, despite their rich social knowledge, baboons "feel no urge to gossip or share information" (Cheney and Seyfarth 2007: 10, 275).

9 Stevens and Price (1996) name these opposed strategies *hedonic* and *agonic*, terms that I find more misleading than mine. Anthony Stevens is the Jungian analyst and psychiatrist who first wrote about Jung's archetypal theory as consilient with recent developments in science. John Price is a former Senior Lecturer in Psychological Medicine at the University of Newcastle-upon-Tyne.

10 The ascription of altruism to non-linguistic animals is much disputed, the definition of altruism often altered to suit one theory or another. It appears to be an area where *talking* primates wish to stake a unique claim for our own species.

11 There are exceptions—younger children can *learn* to have a Theory of Mind, and are particularly liable to do so if they have older siblings (Hauser 2000: 165).

12 Cheney and Seyfarth (2007: 146–98) argue that whether an animal has Theory of Mind is "clearly not a yes/no issue." It is a large area, full of nuance.

13 De Waal calls it "triadic awareness": "the capacity to perceive social relationships between others so as to form varied triangular relationships" (de Waal 1998: 175).

14 Game theorists among evolution scientists may well argue that this solution resembles a "tit-for-tat" game strategy, an "Evolutionarily Stable Strategy"—one that gives its animals an advantage in the struggle to survive. Such strategizing, it may be implied, arises as a simple arithmetical solution and might become established in the genome by natural selection without any consciousness on the part of the rhesus monkey or the chimpanzee (cf. Badcock 2000: 88–106). There is certainly reason to be wary of anthropomorphizing interpretations, but to deny all consciousness to our primate relatives is to suggest that, suddenly and without warning, consciousness and humankind appeared on the evolutionary stage at the same moment.

15 The book on chimpanzees (de Waal 1998, originally 1982) is illustrated with de Waal's own photography and drawings. The bonobo book (de Waal and Lanting 1997) has photos by Frans Lanting.

16 In an even more vivid depiction of our society's division into bonobo- and chimp-like subcultures, Quartz and Sejnowski (2002: 75) report that chimpanzees hunt and eat monkeys for the protein they need in their diet, while bonobos treat monkeys like dolls and get their protein from herbs on the forest floor.

17 The Upper or High Paleolithic (between 40,000 and 10,000 years ago) is the last portion of the "early" (paleo) "stone" (lithic) age. It is called "upper" or "high" because human culture was growing by leaps and bounds in comparison with the relative stasis of the previous two million years.

18 In 1996, Mithen accepted Dunbar's theory that human gossip is a refinement of primate sociality. In *The Singing Neanderthals*, Mithen (2006) expresses opposition, as noted above.

5 The archetypes and the numinous art of the caves

1 For the details of this argument, see Georg Feuerstein, Subhash Kak and David Frawley (1995) *In Search of the Cradle of Civilization: New Light on Ancient India*. See also Haule (1999b).

2 In brief the argument is that sitting in meditation sets up a standing wave in the aorta which causes the body to vibrate and generates a pulsation in the ventricular fluid of the

brain, resulting in stimulation to a sensory map of the body found in the cortex. The sensation of energy rising from the feet to the head is the result of the progressive stimulation of that sensory map in the cortex (Sannella 1992).

3 Paul Bahn was so exercised over the hypothesis that he teamed up with a neuropsychologist to write an article they published privately, being unable to wait on the *Cambridge Archaeological Journal*'s publication schedule. The heart of their argument is that phosphenes are possible only on the basis of drugs that our ancestors in the Upper Paleolithic did not have (Helvenston and Bahn 2002).

4 Noel W. Smith (1992) has a more detailed study of such marks near the nose and mouth of the animals and shamans (as well as others) and concludes they refer to spiritual connections between the dying animals and the entranced humans—a thesis hardly contradictory of the simpler one we are proposing.

5 The actual sockets for scaffolding beams survive in the Lascaux cave (Bahn and Vertut 1997: 12).

6 The role of the brain in psychic process

1 Indeed, atheism is as much a faith position as is found in any religion. For since it cannot be proved that God does not exist, one can only believe it. Strangely, atheists seem just as passionate about their belief as the adherents of organized religion.

2 *Epi-phenomenon*: that which is "above" or "outside of" (epi) the thing that appears (phenomenon).

3 As will become clear in Volume 2, I resist the idea that mysticism is inherently superstitious and anti-rational—not only because the term has been unjustly used against Jung's work for nearly a century, but also because our human capacities for mystical experience can not only be documented, but also investigated with the methods of neurobiology. Rightly understood, mysticism is a real and universal human capacity that can be developed, refined, and used; it is not an irresponsible brand of philosophy.

4 One nanometer $= 1 \times 10^{-9}$ meters, one-billionth of a meter.

5 Glutamate is the excitatory neurotransmitter; neurons can also inhibit one another by releasing GABA (gamma-amino-butyric acid).

6 Canadian psychologist, Donald O. Hebb, in his 1949 book, *The Organization of Behavior*.

7 The same principle used in AM radio.

8 The text reads "preafferent signals" instead of "emotional associations"; but the meaning is roughly the same.

9 Edelman (1992: 6), citing an essay by William James, entitled "Does Consciousness Exist?"

7 Individuation: Jung's phenomenology of psychic process

1 Over and above the twenty-one volumes of the *Collected Works*, volumes of seminars and other writings are still being published.

2 C. A. Meier (1968: 83) traces the origin of this test, which Jung adapted to his own purposes, to the Father of Experimental Psychology, Wilhelm Wundt.

3 The first edition of *Symbols* has been reissued as *CWB* (supplementary Volume *B* of the *Collected Works*). Although it more accurately reflects Jung's thinking as it was in 1912, we shall follow the 1950 revision (*CW5*) because we are interested in the mature idea of individuation.

4 This was the woman's real name, though Jung may have believed it to be a pseudonym. He never met her but acquired her dreams, fantasies, and poems from his mentor in

Geneva, Theodore Flournoy. The accuracy of Jung's diagnosis has been dealt a blow by Sonu Shamdasani (1990).

5 *Das Zeitalter des Sonnengottes*. Berlin 1904, p. 30.

6 *Types* distinguishes extraverted and introverted attitudes, each of which engages with the world through four "functions": thinking, feeling, sensation, and intuition. Thus, there may be both introverted thinking and extraverted thinking, introverted feeling and extraverted feeling, and so on, adding up to eight types; and these can be further differentiated depending on which "auxiliary function" assists the "dominant function."

7 This is how Jung reinterprets Freud's incest principle: it is not a desire to enter our personal mother sexually; it is the need to enter our phylogenetic mother, psyche's unconscious process, symbolically.

8 "The path of the [energy] gradient." (¶78).

9 Clearly this language privileges heterosexuality. In my opinion the gender differences between anima and animus have been far too often the focus of attention—by Jungian analysts as well as by the general public. I think it is a mistake to emphasize gender when, in fact, the function of anima is in large part the same as that of the animus. Both mediate between ego and self. If we focus on this central function, it is not so hard to accommodate the psychological dynamics of homosexual individuals. It will not be hard to accept that the alluring or frightening mediator of the realm of the gods might be of the same gender as the dreamer.

10 Apparently motivated by a desire for simplicity—male chauvinism cannot be ruled out—Jung frequently writes only of the anima when he clearly means to describe the role that is played by both anima and animus.

11 E.g. *CW12*: ¶44, 310; *CW13*: ¶457; *CW14*: ¶41.

8 Reflective process: the ego in neural process

1 Janet's first book, *Automatisme psychologique* (1889), perhaps the most significant contribution to the literature of the dissociation school, was his doctoral dissertation in philosophy. He began medical school on completing it.

2 Some of the most commonly repeated notions in Jung's works are (a) Janet's expression for a drop in ego-function (*abaissement du niveau mental*), (b) Janet's expression for the work of the ego (*fonction du réel*), and (c) Janet's distinction between the "higher" and "lower" psychic functions, which Jung identifies, respectively, with the personal psyche and the collective unconscious (*parties supérieures et inférieures*).

3 Jung does not say where he got the expression *individuation*, but it is likely not Janet, since there are no references to the term in Janet (1903) or earlier, for Janet (1903) is the latest of his publications cited by Jung in the *Collected Works*.

4 When brain scientists speak of "nuclei," they mean a cluster of neurons that cooperate in performing the same function.

5 This detail was inserted into Searle's argument, borrowed from Damasio (1999: 228).

6 PET = positron emission tomography (weakly radioactive tracers were added to glucose; more of the radioactive glucose was used in those regions of the cortex than were being employed for the task; and as a result those regions glowed with the increased radioactivity).

9 Dreams: evidence of dialogic process

1 Essentially "shadow" is Jung's term for aspects of psyche that conflict with ego's plans and ideals. Hostile, deceptive or otherwise challenging dream figures might personify the shadow, and an individual may act out the shadow's intentions when violating conscious moral principles.

2 I refer to Jung's *practice* in handling dreams. As for his speeches in defense of Freud at this time in his career, we find him defending the manifest/latent distinction and the idea of "dream work." After breaking with Freud, he says he decided just to listen to the dreams and see what they had to say (*MDR*: 170f); but the astute reader will see that that was what he had been doing all along.

3 I encountered a strange response of this type from another Harvard professor when a depressed patient of mine asked me to contact the psychopharmacologist who prescribed her antidepressant medication. I did so; but he refused to talk to me, claiming that speaking with a Jungian analyst could be grounds for his being dismissed from the Harvard faculty. On the other hand, I have for years been invited to a monthly Harvard meeting on the history of psychology. Clearly, when Jung's name comes up, strong emotional reactions abound.

4 Elsewhere he gets the names and spellings right (Hobson 1988: 66).

5 For instance, PET scans on men who explored a virtual town with a joystick showed elevated activity in the brain's hippocampus during SWS. This "reflects the processing of memory traces, which eventually leads to an improvement in performance the next day." B. Bower, "Wayfaring Sleepers: Brain Area Linked to Slumber-Aided Recall," *Science News* (June 11, 2004): 294.

6 **PGO** stands for the three brain regions involved: **P**ons, lateral **G**eniculate bodies, and **O**ccipital cortex.

7 Jung made a similar observation in his 1907 discussion of dementia praecox, an earlier term for schizophrenia: "Let the dreamer walk about and act like a person awake, and we have the clinical picture of dementia praecox" (*CW3*: ¶170).

8 "Every view which interprets the symbolic expression as an analogue or an abbreviated designation for a *known* thing is *semiotic*. A view which interprets the symbolic expression as the best possible formulation of a relatively *unknown* thing, which for that reason cannot be more clearly or characteristically represented, is *symbolic*."

(*CW6*: ¶815)

10 Jung's complex theory

1 All translations from books listed in the bibliography with German or French titles are my responsibility.

2 The term "co-conscious" was coined by Prince to refer to subpersonalities that function simultaneously, rather than alternatingly.

3 Blindsight is the ability to respond to objects in a "blind spot" due to neural damage. Prosopagnosia is the inability to recognize faces, although other actions the patient performs seem to indicate that parts of the brain not involved in seeing do respond to the face. Hemineglect is a stroke victim's failure to notice the half of her body afflicted with paralysis. Anosognosia is the condition of being unaware of one's illness.

4 A century ago, many of the multiple-personality patients spoke of feeling a "click" in their heads when the switch occurred.

5 Bleuler and Jung believed that they would have diagnosed nearly all of Janet's patients as schizophrenic (Ellenberger 1970).

6 Modern researchers have verified William James' position on emotion of a century ago (I become scared because I find that my heart is beating rapidly and my palms are sweating)—one of a very few of James' positions that Jung did not adopt.

7 There is a second line, variously described as "experiencing the archetype," "the transcendent function" and "mutual influence," which will be discussed in later chapters.

11 Complexes and the neural substrate

1 The nine are: Charles Darwin (via LeDoux 1996); Silvan Tomkins (Nathanson 1992); Paul Ekman (LeDoux 1996); Robert Plutchik (LeDoux 1996); Philip Johnson-Laird and Keith Oatley (LeDoux 1996); Jaak Panksepp (1998); Antonio Damasio (1999, 2003); Christopher Badcock (2000); and Daniel Goleman (1995).
2 *Amygdala* means "almond" in Greek.
3 *Thalamos* means "bridal chamber" in Greek. We now know it is filled with "convergence zones" (Damasio) where sensory data and emotional valuation are "married"; but the narrow chamber-shaped appearance of the thalamus recommended its name to early anatomists who had no idea of its function.
4 *Hippocampos* means "seahorse" in Greek. Bear in mind that the seahorse has a very long, forward-curving prehensile tail as well as a horse-shaped head and thorax. The hippocampus is likewise a long, narrow, curved structure.
5 In his 1907 book on *Dementia praecox*, Jung speculated that a "toxin" is created when the dominance of a single complex persists for too long a time, and that this toxin renders the condition irreversible and destructive of the personality:

> In such cases one feels tempted to attribute causal significance to the complex, though with the above-mentioned proviso that besides its psychological effects the complex also produces an unknown quantity, possibly a toxin, which assists the work of destruction. At the same time I am fully aware of the possibility that this X may arise in the first place from non-psychological causes and then simply seize on the existing complex and specifically transform it.
>
> (*CW3*: ¶195)

12 Jung's psychotherapy and neuroscience

1 *Schweizerisches Medizinisches Jahrbuch*.
2 Sincere religious beliefs constitute an exception insofar as they remove an issue from the sphere of the merely personal and give it communal and transcendental significance. One says, in effect, "I do not conceal these matters for my own aggrandizement but for the sake of the community and in accordance with the will of God." In Jung's view, sincere religion is unconscious psychology, and psychology is only necessary today because religious claims can no longer be sincerely held by most modern individuals.
3 In this phrasing, Jung deliberately employs the language of Alfred Adler, who, he says, has diminished the role of the unconscious but, by way of compensation, has set up educational institutions and procedures in several countries.

13 Jung on archetypes and altered states

1 Mountain Lake was also known as Antonio Mirabal. Jung carried on a correspondence with his "friend," Mountain Lake, two examples of which have been published (*Letters, i*: 101f; *ii*: 596f).
2 Until Jung met Mountain Lake, these searches had been made primarily in the library. Although he read widely, he was very strongly influenced by the books of Lucien Lévy-Bruhl, who also did not visit the people he wrote about, but exhaustively studied the extant literature from the field. More about Jung and Lévy-Bruhl later in the chapter.
3 In the seminar, he does not identify his cousin, but calls her only a "young girl."
4 There are no references to Husserl or any of the phenomenologists in Jung's *Collected Works*. It is the thesis of my doctoral dissertation that Jung was a naive phenomenologist,

struggling to find a language to describe his observations but without help from what he might have found in the philosophical discipline begun by Husserl and pursued by Heidegger, Merleau-Ponty, and others (Haule 1973).

5 *Vipassana*, the more widely used term in recent Western publications, comes from the classical language of early Buddhism, Pali; the corresponding Sanskrit term is *vipa-shyana*. It means "clear thinking" which leads to recognition of "the three marks of existence": impermanence, suffering, and egolessness (Fischer-Schreiber *et al.* 1989). Jung's interest was clearly about unmasking the ego's illusion of being in control.

6 This formulation is also suggestive of the philosophical school of phenomenology, because four years after Jung's 1925 seminar, Martin Heidegger published one of the great books of the twentieth century, *Being and Time*, which has as its theme that human existence (*Dasein*) is the "Shepherd of Being," for it alone is conscious and forms the "clearing" in which Being appears.

7 Cited in Maurice Leenhardt's Preface to Lévy-Bruhl (1995: xiii).

8 In the three-person God of Christianity, the Son and the Holy Spirit are "of the same substance" as the Father. This makes the three of them "con-substantial."

9 E.g. *CW8*: ¶507, n. 12; *CW9i*: ¶41; *CW11*: ¶817, n. 28.

14 Altered states and transformation

1 I have written about the pursuit of the void as a transcending of more limited altered states in Chapter 11 of my book on Tantra (Haule 1999b).

2 The experience that lies behind my work is discussed in Chapter 3 of *Perils of the Soul* (Haule 1999a).

3 Discussion of these issues will be taken up in Part III of this volume.

4 Described with an accuracy that the rest of us could not know before the satellites and moon shots of a quarter century later.

5 I discuss near-death experiences in much more detail in Chapter 4 of *Perils of the Soul* (Haule 1999a).

6 Exploration of this issue is already developing a rich literature, e.g. Mark S. G. Dyczkowski (1987), N. C. Panda (1995) and Amit Goswami (2001).

7 By *neurognostic*, the authors refer to ways of knowing (*gnosis* = knowledge) that depend upon the neural structure of the brain.

15 Jung on the history of consciousness

1 As the son of a poor country pastor, Jung was certainly not a member of the upper class, but he attended school with the best and the brightest, at the Gymnasium and University in Basel. His "residency" in psychiatry at the Burghölzli, one of the most prestigious mental hospitals in Europe, was officially part of the University of Zurich.

2 Jung quotes, here, from Burckhardt's *The Civilization of the Renaissance in Italy*. Jacob Burckhardt (1818–97) was one of the great intellectuals of Basel, still an authority to be seen on the streets when Jung was a student in Gymnasium and University there. Jung had a high admiration for him.

3 Clearly no such revolution occurred in the 1920s, and it appears to this writer that sickish sentimentality is still with us and is the strongest characteristic of our American response to "terrorism." We continue to try to suppress the masses, though they no longer live so near us. Another revolution is surely due, but no one can predict when or if it will come. I have discussed the evidence that points to our longing for an integration of the irrational and the "Gnostic" in *Perils of the Soul* (Haule 1999a).

4 Neumann's theory of psychology is very clearly derived from Jung, but he systematizes Jung's ideas, solidifies them and reduces their flexibility.

5 It is interesting to note that all three of these books (Campbell 1949; Neumann 1949a, 1949b) were published in 1949.
6 I have discussed these matters at greater length in Haule 1995.

16 History of consciousness: primate rituals

1 They are: A. Alavi, J. B. Ashbrook, M. Baime, E. D. Bigler, A. Brady, S. Brandais, T. Burns, L. Chetelat, M. L. Foster, B. Lex, G. R. Murphy, R. M. Pankin, S. Richardson, R. A. Rubinstein, J. Shearer, W. J. Smith, and M. Webber.
2 Especially Brian Hayden, Professor of Archaeology at Simon Fraser University, British Columbia; David Lewis-Williams, Professor Emeritus and Senior Mentor in the Rock Art Institute, University of the Witwatersrand, Johannesburg; Steven Mithen, Dean and Professor of Archaeology, University of Reading, UK; and Timothy Taylor, Department of Archaeological Sciences, University of Bradford, UK.
3 *The Unconscious in Culture* is the title of a collection of critical papers edited by Ino Rossi (1974).
4 Although they are fairly accurate in their understanding of Jung's archetypes, they tend to reduce archetypes to symbols rather than seeing them in their full reality as tendencies to enact behavioral patterns, whether they be motoric, emotional, or imaginal. D'Aquili and Newberg (1999: 135), for example, reveal their bias toward imagery alone as the nature of archetype when they try to "locate" the archetypes near the junction of the temporal and occipital lobes of the right hemisphere because that region has been shown to produce vivid memories, complex hallucinations, and dream-like states.
5 Minor change is, of course, possible, as we know from listening to "dialects" in birdsong.

17 Ritual and consciousness in the Paleolithic

1 "Moon milk" is a literal translation of *Mondmilch*, which in geology is a descriptive term for calcite (calcium carbonate), on account of its milky-white appearance. It also occurs in a viscous fluid form and is a major component of stalactites.
2 E.g. *CW5*: ¶576; *CW9i*: ¶293; *CW12*: ¶553.
3 E.g. *CW5*: ¶114, 180, 329; *CW6*: ¶201, 788, 814; *CW7*: ¶492; *CW8*: ¶88, 644; *CW9ii*: ¶127.

18 Ritual and consciousness in the Mesolithic

1 Mitochondrial DNA is the genetic material found not in the nucleus of a cell but in tiny structures called mitochondria that produce a cell's energy.

19 Ritual and consciousness in the Neolithic

1 The biogenetic structuralists emphasize the mythic narrative implicit in ritual through an analysis of the Roman Catholic Mass; and here the movement of the priest from one area of the church to another is fundamental (G. R. Murphy 1979: 318–41).
2 /Xan is one of the subgroups of San. Marks such as /, and ! represent "clicks" that their language employs.

20 Ritual and consciousness in the historical era

1 I have discussed some of the variety and applications of the Gnosticisms that have appeared over several centuries in *Perils of the Soul* (Haule 1999a).

2 This is precisely what Reichel-Dolmatoff found among the Tukano people. What they saw in their ecstatic visions was intensely discussed, and meanings were socially agreed upon (Reichel-Dolmatoff 1975).

21 Concluding reflections

1 My much shorter book on Francis of Assisi makes a similar argument (Haule 2004).

References

Aitchison, J. (2000) *The Seeds of Speech: Language Origin and Evolution*. Cambridge: Cambridge University Press.

Aldhouse-Green, M. and Aldhouse-Green, S. (2005) *The Quest for the Shaman: Shape-Shifters, Sorcerers and Spirit-Helpers of Ancient Europe*. London: Thames & Hudson.

Allman, J. M. (1999) *Evolving Brains*. New York: Scientific American Library.

Audi, R. (ed.) (1999) *The Cambridge Dictionary of Philosophy*, 2nd edition. Cambridge: Cambridge University Press.

Aunger, R. (2002) *The Electric Meme: A New Theory of How We Think*. New York: Free Press.

Badcock, C. (2000) *Evolutionary Psychology: A Critical Introduction*. Cambridge: Polity Press.

Bahn, P. G. (1992) "Foreword," in N. W. Smith, *An Analysis of Ice Age Art: Its Psychology and Belief System*. New York: Peter Lang, ix–x.

Bahn, P. G. and Vertut, J. (1997) *Journey through the Ice Age*, 2nd edition. Berkeley, CA: University of California Press.

Bair, D. (2003) *Jung: A Biography*. Boston, MA: Little, Brown.

Barnard, G. W. (1997) *Exploring Unseen Worlds: William James and the Philosophy of Mysticism*. Albany, NY: SUNY Press.

Barnard, G. W. (1998) "William James and the Origins of Mystical Experience," in R. K. C. Forman (ed.) *The Innate Capacity: Mysticism, Psychology and Philosophy*. New York: Oxford University Press, 161–210.

Bellah, R. N. (1964) "Religious Evolution," *American Sociological Review 29*: 358–74.

Bermúdez, J. L. (2003) *Thinking Without Words*. Oxford: Oxford University Press.

Bourguignon, E. (1973) "Introduction: A Framework for the Comparative Study of Altered States of Consciousness," in E. Bourguignon (ed.) *Religion, Altered States of Consciousness, and Social Change*. Columbus, OH: Ohio State University Press, 3–35.

Boyer, P. (2001) *Religion Explained: The Evolutionary Origins of Religious Thought*. New York: Basic Books.

Brody, H. (2000) *The Other Side of Eden: Hunters, Farmers, and the Shaping of the World*. New York: North Point.

Burkhardt, R. W., Jr. (1995) *The Spirit of System: Lamarck and Evolutionary Biology*. Cambridge, MA: Harvard University Press.

Burleson, B. W. (2005) *Jung in Africa*. New York: Continuum.

Campbell, J. (1949) *The Hero with a Thousand Faces*. Princeton, NJ: Princeton University Press, 1972.

Candland, D. K. (1993) *Feral Children and Clever Animals: Reflections on Human Nature*. New York: Oxford University Press.

Chalmers, D. J. (1996) *The Conscious Mind: In Search of a Fundamental Theory*. New York: Oxford University Press.

Chapple, E. (1970) *Culture and Biological Man*. New York: Holt, Rinehart & Winston.

Cheney, D. L. and Seyfarth, R. M. (1990) *How Monkeys See the World: Inside the Mind of Another Species*. Chicago, IL: University of Chicago Press.

Cheney, D. L. and Seyfarth, R. M. (2007) *Baboon Metaphysics: The Evolution of a Social Mind*. Chicago, IL: University of Chicago Press.

Clottes, J. (2001) "Chauvet Cave: France's Magical Ice Age Art," *National Geographic* 200(3): 104–21.

Clottes, J. and Courtin, J. (1996) *The Cave Beneath the Sea: Paleolithic Images at Cosquer*, trans. M. Garner. New York: Harry N. Abrams.

Clottes, J. and Lewis-Williams, D. (1998) *The Shamans of Prehistory: Trance and Magic in the Painted Caves*, trans. S. Hawkes. New York: Harry N. Abrams.

Clottes, J. (2003) *Chauvet Cave: The Art of Earliest Times*, trans. P. G. Bahn. Salt Lake City, UT: University of Utah Press.

Copleston, F. (1960) *A History of Philosophy. Vol. IV, Descartes to Leibniz*. Garden City, NY: Image Books.

Crick, F. (1995) *The Astonishing Hypothesis: The Scientific Search for the Soul*. New York: Touchstone.

d'Aquili, E. G. and Laughlin, C. D., Jr. (1979) "The Neurobiology of Myth and Ritual," in E. G. d'Aquili, C. D. Laughlin, Jr., and J. McManus, with T. Burns *et al.*, *The Spectrum of Ritual: A Biogenetic Structural Analysis*. New York: Columbia University Press, 152–82.

d'Aquili, E. G. and Newberg, A. B. (1999) *The Mystical Mind: Probing the Biology of Religious Experience*. Minneapolis, MN: Fortress.

d'Aquili, E. G., Laughlin, C. D., Jr., and McManus, J., with Burns, T. *et al.* (1979) *The Spectrum of Ritual: A Biogenetic Structural Analysis*. New York: Columbia University Press.

Damasio, A. R. (1994) *Descartes' Error: Emotion, Reason, and the Human Brain*. New York: Avon.

Damasio, A. R. (1999) *The Feeling of What Happens: Body and Emotion in the Making of Consciousness*. New York: Harcourt, Brace.

Damasio, A. R. (2003) *Looking for Spinoza: Joy, Sorrow, and the Feeling Brain*. New York: Harcourt.

Davidson, I. (1997) "The Power of Pictures," in M. W. Conkey *et al.* (eds) *Beyond Art: Pleistocene Image and Symbol*. San Francisco, CA: California Academy of Sciences, 125–59.

Dennett, D. C. (1991) *Consciousness Explained*. Boston, MA: Little, Brown.

de Waal, F. (1996) *Good Natured: The Origins of Right and Wrong in Humans and Other Animals*. Cambridge, MA: Harvard University Press.

de Waal, F. (1998) *Chimpanzee Politics: Power and Sex Among the Apes*, revised edition. Baltimore, MD: Johns Hopkins University Press.

de Waal, F. (2001) *The Ape and the Sushi Master: Cultural Reflections by a Primatologist*. New York: Basic Books.

de Waal, F. and Lanting, F. (1997) *Bonobo: The Forgotten Ape*. Berkeley, CA: University of California Press.

Diamond, J. (1999) *Guns, Germs, and Steel: The Fates of Human Societies.* New York: W. W. Norton.

Dollard, J. and Miller, N. E. (1950) *Personality and Psychotherapy.* New York: McGraw-Hill.

Doniger, W. (ed.) (1999) *Merriam-Webster's Encyclopedia of World Religions.* Springfield, MA: Merriam-Webster.

Dunbar, R. (1996) *Grooming, Gossip, and the Evolution of Language.* Cambridge, MA: Harvard University Press.

Dunbar, R. (2005) *The Human Story: A New History of Mankind's Evolution.* London: Faber & Faber.

Dyczkowski, M. S. G. (1987) *The Doctrine of Vibration: An Analysis of the Doctrines and Practices of Kashmir Shaivism.* Albany, NY: SUNY Press.

Edelman, G. M. (1992) *Bright Air, Brilliant Fire: On the Matter of Mind.* New York: Basic Books.

Edelman, G. M. (2004) *Wider than the Sky: The Phenomenal Gift of Consciousness.* New Haven, CT: Yale University Press.

Edelman, G. M. and Tononi, G. (2000) *A Universe of Consciousness: How Matter Becomes Imagination.* New York: Basic Books.

Eliade, M. (1964) *Shamanism: Archaic Techniques of Ecstasy,* trans. W. R. Trask. New York: Pantheon/Bollingen.

Ellenberger, H. F. (1970) *The Discovery of the Unconscious: The History and Evolution of Dynamic Psychiatry.* New York: Basic Books.

Fagan, B. (1998) *From Black Land to Fifth Sun: The Science of Sacred Sites.* New York: Basic Books.

Fagan, B. (2004) *The Long Summer: How Climate Changed Civilization.* New York: Basic Books.

Feuerstein, G., Kak, S., and Frawley, D. (1995) *In Search of the Cradle of Civilization: New Light on Ancient India.* Wheaton, IL: Quest.

Fischer-Schreiber, I., Ehrhard, F.-K., Friedrichs, K., and Diener, M. S. (eds) (1989) *The Encyclopedia of Eastern Philosophy and Religion.* Boston, MA: Shambhala.

Forman, R. K. C. (ed.) (1998) *The Innate Capacity: Mysticism, Psychology and Philosophy.* New York: Oxford University Press.

Fox, R. (1989) *The Search for Society: Quest for a Biosocial Science and Morality.* New Brunswick, NJ: Rutgers University Press.

Freeman, W. J. (2000) *How Brains Make Up their Minds.* New York: Columbia University Press.

Gladwell, M. (2005) *Blink: The Power of Thinking Without Thinking.* New York: Little, Brown.

Goleman, D. (1995) *Emotional Intelligence.* New York: Bantam.

Goodman, F. D. (1990) *Where the Spirits Ride the Wind: Trance Journeys and Other Ecstatic Experiences.* Bloomington, IN: Indiana University Press.

Goswami, A. (2001) *Physics of the Soul: The Quantum Book of Living, Dying, Reincarnation, and Immortality.* Charlottesville, VA: Hampton Road.

Goswami, A., with Reed, R. E. and Goswami, M. (1993) *The Self-Aware Universe: How Consciousness Creates the Material World.* New York: Tarcher/Putnam.

Gottfried, R. S. (1983) *The Black Death: Natural and Human Disaster in Medieval Europe.* New York: Free Press.

Gray, J. (2002) *Straw Dogs: Thoughts on Humans and Other Animals*. London: Granta.

Greenspan, S. I. and Shanker, S. G. (2004) *The First Idea: How Symbols, Language, and Intelligence Evolved from Our Primate Ancestors to Modern Humans*. Cambridge, MA: Da Capo.

Harner, M. (1980) *The Way of the Shaman: A Guide to Power and Healing*. San Francisco, CA: Harper & Row.

Harris, P. L. (2000) *The Work of the Imagination*. Malden, MA: Blackwell.

Hartman, G. V. (2003) "Archetype: The History and Development of a Concept," *Quadrant: Journal of the C. G. Jung Foundation for Analytical Psychology 33*(2): 59–79.

Haule, J. R. (1973) *Imagination and Myth: A Heideggerian Interpretation of C. G. Jung*. Temple University doctoral dissertation.

Haule, J. R. (1983) "Archetype and Integration: Exploring the Janetian Roots of Analytical Psychology," *Journal of Analytical Psychology 28*(3): 253–67.

Haule, J. R. (1984) "From Somnambulism to the Archetypes: The French Roots of Jung's Split with Freud," *Psychoanalytic Review 71*(4): 635–59.

Haule, J. R. (1986) "Pierre Janet and Dissociation: The First Transference Theory and its Origins in Hypnosis," *American Journal of Clinical Hypnosis 29*(2): 86–94.

Haule, J. R. (1992) "Jung's 'Amfortas Wound': *Psychological Types* Revisited," *Spring 53: A Journal of Archetype and Culture*: 95–112.

Haule, J. R. (1995) "Eros, Mutuality, and the 'New Ethic'," in L. B. Ross and M. Roy (eds) *Cast the First Stone: Ethics in Analytical Practice*. Chicago, IL: Chiron, 9–15.

Haule, J. R. (1999a) *Perils of the Soul: Ancient Wisdom and the New Age*. York Beach, ME: Weiser.

Haule, J. R. (1999b) *Indecent Practices and Erotic Trance: Making Sense of Tantra*, available at www.jrhaule.net/ipet.html (accessed May 28, 2010).

Haule, J. R. (2004) *The Ecstasies of St. Francis: The Way of Lady Poverty*. Great Barrington, MA: Lindisfarne.

Hauser, M. D. (2000) *Wild Minds: What Animals Really Think*. New York: Henry Holt.

Hayden, B. (2003) *Shamans, Sorcerers, and Saints: A Prehistory of Religion*. Washington, DC: Smithsonian Books.

Hebb, D. O. (1949) *The Organization of Behavior*. New York: John Wiley & Sons.

Helvenston, P. A. and Bahn, P. (2002) *Desperately Seeking Trance Plants: Testing the "Three Stages of Trance" Model*. New York: R. J. Communications.

Hobson, J. A. (1988) *The Dreaming Brain*. New York: Basic Books.

Hobson, J. A. (1999) *Consciousness*. New York: Scientific American Library.

Hobson, J. A. (2002) *Dreaming: An Introduction to the Science of Sleep*. Oxford: Oxford University Press.

Hobson, J. A. (2005) *Thirteen Dreams Freud Never Had: The New Mind Science*. New York: Pi Science.

Hobson, R. F. (1980) "The Archetypes of the Collective Unconscious," in M. Fordham *et al.* (eds) *Analytical Psychology: A Modern Science*. London: Academic Press, 66–75.

Hogenson, G. B. (2001) "The Baldwin Effect: A Neglected Influence on C. G. Jung's Evolutionary Thinking," *Journal of Analytical Psychology 46*(4): 591–612.

Horgan, J. (1999) *The Undiscovered Mind: How the Human Brain Defies Replication, Medication, and Explanation*. New York: Free Press.

Hubert, H. and Mauss, M. (1909) *Mélanges d'histoire des religions*. Paris: Alcan.

Hunt, H. T. (1995) *On the Nature of Consciousness: Cognitive, Phenomenological, and Transpersonal Perspectives*. New Haven, CT: Yale University Press.

Husserl, E. (1913) *Ideas: General Introduction to Pure Phenomenology*, trans. W. R. B. Gibson. London: Collier-Macmillan, 1962.

Jaffé, A. (1979) *C. G. Jung: Word and Image*. Princeton, NJ: Princeton University Press.

James, W. (1890) *The Principles of Psychology*. Chicago, IL: Great Books, 1990.

James, W. (1902) *The Varieties of Religious Experience*. New York: Collier, 1961.

Janet, P. (1889) *L'Automatisme psychologique*. Reprinted Paris: Société Pierre Janet, 1973.

Janet, P. (1903) *Les Obsessions et la psychasthénie*, two volumes. Reprinted New York: Arno, 1976.

Janet, P. (1919) *Psychological Healing: A Historical and Clinical Study*, two volumes, trans. unknown, 1925. Reprinted New York: Arno, 1976.

Janet, P. (1924) *Principles of Psychotherapy*, trans. H. M. Guthrie and E. R. Guthrie. Reprinted Freeport, NY: Books for Libraries, 1971.

Jaynes, J. (1976) *The Origin of Consciousness in the Breakdown of the Bicameral Mind*. Boston, MA: Houghton Mifflin.

Jung, C. G. See *Abbreviations page* (p. xii, this volume).

Kuhn, T. S. (1970) *The Structure of Scientific Revolutions*, 2nd edition. Chicago, IL: University of Chicago Press.

Kurtén, B. (1980) *Dance of the Tiger: A Novel of the Ice Age*. New York: Pantheon.

Laughlin, C. D., Jr., and d'Aquili, E. D. (1979) "Ritual and Stress," in E. G. d'Aquili, C. D. Laughlin, Jr., and J. McManus, with T. Burns *et al.*, *The Spectrum of Ritual: A Biogenetic Structural Analysis*. New York: Columbia University Press, 280–317.

Laughlin, C. D., Jr., and McManus, J. (1979) "Mammalian Ritual," in E. G. d'Aquili, C. D. Laughlin, Jr., and J. McManus, with T. Burns *et al.*, *The Spectrum of Ritual: A Biogenetic Structural Analysis*. New York: Columbia University Press, 80–116.

Laughlin, C. D., Jr., McManus, J., and d'Aquili, E. G. (1979) "Introduction," in E. G. d'Aquili, C. D. Laughlin, Jr., and J. McManus, with T. Burns *et al.*, *The Spectrum of Ritual: A Biogenetic Structural Analysis*. New York: Columbia University Press, 1–50.

Laughlin, C. D., Jr., McManus, J., and d'Aquili, E. G. (1990) *Brain, Symbol, and Experience: Toward a Neurophenomenology of Human Consciousness*. Boston, MA: Shambhala.

Laughlin, R. B. (2005) *A Different Universe: Reinventing Physics from the Bottom Down*. New York: Basic Books.

LeDoux, J. (1996) *The Emotional Brain: The Mysterious Underpinnings of Emotional Life*. New York: Touchstone.

LeDoux, J. (2002) *Synaptic Self: How our Brains Become Who We Are*. New York: Viking.

Lévi-Strauss, C. (1969) *The Raw and the Cooked: Introduction to a Science of Mythology*, Vol. 1, trans. J. Weightman and D. Weightman. New York: Harper Torchbooks.

Lévi-Strauss, C. (1982) *The Way of the Masks*, trans. S. Modelski. Seattle, WA: University of Washington.

Lévy-Bruhl, L. (1905) *Ethics and Moral Science*, trans. E. Lee. London: Constable.

Lévy-Bruhl, L. (1910) *How Natives Think*, trans. L. A. Clare. London: Allen & Unwin.

Lévy-Bruhl, L. (1922) *Primitive Mentality*, trans. L. A. Clare. Boston, MA: Beacon, 1966.

Lévy-Bruhl, L. (1927) *The "Soul" of the Primitive*, trans. L. A. Clare. Chicago, IL: Henry Regnery, 1966.

Lévy-Bruhl, L. (1945) *The Notebooks on Primitive Mentality*, trans. P. Rivière. New York: Harper Torchbooks, 1975.

Lewis, T., Amini, F., and Lannon, R. (2000) *A General Theory of Love*. New York: Vintage.

Lewis-Williams, D. (1997) "Harnessing the Brain: Vision and Shamanism in Upper Paleolithic Western Europe," in M. W. Conkey *et al.* (eds) *Beyond Art: Pleistocene Image and Symbol*. San Francisco, CA: California Academy of Sciences, 321–42.

Lewis-Williams, D. (2002) *The Mind in the Cave*. London: Thames & Hudson.

Lewis-Williams, D. and Dowson, T. (1989) *Images of Power: Understanding Bushman Rock Art*, 2nd edition. Cape Town: Struik.

Lewis-Williams, D. and Pearce, D. (2004) *San Spirituality: Roots, Expression, and Social Consequences*. Cape Town: Double Storey.

Lewis-Williams, D. and Pearce, D. (2005) *Inside the Neolithic Mind: Consciousness, Cosmos and the Realm of the Gods*. London: Thames & Hudson.

Lex, B. (1979) "The Neurobiology of Ritual Trance," in E. G. d'Aquili, C. D. Laughlin, Jr., and J. McManus, with T. Burns *et al.*, *The Spectrum of Ritual: A Biogenetic Structural Analysis*. New York: Columbia University Press, 117–51.

Linden, E. (1974) *Apes, Men, and Language*. New York: Saturday Review Press.

Llinás, R. R. (2002) *I of the Vortex: From Neurons to Self*. Cambridge, MA: MIT Press.

MacLean, P. D. (1993) "On the Evolution of Three Mentalities," in J. B. Ashbrook (ed.) *Brain, Culture, and the Human Spirit*. Lanham, MD: University Press of America, 15–44.

McManus, J. (1979a) "Ritual and Human Social Cognition," in E. G. d'Aquili, C. D. Laughlin, Jr., and J. McManus, with T. Burns *et al.*, *The Spectrum of Ritual: A Biogenetic Structural Analysis*. New York: Columbia University Press, 183–215.

McManus, J. (1979b) "Ritual and Social Power," in E. G. d'Aquili, C. D. Laughlin, Jr., and J. McManus, with T. Burns *et al.*, *The Spectrum of Ritual: A Biogenetic Structural Analysis*. New York: Columbia University Press, 216–48.

McManus, J., Laughlin, C. D., Jr., and d'Aquili, E. G. (1979) "Concepts, Methods, and Conclusions," in E. G. d'Aquili, C. D. Laughlin, Jr., and J. McManus, with T. Burns *et al.*, *The Spectrum of Ritual: A Biogenetic Structural Analysis*. New York: Columbia University Press, 342–62.

Marcus, G. (2004) *The Birth of the Mind: How a Tiny Number of Genes Creates the Complexities of Human Thought*. New York: Basic Books.

Marks, J. (2002) *What It Means To Be 98% Chimpanzee: Apes, People, and their Genes*. Berkeley, CA: University of California.

Marshack, A. (1972/91) *The Roots of Civilization: The Cognitive Beginnings of Man's First Art, Symbol, and Notation*, 2nd edition. Mount Kisco, NY: Moyer Bell.

Meier, C. A. (1968) *Die Empirie des Unbewussten*. Zurich: Rascher.

Mithen, S. (1996) *The Prehistory of the Mind: The Cognitive Origins of Art, Religion, and Science*. London: Thames & Hudson.

Mithen, S. (2003) *After the Ice: A Global Human History, 20,000–5000, BC*. London: Phoenix.

Mithen, S. (2006) *The Singing Neanderthals: The Origins of Music, Language, Mind, and Body*. Cambridge, MA: Harvard University Press.

Moody, R. A., Jr., (1975) *Life After Life: The Investigation of a Phenomenon—Survival of Bodily Death*. Covington, GA: Mockingbird.

Murphy, G. R., SJ (1979) "A Ceremonial Ritual: The Mass," in E. G. d'Aquili, C. D. Laughlin, Jr., and J. McManus, with T. Burns *et al.*, *The Spectrum of Ritual: A Biogenetic Structural Analysis*. New York: Columbia University Press, 318–41.

Murphy, M. and White, R. A. (1978) *The Psychic Side of Sports*. Reading, MA: Addison-Wesley.

Nathanson, D. L. (1992) *Shame and Pride: Affect, Sex, and the Birth of the Self*. New York: W. W. Norton.

Neumann, E. (1949a) *Depth Psychology and a New Ethic*, trans. E. Rolfe. New York: G. P. Putnam's Sons, 1969.

Neumann, E. (1949b) *The Origins and History of Consciousness*, trans. R. F. C. Hull. Princeton, NJ: Princeton University Press, 1954.

Panda, N. C. (1995) *The Vibrating Universe*. Delhi: Motilal Banarsidass.

Panda, N. C. (1999) *Maya in Physics*. Delhi: Motilal Banarsidass.

Panksepp, J. (1998) *Affective Neuroscience: The Foundations of Human and Animal Emotions*. New York: Oxford University Press.

Paulhan, F. (1889) *L'Activité mentale et les éléments de l'esprit*. Paris: Alcan.

Pfeiffer, J. E. (1982) *The Creative Explosion: An Inquiry into the Origins of Art and Religion*. New York: Harper & Row.

Pinker, S. (1994) *The Language Instinct*. New York: HarperCollins.

Pinker, S. (1997) *How the Mind Works*. New York: W. W. Norton.

Pinker, S. (2003) *The Blank Slate: The Modern Denial of Human Nature*. New York: Viking.

Pinker, S. and Bloom, P., with commentators (1990) "Natural Language and Natural Selection," *Behavioral and Brain Sciences 13:* 707–84.

Plotkin, H. (1998) *Evolution in Mind: An Introduction to Evolutionary Psychology*. Cambridge, MA: Harvard University Press.

Preuss, K. T. (1904) "Der Ursprung der Religion und Kunst," *Globus* [Brunswick] *86:* 355–63.

Price, N. S. (2001) "An Archaeology of Altered States: Shamanism and Material Culture Studies," in N. S. Price (ed.) *The Archaeology of Shamanism*. New York: Routledge, 3–16.

Prince, M. (1905/08) *The Dissociation of a Personality: A Biographical Study in Abnormal Psychology*. New York: Johnson Reprint Corporation, 1968.

Prince, M. (1914/21) *The Unconscious: The Foundations of Human Personality, Normal and Abnormal*. New York: Macmillan.

Prince, M. (1929/39) *Clinical and Experimental Studies in Personality*. Westport, CT: Greenwood Press, reprinted 1970.

Prince-Hughes, D. (2004) *Songs of the Gorilla Nation: My Journey Through Autism*. New York: Three Rivers.

Quartz, S. R. and Sejnowski, T. J. (2002) *Liars, Lovers, and Heroes: What the New Brain Science Reveals about How We Become Who We Are*. New York: HarperCollins.

Reichel-Dolmatoff, G. (1971) *Amazonian Cosmos: The Sexual and Religious Symbolism of the Tukano Indians*. Chicago, IL: University of Chicago Press.

Reichel-Dolmatoff, G. (1975) *The Shaman and the Jaguar: A Study of Narcotic Drugs Among the Indians of Colombia*. Philadelphia, PA: Temple University Press.

Reichel-Dolmatoff, G. (1987) *Shamanism and Art of the Eastern Tukanoan Indians*. Leiden: E. J. Brill.

Restak, R. (2003) *The New Brain: How the Modern Age is Rewiring your Mind*. Emmaus, PA: Rodale.

Richerson, P. J. and Boyd, R. (2005) *Not by Genes Alone: How Culture Transformed Human Evolution*. Chicago, IL: University of Chicago Press.

Ridley, M. (1996) *The Origins of Virtue: Human Instincts and the Evolution of Cooperation*. New York: Penguin.

Ring, K. (1982) *Life at Death: A Scientific Investigation of the Near-Death Experience*. New York: Quill.

Ring, K. (1984) *Heading Toward Omega: In Search of the Meaning of the Near-Death Experience*. New York: Quill.

Ripinsky-Naxon, M. (1993) *The Nature of Shamanism: Substance and Function of a Religious Metaphor*. Albany, NY: SUNY Press.

Rose, S. (2005) *The Future of the Brain: The Promise and Perils of Tomorrow's Neuroscience*. New York: Oxford University Press.

Rossi, I. (ed.) (1974) *The Unconscious in Culture: The Structuralism of Claude Lévi-Strauss in Perspective*. New York: Dutton.

Rozwadowski, A. (2001) "Sun Gods or Shamans? Interpreting the 'Solar-Headed' Petroglyphs of Western Siberia," in N. S. Price (ed.) *The Archaeology of Shamanism*. New York: Routledge, 65–86.

Rudgley, R. (1999) *The Lost Civilizations of the Stone Age*. New York: Free Press.

Sannella, L. (1992) *The Kundalini Experience: Psychosis or Transcendence?* Lower Lake, CA: Integral.

Savage-Rumbaugh, S., Shanker, S. G., and Taylor, T. J. (1998) *Apes, Language and the Human Mind*. New York: Oxford University Press.

Schwartz, L. (1951) *Die Neurosen und die Dynamische Psychologie von Pierre Janet*. Basel: Benno Schwabe.

Searle, J. R. (2004) *Mind: A Brief Introduction*. Oxford: Oxford University Press.

Shamdasani, S. (1990) "A Woman Named Frank," *Spring 50: A Journal of Archetype and Culture*: 26–56.

Shamdasani, S. (2003) *Jung and the Making of Modern Psychology: The Dream of a Science*. Cambridge: Cambridge University Press.

Shore, B. (1996) *Culture in Mind: Cognition, Culture, and the Problem of Meaning*. New York: Oxford University Press.

Siegel, D. J. (1999) *The Developing Mind: How Relationships and the Brain Interact to Shape Who We Are*. New York: Guilford.

Smith, J. M. and Szathmáry, E. (1999) *The Origins of Life: From the Birth of Life to the Origin of Language*. Oxford: Oxford University Press.

Smith, N. W. (1992) *An Analysis of Ice Age Art: Its Psychology and Belief System*. New York: Peter Lang.

Smith, W. J. (1979) "Ritual and the Ecology of Communicating," in E. G. d'Aquili, C. D. Laughlin, Jr., and J. McManus, with T. Burns *et al.*, *The Spectrum of Ritual: A Biogenetic Structural Analysis*. New York: Columbia University Press, 51–79.

Soffer, O. and Conkey, M. W. (1997) "Studying Ancient Visual Cultures," in M. W. Conkey *et al.* (eds) *Beyond Art: Pleistocene Image and Symbol*. San Francisco, CA: California Academy of Sciences, 1–16.

Solms, M. and Turnbull, O. (2002) *The Brain and the Inner World: An Introduction to the Neuroscience of Subjective Experience*. New York: Other Press.

Stevens, A. (1983) *Archetypes: A Natural History of the Self*. New York: Quill.

Stevens, A. and Price, J. (1996) *Evolutionary Psychiatry: A New Beginning*. London: Routledge.

Taylor, E. I. (1996) "The New Jung Scholarship," *Psychoanalytic Review 83*(4): 547–68.

Taylor, E. I. (1999) *Shadow Culture: Psychology and Spirituality in America*. Washington, DC: Counterpoint.

Taylor, T. (1996) *The Prehistory of Sex: Four Million Years of Human Sexual Culture*. New York: Bantam.

Taylor, T. (2002) *The Buried Soul: How Humans Invented Death*. Boston, MA: Beacon.

Thain, M. and Hickman, M. (eds) (2000) *The Penguin Dictionary of Biology*, 10th edition. London: Penguin.

Tooby, J. and Cosmides, L. (1992) "The Psychological Foundations of Culture," in J. Barkow, J. Tooby and L. Cosmides (eds) *The Adapted Mind: Evolutionary Psychology and the Generation of Culture*. New York: Oxford University Press, 19–136.

Vitebsky, P. (1995) *The Shaman*. Boston, MA: Little, Brown.

Wallace, A. F. C. (1966) *Religion: An Anthropological View*. New York: Random House.

Watson, A. (2001) "The Sounds of Transformation: Acoustics, Monuments and Ritual in the British Neolithic," in N. S. Price (ed.) *The Archaeology of Shamanism*. New York: Routledge, 178–92.

White, R. (2003) *Prehistoric Art: The Symbolic Journey of Humankind*. New York: Henry N. Abrams.

Whitehead, A. N. (1929) *Process and Reality: An Essay in Cosmology*. New York: Free Press, 1969.

Whitley, D. S. (2000) *The Art of the Shaman: Rock Art of California*. Salt Lake City, UT: University of Utah Press.

Wilson, E. O. (1998) *Consilience: The Unity of Knowledge*. New York: Vintage.

Wilson, P. L. (1988) *Scandal: Essays in Islamic Heresy*. New York: Autonomedia.

Wilson, T. D. (2002) *Strangers to Ourselves: Discovering the Adaptive Unconscious*. Cambridge, MA: Harvard University Press.

Winkelman, M. (2000) *Shamanism: The Neural Ecology of Consciousness and Healing*. Westport, CT: Bergin & Garvey.

Wittgenstein, L. (1958) *Philosophical Investigations*, 3rd edition, trans. G. E. M. Anscombe. New York: Macmillan.

Zeman, A. (2002) *Consciousness: A User's Guide*. New Haven, CT: Yale University Press.

Zimmer, H. (1946) *Myths and Symbols in Indian Art and Civilization*, ed. J. Campbell. Princeton, NJ: Princeton University Press, 1972.

Index